W9-COB-121

Managing the Systems Development Process

Charles L. Biggs
Evan G. Birks
William Atkins

Touche Ross & Co.

Prentice-Hall Inc., Englewood Cliffs, N.J. 07632

Library of Congress Cataloging in Publication Data

Biggs, Charles L
   Managing the systems development process.

   (The Touche Ross management series)
   Includes index.
   1. Electronic data processing.   2. Management
information systems.   3. Industrial project management.
I. Birks, Evan G., joint author.   II. Atkins,
William, 1938–   joint author.   III. Title.
IV. Title: Systems development process.   V. Se-
ries: Touche Ross and Company.   Touche Ross management
series.
HF5548.2.B463   658.4'04   79-18981
ISBN 0-13-550830-4

Interior design and editorial/production supervision: Steven Bobker
Editorial Consultant: Dan Serebrakian
Manufacturing buyer: Gordon Osbourne
Cover design: Edsal Enterprises

Printed in the United States of America

10 9 8

Prentice-Hall International, Inc., *London*
Prentice-Hall of Australia Pty. Limited, *Sydney*
Prentice-Hall of Canada, Ltd., *Toronto*
Prentice-Hall of India Private Limited, *New Delhi*
Prentice-Hall of Japan, Inc., *Tokyo*
Prentice-Hall of Southeast Asia Pte. Ltd., *Singapore*
Whitehall Books Limited, Wellington, *New Zealand*

Contents

Foreword

The Touche Ross Management Series — of which this book is a part — is a growing library designed to present the latest management techniques. These techniques are intended to provide valuable assistance to executives in every type of organization who must face the challenges of change.

Change is ever-present and causes management techniques to lag behind current problems and technologies. The books in this series bridge specific portions of this gap and enable both policy-level and operations executives to minimize the interval between recognition of an emerging technology and its successful application.

Concentrating on change-related technology, each volume explains how to apply the latest management techniques in terms that are familiar to the average manager. The approach may be described as common-sense: It covers those theoretical or philosophical aspects helpful to gaining a sound understanding of the techniques. The emphasis is on describing system requirements and actually translating the theory to practical solutions.

Touche Ross sponsors this series in the same spirit that guides its own consulting practice: A dedication to *doing*. By blending writing skills with an in-depth knowledge of how to make new techniques work on the behalf of management, we hope to provide timely and understandable solutions that are able to meet the challenges of change.

Donald A. Curtis
National Director, Management Services
Touche Ross & Co.

Preface

Systems development has come of age in the past two decades. Computers, once held in awe by management, are now used routinely as management tools. As this transition occurred a project approach was used to control and apply the new technology. Although project management itself is not new and has been used in areas as diverse as putting a man on the moon and running election campaigns, special adaptations are required for systems applications. That is what this book is all about.

The authors and contributors of this book are working consultants, dedicated to successfully implementing computerized systems. The emphasis throughout is on the practical. The philosophies, approaches, and techniques by which management methods may be used to effectively control the development of computer-based processing and information systems have been proven. In fact, credit for the methodology offered in these pages belongs primarily to those business, industrial, and governmental organizations that have successfully managed computerized systems.

Designed to suit the needs of a varied audience, this book should be of particular interest to corporate and government executives whose activities interrelate with the systems function; to individuals within systems departments — including systems and operations analysts — who are responsible for project development or implementation; and to upper- and graduate-level students who have had courses in programming. This book may be used either as the primary or as a supplementary text for a course in systems planning and development.

Although literally scores of systems professionals, project managers, and practical-minded consultants contributed to this effort, a few did so at a level that warrants special mention. Two books in this series paved the way for this one:

Managing Computer System Projects, by John C. Shaw and William Atkins (McGraw-Hill, Inc., New York, N.Y., 1970).

Managing the EDP Function, by Arnold E. Ditri, John C. Shaw, and William Atkins (McGraw-Hill, Inc., New York, N.Y., 1971).

Allen E. Haight, Jr. and John P. Demetra, Partners in the Management Services Division of Touche Ross & Co., were prime movers in bringing this methodology up to date. We gratefully acknowledge the intellectual and technical leadership they lent to this effort.

Other members of the dedicated group that initiated the methodology for the systems management techniques presented in this book include Stephan E. Hall, M. Victor Janulaitis, David L. Caudill, and James E. Barlett. In addition, Mary K. Egbertson provided the primary secretarial support for the typing and never-ending process of revision. Challenges, assistance, and contributing interaction came from other sources that are far too numerous to be listed here. To all we give thanks.

Charles L. Biggs
Evan G. Birks
William Atkins

1

Managing the
Systems Development Process

INTRODUCTION

BACKGROUND In 1513 Machiavelli observed: "There is nothing more difficult to plan, more doubtful of success, nor more dangerous to manage than the creation of a new system. For the initiator has the enmity of all who would profit by the preservation of the old system and merely lukewarm defenders in those who would gain by the new one." The words of Machiavelli continue to hold true today for those who strive to develop new systems.

Over the last few decades, most new systems have involved automated data processing techniques. Starting with the early punched card tabulating machines and progressing to today's sophisticated general-purpose, mini and microcomputers, the term "system" has gained a broad spectrum of usage and meaning. Hence, we have grown familiar with terms such as: unit record systems, IBM systems, data entry systems, operating systems, data base management systems, telecommunications systems, and many more. The context in which this book uses the term "system" is in the general sense applying to all of the components which make up a system, i.e., the people, policies, practices, procedures, and processing techniques. Webster includes the following definitions of system: "a whole formed of related things; a set of organized facts, rules etc.; an orderly way of doing things."

It is important for the manager not to lose sight of the many aspects which must be considered when developing a new system. It is not just a technical computer process; to the contrary, it often drastically affects and changes the basic fabric and operation of the organization. Therefore, the manager responsible for developing a new system must be more than a

1

skilled technician applying his trade. The manager must deal with the organizational, operational, and economic factors, as well as the technical considerations.

In the early years (the late 1950s and early 1960s) of computerized data processing, the vast majority of business "systems" were intradepartmental financial applications which had been designed for and converted from unit record punched card systems. Many of the early general-purpose computer systems did not have magnetic tape or disk storage and were simply a faster method for processing the punched cards, making the computations, and printing the reports in one step. These application systems, much as the earlier unit record punched card systems, were economically justified on the basis of eliminating steps and clerical effort. As computers became more in vogue in the early 1960s, management went through a subtle change in their decision making related to EDP (electronic data processing). The change related to a shift away from requiring economic justification prior to embarking on new application systems development projects or on upgrading computer hardware. Management seemed to take the position that even though they would not necessarily save money, the use of computers would represent an improved method of operation and provide for future growth. When economics were considered, they were often relegated to future cost containment. At the same time, data processing personnel were mostly specialized technicians programming and operating the computers. They showed few signs of being able managers and in general followed the direction and recommendations of the computer manufacturer's sales personnel. Management, during this period, tended to abdicate its responsibility for EDP due to a lack of technical understanding presumed to be required.

As the second era (the mid-1960s through the mid-1970s) of computerized data processing arrived, it was heralded by third-generation computers which were to provide comprehensive MIS (management information systems). These general-purpose computers with miniaturized solid logic technology and integrated circuits captured the attention of most management in larger organizations, who by now felt compelled to keep current with the ever-changing world of computers and data processing. The concept of the new MIS crossed organizational lines and integrated all information elements necessary for timely management decision making. To achieve this concept the development and implementation strategy in most cases was to convert the existing application systems to operate on the new computers and concurrently begin planning for an integrated MIS. Needless to say, few MIS projects were ever completed. In the meantime, increasing volumes and new application systems, combined with less processing throughput than anticipated, caused healthy growth for the computer manufacturers.

In the 1970 recession, the future promise of the computer was for the first time insufficient to maintain the pace of demand. Management seemed to be taking a second look and asking how to get more results for the cost. Third-party leasing companies rapidly appeared and experienced significant growth by being able to offer 10 percent, 15 percent, 20 percent, and more savings on computer equipment. However, these savings provided only temporary relief from the ever increasing costs of EDP. Data processing personnel were beginning to face the demands of being managers. They were being asked to justify expenditures, to get more results from the costs being incurred, to reduce costs, to provide reports on a timely basis and to explain the seemingly inescapable cost and time overruns on application development projects and hardware conversions.

The late 1970s and early 1980s appear to be a new era. This new era is one that will be characterized by *management* — management that effectively utilizes computer technology to achieve cost-effective results. For example, minicomputers and microcomputers have proven themselves technologically, and the capability exists for efficient teleprocessing over computer-controlled communications networks. The data capture and data entry technology exists to provide more efficient and accurate input. Vastly improved efficiency is becoming available in operating systems software, data base management software, and programming languages. Yet with all this technology, many of the application systems being processed today have not been resystematized or substantially redesigned to be cost-effective in this new era. New releases of systems software frequently occur to keep pace with technological improvements without requiring complete changes to data processing operations. In this new era, new releases of applications software also need to be developed to evolve existing systems in realistic and manageable steps. The origin of this book goes back to the early era, when as management consultants, we began working with our clients to introduce this now recognized need for "management" in data processing and computer systems development projects.

THE NATURE OF THE PROBLEM

The fundamental problem in early computer systems development projects was that they were considered to be mostly technical and, therefore, were almost completely turned over to technically trained computer personnel. Little thought was given to the needs of the user and the environment the new computerized application system would be serving. In many cases, technically successful computer system projects were operationally cumbersome and difficult for the users, and they never achieved the originally forecast results. During the second era, computer system projects were becoming increasingly complex, crossing organizational lines, and affecting the traditional methods of operation. The authors, in our management consulting role, helped our clients define the basic methodology necessary for managing the planning, development, and implementation of new computerized application systems. In 1970, Touche Ross & Co. partners John C. Shaw and William Atkins authored a book entitled *Managing Computer Systems Projects* and, in 1971, joined by partner Arnold E. Ditri, they authored a book entitled *Managing the EDP Function*. The purpose of both books was to relate our experiences that resulted in a successful methodology and process for managing computer systems projects and the EDP function. These books were well received and established the basis for the more recent experiences which have resulted in this book. Touche Ross & Co. partners and clients have worked together in recent years to improve the management of the systems development process so that it will be more effective during the current era.

One of the primary reasons underlying the often unfulfilled promise of computers and data processing is the lack of attention to basic management techniques by systems and data processing personnel. Even the rudimentary fundamentals of management (planning, organizing, executing, measuring, and correcting) are often disregarded by systems and data processing organizations. These basic management techniques must be introduced, practiced, ingrained, and enhanced if the promise of the computer is to be fulfilled. These management techniques are integral to successfully managing the systems development process.

The first step toward improving the management of the systems development process is to define the thing to be managed in an orderly and logical fashion. This is done with the full awareness that all computer systems projects are different, just as people's fingerprints are different. The definition recognizes that the systems development process could be categorized into its logical components, just as most people's ten fingers can be classified, e.g., two index fingers, one left and one right, etc. It is also clear that not every step in the systems development process would apply to every situation and that the size and complexity would vary by project. Additionally, the strategy for accomplishing useful results in achievable segments, phases, or releases also varies by project.

The second step to improving the management of the systems development process is to define a methodology or management process for managing a systems project. This management process is designed to accommodate a wide variety of project planning, measuring, and reporting techniques including PERT, CPM, and many commercially available approaches.

These two steps, defining the process to be managed and defining the management process to be utilized, created the bridge connecting general management and technical resources. Section Two of this book illustrates both the systems development process and a proven step-by-step methodology for managing it. These are guidelines, not absolutes, which are intended to strengthen the management process. These guidelines will not resolve specific technical problems nor settle policy and procedural issues. But this methodology will help get them identified earlier, analyzed more thoroughly, evaluated more practically, and decided on a more businesslike basis. This book is about a methodology which, when judiciously applied by capable people, should dramatically improve the effectiveness of the management of the systems development process.

Management should continually be aware of certain risk exposures that exist whenever systems development activities occur. The more common of these include:

— Exposure to fraud (systems that include deliberate misapplication of transactions).

— Exposure to inadequately defined systems that result in competitive disadvantages to an organization.

— Exposure to projects that consume excessive costs in development or ongoing operations.

— Exposure to erroneous business decisions based on inaccurate, misleading, or untimely information from a new system.

— Exposure to costly interruptions of ongoing business operations that result from insufficiently tested new systems, poor backup and recovery procedures, or inadequate conversion and implementation plans.

— Exposure to systems that produce unacceptable accounting information or inadequate audit trails.

Although implied from the above risk exposures, it is important to summarize the primary causes:

— Incomplete economic evaluations.

— Inadequate user or technical specifications.

— Systems design errors.

— Unmaintainable application systems.

— No project kill points.

— Poor communications.

— Technical self-gratification.

— Personnel incompetency.

— Temptations for fraud.
— Management abdication.

Existence of these exposures should not deter management from seeking to obtain new information systems for the organization. Rather, awareness of these exposures should encourage management to establish and maintain adequate controls to minimize the inherent risks associated with the systems development process. In general, these controls involve:

— A structured systems development methodology.
— A formalized project management process.
— Adequate systems documentation.
— Frequent management and user reviews and approvals.
— Timely technical reviews and approvals.
— Appropriate auditor participation.
— Comprehensive systems tests.
— Controlled staff hiring and training programs.
— Thorough post-implementation reviews.

The systems development process and management controls over this process are the primary subjects of this book.

This book does not explain how to operationally manage the systems and data processing function in an organization. Nor is it intended to be a cookbook of pro forma standards applicable to all situations in all environments. The unique characteristics of each systems development project must be carefully considered and the level of detail appropriate in each step clearly defined. The results should provide sufficient documentation at each step for meaningful review and decision making consistent with organizational and operational needs. The level of detail increases as the project moves from planning through implementation, building on the documented results completed in prior steps.

WHERE DOES THIS METHODOLOGY FIT?

Most organizations larger than the smallest proprietorships and professional groups have begun to develop some interest in strategic planning. In very large, complex organizations, planning has often become the competitive difference in the marketplace. Other organizations continue to talk a lot about planning without achieving much in the way of results. Some smaller organizations view planning as having the chief executive officer hold discussions about a decision before it is made public. In any event, there seems to be an emerging consensus that top management should be responsible for establishing long-term objectives; defining general business or operational strategies; and setting specific measurable goals or tactical targets to be achieved within a given time period. The objectives and goals — supported by strategies and tactics — require plans and programs that specifically define what is to be done, when, who is responsible, and what resources are to be applied.

This methodology is appropriate for developing the specific plans and programs called for by the systems projects that support an organization's objectives and goals. It specifically defines the phases of the systems development process — planning, requirements, development, implementation, and maintenance. The definition includes the standard activities that should be performed and the results or end items that should be produced. These standards provide for a controlled approach to the definition and development of information systems required to meet objectives and goals. The end items specify a structured method for establishing how the organization will utilize the system and what costs and benefits should result from various alternatives. In many cases, the planning process will identify a number of versions, or releases of a new system over a time period that meets existing needs, allows for evolutionary change, and permits a realistic scope of development effort.

WHO SHOULD BE INVOLVED?

The systems development process should be consistent with top management's objectives, goals and operating plans. This requires an appropriate involvement by each level of management. Just as it would not normally be expected that the chief executive of an organization would make specific decisions on technical details, it should not be expected that technical personnel and a project team make decisions on the organization's objectives, goals, and operating plans.

In most cases, however, all of the parts of the organization that will be affected should be involved in managing the systems development process. This begins at the top with senior management and includes all levels of management. Generally, senior management establishes the objectives and goals of the programs. Then middle management conducts programs and projects.

The appropriate organizational checks and balances that normally exist for other operations are also required in systems development projects to reduce the risks of partial or complete failure. In many cases, though, organizations have gone overboard in attempting to get management involvement either directly or on steering committees. Examples of inappropriate top management involvement include: making detailed technical presentations on systems design to management who lack sufficient exposure or background to make a competent evaluation of the result; asking top management to approve the purchase of hardware and software components without proper costs and benefits analyses to support the request; and generally approaching management with technical issues which are not put into proper context with the mission of the overall organization.

As consultants to management, we stress the need for "appropriate" involvement in managing the systems development process. In general, top management should view systems plans in the context of objectives, goals, and strategic plans for the organization. In a practical sense, these elements are somewhat interactive and modifications to each occur as they both mature.

Middle management's programs, projects, and operating plans should cause them to have very direct involvement in assessing, approving, and "owning" the systems plans. All of these elements—programs, plans, and systems—should be presented in context to top management for their review and decision. Operating management should then be responsible for the detailed planning, execution, and management of approved systems projects.

All three levels of management require an agreed upon methodology to effectively communicate systems development plans and progress. They should all understand what the phases of the systems project will be, what the standard steps are that will occur in each phase, and what "end items" or results will be accomplished. Then when communicating between the project team and various levels of management on project plans or status, reasonable understanding should result.

The project team in most cases should include personnel from the user organization, from the technical organization, and from other outside re-

SYSTEMS PROJECT
SUMMARY OF EXPERIENCE AND SKILL REQUIREMENTS

Experience and Skills	*Operations Analyst*	*Systems Analyst*	*Technical Analyst*	*Programmer Analyst*
General operations and organization	A	B	C	C
Situation analysis/problem definition	A	B	C	C
Systems concepts/problem solution	A	B	C	C
Systems analysis/general design	A	B	C	C
Cost benefits/feasibility	A	B	C	C
Systems projects planning and management	A	A	C	C
Computer techniques to solve business problems	B	A	B	C
Applications system design	B	A	B	C
Systems specifications	B	A	B	C
Procedures, controls, and training	A	A	B	C
Programming management	B	A	B	B
Systems testing	A	A	B	B
Systems conversion	A	A	B	B
Technical specifications	C	B	A	A
Programming and testing	C	B	A	A
Hardware evaluation and selection	C	B	A	B
System software evaluation and selection	C	B	A	B
Data base design and selection	C	B	A	C
Data communications analysis and network design	C	B	A	C

A = Demonstrated capability
B = General awareness
C = Limited exposure

source organizations as required. In many cases, representation from the user organization is the missing link. Often the systems organization tries to make up for this missing element by having a systems analyst be responsible for both the operational and systems aspects of the project. This becomes increasingly difficult as more systems projects address basic business operations such as order processing, logistics management, and production control. These projects require more operations analysis and result in more significant impacts throughout the organization. Requiring a systems analyst to be responsible for both roles seldom accomplishes the results that were initially anticipated. Therefore, a new function has emerged to which we refer as our "operations analyst." The operations analyst is preferably a member of the user organization, but may be a member of the systems group.

The operations analyst is the catalyst for and the agent of change for improvements in operations, systems, and management. The operations analyst works in concert with line management to identify and evaluate opportunities for cost-effective improvements and subsequently works with operations management to implement approved recommendations. Clarity of thought and expression coupled with effective interpersonal skills are mandatory. The operations analyst is project-oriented and works hands-on throughout implementation to achieve results. Implemented results are the measure of the operations analyst's success even though operations management has ongoing responsibility. The operations analyst's career path is into line management from a background that could include engineering, manufacturing, accounting, finance, or systems analysis.

The operations analyst should have demonstrated capability in: organization and operations; situation analysis and problem definition; operations and systems concepts for problem solving; systems analysis and conceptual design; feasibility analysis and cost benefits evaluation; and systems project management including planning, requirements, development, and implementation. The operations analyst should also have general awareness of: computer systems technical design; systems specifications and procedure preparation.

Due to the variety of definitions of the experience and skills appropriate for the members of a systems project team, the chart on page 7 summarizes the general mix that is appropriate. As any project progresses through the various phases and steps, the experience and skill requirements change. This normally results in personnel changes for the project team in order to complete the necessary activities and tasks.

SUMMARY Managing the systems development process is a complex business. The process should be integral to the organization's overall planning and operation. As shown on the facing page, application systems plans should flow from strategic and tactical plans that include organization objectives, competitive strategies (including potential mergers, acquisitions, and divestures), market growth and changes (including legislative trends), forecast economic changes, and new and planned technological developments.

The application systems plans should then be supported by plans for hardware, software, personnel, facilities, financing, and overall implementation approaches. Application systems plans lead to development projects that impact future systems plans. Similarly, the plans lead to new data processing operations that, in the future, impact new support plans for hardware, software, personnel, and facilities. Overall the plans lead back to influencing future tactical planning. The process is integrated and continuing. It should be applied by all levels of management to be effective in an organization.

The remainder of Section One presents an overview of the systems development process followed by a discussion of project management and estimating. Section Two then presents the details of the systems development process and Section Three supports this process with a comprehensive set of standard forms. Properly applied, these guidelines should significantly improve the management of the systems development process.

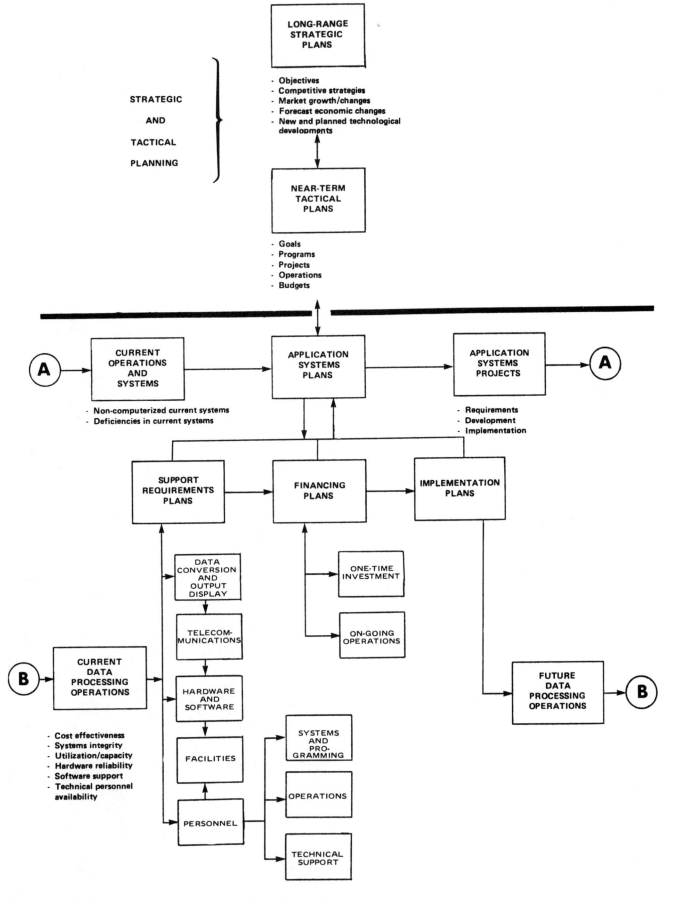

STRATEGIC

AND

TACTICAL

PLANNING

LONG-RANGE
STRATEGIC
PLANS

- Objectives
- Competitive strategies
- Market growth/changes
- Forecast economic changes
- New and planned technological
  developments

NEAR-TERM
TACTICAL
PLANS

- Goals
- Programs
- Projects
- Operations
- Budgets

A

CURRENT
OPERATIONS
AND
SYSTEMS

APPLICATION
SYSTEMS
PLANS

APPLICATION
SYSTEMS
PROJECTS

A

- Non-computerized current systems
- Deficiencies in current systems

- Requirements
- Development
- Implementation

SUPPORT
REQUIREMENTS
PLANS

FINANCING
PLANS

IMPLEMENTATION
PLANS

DATA
CONVERSION
AND
OUTPUT
DISPLAY

ONE-TIME
INVESTMENT

TELECOM-
MUNICATIONS

ON-GOING
OPERATIONS

B

CURRENT
DATA
PROCESSING
OPERATIONS

HARDWARE
AND
SOFTWARE

FUTURE
DATA
PROCESSING
OPERATIONS

B

- Cost effectiveness
- Systems integrity
- Utilization/capacity
- Hardware reliability
- Software support
- Technical personnel
  availability

FACILITIES

SYSTEMS
AND
PRO-
GRAMMING

OPERATIONS

PERSONNEL

TECHNICAL
SUPPORT

OVERVIEW OF THE SYSTEMS DEVELOPMENT PROCESS

INTRODUCTION The systems development process is a comprehensive guideline for creating new information systems. It is a generalized process that is appropriate for all systems development projects. It is also highly flexible and adaptable to individual situations. Although technical in nature, the systems development process is primarily a business management process that provides a structured approach for a multidiscipline group involved in any project.

The approach to systems development is characterized by breaking down the total job into a series of manageable units, each of which is further broken down into controllable job assignments that can be defined, analyzed, evaluated, and budgeted with a degree of assurance. Further, the approach recognizes the importance of structuring the individual work segments to produce end products and of determining these end items in advance. Uniform, predefined end products do not limit or preclude creativity. They provide instead a consistent structure within which to display creativity. The end products also give management something against which to compare progress and quality. Thus, no matter what the systems project is to produce, there are interim points at which results can be evaluated and measured against known standards.

The systems development process uses a consistent set of terms to describe this top-down approach to breaking the total job into logical, functional parts. The complete development process has four *phases*, each of which has several *steps* containing a group of standard *activities*. Project work assignments are created by developing a specific set of *tasks* that are to be completed in the individual project situation in order to accomplish each standard activity.

A *phase* is a major self-contained component of the systems development process. Four phases encompass the entire systems project:

Phase I: Systems Planning.

Phase II: Systems Requirements.

Phase III: Systems Development.

Phase IV: Systems Implementation.

At the completion of each of the first three phases, a major end product has been created containing the results of that particular phase and plans for subsequent phases. These products are key factors in management's review, evaluation, and determination of whether or not to proceed to the next phase. A project may be terminated or redirected at each point if it is not economically, technically, or politically viable (or if it is not important enough to warrant the use of available project resources). At the end of the fourth phase, the new system is in operation and an evaluation is prepared for management to review actual versus planned results. A fifth phase — Systems Maintenance — contains the repetitive process used to maintain and enhance a system after it is installed.

A series of steps exists within each phase. The steps will be individually discussed below. Each step is a logical part in accomplishing the objectives of the particular phase. For example, within Phase III — Systems Development — separate steps exist for specifications, programming, procedures, training, systems testing, and others. In general, each step consists of a functional group of activities that may be assigned to specific members within the project team. Some of these steps primarily involve users, such as Phase II, Step 2 — User Requirements; and Phase III, Step 5 — User Procedures and Controls. Other steps are highly technical in nature, such as Phase III, Step 2 — Technical Support Development; and Phase III, Step 4 — Applications Programming and Testing. Still others are oriented to the project manager, as in Phase III, Step 8 — Conversion Planning. Finally, steps such as Phase III, Step 9 — Systems Testing — require a variety of skills and involve all participants in the development project. The quantity and mix of project personnel is generally constant within any given step. However, because of the variety of steps (some of which may be conducted simultaneously), the overall size and mix of the total project team may frequently change. The structured approach to phases and steps permits these changes to occur in a planned and controlled environment.

A group of standard activities has been included with our analysis of each step in the systems development process. These activities provide the project team with guidelines and methods to accomplish the step's desired end results. Toward this end, a "standard activities/end items" matrix has been included with each step to guide the project team in the completion of the project work. As previously noted, end items are expected to produce specific results for each activity. They provide structure, uniformity, and predictability without inhibiting the analytical or technical creativity necessary in any successful systems project. For example, in Phase II, Step 4 — Conceptual Design and Package Review — a standard activity designed to evaluate packages includes an approach to the evaluation, suggested criteria, and a methodology for ranking results. Although this activity is structured and has definable end products, it does not eliminate the requirement for significant analytical effort in order to produce quality results.

In many cases, activities must be broken down further in order to properly assign and control project work. This involves identifying specific tasks with definable work efforts. Often, the major tasks have been included in describing the standard activities. Thus, an activity in the Feasibility Study (Phase I, Step 2) to "Determine Preliminary User Requirements" includes such tasks as "Identify minimum objectives" and "Outline changes in functions." For some projects, even these tasks will be too general to use for individual work assignments. In such cases, an additional breakdown into subtasks is required. The lowest level of work definition varies within any project. The key, however, is to end with a specific piece of work to produce a tangible end item which can be readily assigned, measured, and evaluated.

The end-item orientation also includes an important cumulative documentation concept. That is, documentation created in any given step is based on the existing level of knowledge and is sufficient to make the decisions required at that point. In subsequent steps, this same documentation is expanded with sufficient additional detail to accomplish the goals at each point in the overall process. Used properly, this orderly approach to documentation not only provides the necessary detail when needed, but also permits temporary in-process terminations to the project and changes in project staffing without starting over or redoing major efforts.

The standard approach to phases, steps, activities, and tasks makes it possible to plan, control, and evaluate progress during the systems development process. Use of a consistent approach throughout all projects improves communication with management and users. The structure allows management to make and monitor incremental commitments and the ability to impact interim results. Thus, adopting a uniform structure is the key to an organization's effective management of the systems development process.

PHASE I — SYSTEMS PLANNING

The systems development process begins with a planning phase to formalize conceptual changes and determine the feasibility of pursuing further development. Requests for information changes and new systems may originate from many sources within an organization—management, users, other projects, etc. Typically, these requests are received by the systems department, where it is determined whether they can be met through maintenance or minor enhancements to existing systems. If they cannot, they form the basis for initiating the first step in the development process.

Step 1 — Initial Investigation

An initial investigation gives management the opportunity to evaluate new systems requests at a preliminary level without major commitments of personnel or dollar resources. It provides enough of an analysis to conclude whether the request warrants a formal feasibility study. In many organizations, general management uses a steering committee mechanism to guide the systems development process. In such cases, the committee assigns the responsibility and priority for conducting an initial investigation. The committee also has the perspective and authority to eliminate all inappropriate requests at this early stage. Thus, properly used, the initial investigation step can save a great deal of time and effort, since many decisions to terminate are made at this point after minimal investment. However, if the request warrants a feasibility study, preparation of the detailed work plan for Step 2 is included so that specific commitments may be made for user and systems project personnel as an integral part of the approval to proceed.

Step 2 — Feasibility Study

The objective of the feasibility study is to report to management the probable characteristics, costs, and benefits of implementing a specific system and to provide generalized project requirements in the form of a formal report. If practical, the study results should offer alternative conceptual solutions with associated costs and benefits, such as a complex approach offering long-term improvements and a less sophisticated approach with short-term improvements.

Determination of project costs includes planning project activities in subsequent phases and estimating time, staffing, and equipment requirements. User involvement in this step is critical to judge the impact of alternative solutions and to substantiate much of the economic evaluation. In addition, experienced senior systems analysts are required to gather and analyze the proper information and reach practical conclusions. The major responsibility of this combined project team is to determine the operating and technical feasibility of the requested system and to find out whether it will produce an acceptable return on the investment.

The end result of a feasibility study is a decision by the steering committee to either approve or terminate the next phase of the project — Systems Requirements. This decision is critical because a major commitment of resources is required for the following phases. Thus, the intent should be to eliminate those projects that are not feasible. If approved, the steering committee assigns priorities in relation to other approved projects and available resources.

PHASE II —
SYSTEMS REQUIREMENTS

The second phase of the systems development process provides the detailed foundation upon which the technical programs and procedures will be developed. Since the new system is to be created for the user's benefit, the initial emphasis is directed entirely to an analysis of user operations. Once user environment and requirements are understood in detail, the technical approaches are determined. Alternatives are evaluated and detailed plans are prepared for development. The phase ends with another review by the steering committee and a decision to either terminate or proceed.

Step 1 — Operations and
Systems Analysis

Current user business objectives, functions, and information flows are analyzed in this step to obtain a detailed understanding of user operations, complexities, problems, and interrelationships. Basic documentation covering user organization, functions, workflows, reports, forms, and files is prepared. In addition, detailed analyses are conducted to understand exception processing, impact of incomplete reports, quality of existing files, controls used to identify and correct errors, relevant business policies, operating constraints, and current levels of system performance. The end product of the Operations and Systems Analysis step is a comprehensive document that provides a reference capability and a base of information from which to prepare requirements and designs for new systems.

Step 2 — User Requirements

The User Requirements step produces a detailed definition of the proposed system's end products in terms of its impact on user operations. User objectives are defined to ensure that alternative technical approaches will be evaluated in terms of their utility in meeting the target requirements. It is critical that these requirements reflect the essential functions and strengths of existing operations and resolve current system shortcomings. The end product of this step is a manual that specifies what the new system will do for its users in terms of functions, information to be maintained and reported, workflows, assumptions, constraints, and impact on user organizations.

Step 3 — Technical
Support Approach

The objective of this step is to determine the technical environment in which the proposed system must operate. Thus, emphasis is on hardware and non-application systems software — operating system, data base management system, communications control programs, etc. This step requires specialized technical expertise and an understanding of existing hardware and software environmental constraints. It may require sufficiently detailed analysis to generate formal requests for proposals from potential hardware and software vendors. Alternative technical approaches may be created and evaluated in terms of technical staff requirements, benefits, costs, education requirements, and project schedule implications.

The Technical Support Approach step is normally conducted in parallel with Step 4 — Conceptual Design and Package Review. The end products of both steps are then used to complete this phase in Step 5 — Alternatives Evaluation and Development Planning.

Step 4 — Conceptual Design and Package Review

The Conceptual Design and Package Review step contains the first-level technical definition of the new application system. This consists of translating user requirements into a conceptual application approach for their implementation. If the feasibility study in Phase I identified potential application packages, then a detailed review of these packages is also included in this step. The relative distribution of effort between reviewing packages and designing new systems depends on the likelihood that a package will fulfill stated user requirements. The proposed system may consist of several major subsystems, some of which may be candidates for package use and others that may require complete redevelopment.

Conceptual design activities include determining the EDP functions and flows required to relate all inputs, outputs, and data element groups previously identified in the User Requirements step. These flowcharts are not intended to identify every program that may eventually be developed, but only to depict the required primary processing functions. The design effort also includes documenting approaches for security, privacy, and control constraints.

Package review activities include preparation of requests for proposals to potential vendors, development of evaluation criteria, and the review of candidate packages. This step concludes with a summary of design and package alternatives for use in the following step.

Step 5 — Alternatives Evaluation and Development Planning

This final step in Phase II has two primary objectives. First, all technical and systems design approaches must be finalized, including make-versus-buy decisions. Second, a detailed project plan for the subsequent Systems Development phase must be prepared. This planning process includes preparation of a revised economic evaluation of the project. That evaluation — along with development plans and approaches — is finally presented to the steering committee for formal approval before proceeding to the development phase.

In many respects, the entire Systems Requirements effort has been directed towards refining and verifying the concepts and plans that were originally presented at the end of the Systems Planning phase. This new economic evaluation may therefore be expected to confirm that the initial assumptions and concepts are still valid. If the more detailed review and design activities resulting from this phase have substantially modified earlier estimates of costs, benefits, or expected system performance, the steering committee may find it appropriate to reevaluate its original decision.

PHASE III — SYSTEMS DEVELOPMENT

The Systems Development phase is generally the largest and most complex segment in the process of creating a new system. The phase begins with an accepted conceptual design approach and perhaps even an agreement to acquire new hardware, software, or application packages. It ends with a completely developed new system that has been thoroughly tested and prepared for implementation. This phase includes nine steps that encompass detailed design specifications, implementation of the technical support functions, writing application specifications and programs, preparing procedures, training users, planning the conversion and implementation, and testing the system. For many projects, this phase may be repeated several times in order to develop multiple subsystems identified during the previous Systems Requirements phase. Purchase of an application package may change the scope and reduce the effort in many of these steps, but seldom eliminates any step altogether.

This phase ends with a presentation to management—the steering committee—summarizing the results of the development and testing efforts, and agreement by all parties (users, systems department, data processing operations, internal audit, etc.) that the new system should be implemented. The steering committee then makes the final decision to terminate or implement the new system.

**Step 1 — Systems
Technical Specifications**

This step includes preparation of the detailed specifications required for both the new application system and the technical software support. The conceptual design prepared in Phase II is used to develop detailed specifications for each output and input, to identify all the functional components of the application, and to define all the data elements and files. The technical software specifications are also prepared, including (if necessary) a data base design and a network design. This step concludes with a finalization of hardware/software delivery commitments and costs. If significant changes from the accepted plan for Phase III occur, additional review and approval by the steering committee is required.

**Step 2 — Technical
Support Development**

The major objective of the Technical Support Development step is to finalize technical procedures and programming policies so that the large project team involved in the subsequent development steps can be efficiently and effectively managed. A secondary objective of this step is to minimize the risks inherent in any previous assumptions about the operation or efficiency of the hardware or software. As such, this step includes generating and testing generation of a prototype data base and the on-line software. These are used to test all critical operating assumptions and characteristics before starting the major programming efforts. Once completed, they also form a basis for use in applications program testing and user training.

This step marks a transition from the analytical and creative process to one where the new system is actually constructed, tested, and implemented. It represents the last chance to make significant changes to the detailed design without incurring major costs in reprogramming or reimplementation.

**Step 3 —
Applications Specifications**

The basic activities associated with this step are to convert the detailed systems specifications prepared in Step 1 of this phase into detailed programming specifications. This step is very technical and hardware-oriented and is often planned and controlled together with the subsequent programming step. Documentation prepared for applications specifications includes finalization of all input and output records and file layouts, detailed description of all program functions, program test plans and test data, and planned requirements for computer operations personnel and equipment.

**Step 4 — Applications
Programming and Testing**

The Applications Programming and Testing step includes the conversion of applications specifications into machine-executable instructions, the conduct of unit and string testing of those instructions, the completion of necessary program documentation, and preparation of the completed operational programs or modules for systems test. Much of the work in this step can often be carried on at the same time as the preceding step, particularly if a top-down approach has been followed in systems design. This overlap gives project managers a chance to save time because these two steps generally account for a very substantial portion of the total time in this phase.

Step 5 – User Procedures and Controls

This step concentrates on developing the detailed manual procedures that must be performed in the new system. A variety of procedures and control documents is generally required to assure adequate operation of the entire system. This includes manual controls for input/output, data files, system access, file maintenance, and recovery. User procedures are developed for normal operations, manual backup, error correction, report usage, and terminal operations.

The User Procedures and Controls step and the User Training step that follows it are primarily performed by user members of the project team. These two steps occur at the same time as the applications specifications and programming are being completed.

Step 6 – User Training

This step uses the completed manual procedures to prepare users for systems testing and subsequent implementation. It includes preparation of an organized training program with supporting material and training activities for an initial group of users.

Step 7 – Implementation Planning

The Implementation Planning step and Conversion Planning (Step 8) are conducted as final preparation before initiating the Implementation phase. Previous steps throughout the development process have included conceptual approaches and strategies for conversion and implementation. These two steps are now required to finalize plans and obtain clear commitments from all affected areas as to both the required effort ant the schedules. They are performed primarily by project management personnel at the same time that specifications, programs, and procedures are being developed.

Implementation planning includes activities for preparing systems test plans, hardware/software installation plans, site preparation schedules, and final systems acceptance criteria.

Step 8 – Conversion Planning

The Conversion Planning step is the second major planning step conducted during the preparation for systems implementation. Previous steps throughout the development process have included conceptual approaches and strategies for conversion. They may also have included identification of special conversion programs and manual procedure requirements. This step is required to review the status of special preparation activities and to finalize detailed plans for converting to the new system.

Step 9 – Systems Test

The purpose of this step is to perform an efficient, accurate, and complete test of all new system components — both computerized and manual — in an integrated fashion. This step begins with programs that have already been individually and string tested, and with procedures that have also been tested. However, actual operational considerations are the key to a systems test because they place the new system under the same daily conditions and stresses that will be encountered during regular operations. To fully explore these conditions, the test includes deliberately caused errors and difficulties that are specifically intended to force the system to fail as a way to test error detection and recovery capabilities. In each case, the objective is to ensure that risks have been anticipated and that the system can recover from failure.

The systems test ends when all involved personnel — users, systems analysts, data processing operations, internal audit, etc. — agree that the new

17

system meets all requirements and a recommendation is made to the steering committee to proceed with implementation.

PHASE IV — SYSTEMS IMPLEMENTATION

The last phase in the new systems development process is Systems Implementation. During this phase, files are converted, final training is conducted, new programs and procedures are initiated, and old processes are discontinued. Certain refinement and tuning operations are then performed to make the new system operate effectively. For many new systems projects, this phase is repeated several times in order to implement the new system in multiple locations or to implement several related subsystems.

Finally, after the new system is in stable operation, a post-implementation review is conducted to compare actual results to the original concepts and plans.

Step 1 — Conversion and Phased Implementation

The goal of the conversion portion of this step is to attain a state of operation of the new system covering three primary areas. First, the equipment required to implement the system must be installed, tested, and accepted. Second, construction and validation must occur on the new data files. Third, final training for user and data processing operations personnel must be conducted in their new or modified job junctions. In many systems projects, this step occurs several times and may also occur at the same time as some portions of the previous phase. In addition, some conversion activities may actually have been initiated very early in the project, where, for example, major data purification efforts are required.

This step also includes implementation of the new system. Its basic purpose is to bring the newly converted system to the point where it is a routine ongoing part of both the user operations and the data processing department.

Step 2 — Refinement and Tuning

Refining and tuning the system that has just been implemented is a critical but frequently ignored step in the systems development process. As users become familiar with the new system, they can and do identify areas that need to be changed and corrected. This refinement and tuning process improves the system to meet performance and requirements criteria established during Phase II — Systems Requirements.

At the conclusion of this step, the programs, procedures, and documentation are turned over to those responsible for ongoing systems maintenance.

Step 3 — Post-implementation Review

This step is conducted after a new system has been implemented so that management may assess the successes and shortcomings of the systems development efforts. Since the objective is assessment, timing is important. It is impractical to perform this step until the system has operated long enough to produce measurable results. The timing varies but should be clearly stated in the original economic evaluations. The steering committee generally has responsibility for authorizing this step and receives the results of the review.

SYSTEMS MAINTENANCE

Maintenance is playing an increasingly important role in most data processing installations as greater numbers of systems are produced. The complex relationship among systems in a typical environment requires more maintenance overhead. Meeting these needs is an important challenge and a vital extension of the systems development process. The approach is structured and consists of prioritization, analysis, specification, programming, and documentation. Extensive systems tests are often appropriate to assure that unforeseen problems have not been created. Training, conversion, and implementation are then planned and conducted.

PROJECT-RELATED PERSONNEL

In any given systems project, a variety of personnel and groups representing different skills and backgrounds and having specified roles and responsibilities may be involved. In general, however, four groups are directly involved in the systems development process—the project team, steering committee, data processing operations, and a quality assurance function.

The Project Team

For most projects, the size and mix of skills in the project team fluctuates—based on the needs of the phase and step and the requirements of the particular project. Adding and removing project team members is usually a difficult management process. It may be accomplished, however, given two basic fundamentals of the systems development process. First, the process uses a standard approach enabling the project manager, systems department, and user departments to understand the current status in the development process, activities that have been completed, and work to be done. Second, the process uses a cumulative documentation approach. This reduces dependence on individual team members by producing consistent documentation in standard formats and adding successive amounts of detail at specific steps in the process.

Virtually all systems project teams require a mix of user and technical personnel. Since new systems ultimately belong to the users, their participation in creating the system is essential. The early steps in Phases I and II require significant user involvement. They contribute in areas such as detail requirements, economic impact, operational feasibility, conversion timing, and implementation location.

As the project progresses into the development phase, the project team size generally increases, with a much greater proportion of technical personnel. User involvement continues, however, for procedures, training, and systems test. The project team for the implementation phase varies depending on the particular environment, but requires both user and technical personnel.

Steering Committee

The steering committee is a mechanism established by general management to provide corporate direction over the planning, development, and implementation of new systems. It is required for systems departments serving multiple users in multiple disciplines. At one time, the systems department of many organizations concentrated primarily on financial applications for a single user, and there was no real need for a steering committee. More recently, however, systems departments have been addressing applications in manufacturing, marketing, distribution, and other areas. Thus, a decision-making mechanism for allocating limited resources among multiple departments is required.

Steering committee members should be able to commit departments to using new systems and should be able to speak for individual department policies. They establish project priorities and provide policy direction—not direct management control—over individual projects. The committee monitors project status. It conducts a project review at the end of each phase and decides to either terminate or continue the project. Reviews are conducted at other points in the development process only when significant changes occur. An important role of the steering committee is to resolve policy conflicts among departments that may occur when new systems are developed for multiple users.

A steering committee may oversee data processing operations and evaluate equipment acquisitions. However, this may be a different group than the systems steering committee.

Data Processing Operations

For most new systems, the current data processing operations department will become ultimately responsible for ongoing production after successful implementation. Thus, it is critical for representatives from that department to participate throughout the development process. They should ensure that the new system is developed to conform with existing operations standards.

Commitments of equipment resources and schedules are critical to project progress and timely completion. Operations management must be sufficiently knowledgeable about a new system to make realistic commitments of resources for program development and testing, systems testing, conversion, and ongoing production.

Quality Assurance

The need for a quality assurance function is more and more frequently recognized as an integral part of the systems development and project management processes. This individual or team fulfills a role that is similar to that of the engineering and manufacturing quality control inspection and approval function. The quality assurance team reviews the development efforts for a technically sound approach and a strong business rationale. It is not integrated within the project team but operates at a level equivalent to that of the project manager.

The quality assurance manager also provides a valuable review and advisory role to the project manager in defining project end products, modifying schedules and budgets, and enforcing adherence to standards among the project team members.

IMPLEMENTING STANDARDS

The definition and effective implementation of a standard systems development process is a major undertaking for any organization. There are many challenges to meet and requirements to fill for the installation of a system of standards. With any approach, the business requirements to be addressed and the capacity of the approach to meet those requirements warrant a careful analysis. No two organizations are identical in their procedures or policies. The successful development and implementation of a standard systems development process is enhanced by efforts to customize a methodology to the organization rather than by simply adopting a generalized package.

The logical first step is to form a standards development project team. Those selected to establish new systems development standards should have extensive skills in project management, systems development, and systems maintenance. They should be highly regarded by their peers within the systems and data processing organization. As appropriate, team members should include users, internal auditors, computer operations, technical support, application development and system support groups. When available, a technical writer should also be assigned to the project team. This increases the productivity of the group and enhances the quality of the documents produced. It may also be desirable to establish a special review group drawn from experienced project managers.

There are standards within almost any organization that develops new systems on a continuing basis. They may be formal or informal and exist as multiple sets of standards for different individuals or functional groups. The project team identifies past successes and failures in the use of existing systems development techniques. The team meets with every organizational entity affected by the Systems Development Process, including:

— User management and line operating personnel.
— Internal audit personnel.
— Members of the steering committee.
— General managers whose functions are not represented on the steering committee.
— Systems development project managers.
— Analysts and programmers with maintenance responsibilities.
— Computer operations personnel.
— Systems and data processing management.

Data is gathered and analyzed to establish the parameters within which new systems development standards are to be implemented in the specific organization. For example, a review of maintenance activities should be performed to determine the types, causes, and frequency of systems revision. A review of this type often identifies weaknesses in the existing systems development methodology. By reviewing past maintenance, the project team's understanding of current documentation and procedures is enhanced. In addition, any post-implementation review reports from previous development and implementation efforts should be reviewed to identify trends in cost estimation and their relation to benefits. If problems reappear, understanding these situations can help shape future systems development standards.

The project team should also analyze past and current systems development projects to profile the type of work being done within the organization. This includes the number of projects and their duration, personnel resources in use, technologies applied, etc. Such a profile may indicate that most of the projects within the organization are relatively short. A comprehensive development structure (such as that presented in this book) may be more than is needed except for a few major efforts. Within an organization such as the one just described, the major development project will be the exception rather than the rule.

A set of specifications, or requirements, is than developed for use in adapting the general approach to the organization's specific needs. Any weaknesses in the current methodology are identified for special attention by the project team.

The most effective approach to developing new systems standards is similar to that used in the systems development process itself — a top-down approach. In effect, the outlining of standards proceeds from the general to the specific, beginning with a table of contents, such as:

— Overview.
— Administration of standards.
— Identification and listing of the phases and steps.
— Identification of the procedures and conditions which permit deviating from standards.

The next activity is to create outline structures for the phases and steps identified for the specific methodology. Significant attributes are identified for each, including:

— Primary objectives.
— Key end products.

— Types of skills required to produce the end products.

— Types of reviews to conduct at the end of the phases and steps.

— Interrelationships between this step and those that precede and follow it.

The process of describing phases and steps in this format leads to discovery or further modification. Some steps are combined, others are added.

Having defined the phases and steps, the team then determines work to be done at the activity level and describes the interim end products associated with those activities. The standard activities/end-item matrices included in this book will indicate the level of detail appropriate in defining both activities and end products. In addition, the end products themselves are broken down to identify the elements of information of which they are comprised.

The standards development effort then concentrates on adding detail to the outline completed previously — to the point where a technical writer can begin to draft the actual standards. This activity produces a detailed text that is reviewed by the entire standards team, the project review group, and other interested parties. Comments and recommendations produced by these reviews are incorporated in the text before actual drafting of final standards documentation begins.

As the last activity before drafting the final standards, some decisions are required on the style and format of the manuals and forms to be produced by the technical writer. The major issues concern who will use the manuals and forms. This impacts on both the writing style and the format of the documents. Once the users are defined, the manual can be written so as to best communicate with that group. The matters of style concern themselves with language complexity, sentences and paragraph length, and other details. Format decisions deal with the organization of the manual, how the sections are presented within each segment, the use of overview summaries to begin each chapter, and the presentation of objectives, activities, skill requirements, and end products. In addition, decisions are needed on how to organize forms, what numbering structure to use, and how to present illustrations.

These seemingly mundane topics make up an important part of the preparation of the standards manuals because the packaging of any product has a major impact on its acceptance. Nothing can destroy the communicative ability of a written document faster than inconsistent or poorly developed style or format. From the writer's standpoint, these decisions must be made before the final standards are drafted to avoid extensive rewriting. If questions about format or style remain unanswered, the team may draft a short chapter or sequence from the manual and use this draft as a tool to develop final edits of style and format.

Standards manuals are generally used as reference documents. They are rarely read through from start to finish by anyone not actually engaged in their drafting. Thus, it is critical for standards programs to include training materials for all personnel involved in systems development projects and maintenance to which the standards apply. Training materials should also include at least one case study to illustrate the points being made and to demonstrate how standards are used. A common approach for the development of this case study is to document work done during the piloting of the standards.

Based on pilot results, the standards manual is revised and/or corrected as required. The final document is then published and distributed. Preparation of distribution lists for standards manuals is an important consideration and is done either before the manual is finalized or during final editing and printing. Once the recipients of the manual are identified, a program that combines distribution of the document and training of its users should be developed. Actual distribution of standards manuals, insofar as is possible, takes place at overview training sessions. Training associated with standards for specific project phases can thus be integrated with actual schedules within the organization. It is best to begin detailed training at the inception of a project and follow along phase by phase, but this is not always possible. Where extensive projects are at interim points, it may be best to initiate the standards at the start of a major phase.

It is important to remember that standards should be flexible. There should be constant interaction among programmers, analysts, and users. This kind of communication can enable the organization to spot trends and potential improvements more quickly. Changes in technologies and people will bring about new opportunities for improvement. These changes will also require modifications in standards and documentation. The documentation approach is really a question of substance, not of form. The forms may already exist, but the point is that they provide information on how something works.

NOT TOO STANDARD

Taken together, the systems development and project management processes described in this book can appear quite formidable — possibly overwhelming. The development structure itself involves four phases, 19 steps, a long list of activities to be performed more or less in established sequence, a well-defined set of end products, and a number of formal and informal reviews and approvals.

One frequently encountered reaction is that all of these tasks, activities, steps, and phases are not appropriate every time. Situations may occur where certain reviews or tasks are skipped, where procedures are abridged, or where activities are performed in a different sequence. Where such optional alternatives are applied, does this mean that the systems development process itself is inappropriate?

The answer depends on the perspective of the respondent. If a rigid, all-or-nothing approach to the implementation of standards is taken, then changes in structure, activities, or end items become intolerable. Given such an attitude, a system of standards will ultimately break down. On the other hand, if the respondent regards system standards as statements of policies or guidelines which can be interpreted or adapted to the realities of special situations, then these types of changes are easily accommodated.

The ability to deal with exceptions is built into most effective systems. This is particularly true for the systems development process described in this book. The framework is universal, but can accommodate exceptions where a situation demands it. The standards presented here are not so rigid as to inhibit responsiveness to business demands. At the same time, they should not become so flexible as to destroy standardization and lose management control over the quality of work, adherence to schedules, and/or costs. Few experienced managers would support positions that favor either complete rigidity or total flexibility.

It is, or course, impossible to identify in advance all of the conditions that could require deviation from standards. However, it is possible — highly desirable in fact — to establish a series of questions that can be addressed in determining when and whether such deviations are appropriate. These include:

— Would the change or omission being considered reduce the ability of the project manager to meet responsibilities for management and control?

— Does the change or omission under consideration impair management's ability to compare this project with others under development?

— Is communication about the system under development changed in any way? What effect is there upon the understanding of the evolving system by users, EDP operations, project team members, and others?

— Are apparent gains in efficiency offset by reductions in quality?

— Is system maintenance impaired by the proposed change? If so, how? What risks are involved?

If the answers to questions like these indicate the need to suspend system standards, it is important to substitute procedures and documents that maintain manageability and control of the affected project. Appropriate criteria and procedures for suspended standards include:

— The decision should be specific. There should be a definite awareness of what standards are being suspended and what procedures, if any, are being substituted.

— The consequences of the suspension or change should be understood.

— Value should be identified and established for the action.

— Reasons and procedures associated with the suspension or change should be documented and included in the project work papers.

— Appropriate levels of management approval should be secured and documented.

The source or level of management approval for a suspension of standards depends on the nature and scope of the decision. If a standard to be suspended only affects the activities of a project team, the project manager may make this decision. If external parties are affected, they should be consulted.

Since situations in which standards are substituted or suspended are highly individual and judgmental, it is obviously impossible to set any firm rules for covering such actions.

The systems development process described in this book is designed to accommodate major projects. However, many smaller, shorter projects are encountered, for which the project structure discussed here can be condensed. Such practices conform to the realities of shorter projects. On a major project, the phase and step structures are established to reflect skill-level differences of the personnel in the project team. Further, phases and steps are established as a checkpointing mechanism, based upon estimated amount of work which can be managed and controlled under typical circumstances. If a project can be completed in a relatively short time frame, it becomes more practical to assemble a small project team that will be together from start to finish. It becomes possible to let individual team members carry through activities spanning several steps within the conventional structure. Furthermore, steering committee reviews need not be as frequent in a smaller, shorter project as for a major undertaking. In summary, the systems development process is a tool designed to be adapted to individual needs and situations.

PROJECT MANAGEMENT AND ESTIMATING

OVERVIEW The systems development process is a series of phases and steps designed to guide a project team from the concept to the implementation and maintenance of a new system. Equally important, and needed with this set of guidelines, is a formalized project management process. Just as the systems development process structures the creation of change, so project management structures the process of managing that change. The project management process is not limited to systems projects; however, its concepts apply equally well in virtually any project-oriented environment. It is really a process of *managing people within a project* — not one of completing forms and counting hours against completed tasks.

An important key to this process is the fact that it is *project-oriented*. Whether large or small, long or short in duration, complex or straightforward in organization or technical implications, all projects share certain minimal basic criteria:

— They have specific objectives to create end products and results.
— They exist for a specified length of time.
— They are not a normal ongoing operation in any part of the organization.

Likewise, the management concepts are basic: planning, organizing, staffing, directing, coordinating, controlling, measuring, reporting, and evaluating. These concepts apply to large projects and small ones. They are not the techniques used to manage ongoing operations, however — with any given project, there is usually but one chance to succeed. Project management further differs from ongoing departmental management in that it normally excludes administrative and personnel functions such as promotions, terminations, salary reviews, and career development. Thus, two sets of management controls should be in operation whenever projects exist in an organization. Since projects are transient operations, controls developed for each unique situation must consider existing departmental management controls.

The project management process is in force throughout the entire life of a project and must be applied carefully and thoroughly. This is particularly important for systems projects which have in the past established a record of late completions, excessive costs, end products that did not meet user needs, and failure to realize expected benefits.

Many systems being developed and planned today are much more complex than their predecessors. For example, single-user systems projects to convert fixed bookkeeping procedures from manual to mechanized approaches are no longer the commonest. Instead, more of today's systems projects address complex issues involving the application of computer assistance to order processing, logistics management, quality control, financial planning, etc. Such projects require a greater degree of expertise and the ability to understand complex business environments and complex technical issues, such as data base approaches, networking, distributed processing, minicomputers, intelligent terminals, and so on. Equally important, they require project skills to deal effectively with multiple users having different and perhaps conflicting interests, goals, and priorities. Nevertheless, the basic concepts of project management are valid and apply to managing a process of change with the following characteristics:

- it is innovative;
- it may operate within critical time schedule constraints;
- it successfully impacts ongoing systems involving people, procedures, and equipment;
- it provides economical improvements and meets the real needs of its users;
- it addresses technical, economic, psychological, and political implications.

The project management process implies the current or impending existence of a project, and thus a user (department, division, client, customer, etc.). It therefore assumes that both users and user management want the new system and want to make it work. If they do not, the project will probably fail, even with an otherwise sound project management approach. Conversely, a high degree of user support and commitment is not likely to produce a successful new system if project management is not sensitive to the user environment. A specific project management approach must be developed based on a complete understanding of the user's business, including knowing how results in that business are measured, how good (or bad) results have been and are projected to be, and how other factors may affect these results.

In essence, the project management process is itself a system involving:

- management, project staff, and users;
- procedures for planning, scheduling, monitoring, control, coordination, direction, measurement, reporting, and corrective action;
- forms, reports, and other materials;
- facilities and equipment support.

The components of this system and application of its concepts are discussed in the following three subsections on project organization, planning, and control. Although presented separately, these three activities are closely interrelated and take place simultaneously and continuously throughout the life of any project.

PROJECT ORGANIZATION

General Concepts Within any systems project, an organization of people is created to perform the required activities and tasks. The precise structure of this organization varies and depends on the unique environment and needs of the specific project. However, any project management approach should contain certain basic organizational concepts:

— The project should receive authority from, and be accountable to, general management.
— A project manager should be designated with clearly assigned responsibility to plan and control the project.
— All team members should have specifically defined roles and responsibilities.

General management controls the planning, development, and implementation of new systems in a variety of ways. However, as discussed in the subsection on Initial Investigation (Phase I, Step 1), the term "steering committee" is used in this book to represent this organizational control mechanism. Note that this does *not* imply that project management is a "committee" process. It is not. Whereas committees are created to recommend acceptable compromises, projects are expected to produce defined results.

Organization of a project may also vary in the extent to which it is a separate physical entity with its own support staff. Some projects are so large, take so long, or are so remote from their team members' own department locations that separate facilities and support are clearly required. Others may need to be physically separated because of project characteristics such as:

— The priority and attention given by general management or the steering committee that may dictate the need for special arrangements.
— A lack of successfully completed projects without physical separation.
— A lack of flexibility normally required to perform project work activities within the team members' departmental environments.
— A need to demonstrate objectivity through physical separation from a specific user or department.

Project Manager Selecting the right project manager is key to the success of any project. First a manager — not a technician — this person must possess the normal management skills of planning, organizing, controlling, and effectively using the unique talents of each individual assigned to project tasks. The project orientation also requires the manager to resolve problems as they occur and to make timely and firm decisions while handling other problems and decisions that will lead to the successful completion of the project. Those who cannot cope with the constant pressure of change over the course of an entire project should not be candidates for project managers. Other management qualifications (such as leadership, technical competence, staff loyalty and trust) are just as applicable to project managers as they are to departmental managers.

The selection of a project manager may be carried out by general management or by the steering committee control mechanism, but must be made carefully since it is an important key to project success. The manager cannot be a person who is simply available, or one who lacks people orientation or desire to improve operations. Rather, the successful candidate must be a proven manager with a demonstrated history of successful projects, and with an ability to obtain the respect and confidence of the users. The most qualified individual to manage a systems project may be found in either the systems or user departments, since competence and knowledge is required in both the business environment and the technical environment. This is necessary to communicate summary results and plans to the steering committee and to provide direction to the project team.

Finally, the project manager should have the perspective of general management and the steering committee. This allows the multitude of short-term decisions required to be viewed in the context of longer-range goals and objectives.

Project Team

Staffing and selecting project team members is a process that may be repeated several times over the duration of a systems project. At project initiation, the project manager is selected and assigned the responsibility to update the general plans and add the detailed activities and tasks necessary to produce desired end products. As the project progresses through various activities and tasks, this planning process is repeated as new activities and tasks are identified. Thus, the primary determinant of staffing levels and skill requirements for the project team is the current project plan.

In general, the size of a project team varies by phase and step and conforms to a bell-shape curve. That is, only a few key people are generally involved in Phase I — Systems Planning, with more team members added for Phase II — Systems Requirements, possibly followed by more additions for Phase III — Systems Development, then tapering off to a much smaller team by the end of Phase IV — Systems Implementation. Likewise, the mix of background and experience requirements change throughout the project, with Phases I and II requiring a small number of more senior team members.

After detailed plans have been finalized, the project manager meets with the appropriate department managers to determine staff assignments. This generally involves a review of objectives, priorities, and plans to allow joint decisions by both managers as to which personnel will be assigned. This approach requires that the project manager maintain a spirit of enthusiasm and dedication among the users and presents carefully prepared project plans.

Selection of project team members is a difficult task. Successful projects require good people, not simply those who have available time. Skills must be matched to specific tasks. Underutilized or overextended individuals generally cause problems. Ideally, staff assignments will permit a controlled growth in the career of each team member.

Unfortunately, a perfect match of skills to tasks in the desired time frame hardly ever occurs. Some adjustments to schedules and approaches to activities are usually required to adapt to the capabilities of the selected project staff. The project manager should carefully determine the talents and limitations of every team member before making final activity and task assignments. As new team members are added to the project, the role and responsibility of each individual should be clearly defined, documented, and communicated.

Project staffing does not require the assignment of permanent team members for all personnel resources required by a project. For example, computer operators are not normally on the project team even though they take part in completing certain project activities.

PROJECT PLANNING AND ESTIMATING

General Concepts

An effective project management process requires a good project plan. The objective of the planning process is to translate project goals into detailed work activities which, when combined with time constraints and personnel and equipment resources, will produce the defined end products in the most cost-effective manner. The plan provides a map displaying one or more routes that may be followed to attain the required results. It may not suggest taking the lowest-cost approach if doing so has a negative impact on benefits. Furthermore, it may not suggest the most desirable staffing, because of resource availabilities. In some cases, it may even result in project cancellation if the only alternatives are shown to be those that result in large expenditures or that have a low probability of success.

All projects require a current, updated plan before the start of any phase or step. This plan identifies all activities, schedules, and resource assignments. It is constructed or revised primarily by the project manager, with assistance as required by user management and project team members. The plan should identify all high-priority or risk areas, and should concentrate effort in these areas. The defined activities must be discretely measurable as to completion and be sufficiently small in scope to be effectively controlled.

The plan must be reviewed and approved by user management and the steering committee at the start of each phase or whenever any significant changes occur. The updated plan then provides the current basis for calculating the one-time investment cost of the project. Thus, it should be a tool that continually communicates to management where the project is going and what it is expected to cost.

Problems encountered in revising the plan, defining all the required activities, allocating time to work on the plan, presenting the plan, or obtaining approvals must not be ignored simply because they are difficult. It is generally true that a project that cannot be planned cannot be done. Unresolved issues or unclear assignments will only lead to larger problems, a less controlled environment, and a high potential for project failure. Properly constructed and approved plans should lead specifically to initiating work tasks, directing activities, and measuring status. If an approved plan cannot answer the question, "What must each team member do tomorrow?" it is not effective as a project management tool.

This does not mean that a good plan guarantees that there will not be any problems during the project. It does provide a basis from which to make timely decisions and revise plans when problems are encountered. This suggests three fundamental characteristics of the plan and planning process:

— The plan must be flexible, and the administrative process used to make modifications and updates must be easy to use.

— The planning process occurs several times during a project, and may have to be repeated during any given step.
— The planning process creates several levels of detail within the overall project plan:
  · Specific task and subtask identification for the current step
  · Specific activities for other steps in the current phase
  · General activities and steps in future project phases.

These planning characteristics recognize the fact that little may be known about future detailed project activities at any given point during the systems development process. It is unreasonable to spend a great deal of effort in preparing a plan if the risk of creating a wrong plan is significant or if decisions are based on inadequate knowledge. For example, detailed estimates of programming effort should not be made during the feasibility study, since a detailed knowledge of user requirements and conceptual designs does not exist at that point. The primary investment risk at conclusion of the feasibility study is the cost of the Systems Requirements phase, which can be planned and estimated in detail at this point in the process.

Planning project time requirements is performed at the same level as identification of work activities. Although certain time constraints generally exist, they cannot simply be mandated to produce a successful project. The planning process develops a logical work sequence and identifies interdependencies which are then related to elapsed time. This information is adjusted to reflect committed end dates, critical periods in user and data processing operations, and management's sense of urgency for the completed end products. For complex projects with many interrelated activities, a critical path determination is often very desirable.

Relationship to Systems Development Process

Project planning is an integral part of the systems development process and is reflected in the standard activities associated with virtually every step. A detailed work plan is prepared near the start of almost every step. It is based on project plans which are generally developed as one of the last activities in the previous phase. That is, the project plans for all five steps in Phase II are prepared as one of the last activities in the feasibility study of Phase I. These project plans identify the specific activities to be performed, skills and effort required, and elapsed time estimates. As each step in Phase II is initiated, the applicable project plan is used to develop a detailed work plan. This plan makes any adjustments required in the specific activities, identifies all individual tasks and subtasks necessary to perform the activities, specifies the end products to be produced, determines the start and end dates of each task, the effort required, and the team member assigned to the work.

The same process is used at the end of Phase II — Alternatives Evaluation and Development Planning — to plan for Phase III. However, since Phase III — Systems Development — is generally the largest phase in terms of elapsed time and required effort, and is technically the most complex, an important addition to this planning process has been included. At the conclusion of Step 2 — Technical Support Development — the project plans for the remaining steps of the phase are reviewed and adjusted based on results of completed technical development (data base, network, etc.). This should provide the most realistic plans for the remaining steps: specifications, programming, procedures, training, and systems testing.

Phase IV — Systems Implementation — is generally the most complex phase from a logistics management viewpoint because of the changes required, the variety of people involved, and the number of functions impacted. For this phase, two complete steps in Phase III are devoted entirely to the planning process: Step 7 — Implementation Planning, and Step 8 —

Conversion Planning. The planned conversion and the implementation activities are tested during the Systems Test step at the end of Phase III. Thus, at the beginning of Phase IV, all the detailed plans are again reviewed and updated to reflect actual experience and current schedules.

Detailed work plans developed for each step break down all activities and tasks into discrete units of work with definable end products. This emphasis on end products should not be ignored since it provides both a basis to perform quality assurance and a method to measure status. If a task does not have its associated end product, there are no visible means of telling when it is complete. For example, a task that requires review of a research document on a particular data entry technique would not be measurable unless it specified an end product—such as a written summary of techniques to be used in the system, or reasons why it cannot be applied. The forms suggested to document work during the systems development process provide a method to obtain these end products. However, it should always be remembered that merely filling out forms is not the objective: forms only provide a structured approach to recording the results of work performed and organizing it in a manner which is useful for review and future reference.

Critical work sequences, alternative paths, and task interrelationships must be determined in the detailed work plans. Network displays may be useful in describing these relationships—but like any other planning tool, they must be flexible and easy to use.

The level of detail required must be sufficient to minimize the risk of unknowns. However, some unknowns must be provided for, although this is not to suggest the acceptance of vague tasks or ill-defined end products. The project manager should plan a budget reserve for unknown tasks or significant estimating errors on an activity. This reserve should be properly managed and not used to cover inefficient or incorrect project work.

Detailed and thorough planning used to minimize unknowns must consider *all* the activities related to a project, not simply the obvious main-line activities such as interviews, program coding, etc. Other frequently ignored or underestimated time required includes:

— Time spent preparing plans and estimates for subsequent phases and steps.
— Effort on the part of the project manager and the project team to prepare, review, revise, and present material at status meetings.
— Time required to summarize interviews and analyze data gathered.
— Effort required of support staff to prepare presentation materials and status reports.
— Delays in interfacing with existing computer operations.
— Security and access restrictions to facilities during nonstandard hours.

In addition, all critical schedule assumptions, both internal and external to the project, should be specifically identified and documented. These may include availability of persons to be interviewed, frequency of project meetings, frequency and type of status reporting, availability of support services, etc.

Scheduling and staffing should also consider practical limitations on the number of people involved, the reasonable rate of absorption of users and the project team, the degree of risk resulting from poor-quality work, and the impact of other changes concurrently taking place within the organization.

Project Estimating

One of the major tasks associated with project planning is estimating the effort required to complete the remaining phases, steps, and activities. This task has frequently been the cause of significant project management problems. Use of top-down approaches that are too broad may overlook significant levels of effort required by the project and thus may produce low estimates and subsequent project overruns. Alternatively, use of extremely detailed bottom-up approaches may ignore the possibility of combining or eliminating certain activities, thus producing excessively high estimates and possibly causing project cancellation. Neither extreme is acceptable — nor is it reasonable to assume that any approach can accurately predict the future. However, a structured approach to the problem can provide a reasonable framework for the project planning process.

Project estimates are used in several important areas within systems projects and are integral to producing a meaningful project plan. They form a basis for measuring project status and provide a significant component when calculating investment cost and economic viability. Thus, it is important to realize certain basic estimating concepts:

— Estimates cannot be more detailed than the information available for developing a project plan. It is unreasonable to plan the number of programs and estimate the coding effort associated with each program during the Feasibility Study step of a project.

— The activities described here should be addressed regardless of the degree to which the standards in the systems development process are applied within any given project. Ignoring them results in improper estimates. The Refinement and Tuning step that follows implementation (Phase IV, Step 2) is always part of a systems project. If that step is not estimated, the project will encounter a cost overrun and possibly a dissatisfied user.

— The effort required to develop good project plans and estimates requires a significant amount of time that must be planned in project management. Conversely, no more time should be spent estimating a project than is needed to minimize the potential risk of a bad estimate.

— The estimate of the effort required to perform any given project can vary simply because of the planned project duration. Reducing the time frame (to speed up realization of benefits, for example) may increase total effort by making coordination more complex and reducing individual efficiency. Extending the time frame (to account for minimal project staff availability, for example) may also increase total effort as a result of lost time in startup/shutdown, reduced momentum on the part of the team, and extended duration of project management.

— The total estimated effort required to develop a given system is not fixed but is highly dependent on the environment and people involved: general management, users, project manager, and project team. Such factors as management commitment, the number of users in computer-based systems, the technical complexity of the application, and the prior involvement of analysts and programmers in similar systems, will affect the estimates. Reliable project estimates cannot be developed without considering variables such as these.

— Project estimates must reflect losses of productivity on the part of individual team members (because of administrative requirements, training, vacations, and other time off) and for team members as a group (because of an imperfect fit of all project activities and the impact of staff turnover).

— The systems development process does not proceed from beginning to end to create a new system. It may include multiple occurrences of Phase III — Systems Development — if several major subsystems are involved. It may include multiple occurrences of Phase IV — Systems Implementation — if several locations are involved.

Since project estimates can only be developed based on the level of current project knowledge, different estimating approaches may reasonably be used, at different points in the systems development process. In the beginning, a plan and estimate are required to perform an initial investigation — Phase I, Step 1. However, since this step is very short in duration and conducted by one person or a very small team, the planning and estimating process is brief and straightforward. It consists simply of constructing a small work plan to conduct the investigation, and including enough time to prepare the plan and estimates for the Feasibility Study step that follows (if that step is appropriate).

Plans and estimates prepared in the intital investigation are only for conducting the feasibility study, not for developing and implementing a new system. That is, the resource investment decision made by management or the steering committee concerns only Phase I. Thus, the estimating process is again related directly to preparing a detailed work plan to conduct the feasibility study. This work plan may be developed based on results of the initial investigation and the standard activities described in Phase I, Step 2 of this systems development process. Some activities will vary in length or effort required depending on the number of users, potential for available packaged software, expected technical complexities, etc. The plan and estimates must be sufficiently detailed to permit staffing and initiation of work immediately following project approval.

During the feasibility study, an estimate is required for the total systems project — requirements, development, and implementation. This estimate is primarily dependent on the detailed project plans developed for the five steps in Phase II — Systems Requirements. Since this next phase is basically an expansion of the preliminary work performed in the feasibility study, it should be possible to construct a reasonable plan and estimate. This involves analyzing each activity in Phase II, comparing the effort expended in the feasibility study to that required by comparable activities, and determining additional analyses to be done. Activities which may vary most as to time and effort required involve the number of:

— Interviews to be conducted.
— Inputs, reports, and files to be analyzed.
— Functions encompassed by the system.
— Major alternatives to be evaluated.
— Users and locations involved in the review and approval process.

At this point, estimates for the development and implementation phases must necessarily be more general as are the related project plans. It should be noted, however, that all steps in these two phases will probably be required regardless of the computer systems alternative selected. Using a purchased application package does not necessarily eliminate any step; it only changes the degree of effort. In this case, applications specifications and programming would be reduced to minor systems changes, conversion programs, etc. General estimates should be possible for major activities in each of these steps. In addition, it may be useful to compare resulting estimates with historical averages of the distribution of project effort among phases and steps. For example, a general average among many different environments with many different applications using this methodology is approximately as follows:

	Typical Percent of Total Project Effort
Phase I — Systems Planning	5 — 10%
Phase II — Systems Requirements	20 — 30%
Phase III — Systems Development	40 — 60%
Phase IV — Systems Implementation	20 — 30%

On the same basis, the distribution of effort within each phase is approximately:

	Typical Percent of Total Effort within Phase
Phase I — Systems Planning	
Step 1 — Initial Investigation	10 — 20%
Step 2 — Feasibility Study	80 — 90%
Phase II — Systems Requirements	
Steps 1 and 2	40 — 50%
Operations and Systems Analysis	
User Requirements	
Steps 3 and 4	40 — 50%
Technical Support Approach	
Conceptual Design and Pachage Review	
Step 5 — Alternative Evaluation	20 — 30%
and Development Planning	
Phase III — Systems Development	
Steps 1 and 2	20 — 30%
Systems Technical Specifications	
Technical Support Development	
Steps 3 and 4	40 — 60%
Applications Specifications	
Applications Programming and Testing	
Steps 5 and 6	15 — 20%
User Procedures and Controls	
User Training	
Steps 7 and 8	5 — 10%
Implementation Planning	
Conversion Planning	
Step 9 — Systems Test	10 — 20%
Phase IV — Systems Implementation	
Step 1 — Conversion and Phased	70 — 80%
Implementation	
Step 2 — Refinement and Tuning	15 — 25%
Step 3 — Post-implementation Review	5 — 10%

It should be remembered that these percentages represent averages. No systems project is likely to conform to this precise distribution, but these figures provide guidelines for reviewing the reasonableness of estimates. Also, as noted previously, a particular systems project may require multiple occurrences of Phase III and/or Phase IV. This would obviously change the distribution. The next (and most critical) estimate of the total project occurs at the end of Phase II, in Step 5—Alternatives Evaluation and Development Planning. At this point, approximately 25% of the total project effort has been expended, with approval being sought for the remaining 75%. If approved, significant project staffing allocations will be based on these estimates. It is therefore important that these estimates be as precise as possible.

At this point, the largest single block of work yet to be done in a custom development project is usually applications specifications and programming. Its completion is obviously essential to project success. Although detailed design, systems specifications, and systems software development have not been done (part of Phase III, Steps 1 and 2), the applications specifications and programming effort is probably better understood at this point than any other remaining work. If this work can be estimated, typical effort for the remaining steps can be calculated by using relative ratios such as those described above. In addition, a detailed project plan for Phase III, Step 1 and general plans for the other steps in Phase III can be based on current knowledge at the end of Phase II. A combination and analysis of programming estimates, project plans for the various steps, and relative ratios of effort should produce reasonable total plans and estimates for the remainder of the project.

Precise identification of individual programs and modules required by the new system cannot be achieved at this point, which is performing Steps 1 and 2 of Phase III. An alternative which combines the unique characteristics of the new system with known base information is required.

Systems department management is responsible for establishing a common base of information to use in developing estimates for specific systems projects. An approach to this process is described in the following paragraphs. However, it is not intended to be precisely applicable for a specific department since each has its own unique organizational and operating environment and level of expertise. Thus, the program function types shown in the following example will be somewhat different in a given department. Likewise, the positions of analyst, senior programmer, and programmer vary in title, level of responsibility, and experience; they are used here for illustrative purposes only.

An analysis of all existing programs in any given environment would show that they can be classified into a finite set of logical functions, with any specific program made up entirely of one or more of these functions. The following functions are shown as an example of program classifications:

- Report generator module.
- File dump/restore/backup/reload module.
- Batch data entry edit module.
- On-line inquiry module.
- Screen formatter module.
- On-line entry/update edit module.
- File update/control module.
- Data manipulation module.
- Statistical analysis module.
- Sorts and other utility packages.

In this example, these ten functions are defined to encompass all the logic required in applications programs. Levels of complexity are then assigned to each type of function to provide a more specific breakdown, as shown in the following example:

Complexity	Comments/Examples
Report Generator Function	
1	Basic output report with limited page breaks and totals.
2	Output report on printed form; single file with complex page layout and control totals.
3	Multifile report with complex layout.
File Dump/Restore/Backup/ Reload Function	
1	Basic file unload (disk to tape) with control totals.
2	Large, multisegment file backup routine with file analysis and control totals.
3	Data base restoration from a checkpoint file with transaction analysis updating.
Batch Data Entry Edit Function	
1	Basic input edit: alpha or numeric field checks; uses code tables.
2	Medium complexity edit of multiple inter-related fields.
3	Same as 2 but adding user turnaround document with extensive error messages.
4	Complex edits on front end of a multifile update routine, including large decision tables and validity computations on entered fields.
On-line Inquiry Function	
1	Basic single file access, search, and reply composition.
2	Complex single file access, search, and reply composition.
3	Multiple file access.
4	English language input; Boolean logic search; multifile; search operators; complex reply.
Screen Formatter Function	
1	Normal data-entry-type screen layout.
2	Large, complex screen with several protected data fields.
On-line Entry/Update Edit Function	
1	Basic screen edit; alpha or numeric checks; uses code tables.
2	Medium complexity edit of multiple inter-related fields; simple update.
3	Complex screen with extensive error editing

Complexity	Comments/Examples
	and computations on data for validity checking.
4	Multifile update edits with large decision tables and interrelated fields.
File Update/Control Function	
1	Routine to manage file access and track updates; produces control report.
2	Data base management control routine handling several multi-indexed files.
Data Manipulation Function	
1	Reads data; arranges it to new format; performs minor computations or logical comparisons.
2	Multiple file access and data manipulation; encoding/decoding.
3	Extensive data management and movement using multiple files to obtain necessary information and work it into new formats.
Statistical Analysis Function	
1	Basic arithmetic computations.
2	Simple linear regression or algebraic mathematical analysis.
3	Linear program or multiple linear regression.
Utility Packages	
1	Basic sort/merge utility on single file.
2	File manipulation and data reduction utilities on multiple files.

Function types and levels of complexity form a base of information from which to develop estimates. First, a standard amount of effort must be assigned to each function type and level of complexity. This effort should be classified by skill levels appropriate to the particular organization. The estimates reflect the time required for persons working from systems technical specifications to develop application specifications, to code, test, and document program modules, and to prepare them for integrated systems tests. Standard times will vary for each environment and are influenced by such factors as:

— Programming language.
— Quality of previous steps.
— Availability of programming tools and software aids.
— Relative experience of technical staff.
— Maturity or stability of the technical hardware and software environment.

An example of the resulting estimating bases for three of the function types follows:

	Degree of Complexity (DOC)	Estimated Months of Effort per Function			
		Analyst	Senior Programmer	Programmer	Total
Report	1	0.05	0.05	0.25	0.35
Generator	2	0.10	0.15	0.40	0.65
Function	3	0.20	0.25	1.00	1.45
Batch Data	1	0.10	0.20	0.60	0.90
Entry Edit	2	0.15	0.25	0.80	1.20
Function	3	0.20	0.40	1.50	2.10
	4	0.25	1.50	0.40	2.15
On-line	1	0.10	0.20	0.40	0.70
Entry/Update	2	0.20	0.30	0.60	1.10
Edit Function	3	0.40	1.00	2.00	3.40
	4	0.40	2.00	1.00	3.40

Note that an increase in effort may not vary in direct proportion to an increase in complexity, and that the relative mix among staff classifications may change by level of complexity and by function type. In the preceding example, the two edit modules require about the same amount of effort at DOC levels 3 and 4; but the proportions of time for senior programmers and programmers change significantly.

Base estimates should be developed for all function types and levels of complexity, as illustrated above. These estimates should be independent of the specific system and the specific staff to be assigned. However, as indicated earlier, they must reflect the unique organizational and operating environment. For these reasons, the set of functions types, levels of complexity, and base estimates of effort may be established as department standards (based on historical experience or measurements of current effort, for example) and maintained under the systems manager's responsibility.

Specifications and programming effort for a particular systems project may be developed by determining the number of functions by type and level of complexity. This is accomplished by using the general design and technical approach presented in the completed systems requirements document. Specific program constructions, run sequences, file organizations, etc., need not be determined — only that a number of function types at approximate complexity levels is required in the completed system. These counts may be multiplied by the base estimates per module to obtain total programming. Staff availabilities and other project organization considerations may then be applied to determine reasonable estimates of elapsed time requirements. The skill level mix, staff assignment techniques, and planned time frame may cause the final total estimated effort to be greater or less than the sum derived by simply adding total estimates by function type.

The final specifications and programming plans, along with project plans and relative ratios of effort for other steps, may all be combined to produce the total plans and estimates for Phases III and IV — Systems Development and Implementation. They may be combined with other end products from Phase II — Systems Requirements — for presentation and approval to proceed.

At the conclusion of Systems Technical Specifications—Phase III, Step 1—the estimates are reviewed and adjusted as needed to ensure that the planned costs and schedules are reasonable. Then, at the end of Technical Support Development—Phase III, Step 2—all plans are revised to reflect increased knowledge about on the new system. Actual details of the work plans for specifications and programming are developed at the initiation of these steps. Finally, the detailed plans for systems testing, conversion, and implementation are prepared in Steps 7 and 8—Implementation Planning and Conversion Planning.

PROJECT CONTROL

The third major component of the project management process is project control. An organized, well-planned project doesn't just happen by itself. Motivation and leadership are required to manage the process of implementing change. It involves an ongoing evaluation of the adequacy of the project organization and progress against plan in meeting ultimate project objectives. To do these things, the project manager needs an adequate set of project control tools and techniques. Directing a project requires:

— Assigning specific tasks and monitoring the individual progress of team members.
— Scheduling and conducting project team meetings.
— Determining and reporting project status.
— Scheduling and conducting review meetings with user management and the steering committee.
— Controlling changes required to the planned end products.
— Determining the impact of end product changes and variances from planned progress, and modifying schedules and staffing as appropriate to meet scheduled completion dates.

Completed project work plans contain detailed tasks with scheduled dates, effort requirements, and specified end products. Project execution requires the project manager to assign each task to an individual for completion. This should be accomplished in a manner that allows flexibility and does not dictate the precise manner in which to perform the task. Of course, the degree of creativity allowed depends on the type of task, existing environmental constraints, and the capability of the individual team member. This management decision may be assisted by the pre-identification of specific review points and criteria.

Regular review meetings with each team member are important ingredients of good project control. The project manager reviews each end product for quality and to make sure that results are within standards and supported by sufficient factual data and analysis. This type of control cannot be exercised merely by reviewing status reports or by informally asking if a task is completed. Detailed reviews also provide a basis for assigning subsequent tasks and modifying schedules.

The focus of this control activity must necessarily be on the most difficult and highest risk activities in the current phase or step. However, even activities whose scheduled dates are not critical to meeting overall project schedules must be controlled to assure that they do not become late and thus impact the schedule. For example, the procedures and training activities in Phase III are generally conducted at the same time as the programming activities but usually require much less effort to complete. If not adequately managed, however, they may not be finished on schedule and thus delay the start of systems testing. Likewise, the project manager must complete the implementation and conversion planning steps during this same period to be prepared for systems testing.

Another project control tool that may be needed on large projects is the use of a project room. This may contain visual aid equipment and materials, space to display schedules and end products, storage for project work papers, and facilities for status and review meetings. If used properly by the project manager, a good project room can be valuable for control, communication, and team motivation. Project team meetings (conducted in the project room) can be effective for communicating overall status and schedules.

Determining Status

Once project tasks have been assigned and work has begun, it is necessary to record quantitative data on effort expended in order to properly measure status. This usually involves using time reports to provide a feedback of time actually spent and an estimate of time remaining to be spent on in-process work. These reports are completed by each individual at a task or subtask level. Time reports should be completed often enough (e.g., daily) to allow the individual to clearly recall what was accomplished and how the time was spent. Reports should also provide enough space to record nonproject or overhead time (such as training, departmental staff meetings, time off) so that a complete picture of each individual's time is provided. However, it is important to avoid overly complex or unnecessarily detailed forms, because it is difficult to enforce proper usage and the value of the excessive detail is questionable.

Compiling time report data is often accomplished through automated project accounting systems. These systems assist in maintaining cumulative time data, calculating variances, and preparing reports. They also help enforce a standardized approach to recording time across multiple projects. However, if not flexible or timely enough, these systems may result in unusable reports. Some automated systems that have become unnecessarily complex or too sophisticated require more effort than they should to maintain with accuracy, and produce too much data in too many configurations to be useful. They may also create a false illusion of progress simply because time is being expended and recorded by precise category.

Regardless of the system used to record time, it is essential to remember that it is only a tool for displaying data and not a substitute for proper analysis of results or other project management responsibilities. The issue in determining status is not merely timekeeping. Rather, it is the quality of completed work produced in proportion to the effort reported. This requires more than simply recording hours spent by task. It also requires a method to indicate completion of the task and a control mechanism to assure that a task is not recorded as complete unless it represents a quality end product that meets standards. This is best accomplished by having tangible, well-defined end products associated with each task that may be reviewed for quality assurance.

A recommended approach for minimizing erroneous and misleading status reports is through use of the earned hours concept. This technique does not allow accumulation of earned hours on incomplete tasks. Hours spent on tasks that are not complete are not yet earned. Schedule variances are determined as the difference between the sum of planned time spent on tasks scheduled to be complete to data and the sum of planned time spent on tasks actually completed to date. This measures the degree to which the project is ahead or behind schedule based on completed results. Performance variances can also be determined as the difference between actual and planned time spent to complete these tasks.

These two variances—schedule and performance—provide an indication of current status related to the plan. Predictions of future status can also be made, but require certain assumptions regarding continuation of past trends, the consistency of the estimates contained in the plan, and the probable impact of any schedule changes, staff changes, or other corrective actions taken by the project manager.

A commonly accepted alternate method of measuring status is the use of a percent complete concept. This requires estimating at each reporting interval (e.g., weekly) the percent to which an in-process task is complete. This method is very subjective, however, and open to different opinions on the amount of work that has really been done. It has often resulted in the "90% complete" activity or task that eventually requires much more effort to finish than was expended to date.

Determining status is basically a matter of assuring that each completed task has produced a quality end product, and then comparing (on the basis of planned time) the completed tasks with the tasks planned to be completed to date.

Reporting Status   Once status has been determined, it needs to be reported in a timely and understandable manner. This may at times be difficult if the project is behind schedule and under severe time constraints. However, it must be remembered that project success is ultimately based on user success. Thus, user management and the steering committee must be kept continually informed of project status in a clear, concise, and meaningful way. This allows the user to make critical decisions regarding plans and operations in the same manner that the project manager uses status reports as a basis for critical project decisions.

Project status reports should be in summary form and should contain descriptions of tasks completed, next tasks, outstanding problems, potential solutions, and actual progress compared to plan, using the earned hours concept described earlier. Problem descriptions should use an exception orientation with prioritization to avoid discussing minor problems in detail. This should be consistent with a "no surprises" approach that avoids user discovery of major problems that have existed for some time but have not been addressed in the regular status reports.

Frequent and timely status reporting should precipitate thorough reviews of the project, both by the project manager who prepares the reports and by the user who reviews it. This process is not a mechanical exercise that compares actual time to planned time: it evaluates results and determines what has been accomplished and what important considerations need to be resolved.

When tasks are late or major problems occur, the project manager must determine alternate actions and change schedules. This, too, must be reflected in the status report to provide users with forward visibility on the project. Changes in plans that occur should be included in each status report for good project management. Adequate communication and dialogue are required to keep changes from confusing the user or distort the measurement of actual progress.

In addition to written reports, frequent project status and review meetings should be held with the project team, with users, and with the steering committee. These meetings will vary in length and level of detail, depending on who attends them. However, they should be frequent, regular, and conducted with formal agendas. Topics listed in the status reports should be discussed and problems related to the particular group should be addressed. Properly handled, these meetings result in improved understanding and interaction.

Status reports and review meetings require the project manager to decide when schedule changes are required. These are often difficult decisions. For example, if a critical activity is not going to be completed on time, changing the schedule may cause further delays because of a reduction in pressure to meet the completion date. On the other hand, failure to change the schedule in this situation may cause other team members to spend excessive overtime to complete their activities on schedule, and then to wait for the late activities to be completed.

Schedule changes must be consistent with the project's original objectives and handled on a formal basis. These changes are an integral part of project planning and serve to illustrate the constant interaction of project planning and project control within the project management process.

KEY CONSIDERATIONS

During the entire organization, planning, and control components of the project management process, certain realities must be observed in order to assure a high probability of success. They may be summarized as follows:

- Being a project manager is not the same as being a project entrepreneur—although a noticeable lack of drive and creativity is equally inappropriate.

- Inadequate attention to project management can easily result in "end product drift"—changes to the scope or nature of end products that are not approved, understood, or consistent with project objectives.

- Proposed additions of unnecessary frills to the new system often take place during the development process. The effort that such changes require is usually underestimated; they result in excessive costs and are often of questionable practical value.

- Although an ideal system may be planned, it must be developed and implemented in an imperfect organization.

- Reasonable compromises between pressures of schedule and quality are constant occurrences and must be properly handled by the project manager. Neither extreme is acceptable.

- A lack of sufficient interaction between the project team and user management in organization, planning, scheduling, reporting, or review will result in the creation of a system that belongs to the project team, not the user.

- Project management must provide an active role throughout the entire project in anticipating problems, and not simply record results and react to problems after they occur.

- Interacting primarily with only one level of user management often results in subsequent changes and requires additional efforts to obtain final reviews and approvals.

- Maintaining effective communications with users is essential to obtaining continuing cooperation and a sense of responsibility for the project.

- Project management is a difficult and demanding task, and thus tends to become less effective over a long period of time, resulting in inefficient project work effort.

- It is easy to lose sight of original project goals in the face of current hot issues. Although it is important to be sensitive to these issues, they must properly relate to the project.

— Good mechanical tools and techniques are no substitute for realistic
and sensitive human relations required by any project management
process.

Properly applied, the project management process becomes a valuable
tool in managing the systems development process. Its techniques should be
remembered throughout the next section of this book, which describes the
details of the planning, development, and implementation process.

Section

2

The Systems Development Process

Section Two of this book presents the systems development process. It is a structured and comprehensive guideline for use in developing new information systems. As shown in the following chart, the approach presented is characterized by breaking down the total development effort into a series of manageable units. Four major self-contained components encompass the complete approach:

Phase I: Systems Planning
Phase II: Systems Requirements
Phase III: Systems Development
Phase IV: Systems Implementation

Within each phase, a series of steps exists each of which is a logical part in accomplishing the objectives of the particular phase. The approach emphasizes controllable work units that can be defined, analyzed, evaluated, and budgeted with a degree of assurance. In addition, it is structured to produce predefined end products that document results and provide a basis to measure progress and quality.

The phases and steps depicted on the following chart are each presented in detail in this section. Each step is described in a separate chapter. The organization may be summarized as follows:

Phase I — Systems Planning begins the systems development process by formalizing conceptual changes and requests received for new systems. The feasibility of pursuing further development is determined through identification of the probable characteristics, costs, and benefits of implementing the requested system. The phase ends with a decision to terminate or approve the next phase. The steps in Phase I are:

— Step 1: Initial Investigation
— Step 2: Feasibility Study

Phase II — Systems Requirements provide the detailed foundation upon which the technical programs and procedures will be developed. Its primary emphasis is on user operations and environment. It ends with another review and decision to terminate or proceed to the next phase. The steps in Phase II are:

— Step 1: Operations and Systems Analysis
— Step 2: User Requirements
— Step 3: Technical Support Approach
— Step 4: Conceptual Design and Package Review
— Step 5: Alternatives Evaluation and Development Planning

Phase III — Systems Development begins with an accepted conceptual design approach and ends with a completely developed new system that has been thoroughly tested and prepared for implementation. For many projects, this phase may be repeated several times in order to develop multiple subsystems identified in the previous requirements phase. Purchase of an application package generally reduces the scope of work in this phase but seldom completely eliminates any step. Phase III ends with a review of development and testing results and an agreement by all parties that the new system should be implemented. The steps in this phase are:

— Step 1: Systems Technical Specifications
— Step 2: Technical Support Development
— Step 3: Applications Specifications
— Step 4: Applications Programming and Testing
— Step 5: User Procedures and Controls
— Step 6: User Training
— Step 7: Implementation Planning
— Step 8: Conversion Planning
— Step 9: Systems Test

Phase IV — Systems Implementation contains the actual initiation of new programs and procedures and the termination of old processes. For many projects, this phase is repeated several times to implement multiple subsystems or to install the system in multiple locations. The steps in Phase IV are:

— Step 1: Conversion and Phase Implementation
— Step 2: Refinement and Tuning
— Step 3: Post-implementation Review

A final subsection is included in Section Two for systems maintenance. It describes the repetitive process used to manage the ongoing maintenance and enhancements to a new system after it is installed.

Each subsection in Section Two is organized into several major compononents. First, a chart is presented to display the relationship of the step to all other steps and to provide an outline of the step contents. Second, the step is described in detail. Each standard activity is presented with discussions of proven approaches that may be used to accomplish the work objectives. Following these items a "standard activities/end items" matrix is included to associate standard activities and tasks within the step with the potential end products and the standard forms presented in Section Three. The subsection concludes with a list of key considerations that describes unique concerns often encountered at that point in the development process. The failure of many systems projects may be traced to ignoring one or more of these key concepts.

Finally, it is important to remember that the systems development process as presented in this section is intended to be a guideline, not a rigid set of instructions. To be most effective, this section should be used for the following purposes:

— As a basis for introducing the concepts involved in developing new systems to those unfamiliar with the process, such as first-time users.

— As a reference guide to review when developing project work plans for phases and steps, to assure that all appropriate activities and tasks have been identified.

— As a reference guide to assist project participants in producing quality results for their assigned activities.

— As a source for the development of standards within an organization.

The standard approach to phases, steps, activities, and tasks makes it possible to plan, control, and evaluate progress during the systems development process without inhibiting the necessary analytical and creative work required to produce successful new systems. The structure allows management to make and monitor incremental commitments and the ability to impact interim results. It is an important key to an organization's effective management of the systems development process.

THE SYSTEMS DEVELOPMENT PROCESS

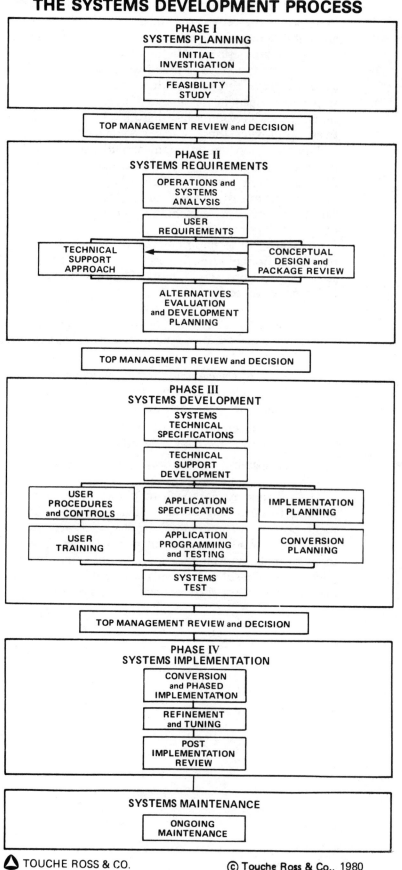

PHASE I
SYSTEMS PLANNING

INITIAL INVESTIGATION

FEASIBILITY STUDY

TOP MANAGEMENT REVIEW and DECISION

PHASE II
SYSTEMS REQUIREMENTS

OPERATIONS and SYSTEMS ANALYSIS

USER REQUIREMENTS

TECHNICAL SUPPORT APPROACH

CONCEPTUAL DESIGN and PACKAGE REVIEW

ALTERNATIVES EVALUATION and DEVELOPMENT PLANNING

TOP MANAGEMENT REVIEW and DECISION

PHASE III
SYSTEMS DEVELOPMENT

SYSTEMS TECHNICAL SPECIFICATIONS

TECHNICAL SUPPORT DEVELOPMENT

USER PROCEDURES and CONTROLS

APPLICATION SPECIFICATIONS

IMPLEMENTATION PLANNING

USER TRAINING

APPLICATION PROGRAMMING and TESTING

CONVERSION PLANNING

SYSTEMS TEST

TOP MANAGEMENT REVIEW and DECISION

PHASE IV
SYSTEMS IMPLEMENTATION

CONVERSION and PHASED IMPLEMENTATION

REFINEMENT and TUNING

POST IMPLEMENTATION REVIEW

SYSTEMS MAINTENANCE

ONGOING MAINTENANCE

TOUCHE ROSS & CO.

THE SYSTEMS DEVELOPMENT PROCESS

**PHASE I
SYSTEMS PLANNING**

INITIAL
INVESTIGATION

FEASIBILITY
STUDY

TOP MANAGEMENT REVIEW and DECISION

 TOUCHE ROSS & CO.

THE SYSTEMS DEVELOPMENT PROCESS

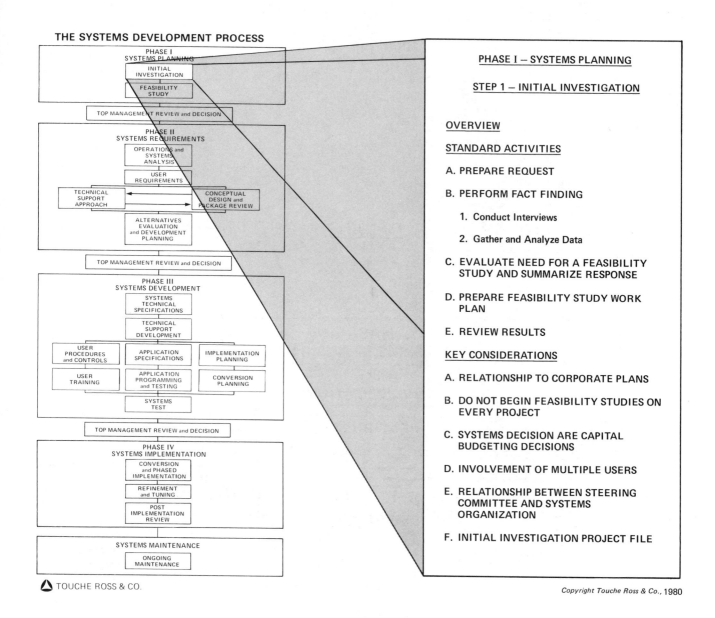

**PHASE I
SYSTEMS PLANNING**

INITIAL INVESTIGATION

FEASIBILITY STUDY

TOP MANAGEMENT REVIEW and DECISION

**PHASE II
SYSTEMS REQUIREMENTS**

OPERATIONS and SYSTEMS ANALYSIS

USER REQUIREMENTS

TECHNICAL SUPPORT APPROACH

CONCEPTUAL DESIGN and PACKAGE REVIEW

ALTERNATIVES EVALUATION and DEVELOPMENT PLANNING

TOP MANAGEMENT REVIEW and DECISION

**PHASE III
SYSTEMS DEVELOPMENT**

SYSTEMS TECHNICAL SPECIFICATIONS

TECHNICAL SUPPORT DEVELOPMENT

USER PROCEDURES and CONTROLS

APPLICATION SPECIFICATIONS

IMPLEMENTATION PLANNING

USER TRAINING

APPLICATION PROGRAMMING and TESTING

CONVERSION PLANNING

SYSTEMS TEST

TOP MANAGEMENT REVIEW and DECISION

**PHASE IV
SYSTEMS IMPLEMENTATION**

CONVERSION and PHASED IMPLEMENTATION

REFINEMENT and TUNING

POST IMPLEMENTATION REVIEW

SYSTEMS MAINTENANCE

ONGOING MAINTENANCE

TOUCHE ROSS & CO.

PHASE I – SYSTEMS PLANNING

STEP 1 – INITIAL INVESTIGATION

OVERVIEW

STANDARD ACTIVITIES

A. PREPARE REQUEST

B. PERFORM FACT FINDING

    1. Conduct Interviews

    2. Gather and Analyze Data

C. EVALUATE NEED FOR A FEASIBILITY STUDY AND SUMMARIZE RESPONSE

D. PREPARE FEASIBILITY STUDY WORK PLAN

E. REVIEW RESULTS

KEY CONSIDERATIONS

A. RELATIONSHIP TO CORPORATE PLANS

B. DO NOT BEGIN FEASIBILITY STUDIES ON EVERY PROJECT

C. SYSTEMS DECISION ARE CAPITAL BUDGETING DECISIONS

D. INVOLVEMENT OF MULTIPLE USERS

E. RELATIONSHIP BETWEEN STEERING COMMITTEE AND SYSTEMS ORGANIZATION

F. INITIAL INVESTIGATION PROJECT FILE

OVERVIEW   Planning, developing, and implementing a system is like trying to guess what the core of an onion will look like as you peel away its outside layers. Successive layers are examined and analyzed while, simultaneously, costs and benefits are continuously monitored. Using this procedure gives management the advantage of being able to stop a project at frequent points.

The initial investigation — the first stage of the planning process — provides an overview of the system. This allows management to estimate system potential in terms of approximate costs and benefits and to evaluate requests at a preliminary level without major commitments of personnel or money.

Although less formal than the steps that follow, a successful initial investigation requires an organized approach. Typically, a top-level steering committee guides the planning, development, and implementation of systems. Whatever the mechanism, requests for new systems call for careful review in order to determine if they warrant an initial investigation. An organization's systems director often screens requests if no formal mechanism exists, or top management may choose to create such a mechanism as a way to establish corporate control over systems planning, development and implementation activities. This book uses the "steering committee" to perform this function.

Initial investigations are usually short — taking perhaps a few days, or at most a few weeks, to complete. The steering committee reviews the results and decides whether or not the project should proceed to the Feasibility Study step (as shown on the process flowchart). Members of the committee must have a broad understanding of the company to be able to weed out inappropriate requests at an early stage. Terminating a project at the initial investigation stage obviously minimizes the expenditure of corporate resources.

Steering committee candidates should have specific credentials, including the following:

— *Knowledge of and access to plans (both strategic and tactical, intra-departmental and corporate-wide).* This is necessary because proposals might conflict with or duplicate plans unknown to parts of the organization, including the person making the proposal.

— *Objectivity in assessing corporate priorities.* This includes the need to have both the ability and the reputation of being objective, since the steering committee's recommendations affect corporate direction. The greater the credibility of the steering committee's individual members, the more likely its recommendations will be approved by top management.

— *A high level of experience.* The initial investigation should require a minimum of time and effort in order to keep preliminary expenditures low and yet provide a clear, accurate, and timely response to the request.

At the conclusion of this brief step, the steering committee reviews and issues a letter of findings and recommendations. This letter constitutes the group's response to the original request and is directed to the manager of the originating department as well as to the managers of any other departments that may be affected. The letter:

- Includes a preliminary identification of costs and benefits as well as an overview of the operational consequences of the request.
- Recommends to either terminate the project or continue to the next step—the feasibility study.
- Specifies the user and technical effort required for the feasibility study step.
- Assigns systems planning priorities to the request.

The requesting department then reviews the steering committee's recommendation. If the recommendation is to terminate the project, the user may elect to resubmit the request, including new facts. If the committee recommends going on to the feasibility study, the user must commit the specified personnel and resources accordingly.

STANDARD ACTIVITIES

Prepare Request   Improvements in a company's systems and services are theoretically the business of everyone within the company who stands to be affected by the changes. However, in actual practice, the manager of the user department usually bears primary responsibility for initiating and reviewing requests for systems development.

It is that same manager's responsibility to develop a climate that encourages employees within his or her department to come forward with suggestions that can be transmitted to the steering committee for review. A situation must be brought about in which anyone within the company, regardless of individual responsibility, feels free to recommend improvements or opportunities for new systems. Creating the proper climate results in activities that enhance the likelihood of employee initiation of suggestions. For example, recognition of an employee who develops a progressive idea encourages others to follow suit.

Once a suggestion has been made, the manager should authorize the department staff, in conjunction with the individual making the proposal, to prepare a letter of request. The letter should contain:

- A clear description of the objectives or purposes served by the request.
- The specific service improvements or economic and operational benefits to be derived. These improvements and benefits should be quantified to the greatest possible extent.
- A functional description of the operational area proposed for investigation. This should include a brief summary of the reports currently being produced and present functions being performed. Any major problem areas should be identified and described in this section of the letter of request. The section should identify organizational areas that could be impacted by the proposed change and organization charts should be provided to illustrate this point.
- A prioritization of this request as compared to other systems development requests or projects within the recommending department.
- The identification of the person or persons within the department

who will provide liaison with the steering committee during the initial investigation.

In many organizations, the letter of request is first reviewed by the systems department to determine if the request can be satisfied by maintenance or a minor enhancement to an existing system. When the request calls for a major enhancement to an existing system or a new system, the steering committee assigns the responsibility and priority for the initial investigation step in light of the backlog of requests and availability of resources.

Perform Fact-Finding Fact-finding should be performed by analysts with enough business and technical experience to gather quantifiable information and apply value judgments to the needs identified by the request. Fact-finding includes interviews, background research, and documentation tasks. Each interview identifies information gaps that may require additional research which, in turn, may highlight the need for still more interviews.

The activity begins with a detailed review of the letter of request, the contents of which determine initial research. The iterative process described in the last paragraph continues until the project team is satisfied that the extent of the fact-finding is sufficient to answer all basic questions (keeping in mind that this is a preliminary step).

Conduct Interviews. The team, while interested in specifics, should acquire a general understanding of the objectives and goals underlying the request as a result of these interviews. Interviewees are generally selected from executive and operating management, including:

- Top-level managers of the department or function from which the letter of request originated, and
- Operating managers in the areas most likely to be impacted by the request.

For example, if a proposed system involved a company's warehouse distribution system, interviewees should include the top executive responsible for distribution, a warehouse superintendent, and possibly, shift or departmental supervisors within the warehouse.

The success of the interview process depends on a tightly planned approach to the gathering of information. In this step, the level of detail of the information need not be as great as in later steps, but the insight gained from the interviews is of unquestioned importance. During this initial investigation, the interview effort determines whether enough quantitative and qualitative information is available to evaluate the cost and benefit impact of the project. A predefined structure and a written summary improves the accuracy and completeness of the interviews. Topics covered include:

- Review of the functions currently performed, along with their associated forms, files, reports and procedures.
- Clarification of the problems identified in the letter of request.
- Detailed analysis of the potential improvements itemized in the letter of request.
- Identification of all organizational units, budgets, and personnel affected by the proposed change.
- Analysis of the relationship of the proposed change to established corporate or departmental long-range plans.

Gather and Analyze Data. In the course of interviewing personnel, study team members collect documentation typical of any systems analysis effort, including organization charts, prime or key output documents and reports describing the area under investigation. Among these are management advisory letters from the external auditor, internal audit or consulting reports, analyses and recommendations by outside consultants, and other documents of this type. These documents are collected at interviews during which written notes are also accumulated. The interviewer summarizes these interviews, indexes the documents, performs analyses, and records observations and findings for later use by other project team members. These observations, interview summaries, and other documents become a part of the project file.

Evaluate Need for a Feasibility Study and Summarize Response

Based upon the analyses performed in the preceding task, the study team for the initial investigation concludes its task by summarizing its findings and reviewing them with key persons in the originating department and other departments impacted by the proposed change. Assuming no exceptions are taken to the findings, the study team then drafts a document focusing on the following:

— Current systems in the affected areas are listed and described.

— Major existing problems and needs are identified.

— Potential benefits are identified both for the departments involved and the entire company or organization.

— The relationship between the proposed change and long-range plans of both the departments and company is described and an analysis of the potential impact on these long-range plans is prepared.

— An initial review of the strengths and weaknesses of the proposal is prepared, including a preliminary identification of costs and benefits, wherever possible.

— Budgets are quantified, where possible.

If, as often happens, the project team concludes that the request should be turned down or delayed, the decision can be made at this time with a minimal outlay of money or resources and presented to the steering committee. However, if the decision is to continue, the project team's next activity is the preparation of a feasibility study work plan.

Prepare Feasibility Study Work Plan

As indicated earlier, the development of a system follows a process in which every successive step results in more detailed end products. Also at every step, the overall project budget and work schedule are reviewed and updated while itemized budget estimates and work schedules are simultaneously prepared for the next step. In order to prepare this plan, the team should first review the following chapter to assure that all major activities required in the next step are identified and understood. For the feasibility study work plan, these activities include documentation of the present system's functions, inputs, files, outputs, costs, and problems; identification of alternative approaches for a new system; and preparation of an economic evaluation. The work plan itself includes an identification of each activity and task to be performed, qualifications and effort required by personnel responsible for each activity and task, and an estimate of the elapsed time required to conduct the entire Feasibility Study step. Because this study is highly dependent on appropriate user involvement, it is essential that detail activities and tasks be thoroughly understood. This work plan is then reviewed by both user and systems management and should be approved by both before presentation to the steering committee.

Review Results   The initial investigation report includes the following:

- — A management summary restating the problems
- — An identification of alternative approaches
- — A preliminary identification of costs and benefits
- — A preliminary summary level Gantt Chart for the entire proposed project
- — A detailed work plan for the next step.

The report is presented to the steering committee jointly by user management and the project team. The team's findings can be explained and, if necessary, jointly defended. This necessitates that the user department fully accept the project team's findings and recommendations. It also signals that the user department supports the project and assumes major responsibility for planning, development, and implementation of the proposed project.

The project team's presentation does not ask for final commitment to the project. It seeks only the limited authority to continue the planning step started during initial investigation through to the next step, the feasibility study. It recognizes that the initial investigation does not provide sufficient information for a full-scale commitment. Steering committee approval constitutes acceptance of the work plan for the feasibility study effort, including the resource allocations and a timetable.

KEY CONSIDERATIONS   Regardless of the degree to which the management process is structured and standardized, the involvement of human judgment will cause substantial variances. Experience has shown that human judgmental criteria, although unpredictable and difficult to communicate within this structured process, are particularly important. Thus each chapter dealing with the steps of these standards for the planning, developing, and implementing of systems will identify the key considerations and precautions needed to deal with these human characteristics. Whatever the nature of the project, special attention to these key considerations will improve the probability of achieving an effective result.

As additional steps and phases are performed, the project team risks losing sight of the original request. A preliminary set of end products which satisfy the original request should be prepared to help keep the project on track. During the remainder of the project, these can be used as a benchmark against which to check the actual results and the degree to which the original request is satisfied.

Relationship to Corporate Plans   Members of the project team should understand the objectives and goals of the department(s) and overall organization. They must know the philosophies that guide the organization and its various functional groups. This input may come from the initial interviews and/or be accessed through the steering committee. These elements of corporate direction guide the steering committee in its analysis of the initial investigation report and are an important part of the periodic analyses conducted as each step in the systems development process is completed.

It should be noted that not all organizations have clear-cut objectives, goals, or philosophies. In many cases, these items are (at best) understood only informally. It may be necessary for the steering committee to attempt to conceptualize them in a more formal manner in order to better analyze the potential impact of the proposed projects on the overall organization.

What can be done when goals and objectives are not clearly stated? The team leader can assist the steering committee by collecting and analyzing information that leads to a clearer understanding of corporate direction. Without this activity, no matter how frustrating and inexact it may be, the risk of failure increases greatly.

Do Not Begin Feasibility Studies on Every Project

At the conclusion of the initial investigation, it is often evident that the project cannot be justified. Thus, the project team must avoid initiating detail feasibility studies on projects that clearly have little change of being justified or approved. The purpose of this step is just as much to eliminate unnecessary feasibility studies as it is to plan for the orderly continuation of the systems planning process.

Systems Decisions Are Capital Budgeting Decisions

Reviewing and approving system proposals is similar to the process of making capital budgeting decisions. This is a particularly important concept because, in many organizations, approval of systems development activities has tended to be informal—resulting in major commitments of expenditures without the benefit of review procedures usually followed for major expenditures. Evaluating a proposal at increasing levels of detail after every step and reassessing its economic viability ensures that major commitments of resources are not made without adequate management review. Many managers are aware of the startup costs involved in the planning, development, and implementation process. However, they may not understand quite as well the cost of ongoing operations.

It is therefore necessary that managers at every level understand both the estimated startup and the ongoing commitment for every project—either as members of the project team, the steering committee, or the user department. Thus, each project submitted for management approval must have its own built-in business rationale, just as each capital investment is viewed on its own merits. The function of the initial investigation is to identify those potential systems development projects which have sufficient merit to warrant a full-scale feasibility study of their economic viability and potential contribution to the organization.

Involvement of Multiple Users

As new systems grow in complexity and sophistication, multiple user involvement becomes more common. Users may be identified as a normal result of the initial investigation activities. Requests for studies may come directly from the systems department through identification of systems improvement opportunities that cross user organization lines. Although the individual activities and tasks within the systems process are essentially the same for individual or multiple users, the review, approval, and budgeting requirements are more complicated for the latter. In multiple user environments, the steering committee may need to take a more global view in its decisions and recommendations to top management. The steering committee may recommend to proceed with the Feasibility Study step even when individual user objections exist. In addition, the planning, development, and implementation of multi-user systems may suggest the need for different budgeting approaches to funding these efforts.

Relationship Between
Steering Committee and
Systems Organization

The difference between a maintenance systems request and one requiring an initial investigation is not always clear. For this reason, every request must be reported to the steering committee. This includes maintenance that is deferred or scheduled to be completed beyond a reasonable period (e.g., six months or longer).

This cycle subjects all user requests to equal review. It also lets the steering committee see the service level given to each user organization by the systems group. In addition, it enables the systems organization to screen out proposals that are inappropriate for steering committee review without relinquishing steering committee control.

Initial Investigation
Project File

A substantial amount of information that may be relevant to later steps in the systems development process is gathered during the initial investigation. This information includes interview summaries, organization charts, budgets, reports, and other documents. This information should be placed in a carefully organized and indexed project file to ensure its accessibility later in the project.

STANDARD ACTIVITIES/END ITEMS

TOUCHE ROSS

ORGANIZATION __PHASE I,__
   STEP 1
SYSTEM __PLANNING__
USER REP _____

ID/TITLE __INITIAL INVESTIGATION__

☐ PHASE   ☒ ACTIVITY   ☐ SUBTASK
☐ STEP   ☒ TASK   ☐

PREPARED BY __MVJ__
REVIEWED BY __CB__   __SH__
DATE __3/29/80__ __CB__ __11/1/80__
PHASE __I-1__ __I-1__

NUMBER	PHASE/STEP/ACTIVITY/TASK/SUBTASK NAME	END ITEM	FORM NO.	PERFORMED BY	DUE DATE	APPROVED BY	DATE
A.	Prepare Request	Letter of Request	112				
		Work Outline	101				
		Work Schedule	102				
		Interview Schedule	120				
B.	Perform Fact Finding						
B.1	- Conduct Interviews	Project Files and Index	100				
		Updated Interview Schedule	120				
		Interview Summary	121				
B.2	- Gather and Analyze Data	Statement of Benefits	146				
		Key Inputs and Outputs	130				
		Data Flows	127				
		Organization Charts	142				
		Budgets						
C.	Evaluate Need for a Feasibility Study and Summarize Response	Economic Evaluation	148				
		Project Plan	102				
		Management Summary	149				

58

STANDARD ACTIVITIES/END ITEMS

TOUCHE ROSS

ORGANIZATION __PHASE I__
STEP __1__
SYSTEM __PLANNING__
USER REP _____

ID/TITLE __INITIAL INVESTIGATION__

☐ PHASE ☐ STEP ☒ ACTIVITY ☒ TASK ☐ SUBTASK ☐ _____

PROJECT NO. _____

	PREPARED BY	__MVJ__	__SH__
	REVIEWED BY	__CB__	__CB__
	DATE	__3/29/80__	__11/1/80__
	PHASE	__I-1__	__I-1__

NUMBER	PHASE/STEP/ACTIVITY/TASK/SUBTASK NAME	END ITEM	FORM NO.	PERFORMED BY	DUE DATE	APPROVED BY	DATE
D.	Prepare Feasibility Study Work Plan	Work Outline	101				
		Project Schedule	102				
E.	Review Results	Initial Investigation Report					

59

THE SYSTEMS DEVELOPMENT PROCESS

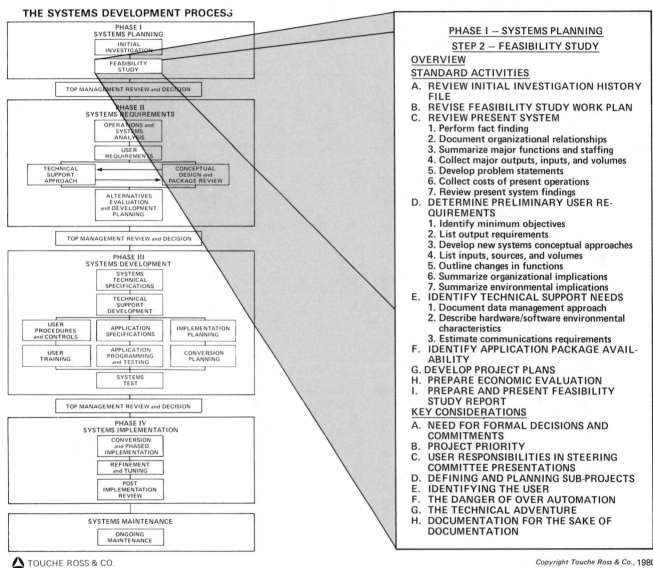

PHASE I
SYSTEMS PLANNING

INITIAL INVESTIGATION

FEASIBILITY STUDY

TOP MANAGEMENT REVIEW and DECISION

PHASE II
SYSTEMS REQUIREMENTS

OPERATIONS and SYSTEMS ANALYSIS

USER REQUIREMENTS

TECHNICAL SUPPORT APPROACH

CONCEPTUAL DESIGN and PACKAGE REVIEW

ALTERNATIVES EVALUATION and DEVELOPMENT PLANNING

TOP MANAGEMENT REVIEW and DECISION

PHASE III
SYSTEMS DEVELOPMENT

SYSTEMS TECHNICAL SPECIFICATIONS

TECHNICAL SUPPORT DEVELOPMENT

USER PROCEDURES and CONTROLS

APPLICATION SPECIFICATIONS

IMPLEMENTATION PLANNING

USER TRAINING

APPLICATION PROGRAMMING and TESTING

CONVERSION PLANNING

SYSTEMS TEST

TOP MANAGEMENT REVIEW and DECISION

PHASE IV
SYSTEMS IMPLEMENTATION

CONVERSION and PHASED IMPLEMENTATION

REFINEMENT and TUNING

POST IMPLEMENTATION REVIEW

SYSTEMS MAINTENANCE

ONGOING MAINTENANCE

TOUCHE ROSS & CO.

PHASE I — SYSTEMS PLANNING
STEP 2 — FEASIBILITY STUDY

OVERVIEW

STANDARD ACTIVITIES

A. REVIEW INITIAL INVESTIGATION HISTORY FILE
B. REVISE FEASIBILITY STUDY WORK PLAN
C. REVIEW PRESENT SYSTEM
  1. Perform fact finding
  2. Document organizational relationships
  3. Summarize major functions and staffing
  4. Collect major outputs, inputs, and volumes
  5. Develop problem statements
  6. Collect costs of present operations
  7. Review present system findings
D. DETERMINE PRELIMINARY USER REQUIREMENTS
  1. Identify minimum objectives
  2. List output requirements
  3. Develop new systems conceptual approaches
  4. List inputs, sources, and volumes
  5. Outline changes in functions
  6. Summarize organizational implications
  7. Summarize environmental implications
E. IDENTIFY TECHNICAL SUPPORT NEEDS
  1. Document data management approach
  2. Describe hardware/software environmental characteristics
  3. Estimate communications requirements
F. IDENTIFY APPLICATION PACKAGE AVAILABILITY
G. DEVELOP PROJECT PLANS
H. PREPARE ECONOMIC EVALUATION
I. PREPARE AND PRESENT FEASIBILITY STUDY REPORT

KEY CONSIDERATIONS

A. NEED FOR FORMAL DECISIONS AND COMMITMENTS
B. PROJECT PRIORITY
C. USER RESPONSIBILITIES IN STEERING COMMITTEE PRESENTATIONS
D. DEFINING AND PLANNING SUB-PROJECTS
E. IDENTIFYING THE USER
F. THE DANGER OF OVER AUTOMATION
G. THE TECHNICAL ADVENTURE
H. DOCUMENTATION FOR THE SAKE OF DOCUMENTATION

OVERVIEW   The initial investigation has determined that the requested project warrants a more detailed study. The feasibility study now begins to consider the technical aspects of the project and provides a firmer basis on which to decide whether or not to undertake development. The feasibility study is a detailed review of a potential system's probable characteristics and costs. Its purpose is to:

- Plan the system's project development and implementation activities.
- Estimate the probable elapsed time, staffing, and equipment requirements.
- Identify the probable costs and consequences of investing in the new system.

If practical, the feasibility study results should offer alternative conceptual solutions along with associated benefits and costs (one of which may be to continue with the present system). The study normally compares two new systems' projects: one that is more complex and offers mostly long-term improvements, and another which is less sophisticated, with short-range improvements.

The objective of this step is to provide management with the predictable results of implementing a specific system and to provide generalized project requirements. This — in the form of a feasibility study report — is used as the basis on which to decide whether or not to proceed with the costly Systems Requirements, Development, and Implementation phases.

User involvement during the feasibility study is critical. The user must supply much of the required effort and information and, in addition, must be able to judge the impact of alternative approaches. Solutions must be operationally, technically, and economically feasible. Much of the economic evaluation must be substantiated by the user. Therefore, the primary user must be highly qualified and intimately familiar with the workings of the organization and should come from the line operation.

The feasibility study also deals with the technical aspects of the proposed project and requires the development of conceptual solutions. Considerable systems experience and technical expertise are required to gather the proper information, analyze it, and reach practical conclusions. This technical work requires too much judgment to be conducted by anyone but an experienced systems analyst.

Improper technical or operating decisions made during this step may go undetected or unchallenged throughout the remainder of the process. In the worst case, such an error could result in the termination of a valid project — or the continuation of a project that is not economically or technically feasible.

The success of the entire project may depend on the quality and capabilities of the systems analysts and users responsible for the feasibility study. Some of the critical steps taken in establishing the feasibility study project team are:

- Identifying a project leader. This person could come from either the systems or user organization. One of the criteria for selection is that this person is an acceptable candidate to manage the project if it is subsequently approved for Systems Requirements (Phase II), Development (Phase III), and Implementation (Phase IV).

— Selecting a project team made up of qualified personnel from both the user and systems organizations. This staff should include participants from the initial investigation, although additional personnel are normally required. The feasibility study cannot start until commitments of time will clearly allow user and systems personnel to participate effectively.

— Determining when the project activities should begin. Many feasibility study projects require data that does not currently exist or cannot be assembled from historical information. For example, orders received may need to be counted by day, or by time of day, for a month. If this is the case, the full project team may not have to be assembled until after the data collection activities are completed.

The major responsibility of the project team is to determine the operating and technical feasibility of the requested system and whether the new system will produce an acceptable return. To this end, the project manager must assure that the feasibility study addresses:

— What needs to be done (the operating considerations).
— How it could be done (the technical considerations).
— The value of doing it (the economic considerations).

In order to find these answers, it is necessary to define for the system's basic approaches and its boundaries or scope.

The feasibility study may take several weeks or several months on any given project. The length of time is determined by many factors, including:

— The extent of problems in current operations.
— The number of functions to be reviewed.
— The time frames over which data collection is required.
— The interrelationships with other systems.
— The potential operating complexity of the requested system.
— The technical complexity of the alternative solutions.

The end result of the feasibility study is a steering committee decision on whether to terminate the systems project or to approve its next phase. Although the steering committee can stop the project at several later phases, the decision is especially critical at this point because later phases require a major commitment of resources. All too often, management review committees approve the continuation of systems projects merely because termination at this point might cast doubt on the group's judgment in giving an earlier approval.

The decision made at the end of the feasibility study should identify those projects that are to be terminated. Once a project is deemed feasible and is approved for development, it must be prioritized with previously approved projects waiting for development (given a limited availability of capital or other resources). As development gets under way, management is given a series of checkpoints to monitor the project's actual progress as compared to the plan.

Review Initial Investigation
Project File

The project team forms a basis for launching the feasibility study by reviewing all previous documentation. Similar activities are established at the startup of other phases and steps. They are planned at stages where a pause may occur in the flow of a project—perhaps the result of a decision point requiring top management review of a steering committee recommendation. Where such pauses occur, it is important that the beginning of the next phase of step include this review because changes that may have taken place during the interim could impact the project or alter its earlier conclusions. Likewise, increasing the project team requires additional time to allow new members to familiarize themselves with the project. Any changes arising from this checkpointing activity may require new interviews with operating unit managers.

Revise Feasibility Study
Work Plan

Constant checking and rechecking of prior assumptions is a key to effective systems planning. Project tasks and associated estimates of schedules and budgets should be continually updated as more details become known. The project manager must, therefore, recognize that work plans require continuous updating and verification.

During the review of the feasibility study work plan, the project team delineates specific tasks required to execute the work plan. For example, the work plan that serves as an input to this activity might specify that a number of current operations be reviewed. The plan is updated to designate the interviewees, the interviewers, the topics, the planned interview durations, the estimated documentation effort, and the specific start and target completion dates. Use of the work plan as the transition from one step to the next is a reminder that the end product of each step serves as the basis for starting the next.

Review Present System

Many decisions about the design of the new system depend on how well the present system is understood by project team members. The primary purpose of this activity is, therefore, to survey current systems and operations well enough to understand generally what the systems do and how they do it. This should be achieved with a minimal level of effort.

The tasks in this review are iterative in nature. For example, interviewing is a process whereby new things are learned, new data are gathered and new insights are gained that may require additional interviews—which produce additional data, and so on. Care must be taken not to expend more effort than is necessary to achieve a general level of understanding.

Perform Fact-Finding. Every activity in the feasibility study is more detailed than those conducted in the initial investigation. The fact-finding interviews in this task are more probing and reach a greater organizational depth. Where the initial investigation concerned itself with top-level managers in the user department(s), feasibility study interviews include the operating level managers and, in some cases, first-line supervisory personnel of areas where the most critical functions are performed.

It is not unusual during this process to discover key people whose relative importance to the system far exceeds their rank and position. It is not effective to schedule interviews merely on the basis of an organization chart. Key names come up in interviews as "the person who can answer this question" or "the person to see for information." Identifying and interviewing key personnel can save project team members many hours of work. The point here is that considerable judgment and thought are needed to perform interviews and follow leads.

In addition to interviews, the fact-finding task also includes background research. Relevant documents may include management advisory letters from the external auditor, internal audit or consulting reports, and operational analyses and recommendations by outside consultants. The auditors' files may contain flowcharts and control requirements documentation, and may identify information needs of external parties who might not normally be interviewed.

Document Organizational Relationships.   In any organization there exists both a formal and an informal organizational structure. Some firms, in fact, have no organizational chart at all. It is important that the project team document and understand both the formal organizational structure and the "real world" way that things get done. The differences between how the organization appears on paper and the way it really works is vitally important to determining the feasibility of the requested system because, without a clear understanding of the functions being performed, the project team is unable to develop realistic cost schedules — a major input to the financial planning for the requested system. One side benefit of this effort is the identification and elimination of unnecessary activities by the requested system.

The data gathered during this activity includes the following elements:

— Organization charts.
— Summaries of functions performed (including position descriptions, if available).
— Staffing levels.
— Budgets.

Summarize Major Functions and Staffing.   Many functions of organization units within a company are interrelated, and the project team must identify and schematically show these interrelationships in its analysis. An overview of the work flow should be prepared along with a summary of the functions performed and the staffing required. Two forms — the general-purpose chart and the summary of functions — are provided for this purpose. The work flow is diagrammed on a top-down basis, beginning with the major functions and showing the relationship of subfunctions. These diagrams should communicate functions, responsibilities, and timing. A line manager or supervisor should be able to identify his or her area of responsibility in sufficient detail to describe functions across several organizational units. As the project team uncovers details that require additional information, more interviews may be conducted. For example, if the project leader believes that more information about a specific function is needed, the person responsible for that function should be interviewed and additional levels of detail added. However, a great deal of time must not be spent determining the precise functions and time makeup of the jobs of all the people in the organization. First of all, the project is only concerned with those people whose job description is potentially affected by the new project and, second, a high level of precision is not necessary at this stage in the project. Much of this work will have to be confirmed or even redone during the Systems Requirements phase.

Collect Major Outputs, Inputs, and Volumes.   Following the function descriptions developed in the preceding task, the project team must next identify the information needed by the system, that produced by it, and their respective volumes. The Computer Output/Report Form, Document Definition Form and Transaction/Data Base-File Activity Form are suggested devices for organizing this data. The appropriate form can be attached to copies of live examples as a cover sheet describing each major input or output document. The cover sheet provides a standard method of recording essential data on inputs and outputs including purpose, volume, distribution, and frequency. Security and privacy requirements are also described, as are control considerations or constraints involved in the preparation and use of the forms and/or data content.

Develop Problem Statements. Throughout the course of interviewing and data gathering on the current system, members of the project team identify business problems and improvement opportunities. This task is specifically structured to consolidate documentation of all of these problems and opportunities and to rank them in order of importance.

Because the scope of this task encompasses the full range of the current system, the entire project team should be involved. Discussions center around organizational impact and the magnitude of the problems and opportunities. Problem documentation should be precise, specific, and quantified. This is easily illustrated:

— Example of a vague problem statement: "Information necessary to make management decisions is not available."

— Example of a precise statement covering the same situation: "The warehouse superintendent is not provided with a forecast of next week's shipments. This results in unplanned overtime averaging 5 percent weekly."

Collect Costs of Present Operations. This task calls for collecting budget and actual cost data related to the current operations under study. To the extent feasible, these cost data should be related directly to the functions, transaction volumes, and staffing previously documented. Cost data for present operations should be collected in view of the eventual need to make cost comparisons with alternative systems approaches. Data compiled during this task should at the very least separate staffing and operating costs for each organizational entity.

Review Present System Findings. A formal meeting with user management concludes the present system review. The objective of the meeting is to communicate the project team's cumulative understanding of the present system, its costs, functions, outputs, inputs, problems, and opportunities for improvement. Since decisions that impact the direction of new systems are based on present understandings, user management must carefully review and approve the findings before initiating the next activity.

Determine Preliminary User Requirements

Reasonable estimates of new systems benefits and the cost of subsequent project phases are highly dependent on the project team's determination of user requirements. However, since the objective of this step is only to determine the system feasibility, only a preliminary identification of user requirements is necessary. The challenge is therefore to perform these tasks in sufficient detail to enable completion of the feasibility study without, in fact, conducting the entire Systems Requirements (Phase II) activities. Active project management is essential to assure that adequate but not excessive effort is expended in appropriate areas. As implied by its name, a significant amount of user orientation and, conversely, a minimal amount of technical orientation are required to complete this activity.

The processes associated with this activity may be repetitive. That is, at any point in the performance of the tasks described below, a prospective approach may be found to be impractical. Whenever this happens, separate approaches are typically identified and analyzed. Time should therefore be allocated for this type of review and for a repetitive consideration of alternatives. In addition, it may be appropriate for some projects to research the "state-of-the-art" and determine whether other organizations have addressed and solved the same business problems.

Identify Minimum Objectives.   In order to develop new systems conceptual approaches, the team must first identify what the system is to accomplish — that is, what business objectives are to be achieved. The objectives defined as a result will establish the scope of the project.

Consider, for example, a customer order processing system. Given the assignment of establishing objectives for this application, the project team would likely consider level of service as a key area. Another key area might be to solve existing operational problems. Thus, for the level of service area, a team working on a customer order entry system might define the objective as "provide the capability to ship 95 percent of class A orders within 24 hours of receipt." In approaching a current problem, the team might identify excessive overtime in warehouses as something that should be addressed, and might further define the objective as "provide warehouse superintendent with shipping schedules that make it possible to cut unplanned overtime by 50 percent."

Stipulating these formal objectives forces the project team to focus on essentials. This instills a project discipline that focuses exploration within the established parameters of the project. It is not unusual for a project team to discover many attractive but optional opportunities for other systems projects. These ideas may impact later stages of the current project or may generate new projects.

List Output Requirements.   Based on the objectives and scope described in the previous task, all major outputs associated with the requested system are identified and listed. Outputs may include printed reports and video displays, depending on the user's requirements. The list should include brief statements of purpose, descriptions (e.g., contents, frequency, timeliness of data, special form requirements, etc.), and primary distributions. Specific report names, identification of data elements, specification of totals, and similar items are not normally appropriate for the feasibility study. In fact, many of the outputs listed at this point may be considerably different from actual outputs developed later during User Requirements in Phase II. One output listed in the feasibility study may often describe an entire class or set of reports to be produced, such as control reports. As stated previously, the preliminary requirements need only be described in sufficient detail to permit adequate assessment of system and project feasibility. This does not preclude limited circumstances in which a specific output is described in order to effectively communicate with users, to adequately assess operational impacts, or to reasonably estimate developmental requirements.

Develop New Systems Conceptual Approaches.   This task involves developing one or more acceptable approaches to performing required functions, producing the outputs, and meeting the objectives of the requested system. This process involves identifying and considering a range of alternatives that assure recommendation of the most practical approach. Each reasonable alternative must be adequately and consistently documented at a level of detail comparable to the present system documentation.

Identifying alternative approaches is a creative process and should be treated accordingly. It is important to the success of the project team's mission to encourage a free-flowing thought process that extends to any reasonable type of approach, whether it involves computer or manual techniques. Because team members have detailed expertise in specific areas, they should be able to explore a variety of alternatives. The success of this activity will depend on how well the project manager has established the right atmosphere for the exchange and development of ideas.

Once the reasonable range of alternatives has been developed, the project team conducts a final analysis and selects the approach best suited to the objectives of the system. Often, more than one approach will meet the stated objectives. Thus, the project team's final recommendations may include one approach as the most cost-effective in the long term and another approach as easier to implement and beneficial in the short term.

List Inputs, Sources, and Volumes. Identification of required inputs may now be determined to fulfill the output requirements using the selected approach. The list of inputs is oriented to complete documents (e.g., customer order) as a single input, even though a document may technically incorporate several input records (e.g., customer name and address, shipping instructions, line items, etc.). The list should include brief descriptions of contents, sources of information, major processing steps and interfaces required, frequency and volumes anticipated — at both peak and average periods. As with the list of outputs, specific transaction record names, identification of data elements, and similar items are not normally appropriate at this time.

Outline Changes in Functions. The output requirements, inputs, and approaches to be recommended for the new system generally require changes in functions performed by the user organizations. Thus, the project team must compare the preliminary user requirements as developed in the above tasks to the previously documented summaries of functions presently performed in order to outline resultant functional changes. Care must be exercised in the analysis of staffing impacts related to these functional changes. For example, elimination of specific functions from one user person (or group) that appears to reduce workload by 50 percent may or may not result in a realizable benefit equal to 50 percent of the current staff cost, depending on the complexity and redistribution of the workload over the remaining functions. Conversely, addition of functions to an existing user group may add, reduce, or not change incremental costs because of content, timing, and/or employment restrictions.

Summarize Organization Implications. Once staffing impacts and functional changes have been identified, overall organizational implications are determined. In some cases, entire groups and their associated supervisory and management personnel may be eliminated. In other cases, staff requirements may increase or decrease to such an extent as to imply changes to the quantity or level of management and supervisors. Finally, new systems may involve such a significant new approach to the business operation as to suggest a major realignment of responsibilities and a physical relocation of operations. All implications must be analyzed, costed, and summarized for presentation in the feasibility study report.

One key implication to be explored at this point is the emotional environment — the human factor considerations. Depending on user personnel and the nature of the system, anxieties over job security or job changes may require special analysis or specific activities and skills during subsequent phases of the project. At the extreme, a project which is "technically" and "economically" feasible may not be "emotionally" feasible because of re-education requirements or because of political implications for management and users.

Summarize Environmental Implications.   Significant environmental factors that may reasonably be expected to impact the final design of the new system are summarized at this time. They include:

— Security and privacy regulations.
— Control considerations.
— Policy, schedule, and other constraints.

To assure that these requirements have been addressed, members of the project team or other resource personnel may be assigned to review applicable legislation, regulations, or policies and practices within the user and data processing organizations. Constraints associated with schedules or timing of projected outputs are also summarized at this time. Additionally, the proposed approach to controls should be reviewed with the internal and external auditors.

Identify Technical Support Needs

The sum total of preliminary user requirements as determined by the previous activity and tasks are now available to help identify technical support needs. The objectives, approaches, and other requirements of the proposed system may imply either minimal or significant needs for technical support. For example, a new batch-oriented application required to maintain records of a simplified, relatively inactive inventory may only require minimal run time on an existing computer facility. Conversely, a new customer order-processing application that interactively accepts and edits orders and provides order status inquiries from a variety of sales offices may imply use of intelligent terminals, interapplication transaction processing, sophisticated data management, telecommunications, distributed processors, or combinations of these and other available technical tools.

It is important to remember, however, that technical capabilities are analyzed in response to identified user requirements and practical environmental considerations. Technical approaches that are not required to fulfill these requirements are not appropriate except in special circumstances. For example, a proposed system may be required to operate in an environment where only transaction processing and a specified data management approach are permitted. In this example, the approach could be constrained primarily by technical issues and not by user requirements. If the technical support required seriously detracts from the economic viability of the project and system, that incremental cost should be documented in the economic evaluation. In addition, in this case, other systems approaches might be considered (e.g., use of a service bureau, time sharing, or a minicomputer).

Three areas of technical support must usually be identified during the feasibility study: (1) data management approach, (2) communications requirements, and (3) hardware/software characteristics. Specialized technical expertise may be required to assist the project team in this activity, even though no actual data base, data communications or hardware/software specifications are to be generated at this time. Thus, technical staff resources must possess sufficient expertise to identify needs without developing detailed solutions. Inappropriate or insufficient technical resources during this activity may produce significantly invalid estimates. For example, new systems may incur substantial unplanned ongoing expenditures or may require several times the estimated developmental effort. On the other hand, new projects could be terminated because of overstated technical requirements and costs or understated availabilities of hardware and software.

Document Data Management Approach.   For proposed computer based systems, the project team needs to document an approach for data management and to develop preliminary estimates of gross file space and updating requirements. Depending on the type of proposed system and the current environment within the data processing function, the approach may be stated in different ways. For example, if the requested system requires only periodic updating and reporting of a minimal set of data elements, the application would be more suited to conventional file processing rather than to a data base management system. In this case, the only additional requirement would be to estimate permanent and temporary disk storage.

In other situations, a proposed system may indicate the need to maintain many data elements with complex interrelationships. This could suggest a sophisticated data base approach. If so, a further task would be required to understand the cost effectiveness of integrating this new system with existing data bases or the need to establish a new data base or data management approach.

Only the approach to data management must be documented and understood in order to predict operating characteristics and estimate costs for the feasibility study. Determining these implications could require significant technical effort and time during this phase. Substantial additional effort may be required later and should be planned for and shown in the economic evaluation and overall feasibility study conclusions.

Describe Hardware/Software Environmental Characteristics.   Many proposed systems imply the use of hardware within the user organizations to supplement or replace existing hardware. These implications are derived from user objectives and conceptual approaches documented in previous activities. In order to describe the hardware and software environmental characteristics, the project team must analyze every major component of the new system.

For example, timing and volume considerations may indicate that planned reports (or COM) are sufficient. Otherwise, low- or high-speed hard copy devices and/or video displays may be planned. For output, then, the project team's end-product descriptions details the hardware and software requirements.

The approach used to analyze hardware and software environmental characteristics may also be applied to data input and data storage. Each component area has specific characteristics related to types and amount of hardware and systems software support. The end product of this task includes alternative uses of hardware and software to fulfill user requirements. The relative advantages and disadvantages of these approaches, considering costs and other implications, are also described. Care must be exercised to assure that the data management approach documented in the previous task is properly reflected in the overall hardware and software characteristics description.

Estimate Communications Requirements.   The need for data communications in the new system is derived from descriptions of hardware and other environmental characteristics completed in the previous task. The requirement could vary from a minimal quantity of "dumb" terminals to systems using complex networks with multiple intelligent nodes. To estimate the potential communications requirements, the Project Team must understand the types and response characteristics of traffic flowing between each point (hardware device) and the approximate number of points involved. This type of information should be available from the previous task and from documentation used to determine preliminary user requirements. Estimates of the quantity, quality, and speed of communications facilities are developed and documented in this task. Based on the current data processing environment, data communications needs may also imply installing new systems software. As in the case of data management, the feasibility study only requires documenting the approach and estimated needs for data communications. Impact should be carefully analyzed, however, since the approach could require significant time and technical effort to implement. If so, this must be planned for and shown in the economic evaluation and overall feasibility study conclusions.

Identify Application Package Availability

A frequent alternative to the complete development of a new system is the purchase and installation of an existing application package. Previous activities in this step have documented preliminary user requirements and technical support needs related to the new system requested. This information will be used in the next activity to estimate development efforts, including all the steps related to specifications and programming. A second development approach could result from package acquisition rather than custom development. Many packages exist, covering a wide variety of applications, either software or packaged (turnkey) hardware/software products. Thus, an important activity within the feasibility study is the identification of package availability for the proposed system.

Packages may be leased or purchased from several sources — computer hardware vendors, third-party software companies, or other organizations involved in the same type of business (especially at the state and local government level and other noncompeting organizations). Using these sources, the project team reviews package features with preliminary user requirements and technical support needs. Packages that match all or some of the requirements may be identified, suggesting that a package is a viable alternative. If minimum objectives are met or if stand-alone modules are available, a package may be an acceptable approach. If package use is an alternative, the project team prepares the following documentation:

— A comparison of package features with preliminary user requirements and technical support needs.
— Potential vendor(s) able to supply the packages.
— Acquisition and/or ongoing fees paid to the vendor(s) of the packages.
— Other critical factors (e.g., requirements for specialized minicomputer hardware, other vendor relationships, etc.).

Develop Project Plans

Documentation prepared up to this point in the feasibility study is used by the project team to develop estimates of effort and timing for completing Systems Requirements (Phase II), Development (Phase III), and Implementation (Phase IV) of the proposed system. One complete project plan is created for each conceptual approach and for package acquisition versus custom development, if applicable. Note that package acquisition generally does not completely eliminate any phase or step in the process; it merely changes the amount of effort in certain areas. For example, Applications Specifications and Programming (Steps 3 and 4 of Phase III) are greatly reduced through use of a package, but are not eliminated since some modifications may be required.

Major assumptions related to any particular phase or step are documented as part of the project plan. This may include assumptions concerning the availability of critical personnel, equipment, or software at certain points in time. The associated risks and consequences of changes to these major assumptions are also considered. Special approaches or strategies required during conversion and implementation are identified and incorporated into the project plans. They may include establishing a logical installation sequence for multiple system segments. These strategies should address the organization's normal reluctance to change and the potential operating risks inherent in large or old manual files. If significant cleanup activities are required prior to new system development, they too should be included in the plans.

The estimated effort required for each phase and step is planned by job type — systems analysts, programmers, technical analysts, user managers, clerical, procedures analysts, etc., as appropriate. The project team must avoid overly detailed project planning: i.e., estimates that cannot be reasonably supported based on the level of understanding attained during the feasibility study. For example, time and work estimates may be more appropriately expressed in months instead of days. Applications development estimates may be based on subsystems or modules, not on the number and complexity of individual programs. As with other activities in this step, development of project plans requires experienced and highly capable personnel.

Prepare Economic Evaluation

The purpose of the economic evaluation is to compare the estimated development and operating costs to identified benefits at a general level of precision that enables management to determine the project's feasibility. If the project is deemed feasible, it is prioritized for development with other projects.

Developmental costs can usually be estimated from personnel and equipment requirements indicated in the project plan prepared in the previous activity. The costs presented are generally incremental in nature and would not, for example, include the cost of training existing personnel, unless temporary help were employed to offset workloads. The cost of dedicated personnel presently on staff would be included. The presentation of costs will vary according to the management style of the organization in which the system is being implemented.

Estimating operating costs and benefits generally presents a far more difficult and critical problem. It is often useful to consider benefits in the following manner: tangible benefits are those for which dollar value may be reasonably quantified and measured. Intangible benefits may either be quantified in units other than dollars, or may be identified and described subjectively. The decision to proceed with the development of a system may rest on any one or all of the following:

- *Current operating costs and benefits:* the cost of operating the system in today's circumstances and the (quantified) expected benefits.
- *Future period costs and benefits:* a projection of today's costs and benefits according to expected or planned operating changes (such as policy, procedure, volume, and organization).
- *Intangible costs and benefits:* other costs and benefits that may be particularly difficult to quantify, or where quantification contributes little to the decision process. These costs and benefits may more properly be categorized as measured and unmeasured.

In most cases, intangible considerations should be identified and documented. Enough care must be exercised during the benefit identification effort to assure that only appropriate benefits are assigned to the proposed systems project. Many benefits may be achieved in an existing environment without the need to develop a new system. For example, if in a manufacturing plant a "kitting" process takes place several weeks before final assembly because the current inventory is unreliable, the process can be eliminated if the existing system is improved. This would bring about an inventory benefit without developing a new materials requirement planning system. The value of the benefit should therefore not be associated with developing the new system.

Identifying and quantifying costs and benefits is a standard part of the feasibility study and should not be glossed over by the project team. Various pitfalls, considerations, and approaches associated with these tasks are described below:

— Personnel costs/benefits: Almost always a factor in systems projects. The conservative approach is to quantify such costs only in those cases where a full time person is either gained or lost. Such determinations of payroll impact should be supported by the functional analysis developed in analyzing current and projected system workflows against current and projected operating volumes. Variable fringe benefits may be appropriately included with estimated salaries in arriving at a total. Fractional time gained by individuals freed for other purposes is more accurately described as an unmeasured benefit. If different skills are required, then cost level must be considered in addition to quantity.

— EDP operating costs: Particularly difficult to estimate, because changes in equipment loading (as a result of changes in other systems or in volume) may impact incremental operating costs if the system is to be implemented with existing hardware. More subjectivity may be introduced by the unknown effects of new software interacting with the current operating environment. In general, the only practical approach open to the project team is to:

  · Carefully document all known assumptions and constraints in developing system costs.

  · Base estimates of equipment and operating costs on the conceptual design and volume estimates developed in the feasibility study. In many cases, the most effective way to assure that EDP operating costs or benefits are reasonable is to obtain formal approval of the estimates by EDP operations management.

— Operating benefits other than personnel reductions are most often the principal reason for new systems development. These benefits are typically (but not necessarily) derived in the general operations of the business rather than in EDP operations. These projected benefits are commonly overlooked by operating management. An examination of the routine causes of such failures also provides a list of potential pitfalls to be avoided in developing these estimates. Examples include:

  · Unrealistic or unrecognized assumptions are often the cause of unrealized benefits. All assumptions and constraints must therefore be documented and verified to the fullest practical extent.

  · Unrealistic or unnecessary operating constraints may artificially cause the proposed system to appear unfeasible. For example, inventory management systems are often based on a prescribed service level without a real understanding of current or necessary service levels. Consequently, inventory levels typically increase rather than decrease with the introduction of new systems. Similarly, response-time requirements are often stated in the absolute rather than within parameters for on-line systems, forcing a higher level of hardware capability to meet peak load processing than is realistically necessary.

The current system, the proposed development project, and the new system may also involve significant intangible costs and benefits associated with management time, staff morale, turnover rates, and competitive postures.

In the final summary of development and operating costs and benefits, it is generally desirable to describe each alternative at a consistent level of detail (including the "do-nothing" alternative) and in comparable terms. For example, the economic description of each specific project should include a complete presentation of all:

— Development costs.
— Quantifiable operating costs.
— Other costs.
— Tangible benefits.
— Intangible benefits (both measured and unmeasured).
— Operating assumptions and constraints.

Management approval and prioritization of potential projects will be based on factors such as:

— Comparative return on investment.
— Probability of success.
— Realism of assumptions and constraints.
— Estimated worth of unmeasured benefits.
— Strategic business needs.

Prepare and Present the Feasibility Study Report

Two levels of review are held as the final activity of this phase. These reviews present the findings and recommendations of the project team to both user management and steering committee members.

In practice, a series of such meetings may be required to complete the necessary, highly detailed review with the system's ultimate users. User organizations must support the accuracy of the observations on the current system and the operation and benefits to be gained from the proposed system. This is an exceptionally valuable exercise for the project team and it will help the team "fine tune" the feasibility study report before its final review and presentation to the steering committee.

The principal vehicle around which the review sessions are organized is the executive summary. This top level summary also provides the introductory and summary level first chapter of the feasibility study report. The remainder of the report should essentially be little more than an organized collection of the documentation and materials developed during the feasibility study effort.

The precise strategy implied in the structure and presentation of the executive summary will be determined by circumstances within each project. Whatever that structure, the executive summary should include, as a minimum, a clear and concise presentation of:

— The scope and objectives of the study.
— Problems and constraints.
— Summary of economic considerations.

The principal creative effort required of the project team in preparing this final document is the development of specific recommendations and the presentation of supporting evidence.

In general, the project team should refrain from giving the steering committee only one alternative. While a clear and unambiguous recommendation is necessary, it is also important to ensure that all major alternatives are presented fairly in a way that permits easy comparison.

At the conclusion of the Feasibility Study, the steering committee is in a position to either accept or reject the recommendations of the project team. If the decision is to proceed into Phase II (Systems Requirements) with any of the alternative approaches identified in the feasibility study, the steering committee should be able to establish priorities consistent with estimated costs and benefits, as well as a target date to begin the Requirements phase.

KEY CONSIDERATIONS

Need for Formal Decisions and Commitments

A project should not move forward without formal approval of the work performed during the feasibility study and an equally formal commitment of resources by the users, the systems organization and top management. External resources may also be required.

It may be tempting to proceed on an informal basis with piecemeal changes. However, the adoption of portions of proposed solutions does not constitute formal approval or acceptance of the team's findings and recommendations. In fact, a piecemeal approach could destroy the entire project since individual parts of the proposal may fail without the needed interconnection of component parts. Additionally, many individual parts may require the completion of prerequisite parts to be practical and cost effective.

Project Priority

Hopes are usually high at the beginning of a feasibility study effort, and its backers support it eagerly. However, in time, eagerness may lessen as supporters become distracted by other developments or lose interest. Each new system project competes with others, and an organization may have many projects in process simultaneously. These projects vie for corporate resources: people, time, money, even the attention of outside vendors.

It is therefore critically important that the project either be shelved or receive an assigned priority at the end of the Systems Planning phase relating this project to others that may be underway. Priority is subject to reevaluation as new projects are undertaken. However, since personnel may be involved in more than one project, time must be allocated to projects according to some priority scale. Successful systems management requires defining and producing clear understandings on these priorities before and during the project.

User Responsibilities in Steering Committee Presentations

It is an old but frequently ignored adage of the business world that systems cannot be imposed upon users without their involvement and support. A system that does not belong to its users will not achieve expected results and attainable benefits.

It is therefore usually desirable during this phase to have the highest-level user in the review process make or participate heavily in the presentation of the findings and recommendations of the team to the steering committee. This technique increases the probability that the project will have the necessary user involvement and support. It also can help guarantee that the system will be developed with user involvement and will belong to user personnel at its conclusion.

Defining and Planning Subprojects

The project techniques described in this section are readily adaptable to special needs. One situation that surfaces frequently is the "spinning off" of additional projects or subprojects on the basis of findings in the System Planning phase. In some instances, these spin-offs will involve totally new areas. In others, they will create additional related systems and will require a considerable effort in time and resources before beginning the System Requirements (Phase II) which follows. When this situation occurs, the steering committee may have to approve a separate project with its own funding to accomplish this task.

For example, if a project is undertaken to develop an inventory forecasting system, a sound approach would be to develop several simulation models to test alternative approaches. It would be possible to conduct this type of modeling on a subproject basis before the initiation of the System Requirements (Phase II).

Identifying the User

It is important to understand that defining the user of a new system in many large companies, will not be an easy task. At its most simplistic level, this problem arises because the operating department uses the data and an EDP department operates the system. On a more complicated level, many systems cut across organization lines. Several departments may be impacted by the change. While one department may be a primary user, other organizations may have to respond to the changes imposed by the new development effort.

The Danger of Over-Automation

When relatively inexperienced systems people play an important role in project definition, the project team often fails to adequately distinguish between those things which should be automated and those things which can be automated. There is a major difference between a systems feature that enhances human engineering and a feature that is unnecessary to obtain benefits or support the business operation. This is particularly true if the designer fails to understand all the exception conditions surrounding the decision or underestimates the volatility of the decision-making process.

The Technical Adventure

All too often, data processing people view a new system as an opportunity to test out some new systems feature or to experiment with a new language or operating system. As a general rule, complex and critical systems are not the appropriate place to test out untried equipment and systems software. Such decisions must be weighed carefully, since it is not likely that they will be challenged at any later stage of the developmental process. Once a formal project plan is adopted, it is likely to be implemented as planned.

Documentation for the Sake of Documentation

The purpose of the review of existing systems is two-fold:

- To develop a sufficient understanding of current systems in order to adequately understand existing problems and to prescribe potential solutions.
- To develop a comparative cost basis for evaluating alternatives.

It is not unusual for a study team to find itself reviewing an existing system that has recently been documented in part or in its entirety as part of another study. Alternatively, it may be evident upon review of the initial investigation effort, that a complete documentation effort covering an entire system may not be necessary to determine its feasibility. If the current operation is not likely to be internally altered by the new system, it may not make sense to document that operation in detail. In such cases the project team should refrain from ritualistic gathering of unneeded or duplicative information simply because the standard methodology calls for certain activities and tasks to be performed, and the end-item documentation produced.

STANDARD ACTIVITIES/END ITEMS

TOUCHE ROSS

ID/TITLE ___FEASIBILITY STUDY___

ORGANIZATION ___PHASE I,___

STEP 2

SYSTEM ___PLANNING___

USER REP ___

☐ PHASE   ☒ ACTIVITY   ☐ SUBTASK

☐ STEP   ☒ TASK   ☐ ___

PREPARED BY MVJ SH

REVIEWED BY CB CB

DATE 3/29/80 11/1/80

PHASE I-2 I-2

PROJECT NO. ___

NUMBER	PHASE/STEP/ACTIVITY/TASK/SUBTASK NAME	END ITEM	FORM NO.	PERFORMED BY	DUE DATE	APPROVED BY	DATE
A.	Review Initial Investigation Project File	Updated Project Plan	102				
B.	Revise Feasibility Study Work Plan	Updated Work Outline	101				
C.	Review Present System						
C.1	– Perform Fact Finding	Updated Interview Schedule	120				
		Interview Summaries	121				
		Glossary of Terms	122				
C.2	– Document Organizational Relationships	Organization Charts	142				
		Summary of Functions	125				
		Position Descriptions						
C.3	– Summarize Major Functions and Staffing	Staffing Requirements	126				
		Updated Summary of Functions	125				
		Work Flow Diagram	127, 128				
C.4	– Collect Major Outputs, Inputs, and Volumes	Input/Output Index	130				
		Input/Output Identification	131				
		Document Definition	132				
		File Description	133				
		Summary of Controls	141				

77

STANDARD ACTIVITIES/END ITEMS

TOUCHE ROSS

ORGANIZATION __PHASE I,__

STEP 2

SYSTEM __PLANNING__

USER REP _____

ID/TITLE __FEASIBILITY STUDY__

☐ PHASE   ☒ ACTIVITY   ☐ SUBTASK
☐ STEP   ☒ TASK   ☐

PREPARED BY __MVJ__ __SH__
REVIEWED BY __CB__ __CB__
DATE __3/29/80__ __11/1/80__
PHASE __I-2__ __I-2__

NUMBER	PHASE/STEP/ACTIVITY/TASK/SUBTASK NAME	END ITEM	FORM NO.	PERFORMED BY	DUE DATE	APPROVED BY	DATE
C.5	- Develop Problem Statements	Operating Constraints	140				
		Problem Statements	142				
C.6	- Collect Costs of Present Operations	Operating Cost Summary	145				
C.7	- Review Present System Findings						
D.	Determine Preliminary User Requirements						
D.1	- Identify Minimum Objectives	Statement of Objectives	142				
D.2	- List Output Requirements	Input/Output Index/ID	130, 131				
D.3	- Develop New Systems Conceptual Approaches	Statement of Approaches	142				
D.4	- List Inputs, Sources, and Volumes	Input/Output Index/ID	130, 131				
		File Description	133				
		Summary of Controls	141				
D.5	- Outline Changes in Functions	Work Flow Diagram	127, 128				
		Summary of Functions	125				
		Staffing Requirements	126				
D.6	- Summarize Organizational Implications	Organization Structure	142				
		Operating Cost Summary	145				

78

STANDARD ACTIVITIES/END ITEMS

TOUCHE ROSS

ORGANIZATION _____

SYSTEM _____

USER REP _____

ID/TITLE ____ FEASIBILITY STUDY

☐ PHASE   ☒ ACTIVITY   ☐ SUBTASK

☐ STEP   ☒ TASK   ☐

PHASE I,

STEP 2

PLANNING

		PREPARED BY	MVJ	SH
		REVIEWED BY	CB	CB
		DATE	3/29/80	11/1/80
		PHASE	I-2	I-2

NUMBER	PHASE/STEP/ACTIVITY/TASK/SUBTASK NAME	END ITEM	FORM NO.	PERFORMED BY	DUE DATE	APPROVED BY	DATE
D.7	– Summarize Environmental Implications	Summary of Controls	141				
		Assumptions and Constraints	140				
E.	Identify Technical Support Needs						
E.1	– Document Data Management Approach	Data Base/File Contents Characteristics	152				
		Data Element Description	134				
		Record/Documents Contents	153				
		Description of Approach	127, 128, 142				
E.2	– Describe Hardware/Software Environmental Characteristics	Description of Approach	127, 128, 142				
E.3	– Estimate Communications Requirements	Description of Requirements	127, 128, 142				
F.4	Identify Application Package Availability	List and Description of Package	142				
G.	Develop Project Plans	Work Outline	101				
		Project Plan	102				
		General Purpose Checklist	183				

79

TOUCHE ROSS

ORGANIZATION	PHASE I, STEP 2
SYSTEM	PLANNING
USER REP	

ID/TITLE ___FEASIBILITY STUDY___

☐ PHASE   ☒ ACTIVITY   ☐ SUBTASK
☐ STEP   ☒ TASK   ☐ _____

PREPARED BY	MVJ	SH
REVIEWED BY	CB	CB
DATE	3/29/80	11/1/80
PHASE	I-2	I-2

NUMBER	PHASE/STEP/ACTIVITY/TASK/SUBTASK NAME	END ITEM	FORM NO.	PERFORMED BY	DUE DATE	APPROVED BY	DATE
H.	Prepare Economic Evaluation	Development Costs	105				
		Operating Costs	145				
		Other Costs	145				
		Tangible Benefits	146, 147				
		Intangible Benefits	146, 147				
		Assumptions and Constraints	140				
		Economic Evaluation Summary	148				
		Problems and Constraints	140				
		Management Summary	149				
I.	Prepare and Present Feasibility Study Report						

80

THE SYSTEMS DEVELOPMENT PROCESS

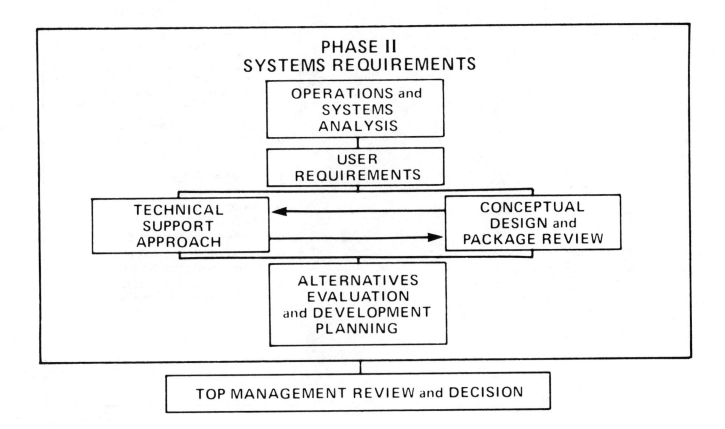

PHASE II
SYSTEMS REQUIREMENTS

OPERATIONS and
SYSTEMS
ANALYSIS

USER
REQUIREMENTS

TECHNICAL
SUPPORT
APPROACH

CONCEPTUAL
DESIGN and
PACKAGE REVIEW

ALTERNATIVES
EVALUATION
and DEVELOPMENT
PLANNING

TOP MANAGEMENT REVIEW and DECISION

TOUCHE ROSS & CO.

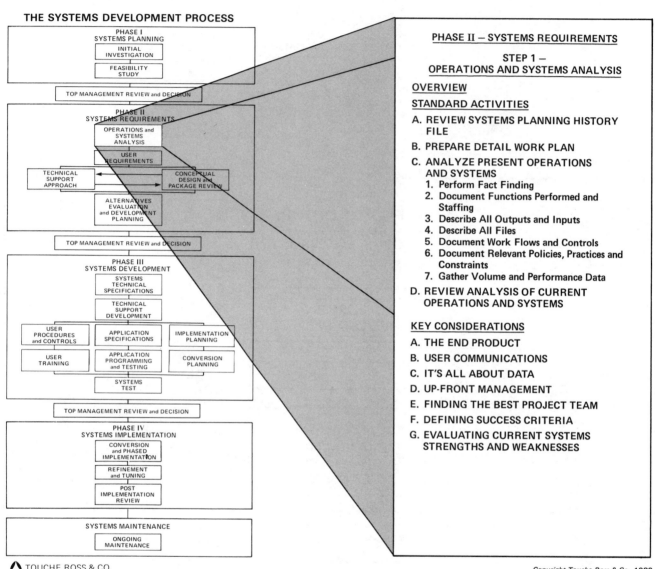

THE SYSTEMS DEVELOPMENT PROCESS

PHASE I
SYSTEMS PLANNING
- INITIAL INVESTIGATION
- FEASIBILITY STUDY

TOP MANAGEMENT REVIEW and DECISION

PHASE II
SYSTEMS REQUIREMENTS
- OPERATIONS and SYSTEMS ANALYSIS
- USER REQUIREMENTS
- TECHNICAL SUPPORT APPROACH
- CONCEPTUAL DESIGN and PACKAGE REVIEW
- ALTERNATIVES EVALUATION and DEVELOPMENT PLANNING

TOP MANAGEMENT REVIEW and DECISION

PHASE III
SYSTEMS DEVELOPMENT
- SYSTEMS TECHNICAL SPECIFICATIONS
- TECHNICAL SUPPORT DEVELOPMENT
- USER PROCEDURES and CONTROLS
- APPLICATION SPECIFICATIONS
- IMPLEMENTATION PLANNING
- USER TRAINING
- APPLICATION PROGRAMMING and TESTING
- CONVERSION PLANNING
- SYSTEMS TEST

TOP MANAGEMENT REVIEW and DECISION

PHASE IV
SYSTEMS IMPLEMENTATION
- CONVERSION and PHASED IMPLEMENTATION
- REFINEMENT and TUNING
- POST IMPLEMENTATION REVIEW

SYSTEMS MAINTENANCE
- ONGOING MAINTENANCE

PHASE II – SYSTEMS REQUIREMENTS

STEP 1 – OPERATIONS AND SYSTEMS ANALYSIS

OVERVIEW

STANDARD ACTIVITIES

A. REVIEW SYSTEMS PLANNING HISTORY FILE

B. PREPARE DETAIL WORK PLAN

C. ANALYZE PRESENT OPERATIONS AND SYSTEMS
1. Perform Fact Finding
2. Document Functions Performed and Staffing
3. Describe All Outputs and Inputs
4. Describe All Files
5. Document Work Flows and Controls
6. Document Relevant Policies, Practices and Constraints
7. Gather Volume and Performance Data

D. REVIEW ANALYSIS OF CURRENT OPERATIONS AND SYSTEMS

KEY CONSIDERATIONS

A. THE END PRODUCT

B. USER COMMUNICATIONS

C. IT'S ALL ABOUT DATA

D. UP-FRONT MANAGEMENT

E. FINDING THE BEST PROJECT TEAM

F. DEFINING SUCCESS CRITERIA

G. EVALUATING CURRENT SYSTEMS STRENGTHS AND WEAKNESSES

TOUCHE ROSS & CO.

There are five steps in Phase II — Systems Requirements — the first of which is analysis of current operations and systems. Phase I (Systems Planning) activities determined that the proposed system is technically and economically viable for development and implementation. Steps 2 through 5 are, respectively: User Requirements, Technical Support Approach, Conceptual Design and Package Review, and Alternatives Evaluation and Development Planning.

Current operations and systems to be analyzed during this step were identified during Phase I. The primary difference between this step and the previous review is the degree of analysis, understanding, and documentation required. For the feasibility study, the current systems review is only sufficient to conceptualize the new system and to adequately assess the costs and benefits associated with subsequent activities. However, once a decision has been made to continue with a new systems project, then a more thorough review of present systems is required.

Documentation resulting from this step should reflect the project team's detailed understanding of the current systems' operations, complexities, problems, and interrelationship with other systems. The documentation must be complete and organized if it is to be of any use in future requirements, development, and implementation activities. Thus, the Operations and Systems Analysis step must be carefully planned and conducted. Because only an understanding of the business requirements and systems considerations of subsequent steps within the systems project, is needed, not too much analysis should be conducted.

Although some changes in the amount of participation may occur to reflect the need for different skills in various activities, project team members involved in this step usually participate in subsequent steps of this phase. The team comprises both user and systems personnel, and preferably includes a core group of Phase I personnel, supplemented by enough additional members to complete the required tasks. An essential ingredient of project success is adequately estimating project resource requirements and obtaining a commitment of individual time that assures effective participation by every team member.

The Operations and Systems Analysis step generally includes four major activities. The first two — team orientation and detailed work plan development — are preparatory.

The third activity involves the actual analysis tasks and requires the most time and effort. The step concludes with a formal review and approval activity. The total time required to perform this step varies from several weeks to several months but is generally less than that required to perform the feasibility study. Time variations are the result of operating complexities and function variety in the current operations, and the degree of interrelationship with other systems.

STANDARD ACTIVITIES

Review Systems Planning
History File

As did the feasibility study — and as will subsequent steps — operations and systems analysis begins with an activity designed specifically to allow project team members to orient themselves and review the work to date. This is a brief activity consisting primarily of a paper review of findings and documentation. If changes have occurred since the conclusion of systems planning, an assessment of their probable impact on the structure and timetable for this step is required. The conclusions should then be reflected in subsequent activity.

Prepare Detailed Work Plan

The project plan for this step was prepared during the feasibility study. However, actual project team personnel assignments and the impact of changes identified in the above review result in a new work plan and project timetable. The steering committee may need to provide a new authorization in order to continue a project that becomes marginally cost effective or less attractive because of the changes uncovered by the first two activities in this step. Less serious changes may require no more than the revision or addition of some tasks in the work plan.

Analyze Present Operations and Systems

One of the keys to successful systems change is a thorough understanding of the way the current system works. The starting point for this process is that portion of the systems planning documentation describing the current system. Several tasks are required to complete this activity as described in the following paragraphs. In practice, these tasks are conducted simultaneously through a repetitive process — as reflected by the detailed work plan.

Perform Fact-Finding. The project team begins its information gathering tasks by starting where it left off in the previous step — with first-line supervisors — and working down through the organization. The process of gathering facts from these people increases the team's understanding of current functions and verifies previous findings. As new information is obtained, any previous documentation should be updated accordingly.

As part of the fact-finding effort, great care should be taken to thoroughly understand exception processing, emphasizing methods used to detect and correct errors. The resulting documentation should extend beyond simply noting clerical procedures and must focus on the impact of incomplete or untimely reporting of data to decision-makers. Whenever exception procedures are not properly considered and included in new systems, significant problems develop during implementation.

In addition to interviews, fact-finding should also include background research. Relevant documents may include management advisory letters from the external auditor, internal audit or consulting reports, and operational analyses and recommendations by outside consultants. The auditors' files may contain flowcharts and control requirements documentation and may identify information needs of external parties who might not normally be interviewed.

Document Functions Performed and Staffing. The additional interviews allow the project team to further detail current functions and their staffing requirements. Staff time required to perform all functions that may be impacted by a new system should be identified through interviews, current productivity or time reports, special data collection logs, or other appropriate methods. This functional analysis and documentation should be supplemented by a copy of relevant existing written procedures and system flowcharts. These items — if they exist — must reflect current operations. Furthermore, they should be updated as necessary.

Describe All Outputs and Inputs. In the feasibility study, only major outputs and inputs were collected. In this step, all outputs and inputs associated with the current system are described. These new items primarily consist of internal or infrequently used documents and reports, since the previous step has identified all the outputs and inputs that are high-volume and key to the current operations. The additional documentation should include samples of actual reports and input forms, complete with logical data, not just a series of alphabetic characters intended to represent logical data.

Describe All Files. This file description task is similar to the above output and input description tasks. The project team identifies all files used in the current system including card index files, file folders, and computer files. A test for the completeness of this task may consist of assuring that the disposition of all copies of inputs and reports is documented and of reviewing the contents of all physical file cabinets in the user areas.

Data in manual files that may be subsequently converted should also be reviewed for quality. If necessary, cleanup activities may be initiated at this point to allow maximum time prior to conversion needs. It is frequently inappropriate to wait until the Conversion Planning step in Systems Development (Phase III, Step 8) to determine data purification requirements, since the time required for cleanup may be extensive.

Document Workflows and Controls. This step is intended to visually depict the interrelationship of functions performed, outputs, inputs, and files used. Once the workflows and the associated documentation are consistent, the project team may be reasonably assured that the current system documentation is complete. This workflow documentation should include a description of all controls used to balance data, identify and correct errors, and test for reasonableness of results.

Document Relevant Policies, Practices, and Constraints. Up to this point, team efforts have concentrated upon gathering and analyzing factual data about what currently takes place. The emphasis during this next task centers more on the reasons, policies, and practices behind the system. Types of information gathered at this point include:

— Business rules. For example, in developing a customer order processing system, the analysis of the present system is expanded to include volume discount practices, pricing policies, and credit decision criteria.
— Data retention. Documentation is gathered on retention cycles and on company procedures for retaining input and output documents.
— Timing constraints related to the receipt of input data and the required availability of reports.
— Regulatory policies and reporting requirements.
— Security, privacy, and control considerations.

Wherever possible, this information should be referenced to the functions, inputs, and outputs of the present system.

Gather Volume and Performance Data. Throughout the previously described analysis tasks, the project team should continually strive to gather all relevant volumes and performance data to use in determining the technical requirements for the new system. For example:

— In addition to identifying the total number of input documents received, it may also be necessary to determine volumes by source and by time of day for use in evaluating source data entry alternatives in subsequent steps.

— In addition to identifying the total number of records in a file, it may also be necessary to determine the frequencies of record addition, change, and removal, and the frequencies and reasons for use as reference or inquiry. This data may be used in developing magnetic storage volume and access requirements.

— The documented workflows should identify points in the information flows where data is physically transferred between departments or between systems. These points should be analyzed to determine the time-related volumes of data transferred. The results should be useful in preparing technical requirements for data transmission and network communications in subsequent steps.

— In systems that provide specific services or produce definitive results, the level of performance currently achieved should be determined. Examples may include:

· How often are order acknowledgments either sent incorrectly or not at all?

· How much time is required to schedule an order after receipt? How often is an order never scheduled?

· How much expediting or exception handling is required because products are not produced when promised?

· How many customer complaints require adjustments to correct misposted payments? How long does this take?

Many new systems do not directly automate present functions, but instead use new techniques to accomplish essential services. Additional volume and data collection activities may thus occur during the systems requirements and design steps. However, the gathering and analysis of current performance data is necessary to provide a basis for identifying and quantifying alternatives for the new system.

Review Analysis of Current Operations and Systems

The project team has now reached a key point in its work. After this step is concluded, there will be no further complete review of the current system. All efforts will be directed toward the new system. Therefore, it is important to validate information and understanding about current procedures and operations. Despite the halt to detailed reviews of the current system, the team leader must stay informed of developments that could impact the new system, because further changes may be made to the current operation during the time elapsed prior to implementation.

The validation of the current system that is concluded during this activity should include:

— Confirmation of the understanding of the current system on the part of both the project team and user management.

— Establishment of mechanisms that alert the project team of any changes taking place in the current operation that will impact the design and implementation of the new system.

Persons who have been interviewed are asked to validate the accuracy of the data gathered, starting with key clerical personnel and then moving through first-line supervisors, operating managers and, finally, top-level managers. At each level, individuals who approve the content of documentation are asked to indicate their approval by signing-off on the appropriate forms. At the conclusion of this activity, user management provides a final sign-off before steps related to the new system are undertaken.

Great care should be taken during the sign-off process to make sure that those indicating their approval truly understand the implications of their approval. It may be easy to get sign-offs without associated understanding. Thus, frequent checkpoints should be set up to ensure that all involved understand what they are approving. A misunderstanding at any level of project development impacts all the work that follows and could severely delay implementation.

KEY CONSIDERATIONS

The End Product The end product of the Operations and Systems Analysis step should be a comprehensive document: an internally consistent description of all current user-based operations. In subsequent steps of Systems Requirements, Development, and Implementation, it is often necessary to refer to this documentation in order to assess alternative approaches and determine tasks to be performed. If the end product cannot provide this reference capability, then the step may not have been a cost-effective investment in the systems development process. In particular, the end product provides a base of information used to prepare requirements and designs of new systems, including considerations of:

— Operational use of existing policies; detailed calculations performed; rules of operation; time frame definitions; etc.
— Exception item handling processes.
— Mandatory report descriptions.
— Internal control procedures.
— Volumes of data retention and activity.
— Developing plans for conversions based on existing file types, sizes, controls, and degree of completeness and accuracy.
— Developing new staff organizations, functions, and personnel requirements.
— Preparing new user procedures and controls.
— Updating cost and benefit analyses.

User Communications End product documentation is not generally an effective vehicle for communication with key users. It is a lengthy, comprehensive, and somewhat intimidating document. It is more appropriately used as a reference document than as a communication device. Formal and informal presentations to the user that rely heavily on visual aids and the ability to respond to questions are much more effective as a general communication tool. Presentations of this nature can stimulate the interest and understanding necessary to make effective use of the document.

Is It All About Data? Identification of current data usages and descriptions of data attributes are critical end products of the activities of this step, since data content is the heart of any system, whether it is manual or computerized. The decision-making mechanisms of most organizations depend upon data content. A thorough understanding of data is particularly critical whenever new systems requirements are developed in a data-base environment. An incomplete understanding of groupings (forms, reports) and interrelationships between data elements (workflows) could lead to extensive rework at later points in the project.

Up-front Management

The Operations and Systems Analysis step requires a significant amount of effort to generate an effective end product that is neither too general nor too detailed to be useful in subsequent project steps. Therefore, it is essential that lead persons assigned to the Project Team during this step include the best, most experienced individuals available from both the user and the EDP organizations. In the long run, this produces the greatest return on an organization's investment of management and senior staff time in the project.

Finding the Best Project Team

Project team participation by users is critical in this step for supplying detailed information and assisting in the analyses and documentation of all pertinent components of the current systems. User personnel must be highly qualified and thoroughly familiar with present operations. They should be selected from the line organizations and may include a cross section of managerial, supervisory, and lead clerical personnel appropriately matched to the tasks to be performed.

Analyst involvement in this step may include personnel with a mixture of talents and experience. Lead analysts should be highly experienced to assure that all appropriate information needed in the next steps is gathered and analyzed. Less experienced analysts may be used to assist in much of the basic data collection and documentation.

The project leader may be selected from either the user or systems organization and is preferably the same person used in the Systems Planning phase. If it is necessary to change project leaders, the same criteria described in the Feasibility Study step should be applied. A potential candidate could be another key member of the feasibility study project team.

Defining Success Criteria

It is too easy to think of the end results of a system entirely in terms of the reports that are generated. When this is done, evaluations of success stop short of ascertaining that the outputs or results of the system are actually used to control and improve business operations. It is therefore important that the current end products for any present system be stated in business management terms and that, during this step, reviews include evaluations of whether the present system meets the business objectives established for the user organizations.

Evaluating Current Systems Strengths and Weaknesses

Evaluations of the strengths and weaknesses of existing systems are often skipped entirely or performed at a very cursory level. In other situations, the project team focuses entirely on weaknesses, overlooking strengths. Evaluations of strengths and weaknesses frequently encounter yet another trap: the work is performed at a technical level and deals with technical content only. In most situations, technical strengths and weaknesses will be readily apparent from the compiling of documentation and analysis of existing operations. By contrast, strengths and weaknesses in nontechnical areas should be derived from user interviews. Beyond focusing entirely on identification of functions, inputs, outputs, and workflows, these interviews should extend to cover problems and successes of current systems. Unless this probing is done, the new system may incorporate the same weaknesses (from a user standpoint) that existed in the current system.

STANDARD ACTIVITIES/END ITEMS

TOUCHE ROSS

ORGANIZATION _____ PHASE II,
STEP 1
SYSTEM _____ REQUIREMENTS
USER REP _____

ID/TITLE OPERATIONS AND SYSTEMS ANALYSIS

☐ PHASE   ☒ ACTIVITY   ☐ SUBTASK
☐ STEP   ☒ TASK   ☐

PREPARED BY	MVJ	SH
REVIEWED BY	CB	CB
DATE	3/29/80	11/1/80
PHASE	II-1	II-1

NUMBER	PHASE/STEP/ACTIVITY/TASK/SUBTASK NAME	END ITEM	FORM NO.	PERFORMED BY	DUE DATE	APPROVED BY	DATE
A.	Review Systems Planning History File	Updated Project Plan	102				
B.	Prepare Detailed Work Plan	Work Outline	101				
C.	Analyze Present Operations and Systems						
C.1	- Perform Fact Finding	Interview Schedule	120				
		Interview Summaries	121				
		Glossary of Terms	122				
C.2	- Document Functions Performed and Staffing	Summary of Functions	125				
		Staffing Requirements	126				
		Written Procedures					
C.3	- Describe All Outputs and Inputs	Glossary of Terms	122				
		Data Element Description	134				
		Input/Output Identification	131				
		Document Definition	132				
C.4	- Describe All Files	File Description and Inquiry	133				
		Data Element Description	134				
C.5	- Document Work Flows and Controls	Work Flow Diagrams	127, 128				
		Summary of Controls	141				

STANDARD ACTIVITIES/END ITEMS

TOUCHE ROSS

ORGANIZATION ___PHASE II,___
___STEP 1___
SYSTEM ___REQUIREMENTS___
USER REP ___

ID/TITLE ___OPERATIONS AND SYSTEMS ANALYSIS___

☐ PHASE   ☒ ACTIVITY   ☐ SUBTASK
☐ STEP   ☒ TASK   ☐

		PREPARED BY	MVJ	SH
		REVIEWED BY	CB	CB
		DATE	3/29/80	11/1/80
		PHASE	II-1	II-1

NUMBER	PHASE/STEP/ACTIVITY/TASK/SUBTASK NAME	END ITEM	FORM NO.	PERFORMED BY	DUE DATE	APPROVED BY	DATE
C.6	- Document Relevant Policies, Practices and Constraints	Assumptions and Constraints	140				
C.7	- Gather Volume and Performance Data	Volume Statistics	131, 132 133, 142				
D.	Review Analysis of Current Operations and Systems						

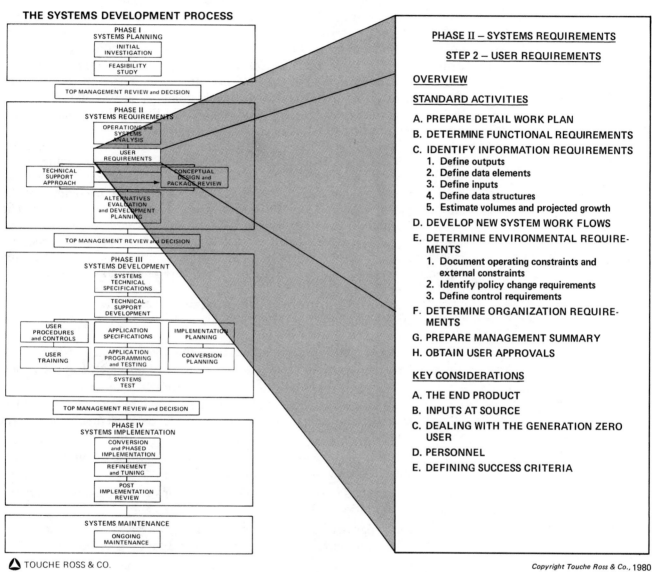

THE SYSTEMS DEVELOPMENT PROCESS

PHASE I
SYSTEMS PLANNING

INITIAL
INVESTIGATION

FEASIBILITY
STUDY

TOP MANAGEMENT REVIEW and DECISION

PHASE II
SYSTEMS REQUIREMENTS

OPERATIONS and
SYSTEMS
ANALYSIS

USER
REQUIREMENTS

TECHNICAL
SUPPORT
APPROACH

CONCEPTUAL
DESIGN and
PACKAGE REVIEW

ALTERNATIVES
EVALUATION
and DEVELOPMENT
PLANNING

TOP MANAGEMENT REVIEW and DECISION

PHASE III
SYSTEMS DEVELOPMENT

SYSTEMS
TECHNICAL
SPECIFICATIONS

TECHNICAL
SUPPORT
DEVELOPMENT

USER
PROCEDURES
and CONTROLS

APPLICATION
SPECIFICATIONS

IMPLEMENTATION
PLANNING

USER
TRAINING

APPLICATION
PROGRAMMING
and TESTING

CONVERSION
PLANNING

SYSTEMS
TEST

TOP MANAGEMENT REVIEW and DECISION

PHASE IV
SYSTEMS IMPLEMENTATION

CONVERSION
and PHASED
IMPLEMENTATION

REFINEMENT
and TUNING

POST
IMPLEMENTATION
REVIEW

SYSTEMS MAINTENANCE

ONGOING
MAINTENANCE

TOUCHE ROSS & CO.

PHASE II – SYSTEMS REQUIREMENTS

STEP 2 – USER REQUIREMENTS

OVERVIEW

STANDARD ACTIVITIES

A. PREPARE DETAIL WORK PLAN

B. DETERMINE FUNCTIONAL REQUIREMENTS

C. IDENTIFY INFORMATION REQUIREMENTS
1. Define outputs
2. Define data elements
3. Define inputs
4. Define data structures
5. Estimate volumes and projected growth

D. DEVELOP NEW SYSTEM WORK FLOWS

E. DETERMINE ENVIRONMENTAL REQUIRE-MENTS
1. Document operating constraints and external constraints
2. Identify policy change requirements
3. Define control requirements

F. DETERMINE ORGANIZATION REQUIRE-MENTS

G. PREPARE MANAGEMENT SUMMARY

H. OBTAIN USER APPROVALS

KEY CONSIDERATIONS

A. THE END PRODUCT

B. INPUTS AT SOURCE

C. DEALING WITH THE GENERATION ZERO USER

D. PERSONNEL

E. DEFINING SUCCESS CRITERIA

OVERVIEW   At this point the project team is ready to begin the definition and documentation of user requirements for the new system. The user requirements document produced during this step defines the end product of the proposed systems project in terms of its impact on the operations of the users. This documentation serves as the basis for the two steps — Technical Support Approach and Conceptual Design and Package Review — that follow. A thorough definition of what the system is to do, expressed in terms of the objectives of its users, is produced at this point to ensure that alternative technical approaches are evaluated on the basis of their utility in meeting the target established by the user requirements document.

The results of the previous Operations and Systems Analysis step form the basis of the User Requirements step. It is critical that the requirements for the new system reflect the essential functions and strengths of the existing system (mechanized or manual) and resolve the shortcomings of the current system which (at least in part) initiated the new systems project. The Phase I feasibility study report provides the most complete description of the new system prepared to date, including both preliminary user requirements and cost/benefit objectives. In addition, the project cost and timing objectives expressed in the feasibility study serve to establish the scope of the User Requirements activities.

The user requirements manual specifies what the new system is to do for its user organizations, including:

— Functions that are to be part of the new system are identified, described in terms of their operation and impact on the users, and related to the functions of the current system.
— Information to be maintained and reported by the new system is described in terms of outputs, inputs, data elements, and data structures.
— The workflow associated with the new system is documented by a flow diagram with supporting narrative descriptions.
— Internal and external assumptions and constraints on the new system are identified and documented.
— The impact of the new system on its target organizations is described in terms of new, revised, and eliminated functions or positions.

The project team for this step should remain essentially unchanged from that used to carry out the previous step. However, it is important to remember that this step requires substantial creative input as to how the organization is to function with the new system. The end result may have a significant long-term impact on the operation of the organization. Therefore, at the very least, the overall blend of experience levels in the project team should be retained for this step. An increase in average experience level, particularly as pertains to systems analysts, is often a desirable modification.

The total time required to complete this step varies from several weeks to several months, but is generally about the same as that required for the previous step. The actual duration of this step is a function of the size and makeup of the project team, the scope and complexity of the new system, the number of functions to be analyzed, and the managerial characteristics of the user organizations.

STANDARD ACTIVITIES

Prepare Detailed Work Plan

This activity starts with a review of the work completed to date, including the project plan for user requirements prepared as part of the feasibility study. The findings and documentation from these previous steps form the basis for initiating the User Requirements step. The project team also identifies and assesses the impact of any business policy or operating changes affecting the work conducted to date. The steering committee is consulted if it becomes apparent that major changes will affect the fundamental premises on which this phase of the project was approved. Marginally productive projects may lose their attractiveness as a result of changes uncovered during the Operations and Systems Analysis step. If this happens, termination of the project should be recommended.

The user requirements project plan prepared during the feasibility study is now expanded into a detailed work plan. This plan provides sufficient detail to direct, control, and coordinate project team activities and tasks throughout this step. Substantial creativity is required to identify and describe the specific tasks to be performed in developing user requirements. It is extremely important that this definition of tasks be carefully done. Even the best of project teams cannot produce an effective end product if important tasks are left out. Important considerations in developing a work plan with specific tasks and responsibilities include:

— Organization of the new system into logical subsystems or components, so that each may be described independently — but with a clear indication of interrelationships.
— Identification of key personnel and information sources needed to complete the standard activities.
— Assignment of staff and time to specific tasks in a manner that reflects the relative importance of every task to the overall end product.
— Identification of end-item documentation to be generated from each activity and task, and its relationship to the overall end-product organization and table of contents.

The user requirements work plan should be end-product-oriented. An end product should be specified for most of the tasks listed on the work plan. Generally, this end product will take the form of documentation suitable for inclusion in the user requirements manual. For each task, the completed work plan specifies a start date, a completion date, end items to be produced, estimated effort required, and an individual responsible for completing the task. After review and approval of the work plan, including user and systems management, the project team proceeds to the next activity.

Determine Functional Requirements

This activity identifies and describes all significant functions to be performed within the new system. If the new system has been segmented into subsystems, the functional requirements are defined by subsystem. The definition of functions to be performed is an expansion of the system objectives and sources of potential benefit that are developed in the feasibility study. The project team defines by subsystem those functions which the new system must perform in order to achieve the objectives and realize the benefits. In addition, the project team reviews the functions performed by the current system to identify those that must continue as part of the new system. In general, the new function definitions encompass two primary categories:

— Functions required in order to perform current functions effectively, or,

— Additional functions that are required and can be included at an attractive cost, in light of the potential benefits likely to accrue from the new system.

Each completed function description clearly identifies both the manual and automated components and their interactions within the user areas. The level of detail at which functions are identified and described should be sufficient to define what the system is to do without necessarily describing how the system will technically perform the function. In general, a function description should specify what is to be done, who is to do it, and how the function interfaces with the overall system.

Identify Information Requirements

The series of tasks which comprise this activity identify the information required to support each function described in the new system or subsystems. This includes reports, other outputs, inputs, data elements, and data structures containing the elements required to support the function. The standard set of tasks associated with this activity is described below:

Define Outputs. This task identifies and describes the reports and other outputs (manual and mechanized) to be generated by the system. The task begins with the output requirements described in the feasibility study and then refines and expands the requirements based on the function definitions just completed. Only outputs directly related to user operations are defined at this point; outputs required for data processing controls are merely identified conceptually here, and are then defined more completely during the Conceptual Design and Package Review step.

Each output identified is described in terms of its purpose, frequency, and distribution. The statement of purpose relates to the system functions defined above. An output can take many forms; in general, however, it is a report, a terminal inquiry, or — in some cases — magnetic media.

In addition, the general data element content of each output is described using a General-Purpose Chart form to define each field. A generalized layout may be prepared without indicating the relative location and format of data, since in most cases, the effort to gather the requisite information and prepare report layouts is not made at this point. However, if a user manager requires a visual representation of a specific report to clarify his understanding, an example should be prepared. If this is done, it should be indicated clearly that this is only a preliminary rendering and that the format may change as the project progresses.

Define Data Elements. This task identifies and describes in general terms each of the data elements within the scope of the new system. Initially, the data elements identified are those contained on the outputs, plus additional data elements required to support automated functions of the system. As the systems project progresses into subsequent levels of detail, this list is refined and expanded as additional data elements are defined.

Each data element identified is described on a Data Element Definition form. The emphasis is on the characteristics of data elements rather than specific formats. The significant items to be described for each data element include:

— "Data Element Number," which uniquely identifies the data element throughout the system and is used to cross-reference data element usage.
— "Data Element Name," which is unique and always applied to the data element. A standard convention is often developed for data element names.
— "Picture," which defines the size and format of the data element.
— "Source," which identifies the input document containing the data element.
— "Definition," including the content and significance of the data element.
— "Edit Criteria," listing the validation rules to be applied for each data element, such as numeric field tests, coded table entries, data validation, reasonableness checks, or others.

As a control to assist in conducting subsequent steps in the project, a Data Element Cross-Reference Listing is generated. Initially, this listing cross references data elements to inputs and outputs. During Systems Development (Phase III), this cross reference is expanded to include records and programs. For large systems, this data element cross-reference capability is most practical to maintain when automated. A number of available software packages can provide this capability with good results if the data element definitions are prepared in the disciplined manner previously described.

Define Inputs.   This task identifies all inputs within the new system and the data elements contained in each input. The input list developed during the Feasibility Study is expanded to include the sources of each data element previously identified. Most inputs are generated as forms or other documents to record activities (transactions) occurring in the environment that are relevant to the system. Input is described in terms of time, space, and organizational responsibility at the point of origin of the activity being reported. Each input identified for the new system is described as follows:

— Source, including form name and responsibility for completing the form.
— Data elements included.
— Method of data collection (e.g., remote terminals, OCR, etc.).
— Manual processing, including edit procedures and distribution.
— Controls required, both manual and automated.

Define Data Structures.   This task establishes a preliminary organization of the defined data elements into logical records and the relationships between these logical records. The data is organized in a way that facilitates the processing of inputs to generate outputs and satisfy other computational requirements. Generally, this is best accomplished by defining data structures that model the way in which data naturally occurs in the environment. Thus, in a manufacturing environment, data is organized around parts and relationships between parts that are contained in products. A criminal justice data structure is organized around incidents (e.g., crimes), people, and relationships between the two.

As a part of this task, the project team organizes required data elements into logical records or schemas and develops an initial specification for these data element groups and group relationships.

A data structure chart is then prepared to illustrate the logical relationships among the records defined above. Connecting lines may be used to indicate that one record can be logically accessed from another. In addition, a key is identified for each record that may be directly accessed. (*Note:* A decision on the use of data base management software is not part of the User Requirements step.) The objective of this task is to define a logical set of records and record relationships that satisfy the user-based requirements of the new system. The next step, the Technical Support Approach, addresses the data base issues.

Estimate Volumes and Projected Growth. The purpose of this task is to provide the data required during the Technical Support Approach step for assessment of terminals required, network requirements, system processing time, and other technical items. The peak and average volume estimates include input transactions, inquiries, reports and other outputs and record volumes for permanently stored records. These volume and growth estimates are normally recorded on the input, output, and record documentation described above.

Volume increases may occur more rapidly in the first few operating cycles following pilot implementation until a steady state of the new system is reached. There are several reasons for this:

— Growth in volumes often occur as additional modules of the system are implemented.
— Growth in volumes often occur as the system is implemented for additional units of the organization.
— The system may maintain history for a fixed period of time (e.g., three years) causing record volume increases due to a buildup of historical data for the entire fixed period.

Volume estimates may also be required for conversion data. Any purification efforts required should be planned and initiated in light of these conversion volume estimates.

**Develop New
System Workflows**

At this point, the new system has been defined in terms of its functions, data structures, inputs, and outputs. The purpose of this task is to integrate these elements of the system definition into an overall description of how the new system will operate in the user environment. During this task, a workflow diagram is prepared for each subsystem or other major system component. This flow diagram illustrates how the affected organizations are to conduct their major functions once the new system is implemented. The primary focus of the flow diagrams is how the work of the organization is to be accomplished rather than how the components of the technical system interact together.

**Determine Environmental
Requirements**

This task requires the project team to consider all significant constraints imposed on the system design by factors external to the scope of the system. The end products of this task are descriptions of each of the relevant constraints and user-based requirements imposed by each constraint.

Document Operating Constraints and External Constraints. The internal system constraints include timing considerations such as reporting deadlines, operating schedules, peak periods, and constraints such as environmental quality, space and staffing limitations. The project team describes each of these constraints in terms of its source and operating implications. The additional system requirements arising because of these constraints are specifically identified.

External constraints include statutory or other imposed restrictions within which the system must operate. These constraints may be reporting requirements imposed by regulatory agencies such as the Internal Revenue Service, the Securities and Exchange Commission, and other state and federal agencies. They also include data security and privacy control requirements imposed by management policy and/or external authority. Finally, management may have some overall growth, diversification, or centralization objectives which impose constraints on the new system. In each case these constraints are identified and fully documented. Additional system requirements arising based on these constraints are described by the project team.

Identify Policy Change Requirements. Situations in which current organization policy is in conflict with the evolving user requirements are identified and fully documented. Both the nature of the policy conflict and the impact on the ability of the system to satisfy its user requirements are defined. Some policy issues require resolution prior to the start of Systems Development (Phase III), while others need not be resolved until implementation of the system in the user organization. For each of these policy issues, the project team defines both the urgency with which resolution is required and the steps to be taken to resolve the issues.

Define Control Requirements. Effective user-oriented controls are an important part of the success of any system—manual or automated. The project team identifies the key points at which controls are to be applied over the quality of input data, the processing of transactions, and the system-generated outputs. In addition to identifying these primary control points, the project team also describes the nature of the controls. While the detail design of systems controls occurs at later steps in the process, the following general types of control—preventive, detective, and corrective— are specified at this point.

- Automated edit and reasonableness controls of a preventive nature to be applied to inputs when first processed by the system.
- Manual review controls, including signatures, to be applied to both inputs and outputs; many kinds of errors can be detected by a knowledgeable person's cursory review.
- Balancing controls to be applied which require certain inputs to balance with certain outputs and control totals, or in which certain outputs must balance with each other or else require corrective action.

Determine Organizational Requirements

At this point, the functions of the new system are defined sufficiently for their impact on the user organization to be evaluated. The evaluations are primarily based on the functions to be performed by users and the work volumes involved. These factors may make it necessary to establish new job functions, to restructure certain jobs, or to terminate existing positions within user organizations. Many new systems—especially those involving extensive automated transaction processing—result in changes to staffing levels within user organizations. These changes often require modifications to the user's organization chart. Significant review and approval by top management of the affected organizations is required to assure that the changes are reasonable and appropriate. To facilitate this review and approval process the project team quantifies organizational impacts as follows:

— New organization charts are developed for any part of the organization that requires significant change.
— Estimates by job classification are developed for new jobs that are to be established and existing jobs that are to be eliminated.
— Summary level job descriptions are prepared for new or revised job classifications.

New systems frequently have greater impact on the distribution of functions or positions than in the total number of personnel in an organization. For example, the new system may call for the replacement of entry level employees with more highly qualified personnel. Although the net result may be the same number or slightly fewer total employees, skill level increases may result in higher total personnel costs. These higher costs may make the proposed system unfeasible and should be carefully analyzed for reasonableness. Both user management and the project team should carefully review these organizational impacts and assure that available personnel savings and cost reductions are identified. If not, the entire new system approach must be reevaluated and adjusted to reflect practical solutions within which the users and systems can reasonably be expected to operate.

Prepare Management Summary

This activity summarizes the User Requirements document as it has evolved through the preceding tasks. Several considerations are of prime importance in developing this summary.

— The summary must be written for management. It should be concise, well written, and oriented to management concerns.
— The summary may be the only part of the User Requirements documentation which is read by most key managers. Therefore, it should provide a complete summation of the critical points in each section.
— The summary should include a brief introduction outlining the key objectives of the system, a brief summary of development efforts to date, and a current estimate of the anticipated costs and benefits of the new system.

Obtain User Approvals

Once the User Requirements document is completed, the project team becomes involved in obtaining user agreement and approval of the results. An enthusiastic endorsement of this document by management of key user organizations is critical at this point for two reasons:

— First, since this document forms the basis for all subsequent technical and development efforts, user approval is required to assure a sound basis for directing future project efforts.
— Second, successful implementation requires commitment of the user organization to the new system. This commitment can only be developed if user management believes that it has provided significant direction to the project from its earliest steps.

In order to obtain necessary user approvals, the project team must actively work to explain the system and its benefits to key user managers.

Approvals are not to be obtained by merely allowing users to read the requirements document. Certain key steps in the explanation process are generally required.

The project team first identifies key individuals and groups whose approval and support is required if the system is to be successfully implemented. They include key operating management directly affected by the system and top management of user organizations. The process of explaining the system to those who will be responsible for it begins here. Whether the system is to be implemented in many autonomous organizations or in a single large organization, a relatively small group can usually be identified as the focus of this review and approval effort. The review and approval group should be knowledgeable across all affected user organizations and should have credibility with those not represented, but who will need to accept their decisions.

Second, the project team organizes a series of meetings with those identified above to present the user requirements document in a step-by-step manner. Formal oral presentations of the system should be made at these meetings, with sufficient time to answer questions, accept recommendations, and discuss potential modifications to the requirements. The project team must be responsive to the questions, comments, suggested changes and concerns of key user personnel. This total review process may require a significant amount of time, but is essential if the user commitment necessary for a successful implementation is to be obtained. The steering committee and top management of user organizations should be kept up to date throughout this process, as they can often be of significant assistance in generating enthusiastic user approval.

Finally, once agreement is reached on the user requirements document, a final revision should be issued bearing the approval signatures of the top management personnel in the affected user organizations.

KEY CONSIDERATIONS

The End Product The end product of the User Requirements step is a comprehensive written document, containing an internally consistent description of all user-based requirements of the system. In the subsequent steps and phases it is often easy to lose sight of the original objectives. When this occurs, the User Requirements document is referenced for the original scope of the system. Any requirement not specifically identified in the User Requirements document will not be considered a requirement of the system unless there is overwhelming evidence that the requirement is a necessity. From this point on, only new requirements must be formally reviewed and approved by user management, so that their impacts on the project and system might be fully understood.

Inputs at Source During the User Requirement step, data input functions are usually described as close to the sources of data as practical. In addition, alternative approaches to source data entry may be described, assuming the alternatives are practical from a business operations viewpoint. Differences in staffing requirements and user-oriented advantages and disadvantages are documented in this step for use in evaluating Technical Support Approaches in the next step.

Dealing with the Inexperienced User The inexperienced user—the user without previous experience in developing or managing a computerized system—should receive special attention during all phases of the project. There is frequently a tendency on the part of members of a project team to act as though all users were alike and equal. However, when a user lacks sufficient background to reach intelligent evaluations and judgments about the impact of EDP systems, special educational efforts are appropriate. It is particularly important during project reviews to ensure that the user has sufficient preparation to allow effective participation with the project team.

Further, continuing education of inexperienced users is necessary for the steps that follow completion of the User Requirements stage. As succeeding steps become increasingly technical, users may feel left out until preparation for implementation begins. The project team should find ways to stimulate and maintain user interest throughout systems development. One way to do this is through user involvement in the systems development steps such as User Procedures and Controls, User Training, Implementation Planning, and Conversion Planning. One approach to user training to develop mechanisms for simulating the basic inputs, functions, and outputs of the new system. This often helps the user gain a better understanding of how the system will work in operational terms. This serves to maintain user interest, to precondition the user organization to the activities that will follow, and also to provide a basis for rechecking earlier decisions about systems functions.

In summary, it is important to identify inexperienced users, to make allowances for their lack of understanding, and — if necessary — to make special preparations for their education.

Personnel

The success of any new system depends heavily on the attitudes and skills of user personnel. Therefore, in considering approaches during the User Requirements step, it is necessary to think about how well user personnel will be able to work with the new system. The ability of user personnel to understand and adapt to change must also be considered. In effect, the project team must assess the extent of change a user organization can absorb over a given period of time and must plan the systems implementation accordingly.

Considerations such as these may not always impact the design of the new system or the way it functions. However, there may be cases in which projects are extended in order to allow for additional user training or for an additional period for implementation of a new system. Under the most extreme circumstances, it may actually prove undesirable to continue a project because it calls for skills and ability that are beyond those of user personnel. The alternatives — should such a situation develop — may well hinge on the availability of new personnel. Otherwise, the project may be significantly delayed or scrapped entirely.

In addition, project staffing changes can alter project timetables. Earlier, it was pointed out that staffing commitments must be established and adhered to if schedules are to be met. If there is a change in this commitment, the project may face serious delays and the steering committee may want to review its previous approval.

Defining Success Criteria

It is all too easy to think of the end results of a system development project entirely in terms of the reports generated. When this is done, evaluations of the system's success stop short of ascertaining that the outputs or results of the system are actually used to control and improve business operations. Therefore, it is important that the end products for any individual project be stated in business management terms and that reviews include continuous evaluation of whether the proposed system will meet the business objectives established for the user organizations.

For example, a material requirements planning information system may be designed to meet an objective of reducing overall company investments in inventory. The system itself could succeed admirably in providing information about inventory control. However, if user managers do not use this information to reduce inventory levels, the system has not achieved its primary objective. It is therefore important that the key business objective of any project be stated clearly and reviewed periodically by all members of the project team and user management.

TOUCHE ROSS

STANDARD ACTIVITIES/END ITEMS

ORGANIZATION __PHASE II,__
__STEP 2__

SYSTEM __REQUIREMENTS__
USER REP _____

ID/TITLE ____USER REQUIREMENTS____

- [ ] PHASE
- [ ] STEP
- [x] ACTIVITY
- [x] TASK
- [ ] SUBTASK
- [ ] _____

	PAGE __1__ OF __2__
PROJECT NO.	
PREPARED BY	__MVJ__
REVIEWED BY	__CB__
DATE	__3/29/80__
PHASE	__II-2__
	__SH__
	__CB__
	__11/1/80__
	__II-2__

NUMBER	PHASE/STEP/ACTIVITY/TASK/SUBTASK NAME	END ITEM	FORM NO.	PERFORMED BY	DUE DATE	APPROVED BY	DATE
A.	Prepare Detailed Work Plan	Work Outline	101				
		Project Plan	102				
B.	Determine Functional Requirements	Functions Definition	142				
C.	Identify Information Requirements						
C.1	- Define Outputs	VDT Screen Layout	161				
		Computer Output/Reports	163				
C.2	- Define Data Elements	Data Element Definitions	134, 150				
		Glossary of Terms	122				
		Data Element Cross Reference	151				
C.3	- Define Inputs	Document Definition	132				
C.4	- Define Data Structures	Data Base File Layout	154				
		Data File/File Contents and Characteristics	152				
C.5	- Estimate Volumes and Projected Growth	Volume Growth Table	177				
D.	Develop New System Work Flows	Work Flow Diagrams	127, 128				
		Summary of Controls	141				
		Code Tables	178				

© Touche Ross & Co., 1980
All Rights Reserved

102

STANDARD ACTIVITIES/END ITEMS

TOUCHE ROSS

ORGANIZATION: PHASE II,
STEP 2
SYSTEM: REQUIREMENTS
USER REP

ID/TITLE: USER REQUIREMENTS

☐ PHASE   ☒ ACTIVITY   ☐ SUBTASK _____
☐ STEP   ☒ TASK   ☐ _____

PREPARED BY	MVJ	SH
REVIEWED BY	CB	CB
DATE	3/29/80	11/1/80
PHASE	II-2	II-2

NUMBER	PHASE/STEP/ACTIVITY/TASK/SUBTASK NAME	END ITEM	FORM NO.	PERFORMED BY	DUE DATE	APPROVED BY	DATE
E.	Determine Environmental Requirements						
E.1	– Document Operating Constraints and External Constraints	Assumptions and Constraints	140				
E.2	– Identify Policy Change Requirements	Policy Definitions	142				
E.3	– Define Control Requirements	Summary of Controls	141				
F.	Determine Organizational Requirements	Staffing Requirements	126				
		Organization Chart	142				
		Summary of Functions	125				
G.	Prepare Management Summary	Management Summary	149				
		Economic Evaluation Summary	148				
H.	Obtain User Approvals						

103

THE SYSTEMS DEVELOPMENT PROCESS

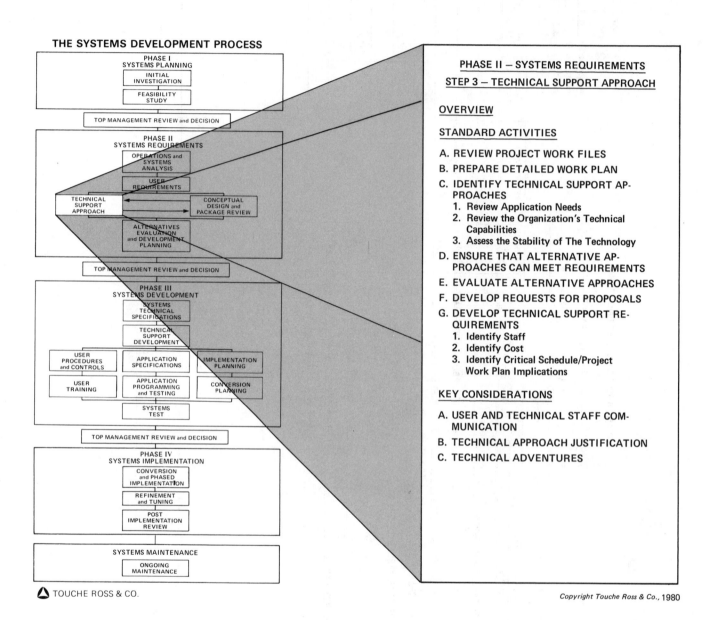

PHASE I
SYSTEMS PLANNING

INITIAL
INVESTIGATION

FEASIBILITY
STUDY

TOP MANAGEMENT REVIEW and DECISION

PHASE II
SYSTEMS REQUIREMENTS

OPERATIONS and
SYSTEMS
ANALYSIS

USER
REQUIREMENTS

TECHNICAL
SUPPORT
APPROACH

CONCEPTUAL
DESIGN and
PACKAGE REVIEW

ALTERNATIVES
EVALUATION
and DEVELOPMENT
PLANNING

TOP MANAGEMENT REVIEW and DECISION

PHASE III
SYSTEMS DEVELOPMENT

SYSTEMS
TECHNICAL
SPECIFICATIONS

TECHNICAL
SUPPORT
DEVELOPMENT

USER
PROCEDURES
and CONTROLS

APPLICATION
SPECIFICATIONS

IMPLEMENTATION
PLANNING

USER
TRAINING

APPLICATION
PROGRAMMING
and TESTING

CONVERSION
PLANNING

SYSTEMS
TEST

TOP MANAGEMENT REVIEW and DECISION

PHASE IV
SYSTEMS IMPLEMENTATION

CONVERSION
and PHASED
IMPLEMENTATION

REFINEMENT
and TUNING

POST
IMPLEMENTATION
REVIEW

SYSTEMS MAINTENANCE

ONGOING
MAINTENANCE

PHASE II – SYSTEMS REQUIREMENTS
STEP 3 – TECHNICAL SUPPORT APPROACH

OVERVIEW

STANDARD ACTIVITIES

A. REVIEW PROJECT WORK FILES

B. PREPARE DETAILED WORK PLAN

C. IDENTIFY TECHNICAL SUPPORT AP-
PROACHES
1. Review Application Needs
2. Review the Organization's Technical
Capabilities
3. Assess the Stability of The Technology

D. ENSURE THAT ALTERNATIVE AP-
PROACHES CAN MEET REQUIREMENTS

E. EVALUATE ALTERNATIVE APPROACHES

F. DEVELOP REQUESTS FOR PROPOSALS

G. DEVELOP TECHNICAL SUPPORT RE-
QUIREMENTS
1. Identify Staff
2. Identify Cost
3. Identify Critical Schedule/Project
Work Plan Implications

KEY CONSIDERATIONS

A. USER AND TECHNICAL STAFF COM-
MUNICATION

B. TECHNICAL APPROACH JUSTIFICATION

C. TECHNICAL ADVENTURES

TOUCHE ROSS & CO.

The Technical Support Approach is the third of five steps in Phase II and is usually performed simultaneously with Conceptual Design and Package Review (Step 4). The purpose of this step is to determine the technical environment in which the system must operate. Consequently, emphasis is on hardware and nonapplication systems software (e.g., operating system, data base management system, communications control programs).

The nature of the activities in this step generally requires the participation of personnel with particular specialties or areas of expertise. Since they may not be oriented toward application system development, close coordination of their activities with the conceptual design team is critical. In fact, depending on the size of the effort, it would not be unusual to have both efforts under the direction of a single project leader.

In most cases, technical questions to be addressed in this step will focus on a single issue, such as the selection of hardware or the evaluation of specific software packages (since most new systems must "fit" into an existing environment). In many cases this step will be relatively minor and its major contribution will be to assure that the development team adequately considers the technical environment. In other cases, this step may include the definition of an entire operating environment, and it could therefore be especially critical to the total systems development effort. It will also have a major effect on total project schedules and costs.

Any hardware and software requirements and configuration defined in this step should be specified to a level of detail that would provide the basis for Requests for Proposals (RFPs) from potential vendors. Although vendor proposals may be accepted and evaluated in this step, decisions may not be finalized until the conclusion of the Requirements phase.

Documentation of alternative approaches should reflect on the evaluation or estimate of:

— Technical support staff necessary to implement and maintain the system or software being evaluated.

— Benefits (tangible and intangible) associated with the approach.

— Costs of implementing and operating the hardware or software under consideration. For example, if a complex data base structure will add operating overhead, it should be identified and estimated in terms of:

· Processing efficiencies/inefficiencies.

· Mass storage requirements.

· Main memory requirements.

· Other specific limitations or restrictions.

— Staff education requirements.

— Schedule and project work plan implications.

The end products of this step are then merged with the Conceptual Design and Package Review end products in the final step of the Requirements phase, where all alternatives are evaluated and final implementation plans are developed.

STANDARD ACTIVITIES

Review Project Work Files This step most often introduces technical personnel to the project effort who have not been associated with the project at any level of depth until this time. This activity includes the effort that familiarizes them with the proposed solution (Feasibility Study) and the detailed requirements (User Requirements). This activity also provides a common ground on which project team members can communicate with the members on the conceptual design and package review team.

Prepare Detailed Work Plan The project team must expand the work plans developed in the feasibility study to the detail necessary for an adequate understanding of the technical approaches available. This knowledge will be used extensively in the following steps and will form the basis for key decisions in the Systems Development phase. With this in mind, emphasis is placed on known technical problem areas or on the areas that are new to the project team or the organization.

This project plan must be coordinated with Step 4 to assure that the technical approaches do not drive the conceptual design process. Rather, a parallel activity with constant interaction should take place with User Requirements providing the driving force. Care should be taken to avoid technical adventures.

To the extent possible, personnel with specific experience on the equipment or software being considered should be assigned to the project team. The need for this type of expertise in the remainder of the effort should also be considered, and personnel who will participate in the on-going project should be identified and added to the project if possible.

Identify Technical Support Approaches The project team usually begins with the technical approaches identified in the Feasibility Study, User Requirements, and Conceptual Design and Package Review steps. Alternative approaches should not be ignored, however, but should be reviewed if they seem applicable. Alternative considerations may include a review of such things as:

- Data base management systems.
- Data base structures.
- Communication facilities.
- Operating systems.
- Hardware.
  - Processing.
  - Input.
  - Output.
- Real time/on-line/batch processing.
- Source data entry.
- Centralized/distributed processing.
- Programming languages.
- "Turnkey" packages combining hardware and applications software.

Tasks to accomplish this activity are to:

- Review the needs of the application.

106

— Review the organization's technical capabilities.

— Assess the stability of the technology.

Review Application Needs.   The key documents to review at this time are the feasibility study and the user requirements manuals. As the application needs are reviewed, the list of alternative approaches is expanded and the options are identified. This activity is carried out together with the conceptual design and package review team. Among the factors reviewed at this time are economics, available equipment resources, and the organization's overall systems plans and business directions. The relationship of the effort under development to the overall plans of the systems organization is a major consideration in this step of the effort. In addition, for some projects it may be appropriate to research the "state-of-the-art" and determine if other organizations have technically addressed the same business problems. This research could provide added insight into how technical issues were resolved and what lessons were learned.

It is highly desirable that specialists in the specific technical areas being evaluated be assigned to this effort. In addition, someone with similar technical experience should review completed work, findings, and any tentative decisions made at this point.

Review the Organization's Technical Capabilities.   The success or failure of any systems development project depends on the people and organization. For a major project requiring complex technical approaches, this is even more of a consideration. Before any technical solution is adopted, the organization to design, develop, implement, and maintain the system must be defined, approved, and in place.

Items to be reviewed include the availability of technical skills, the potential or expected impact of attrition and any special training or education necessary to deal with a specific technical approach. It is important to be realistic about both the quality and quantity of available skills, particularly in dealing with new technology.

Assess the Stability of the Technology.   If a project is to be a "leading edge" application in terms of the technical tools to be employed, the implementation plans must be structured to carefully deal with the potential impacts of:

— Hardware failure.

— Software failure.

— Lack of vendor support.

— Contingency requirements.

— Communication facility failures.

— The "learning curve" required of the in-house technical support staff.

As a general rule, it is unwise to pioneer new technology in an operationally critical system. Particular attention should be given to plans for backup in the event of system failure and to the objectives that lead to the selection of the technology to be employed.

Ensure that Alternative
Approaches Can
Meet Requirements

After the alternatives for technical support have been identified, it is necessary to maintain close liaison with the conceptual design and package review team. Technical considerations may have an impact on the design and/or package selection. This is especially true in "turnkey" approaches combining hardware and applications software. Specific attention should be given to the impact of the selected alternatives on:

- *Inquiry Requirements.* What is acceptable response time? Can these requirements be satisfied?
- *Data Structures.* Will the software support the required data structures? Can the hardware accommodate the required volumes?
- *Data Base Logic.* Can the data base deal efficiently with the required methods of accessing and processing the data?
- *Communication Networks.* What types of communications facilities are required to service necessary locations and provide adequate response time? What are the human engineering considerations?
- *Contingency Plans.* What are backup arrangements and their implications?

Evaluate Alternative Approaches

With alternative support approaches identified and special considerations reviewed, the project team is able to evaluate the approaches. Each has its own set of consequences in terms of operating costs, development costs, speed and level of service, and maintainability.

For example, alternative approaches for an order entry system could include:

- Orders entered at a regional office through use of on-line video display terminals linked directly to the central computer.
- Orders entered at regional offices into video terminals connected to satellite minicomputers for local processing and transmission of batches of data to the central computer.
- Orders typewritten at regional offices and mailed to the central office for input through optical character recognition (OCR) equipment.
- Orders mailed to the central office for capture on key-driven equipment and subsequent input to the central computer.

The evaluation of each option requires that specific considerations be evaluated, documented, and quantified if possible. Items to be evaluated include:

- Potential personnel changes.
- Service level implications.
- Potential impact on technical and nontechnical resources.
- Considerations for future systems development.
- Installation standard approaches.

Develop Requests for Proposals (RFP)

For each approach that requires a purchase from or commitment to a hardware of software vendor, a formal Request for Proposal (RFP) may be necessary. The vendor's response provides the cost, timing, and feature information which will be used in the next step to evaluate alternatives and plan for development. No commitment need be made to any vendor. This is purely an information gathering and analysis activity.

During this activity, the team should learn the lead times for particular pieces of equipment and software needed for the new system. If lead time appears to be a problem, either the technical approach or the schedule for the development and implementation will be changed in the Development Planning stage.

The conceptual design and package review process may include a similar RFP evaluation. The activities associated with this evaluation should be reviewed to determine the applicability to this step. At the end of this activity the project team recommends a "best" technical approach to be followed.

Develop Technical Support Requirements

Once all the RFPs are compiled and the evaluations completed, resource and timing requirements can be defined. This includes staffing, cost and work plan requirements.

Identify Staff. It is essential that technical staff assigned to the project team have the technical and managerial experience necessary to develop and implement the proposed technical approach. In the long run, this generates the best return on an organization's investment of management and senior staff. The consequences of failure to make the proper commitment, especially in technical areas, can be likened to a situation where a newly certified, relatively inexperienced architect develops plans for a new building with little or no support from senior, experienced professionals. Inexperience greatly increases the likelihood of error. Changes or revisions required during construction (System Implementation) or following construction (Maintenance) of the new building become extremely costly. Ultimately, such modifications require much more time on the part of skilled, senior architectural professionals than would have been the case if they had been originally assigned to the project.

The same is true of any new system. Delay is costly—both financially and in terms of the quality of end products. These pitfalls are far less likely to be encountered if the required level of senior managers and technicians are assigned to the project at the onset.

Identify Cost. The costs associated with the technical approach selected are documented at this time. These will then be used in updating the economic evaluation in the next step.

A checklist approach can be used for this process. Examples of the types of costs to be compiled are included on the Operating Cost Checklist form. This can be used as a guide for items to be included, but necessarily is not all-inclusive. A schedule of the operating cost is then prepared for the technical approach. This schedule can be presented in the format of the Operating Cost Summary form.

Identify Critical Schedule/Project Work Plan Implications. The technical approach may cause some schedule and work plan changes. For example, as the technical approach is defined, lead times to implement the hardware and/or software are known and can be scheduled. In the next step these activities are included for the development and implementation plans.

KEY CONSIDERATIONS

User and Technical Staff Communication

Members of the project team must carefully review the proposed technical approaches with the user and EDP personnel involved in data processing segments of the project. The objective of the review is to confirm user and EDP personnel's understanding of the proposed system. This should include acceptance of technical approaches for information processing. Recommitment of the critical organization's resources is obtained. This should include the budgetary consequences of the technical approach selected.

Technical Approach Justification   When reviewing the feasibility or desirability of a technical approach, factors considered frequently go far beyond those associated with the application under development. Actually, it is often difficult to justify the costs or efforts associated with a technical approach for a single application. Instead, a technical approach typically supports a number of applications. For example, there may not be sufficient justification to implement a data base solely for an item master record within a customer order processing system. However, if the company's overall plans call for developing a distribution and inventory control system, there may be no choice but to establish a data base, or to tie in with one already available or under development.

Thus, many decisions about data base or other technical approach feasibilities should be made by the steering committee for compatibility with corporate and/or systems development long-range plans.

Technical Adventures   The technical approach definition activity offers an unusual opportunity for projects to "wander" from their objectives. Quite often, a decision to employ a given technical strategy is the result of a prior policy decision which may have been made for purely technical reasons and is, in fact, severely detrimental to the cost or operation of the system being developed. In such instances the project team must at least document the costs and benefits of other alternatives in order to make the steering committee aware of the business implications of decisions made in a technical vacuum.

110

STANDARD ACTIVITIES/END ITEMS

TOUCHE ROSS

ORGANIZATION __PHASE II.__
STEP __3__
SYSTEM __REQUIREMENTS__
USER REP ____

ID/TITLE __TECHNICAL SUPPORT APPROACH__

☐ PHASE ☐ STEP ☒ ACTIVITY ☒ TASK ☐ SUBTASK ☐ ____

	PREPARED BY	REVIEWED BY	DATE	PHASE
	MVJ	CB	3/29/80	II-3
		CB	11/1/80	II-3
		SH		
		CB		

NUMBER	PHASE/STEP/ACTIVITY/TASK/SUBTASK NAME	END ITEM	FORM NO.	PERFORMED BY	DUE DATE	APPROVED BY	DATE
A.	Review Project Work Files						
B.	Prepare Detailed Work Plan	Work Outline	101				
		Project Plan	102				
C.	Identify Technical Support Approaches						
C.1	– Review Application Needs	List of Application Options	142				
C.2	– Review Organizations Technical Capabilities	Survey of Organizations Technical Skills	125, 142				
C.3	– Assess the Stability of the Technology	Survey of Technical Approach Maturity	142				
D.	Ensure That Alternative Approaches Can Meet Requirements	Identification of all Major Considerations	140, 142				
E.	Evaluate Alternative Approaches	Advantage versus Disadvantage List	142				
F.	Develop Requests for Proposals (RFP)	Draft RFP	142				
G.	Develop Technical Support Requirements						
G.1	– Identify Staff	Job Description	103				
		Summary of Functions	125				
		Staffing Requirements	126				
G.2	– Identify Cost	Operating Cost Summary	145				

STANDARD ACTIVITIES/END ITEMS

TOUCHE ROSS

ORGANIZATION __PHASE II,__
    STEP 3
SYSTEM __REQUIREMENTS__
USER REP

ID/TITLE __TECHNICAL SUPPORT APPROACH__

☐ PHASE   ☒ ACTIVITY   ☐ SUBTASK
☐ STEP   ☒ TASK   ☐

PREPARED BY __MVJ__
REVIEWED BY __CB__
DATE __3/29/80__
PHASE __II-3__

PREPARED BY	MVJ	SH
REVIEWED BY	CB	CB
DATE	3/29/80	11/1/80
PHASE	II-3	II-3

NUMBER	PHASE/STEP/ACTIVITY/TASK/SUBTASK NAME	END ITEM	FORM NO.	PERFORMED BY	DUE DATE	APPROVED BY	DATE
G.3	– Identify Critical Schedule/Project Work Plan Implications	Project Plan	102				
		Data Acquisition Plan	192				
		Personnel and Equipment Plan	193				
		Work Outline	101				

THE SYSTEMS DEVELOPMENT PROCESS

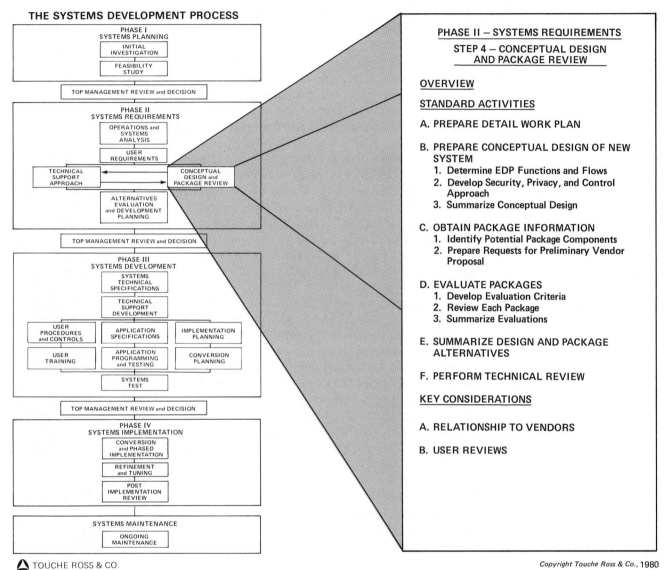

PHASE I
SYSTEMS PLANNING

INITIAL INVESTIGATION

FEASIBILITY STUDY

TOP MANAGEMENT REVIEW and DECISION

PHASE II
SYSTEMS REQUIREMENTS

OPERATIONS and SYSTEMS ANALYSIS

USER REQUIREMENTS

TECHNICAL SUPPORT APPROACH

CONCEPTUAL DESIGN and PACKAGE REVIEW

ALTERNATIVES EVALUATION and DEVELOPMENT PLANNING

TOP MANAGEMENT REVIEW and DECISION

PHASE III
SYSTEMS DEVELOPMENT

SYSTEMS TECHNICAL SPECIFICATIONS

TECHNICAL SUPPORT DEVELOPMENT

USER PROCEDURES and CONTROLS

APPLICATION SPECIFICATIONS

IMPLEMENTATION PLANNING

USER TRAINING

APPLICATION PROGRAMMING and TESTING

CONVERSION PLANNING

SYSTEMS TEST

TOP MANAGEMENT REVIEW and DECISION

PHASE IV
SYSTEMS IMPLEMENTATION

CONVERSION and PHASED IMPLEMENTATION

REFINEMENT and TUNING

POST IMPLEMENTATION REVIEW

SYSTEMS MAINTENANCE

ONGOING MAINTENANCE

TOUCHE ROSS & CO.

PHASE II – SYSTEMS REQUIREMENTS

STEP 4 – CONCEPTUAL DESIGN AND PACKAGE REVIEW

OVERVIEW

STANDARD ACTIVITIES

A. PREPARE DETAIL WORK PLAN

B. PREPARE CONCEPTUAL DESIGN OF NEW SYSTEM
1. Determine EDP Functions and Flows
2. Develop Security, Privacy, and Control Approach
3. Summarize Conceptual Design

C. OBTAIN PACKAGE INFORMATION
1. Identify Potential Package Components
2. Prepare Requests for Preliminary Vendor Proposal

D. EVALUATE PACKAGES
1. Develop Evaluation Criteria
2. Review Each Package
3. Summarize Evaluations

E. SUMMARIZE DESIGN AND PACKAGE ALTERNATIVES

F. PERFORM TECHNICAL REVIEW

KEY CONSIDERATIONS

A. RELATIONSHIP TO VENDORS

B. USER REVIEWS

113

The Conceptual Design and Package Review step consists of the first-level technical definition of the new application system. The first two steps of this phase documented what the new system is to do and how it is to perform in the user's environment. Step 3, the Technical Support Approach, and this step are then carried out simultaneously to document the technical definition of the new application and its associated technical support approaches for systems software and hardware. At the conclusion of these two steps, sufficient systems requirements will exist to permit final evaluations of alternatives, including make or buy approaches, and preparation of developmental plans.

The overall job during this step is to take user requirements and develop a conceptual design for their implementation. Since the feasibility study in Phase I identified the potential for use of application packages, this step may also include a detailed review of application packages. Thus, two primary activities are included in this step: conceptual design and package review. The emphasis and relative effort devoted to these two activities depends on the likelihood that an application package will fulfill the stated user requirements. If package acquisition is virtually assured, then the conceptual design work should be limited to a confirmation of the design approach discussed in the feasibility study. This minimal effort would be performed to confirm that the custom development approach was not reasonable or cost effective.

The proposed new system may consist of several subsystems, some of which may be candidates for package usage. In this case, detailed package reviews would be conducted for some subsystems and conceptual designs would be conducted for remaining subsystems.

Finally, the new system may be implemented through a time-sharing, facilities management, or service bureau approach. Again, the potential use of these alternatives should have been identified in the feasibility study. If they are viable candidates, the review process is conducted in the package review activities of this step.

There is less user participation in this step than in the first two steps of Systems Requirements. This step consists primarily of answering questions raised by the systems analysts who will be performing much of the work. Although users are not participating directly, they remain involved to assure that the project continues to keep user considerations in perspective.

STANDARD ACTIVITIES

Prepare Detailed
Work Plan

This step begins with a review of work completed to date including both the feasibility study and the user requirements document. Any business changes that have occurred and have impacted these documents are also reviewed and noted. Also at this point, project plans from the feasibility study that relate to this step are expanded into a detailed work plan. This plan provides sufficient detail to direct, control, and coordinate project team activities and tasks throughout this step. Substantial creativity is required to identify and describe the specific tasks to be performed; however, even the best of project teams cannot produce a quality end product if critical tasks are left out. Important considerations in developing a work plan with specific tasks and responsibilities include:

— Identification of key personnel with the experience necessary to complete the standard activities.
— Assignment of staff and time to specific tasks that reflect the relative importance of each task to the overall end product, taking into consideration the relative potential of custom development versus package acquisition.
— Identification of end items to be generated by each activity and task, and their relationship to the overall organization of the end product.

Prepare Conceptual Design of New System

This activity, through a series of tasks and subtasks, shapes the conceptual design of the new system. The project team works with both the previously developed user requirements documentation and the parallel technical support approach project team. The end product of this activity should be the documentation necessary to develop the systems technical specifications in the next phase.

The structure of work units during this activity is repetitive in nature, following a top-down pattern. Conceptual design begins with higher-level functions within the new system and moves downward through a series of functions and subfunctions, adding depth and detail at each level.

During the User Requirements step, the outputs, data elements, inputs, and data structures were defined. These items are now used as the basis for developing a conceptual design that will technically integrate the requirements. Modifications may occur to these items during the design activity; if so, the modifications must be reviewed and approved by the user. Data structures are addressed in the Technical Support Approach step.

Determine EDP Functions and Flows. EDP flowcharts are now developed to relate all input, output, data element groups and major processing steps. These charts are developed to a level of detail necessary to describe the entire computer processing flows for the new system. They are not intended to depict program run-to-run or even identify every program that may eventually be developed. For example, the flowcharts may indicate the need for a restart/recovery function, but would not be developed to detail every program and module required to accomplish this function. Also, the flowcharts may indicate one function producing a series of daily control and balancing reports, but would not include identification of the individual print modules or any of the required sorts.

EDP flowcharts are prepared for each subsystem and major processing group of the new system. This may include flowcharts for mainline processing, file maintenance, weekly cycle processing, systems interfaces, and others. The flowcharting task is not complete until all inputs, outputs, data structures, and major processing steps have been included.

Besides creating the EDP flowcharts, the analyst also describes each of the functions identified on the flowcharts. These descriptions are placed on Program/Module Function forms.

Develop Security, Privacy, and Control Approach. This task uses the general environmental constraints documented in the user requirements manual to develop the conceptual EDP approach to handling security, privacy, and control functions. These constraints and controls are documented from a computer processing viewpoint and are incorporated into the EDP flowcharts and function descriptions completed in the previous task. The controls should at least conform to the minimum standards established by the internal or external auditors to minimize the need for subsequent design modifications of the new system. Some of the questions that should be addressed in completing this task include:

— What functions are subject to control?
— Are adequate controls designed for each type of input?
— What tolerance limits have been designed into the system to require special actions for unusual conditions and to control transaction flow?
— Have adequate exception reports been included?
— Have adequate control totals been provided?
— Have functions been identified to check the integrity of data? For example, in order processing systems, it is desirable to include functions that check the contents of open order files against corresponding customer inventory and item master files to ensure accurate and consistent data.
— Have hardware and software safeguards been included to identify unauthorized access to both program and data files?
— Have data retention and recovery functions been identified?

At a minimum, this task is not completed until all of the environmental constraints identified as user requirements have been incorporated into the conceptual design.

Summarize Conceptual Design.   This task concludes the conceptual design activity by organizing into a completed package all of the systems design material developed in this step, plus material from the User Requirements step and the Technical Support Approach, as appropriate.

Obtain Package Information   This activity consists of identifying vendors who may be capable of fulfilling the requirements with application packages or time-sharing, facilities management, or service bureau approaches. It also includes the preparation and submission of a preliminary Request for Proposal (RFP) to each of these vendors.

Identify Potential Package Components.   Using the user requirements manual and the material describing package availabilities from the feasibility study, the analyst identifies potential packages that may fulfill some components of the system's requirements. If sufficient information on package availabilities does not exist, additional research effort is required. This initial task is similar to that included in the feasibility study.

Packages may usually be acquired from several sources, including computer hardware vendors, third-party software companies, or other organizations involved in the same type of business (especially at the state and local governmental level and other noncompeting organizations). Through contact with these sources, the project team reviews package features (as described in brochures or catalogs) with user requirements. In some cases, packages may be found to match virtually all of the requirements. In other cases, package features may address only some of the requirements, or only requirements for certain subsystems or modules. This may or may not suggest that a package is a viable alternative. If minimum objectives are met, or if stand-alone modules are available, then a package may be an acceptable approach. Another approach may include packaged "turnkey" acquisitions consisting of both applications software and hardware. In this case the technical support project team must also be involved in obtaining information and evaluating packages.

Prepare Requests for Preliminary Vendor Proposal. For each potential package, the supplying vendor should be sent a request for proposal (RFP) that will allow the project team to receive sufficient information to conduct a detail evaluation as described in the next activity. The project team planning for this task should strive to provide sufficient background information to the vendors and should be prepared to respond to vendor questions as they attempt to construct their proposals. Thus, adequate time must not only be planned for the vendor but also for project team members. Since the RFP may be included as part of a negotiated contract, it should be carefully prepared. In general, the RFP should include the following:

— Description of current operations and projected growth or changes.
— Specification of requirements for the new system.
— Request for the vendor to describe the application package, its characteristics, method of operation, special features, and technical constraints.
— Request for the vendor to describe the package's ability to meet projected growth and other operational changes.
— Request for detailed costs, including purchase and lease prices, maintenance, and any other costs associated with the package.
— Request for an estimate of typical installation time and a vendor-prepared implementation plan.
— Request for customer reference information.
— Request for a copy of the vendor's proposed contract, including vendor responsibilities, delivery schedules, payment schedules, penalty clauses for not meeting performance claims or schedules, and explicit definitions of what constitutes acceptance.

In some cases it may be beneficial to include the evaluation criteria in the RFP in order to receive appropriate emphasis in the vendors' proposals. A cover letter should also be prepared and sent with the RFP to inform the vendor of the request's intent, the proposed schedules, and persons to be contacted.

Evaluate Packages   This activity includes the development of standard criteria and the measurement of each package against those criteria. Evaluation criteria should be established while the vendors are preparing their proposals, so that the project team may immediately begin the review and evaluation process once responses are received.

Develop Evaluation Criteria. The user requirements manual and, as appropriate, the Technical Support Approach are used to prepare a detailed set of criteria against which each response will be measured. The evaluation criteria should include qualitative factors only. The costs, or financial impact, should be analyzed as a separate task and then combined with the qualitative evaluation at the end of the process. The criteria should include the following areas:

— *User Requirements.* Required features of the new system as documented and approved by the users are listed for comparison against package features.

— *Availability.* Two primary benefits of acquiring an applications package are a reduction in systems development effort and the expectation of error-free operation. These benefits may only be expected if the package is currently operational at a production status in multiple customer locations.

— *Equipment Configuration.* The equipment constraints as outlined in the Technical Support Approach are listed for comparison to package requirements.

— *Software Environment.* The software constraints as outlined in the Technical Support Approach are listed for comparison to package requirements. This includes programming language, operating system, data base, and data communications requirements.

— *Technical Design Features.* Criteria should be established to evaluate application packages on design features such as:

  · Control procedures and audit trails.

  · Input and output options.

  · Provisions for file maintenance and reruns.

  · Ease and flexibility of operation, including absence of many special forms.

  · Straightforward and understandable programming techniques.

— *Flexibility.* Criteria should include items used to review a package's ability to accommodate changing user requirements. Areas include reviews of data element and record length restrictions, report option flexibilities, edit change capabilities for code numbers, etc. Criteria should also consider whether the application was originally designed as a package or developed as a specific system and then subsequently modified for outside sales.

— *Expandability.* Criteria should also include items to review the application packages' sensitivity to increases in production volumes and frequency of operation.

— *Documentation.* The quality of vendor-supplied documentation should be listed for review even though standard documentation usually requires revision prior to implementation to meet the specific environment. Individual documentation categories include:

  · Systems manual.

  · Users manual.

  · Source listing and program documentation.

  · Operations manual.

— *Vendor Support.* This category should include items of support for installation, maintenance, and enhancements.

— *Vendor Reputation.* This category should include evaluation items to assess the risk of vendor business failure and the quality of vendor personnel.

After completing the list of evaluation criteria, the project team must assign relative weights (values) to each of the items. These weights should reflect the relative overall importance of the various items to the total new system. In addition, any criteria that, if unmet, would cause the package to be totally unacceptable are noted. In most cases, however, the inability of a package to fulfill completely a stated criterion will only cause the package to be less acceptable and result in a larger and more complex development and implementation effort.

Review Each Package.   Once vendor proposals have been received, the project team may begin the process of package review and evaluation. Although several tasks are involved, the first is generally to read each response and score the vendor against the evaluation criteria developed in the previous activity. This may be accomplished by establishing a standard rating system to be applied to each evaluation category. For example, the rating system could be from zero to four with four as the best and zero as the poorest. Once ratings have been assigned to each item, they are multiplied by the weights to obtain category scores and thus total scores. This initial review and scoring process accomplishes two objectives. First, it may reduce the number of candidate packages by determining that certain vendor responses are sufficiently inadequate to cause that particular package to be removed from further consideration. Second, it identifies areas where additional followup is required for vendors whose packages continue to appear as potential alternatives.

The evaluation process should be conducted carefully and with more than one analyst if possible. Major considerations in this effort include:

— Packages may contain features that have not been specified as user requirements but appear to be very useful; or features which compromise stated user requirements. This situation may require additional meetings with users and subsequent modification of the requirements document.

— Packages that are unstable in multiple environments, or that appear to require significant modifications in order to meet an acceptable level of requirements, should be considered as high-risk and rated very low.

— Packages may appear to operate in several hardware and software environments, but may have significantly different performance characteristics in these environments.

— Packages that contain a significant amount of flexibility may require substantial efforts to implement and maintain, and may result in considerable operating overhead. Such packages should therefore not arbitrarily be rated high simply because they offer many package options.

The package evaluation process also includes followup meetings with vendors and contacts with other package users. These tasks are conducted to verify and expand information provided in the proposals in order to complete the evaluations. Finally, this activity includes an analysis of all costs related to each package. This contains:

— Purchase or lease price of the basic package.
— Cost of package options.
— Projected maintenance charges.
— Costs of additional hardware and software required to utilize the package.
— Costs of package usage at multiple locations.

Summarize Evaluations.   The summarization process generally includes two major tasks. First, the detail evaluation should be reviewed to identify the significant strengths and weaknesses identified for each package. This includes documenting the special concerns that will impact the development, implementation, and ongoing operations if the package is selected. Second, the cost analysis must be related to the qualitative evaluation in order to develop a cost-effectiveness comparison of the various packages.

Summarize Design and Package Alternatives

This activity consists of combining the previously developed material into comparisons of various viable alternatives for custom development and package acquisition. The alternatives comparison includes such items as relative advantages and disadvantages, cost characteristics, expected performance characteristics, and special development and implementation considerations. It should also include a recommended approach. In addition, special considerations related to conversions with the various alternatives are identified and documented for use in preparing the development plan in the next step.

Perform Technical Review

This final activity is required to assure that the conceptual design, package alternatives, and technical support approaches are consistent and complete. Any modifications or additions must be completed before beginning Step 5 — Alternatives Evaluation and Development Planning.

KEY CONSIDERATIONS

Relationship to Vendors

Although vendors can be very helpful in assisting the project team to understand the applications packages, the project team should always keep in mind that vendors are primarily interested in selling their products or services. Thus, they may be expected to present their material in the most favorable manner and emphasize only the strong points. It is the project team's responsibility to remain objective and perform sufficient analysis to thoroughly understand the packages. This also applies to contacts with vendor customers, since the references supplied should also be expected to provide positive comments regarding the packages.

User Reviews

It is unlikely that any package will exactly match the user requirements specified for the new system. Thus, the project team must carefully review differences with the users in order to understand their potential impact on the development project and new system operation. Requirements that are not fulfilled by the package may be addressed in a different manner by the user or may be incorporated in the package during the Systems Development phase. Conversely, the packages may have additional features that were not stated as requirements but would be very beneficial to the user. In this case, the requirements and cost-and-benefit estimates could be modified to reflect these features.

TOUCHE ROSS

ORGANIZATION __PHASE II__
STEP __4__
SYSTEM __REQUIREMENTS__
USER REP ____

STANDARD ACTIVITIES/END ITEMS

ID/TITLE __CONCEPTUAL DESIGN AND PACKAGE REVIEW__

☐ PHASE ☒ ACTIVITY ☐ SUBTASK ____
☐ STEP   ☒ TASK   ☐ ____

PAGE __1__ OF __2__
PROJECT NO. ____

	PREPARED BY	M T	SH
	REVIEWED BY	CJ	CB
	DATE	3/29/80	11/1/80
	PHASE	II-4	II-4

NUMBER	PHASE/STEP/ACTIVITY/TASK/SUBTASK NAME	END ITEM	FORM NO.	PERFORMED BY	DUE DATE	APPROVED BY	DATE
A.	Prepare Detailed Work Plan	Work Outline	101				
		Project Plan	102				
B.	Prepare Conceptual Design of New System						
B.1	- Determine EDP Functions and Flows	General System Flow Chart	127, 128				
		Program/Module Function	171				
B.2	- Develop Security, Privacy and Control Approach	Assumptions and Constraints	140				
		Summary of Controls	141				
B.3	- Summarize Conceptual Design	Conceptual Design Book	142				
C.	Obtain Package Information						
C.1	- Identify Potential Package Components	Components versus Packages	177				
C.2	- Prepare Requests for Preliminary Vendor Proposal	Request for Proposal	142				
D.	Evaluate Packages						
D.1	- Develop Evaluation Criteria	Requirements versus Vendors	177				
		Scoring Technique	142				
D.2	- Review Each Package	Score of Each Package	177				
		Qualitative Evaluation	142				
		Cost Summary	145				

121

STANDARD ACTIVITIES/END ITEMS

TOUCHE ROSS

ORGANIZATION __PHASE II,__

STEP __4__

SYSTEM __REQUIREMENTS__

USER REP _____

ID/TITLE __CONCEPTUAL DESIGN AND PACKAGE REVIEW__

☐ PHASE   ☒ ACTIVITY   ☐ SUBTASK

☐ STEP   ☒ TASK   ☐ _____

PREPARED BY	MVJ	SH
REVIEWED BY	CB	CB
DATE	3/29/80	11/1/80
PHASE	II-4	II-4

NUMBER	PHASE/STEP/ACTIVITY/TASK/SUBTASK NAME	END ITEM	FORM NO.	PERFORMED BY	DUE DATE	APPROVED BY	DATE
D.3	- Summarize Evaluations	Cost Analysis Per Package	105, 148				
		Strengths/Weakness Listing	142				
E.	Summarize Design and Package Alternatives	Alternatives Analysis	142, 177				
F.	Perform Technical Review	Technical Review Memos	142				

122

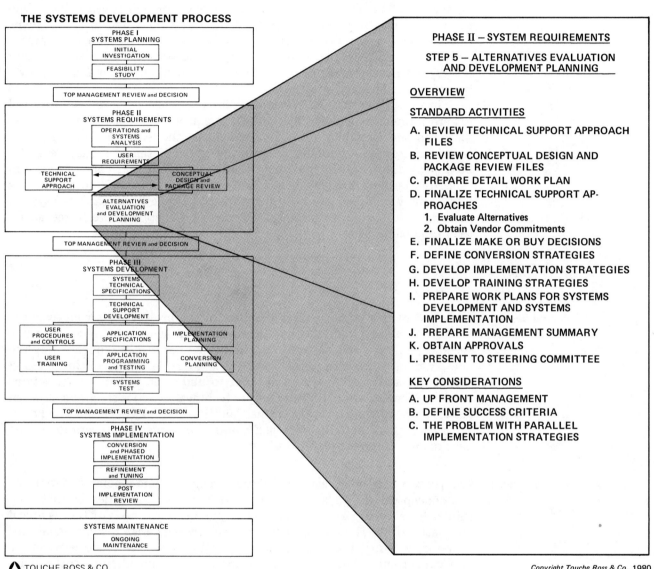

THE SYSTEMS DEVELOPMENT PROCESS

PHASE I
SYSTEMS PLANNING
INITIAL INVESTIGATION
FEASIBILITY STUDY

TOP MANAGEMENT REVIEW and DECISION

PHASE II
SYSTEMS REQUIREMENTS
OPERATIONS and SYSTEMS ANALYSIS
USER REQUIREMENTS
TECHNICAL SUPPORT APPROACH
CONCEPTUAL DESIGN and PACKAGE REVIEW
ALTERNATIVES EVALUATION and DEVELOPMENT PLANNING

TOP MANAGEMENT REVIEW and DECISION

PHASE III
SYSTEMS DEVELOPMENT
SYSTEMS TECHNICAL SPECIFICATIONS
TECHNICAL SUPPORT DEVELOPMENT
USER PROCEDURES and CONTROLS
APPLICATION SPECIFICATIONS
IMPLEMENTATION PLANNING
USER TRAINING
APPLICATION PROGRAMMING and TESTING
CONVERSION PLANNING
SYSTEMS TEST

TOP MANAGEMENT REVIEW and DECISION

PHASE IV
SYSTEMS IMPLEMENTATION
CONVERSION and PHASED IMPLEMENTATION
REFINEMENT and TUNING
POST IMPLEMENTATION REVIEW

SYSTEMS MAINTENANCE
ONGOING MAINTENANCE

△ TOUCHE ROSS & CO.

PHASE II — SYSTEM REQUIREMENTS

STEP 5 — ALTERNATIVES EVALUATION AND DEVELOPMENT PLANNING

OVERVIEW

STANDARD ACTIVITIES

A. REVIEW TECHNICAL SUPPORT APPROACH FILES
B. REVIEW CONCEPTUAL DESIGN AND PACKAGE REVIEW FILES
C. PREPARE DETAIL WORK PLAN
D. FINALIZE TECHNICAL SUPPORT APPROACHES
  1. Evaluate Alternatives
  2. Obtain Vendor Commitments
E. FINALIZE MAKE OR BUY DECISIONS
F. DEFINE CONVERSION STRATEGIES
G. DEVELOP IMPLEMENTATION STRATEGIES
H. DEVELOP TRAINING STRATEGIES
I. PREPARE WORK PLANS FOR SYSTEMS DEVELOPMENT AND SYSTEMS IMPLEMENTATION
J. PREPARE MANAGEMENT SUMMARY
K. OBTAIN APPROVALS
L. PRESENT TO STEERING COMMITTEE

KEY CONSIDERATIONS

A. UP FRONT MANAGEMENT
B. DEFINE SUCCESS CRITERIA
C. THE PROBLEM WITH PARALLEL IMPLEMENTATION STRATEGIES

OVERVIEW   The objective of this step is to finalize all technical and systems design approaches and to develop a formal and detailed project plan for the subsequent Systems Development phase. This is the final step in the Systems Requirements phase. Consequently, it is necessary at this time to prepare a revised economic evaluation of the project and present that evaluation and the revised development plans to the steering committee for final approval before proceeding to the next phase.

In many respects, the systems requirements efforts have been directed toward refinement and verification of the concepts and plans originally presented in the feasibility study that concluded the Systems Planning phase. In that sense, the economic evaluation prepared at this time may generally be expected to confirm that the initial assumptions and concepts are still valid. If the more detailed review and design carried out in this phase has substantially modified prior estimates of costs, benefits, or expected system performance, the steering committee may find it appropriate to reevaluate their original decision.

STANDARD ACTIVITIES

Review "Technical Support Approach" Files

In Step 3 of this phase, several members of the project team were given the task of evaluating alternative technical approaches and recommending specific hardware and software techniques to be used in implementing the new system. A necessary activity now is to review the conclusions and recommendations of that step in order to understand what further actions must be taken to assure that the proper technical facilities are available when system development formally begins. Additionally, the conclusions and decisions reached in the prior step significantly influence the preparation of the developmental project plan.

Review "Conceptual Design and Package Review" Files

The project team must also review the conclusions and recommendations of the conceptual design and package review effort. Activities in that step should have been carried out largely in parallel with those of the technical approach effort. The project team must review the design recommendations, however, to assure that proper communication has taken place between the two concurrent efforts and that the overall recommendations and conclusions of the Conceptual Design and Package Review step are consistent with the recommendations of the Technical Support Approach step. Like the technical approach team, the conceptual design team may also have identified alternative approaches. Thus, it may be necessary to finalize the conceptual design or to formally contract with hardware and software vendors, contingent on steering committee approval, as part of this work plan.

Prepare Detailed Work Plan

Having reviewed the two previous steps, the project team is now in a position to review the initial project plan established for the current step at the conclusion of the systems planning effort and to prepare the detailed work plan. Revisions may be necessary as a result of such factors as unplanned changes in project personnel, as well as changes arising out of the systems requirements effort.

124

Finalize Technical Support Approaches

Because of the nature of potential technical support recommendations, it is usually necessary to finalize all technical approaches and environmental considerations at the outset of this step. For example, vendor commitments must often be obtained for the delivery of equipment and software before developmental planning can be completed and a revised economic evaluation produced. Also, vendors often take a long time to respond to a Request for Proposal (RFP) if such additional procedures are necessary. In any case, this activity may be necessary in order to evaluate alternative approaches and finalize vendor arrangements.

Evaluate Alternatives. If the technical approach team identifies more than one alternative technical approach, the cost and benefit implications of each alternative must be reviewed in order to understand any assumptions or constraints included in the recommendation. In most cases, the final recommendation of the technical approach group will be followed unless major unplanned expenditures are indicated or unless it appears desirable to issue formal requests for proposals to various vendors of hardware and/or software in order to obtain firm price delivery and performance commitments. In this latter case, a draft RFP should have been prepared as an end product of the Technical Support Approach step. If so, the RFP must now be issued to prospective vendors. The evaluation of vendor proposals should be accomplished according to criteria established by the technical approach team. Careful planning is necessary to assure that a four- to six-week delay for vendor responses does not result in a corresponding delay in completion. In addition, the project team must recognize any situation requiring a benchmark and must plan for all the activities and time required for the benchmark process.

Obtain Vendor Commitments. Regardless of how vendor selection is accomplished, final delivery dates and performance commitments must be obtained from the hardware and software vendors during this activity. The identification of optional sources of hardware or software—such as third-party vendors or "software houses"—may be required in order to meet project schedules. Decisions of this nature can potentially affect the economic viability of the system under development.

Finalize "Make or Buy" Decisions

Similarly, any other "make or buy" decisions which may have resulted from the conceptual systems design effort must be finalized early in this step. Additional RFPs to various vendors of application software packages may also be required to finalize the general design. If design alternatives include recommendations to purchase time-sharing services or to enter into facilities management or service bureau contracts, considerable effort is required to solicit proposals, attend presentations and negotiate operating arrangements with vendors. A service bureau, facilities management firm, or time-sharing organization may also be required to develop and recommend approaches to convert files or systems, train personnel, or define an implementation strategy. In those cases, the evaluation and selection of a vendor is necessary for the completion of the next three standard activities in this step.

Define Conversion Strategies

A tentative conversion plan was prepared during the Systems Planning phase. That plan must now be reevaluated in view of the conceptual design and technical approach.

The Conversion Planning form provides a suggested means of identifying major elements of the conversion plan. This document outlines the tasks necessary for the conversion of files, preparation of data collection forms (if necessary), and the creation of conversion programs. It also indicates the desired sequence of the conversion. If conversion programs must be developed during Phase III — Systems Development, that consideration must be reflected in the planning process at this time.

The project team should also recognize that the precise physical structure of a data base may not be finalized until systems technical specifications are developed in Phase III. However, even in the case of complex data base environments, the basic business variables that must be captured are known and should be identified.

Any conversion strategy should also consider the need to "purify" data before accepting it into the new system. Such efforts may require an intensive manual review of existing file contents and may have to be started very early in the development process if it is to be completed in time for conversion. As a rule, data or files that are out of control cannot be converted.

Whatever the approach to file conversion, a strategy must be developed at this point in the project in order to plan for all necessary resources and to identify the attendant costs.

Develop Implementation Strategies

The project team is once again ready to build on the concepts outlined in the systems planning effort in order to develop a final approach to the implementation of the new system. Specific approaches will vary greatly with each organization and application. However, the implementation plans developed at this point should at least take into account such considerations as:

— The timing of implementation for each significant system segment, if modular development and implementation is envisioned.
— The timing of implementation at different locations or organizations impacted by the new system.
— The need for a pilot implementation and site.
— The need for parallel processing between the old and new systems. If parallel processing is required, the plan must also allow for the necessary increased workload to operate both systems and to reconcile differences between them. In addition, the conditions for termination of the parallel operation must be defined.
— Acceptance criteria for the new system.
— The approach taken to phase out current operations. This consideration should also include the outline of a strategy to relocate displaced personnel or acquire new personnel.

The project team developing an implementation strategy should realize that final turnover of a new system is generally dependent on the system's ability to meet stated objectives. Unless these objectives are clearly identified and agreed to prior to the start of implementation, the project team may find itself in a position where both the new and the old system continue to function — at great cost to the organization — simply because user management is emotionally unable to abandon the old system.

Develop Training Strategies

The objective of this activity is to identify the basic approach to training operations personnel. Such strategies should include consideration of the need for new procedures manuals as well as the potential need for formal training. If the system itself is to be used to train users during the Systems Test step, that strategy must now be recognized in order to plan for temporary help or backup to process the normal workload during the training period. The actual efforts to define formal training programs and plans are part of the next phase — Systems Development.

Prepare Project Plans for Systems Development and Systems Implementation

Once all alternatives have been evaluated and all strategies have been formalized, the project team is in a position to revise the systems development project plans. These revised plans should indicate key decision points and resources required at each step. They may also specify the need to have repetitive development phases if multiple system modules are not to be developed at the same time.

As a guide to the development of revised plans for Phase III — Systems Development, the project team is referred to standard activity descriptions in the following subsections that describe each step in the phase. Specifically, there are nine steps in the Systems Development phase for which reasonably detailed plans should be developed. The activities of the subsequent phase, Systems Implementation, should also be outlined at this time although not necessarily at the same level of detail. Final plans for Systems Implementation will be developed in Phase III. The basic steps that require detailed plans at this time are:

- Systems Technical Specifications.
- Technical Support Development.
- Application Specifications.
- Application Programming and Testing.
- User Procedures and Controls.
- User Training.
- Implementation Planning.
- Conversion Planning.
- System Test.

The project team may also find it helpful to review the standard end items and documentation described in each of these steps for additional guidance. Note, however, that the team may easily fall into the trap of blindly executing every standard form. Thus, it should be remembered that the project structure and systems standards defined in this document are designed to have wide application to a large variety of systems projects. Consequently, these standards and activities must be tailored to fit the scope and complexity of each individual situation to which they are applied.

Similarly, the project team should also take this opportunity to carefully review all prior estimates. There are two purposes for having this standard activity at this point in the project. First, the planning effort assures that the developmental project team has realistic project schedules and is not bound by invalidated estimates and commitments made during the feasibility study. Second, since the largest portion of the total expense of a systems project is incurred by Phase III, replanning the project at this time allows all prior cost and benefit estimates to be updated. Management now has the opportunity to terminate an unfeasible project.

Prepare Management Summary

In completing this Systems Requirements phase, the project team has essentially revised or updated the bulk of the documentation that made up the feasibility study in Phase I — Systems Planning. To complete that update, a review and summary of all estimates (costs, benefits, and project timing) presented in the feasibility study report must be made. This task includes challenging all project assumptions and constraints as well as reworking the economic evaluations. Another useful task at this point is to prepare a variance analysis highlighting all significant changes from the feasibility study report and explaining the sources of variances. If the project team is recommending a shift in direction and that shift is responsible for many or most of the changes, the management summary should also present any alternative approaches that might bring costs or performance closer to the original estimates.

Obtain Approvals

Once the Systems Requirements documentation package has been completed, the project team must again review all the requirements, strategies, and timing assumptions with users of the system. In addition, they should review the system in detail with data processing operations personnel who will be responsible for the day-to-day operation. Finally, a review with the internal and/or external auditors is also advisable to assure that internal controls specified for the new system are complete. This last review with the auditors should also assure that the project team has not inadvertently eliminated a checkpoint or control document necessary to another system or activity.

Most of the standard forms provided for documentation of systems provide for formal user review and approval. Even if the project team has conscientiously obtained formal user approvals on every piece of documentation, a single confirmation document should still be obtained from key users. This document should state the user's acceptance or agreement with the systems requirements and set forth any reservations they may have about the planned new operations.

Present to Steering Committee

The report and agreement letters are presented to the steering committee by both user management and the project team. By taking this action, the user signals support for the project and willingness to assume responsibility for final implementation and operation, as long as the developed product meets the specifications in the requirements.

KEY CONSIDERATIONS

Up-Front Management

The final items in this phase shape the remainder of the project. Approximately 60 to 70 percent of the cost and effort of systems development still lies ahead and will be expended on the basis of the output of the Systems Requirements phase. Thus, the project team must include senior, experienced individuals from both the user and data processing organizations in order to assure quality in both business and technical aspects of the system. In the long run, this approach will produce the greatest return on the organization's investment of management and senior staff time. If insufficient attention of senior personnel is given to the project in this phase, there is a high probability that problems that could have otherwise been avoided will require much more attention and time later.

Define Success Criteria

It is often too easy to think of the end results of a systems project entirely in terms of reports and data. To be truly successful, these reports and data must actually be used to improve business operations. In order to keep that objective in focus, the project end products must be stated in business terms. Stating system objectives in terms of business goals not only keeps the proper focus on the systems development process, but also forces the project team and users to think in terms of responsibilities for impiementation. For example, not only must the new system produce prescribed information, but users must also commit themselves to commit to use that information in such a way as to reach the desired goals.

The Problem with Parallel Implementation Strategies

To the uninitiated, operating a new system simultaneously with an old or proven system appears an obvious and fail-safe way to prove out and test a new system. In fact, this approach is very often a very costly and ineffective process.

There are several potential pitfalls in a parallel system operation. First, significant additional effort may be required to operate both the new and the old systems simultaneously. Additional trained personnel may also be temporarily required to reconcile differences between the two systems that are assumed to be explained by errors in the new system. In many cases, the errors are in the old system and are, in fact, among the reasons for the new systems project.

Reconciliation can also be a very complex task when the system carries differences forward through updating cycles. For example, if a tax calculation method changes in a payroll system, minor differences may be discovered in tax deductions on individual paychecks. However, these differences will accumulate into year-to-date totals each time checks are calculated. Reconciling the year-to-date totals involves not only reconciling differences resulting from the current payroll, but also differences from all prior parallel payrolls.

A last—and possibly most serious—drawback to prolonged parallel implementation lies in the attitudes of the user departments. The continued existence of the old system often provides a psychological crutch and unreasonably inhibits the user from discontinuing its operation.

TOUCHE ROSS

STANDARD ACTIVITIES/END ITEMS

ID/TITLE ALTERNATIVES EVALUATION AND DEVELOPMENT PLANNING

ORGANIZATION PHASE II,
STEP 5
SYSTEM REQUIREMENTS
USER REP

☐ PHASE ☐ STEP ☒ ACTIVITY ☒ TASK ☐ SUBTASK ☐ _____

PAGE 1 OF 2
PROJECT NO.

	PREPARED BY	MVJ	SH
	REVIEWED BY	CB	CB
	DATE	3/29/80	11/1/80
	PHASE	II-5	II-5

NUMBER	PHASE/STEP/ACTIVITY/TASK/SUBTASK NAME	END ITEM	FORM NO.	PERFORMED BY	DUE DATE	APPROVED BY	DATE
A.	Review Technical Support Approach Files						
B.	Review Conceptual Design and Package Review Files						
C.	Prepare Detailed Work Plan	Work Outline	101				
		Project Plan	102				
D.	Finalize Technical Support Approaches						
D.1	– Evaluate Alternatives	Approaches versus Requirements	177				
D.2	– Obtain Vendor Commitments	Vendor Commitment Letters	142				
E.	Finalize Make or Buy Decisions	Management Summary	149				
F.	Define Conversion Strategies	Conversion Planning Checklist	181				
		Data Acquisition Plan	192				
		Conversion Plan	191				
		Personnel and Equipment Plan	193				
G.	Develop Implementation Strategies	General Purpose Checklist	183				
		Personnel and Equipment Plan	193				

© Touche Ross & Co., 1980
All Rights Reserved

130

STANDARD ACTIVITIES/END ITEMS

TOUCHE ROSS

ORGANIZATION PHASE II,

STEP 5

SYSTEM REQUIREMENTS

USER REP

ID/TITLE ALTERNATIVES EVALUATION AND DEVELOPMENT PLANNING

☐ PHASE   ☒ ACTIVITY   ☐ SUBTASK
☐ STEP   ☒ TASK   ☐

	PREPARED BY	MVJ	SH
	REVIEWED BY	CB	CB
	DATE	3/29/80	11/1/80
	PHASE	II-5	II-5

NUMBER	PHASE/STEP/ACTIVITY/TASK/SUBTASK NAME	END ITEM	FORM NO.	PERFORMED BY	DUE DATE	APPROVED BY	DATE
H.	Develop Training Strategies	User Procedures and Training Checklist	182				
		User Procedures and Training Plan	195				
		Personnel and Equipment Plan	193				
		Staffing Requirements	126				
I.	Prepare Project Plans for Systems Development and Systems Implementation	Work Outline	101				
		Project Plan	102				
		Programming Estimate	104				
		Standard Activities/End Items	106				
		Measurable Benefits Evaluation	147				
		Operating Cost Summary	145				
		Development Cost Measurement	105				
J.	Prepare Management Summary	Management Summary	149				
		Economic Evaluation Summary	148				
K.	Obtain Approvals	Confirmation Document					
L.	Present to Steering Committee						

THE SYSTEMS DEVELOPMENT PROCESS

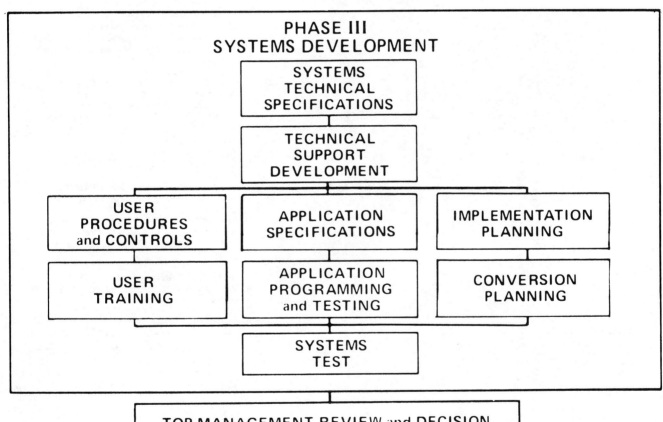

PHASE III
SYSTEMS DEVELOPMENT

- SYSTEMS TECHNICAL SPECIFICATIONS
- TECHNICAL SUPPORT DEVELOPMENT
- USER PROCEDURES and CONTROLS
- APPLICATION SPECIFICATIONS
- IMPLEMENTATION PLANNING
- USER TRAINING
- APPLICATION PROGRAMMING and TESTING
- CONVERSION PLANNING
- SYSTEMS TEST

TOP MANAGEMENT REVIEW and DECISION

 TOUCHE ROSS & CO.

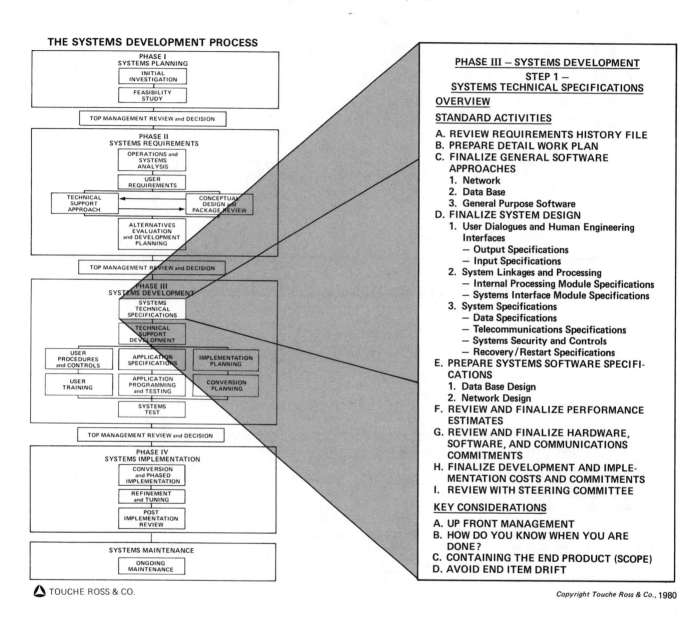

The Systems Technical Specifications step is the first of nine steps in Phase III — Systems Development. Phase II (Systems Requirements) activities formulated the technical and application needs of the proposed system. The steps that follow are Technical Support Development (Step 2), Application Specifications (Step 3), Application Programming and Testing (Step 4), User Procedures and Controls (Step 5), User Training (Step 6), Implementation Planning (Step 7), Conversion Planning (Step 8), and Systems Test (Step 9).

Systems Technical Specifications, which are defined in detail during this step, have been identified in Phase II, Steps 3 (Technical Support Approach) and 4 (Conceptual Design and Package Review activities), and evaluated in Phase II, Step 5 (Alternatives Evaluation and Development Planning) activities. Documentation resulting from this step is the basis upon which technicians implement the technical approach in the next step of this phase. Thus, these specification activities must be carefully planned, conducted, and documented.

Project team members involved in this step generally are involved in all of the technical activities that follow. The team may be expanded from the previous phase by including members who have additional technical skills necessary to complete this detailed specification step.

The specifications step generally includes nine major activities. The first two are preparatory, consisting of project team orientation and detailed work plan development. The next two center around finalization of the technical software and systems design considerations necessary to complete this step. The fifth activity is the actual preparation of the systems software specifications and requires the most time and effort. The last four activities are the review and finalization of performance estimates and commitments, the finalization of cost commitments, and review with the steering committee.

STANDARD ACTIVITIES

Review Requirements History File

As was the case with previous steps, the Systems Technical Specifications step begins with an activity designed specifically to allow project team members to orient themselves and review the work to date. This is a brief activity, consisting primarily of a paper review of findings, recommendations, and documentation. If changes have occurred since the conclusion of Systems Requirements, their probable impact on the structure and the timetable for this step and the remainder of the project is assessed. The changes are then reflected in the work plan that is prepared in the next activity.

Prepare Detailed Work Plan

The project plan for this step was prepared during the last step of Phase II, Systems Requirements: Alternatives Evaluation and Development Planning. However, actual personnel assignments to the project team and the impact of any changes identified in the above review results in a detailed work plan and project timetable. In addition, the steering committee may need to provide a new authorization to continue a project that has become marginally cost effective, or less attractive because changes uncovered during the first two review and planning activities in this Step. Less serious changes may require only a few revised or additional tasks in the work plan.

Finalize General
Software Approaches In the previous Phase, Systems Requirements, several technical approaches were identified and evaluated. In this activity, the approach selected (there may be more than one) is finalized and documented to the level of detail necessary to initiate the next activity, finalization of the systems design.

Network. The communication network environment is defined to the level of detail necessary for an adequate implementation of the network in the next Step, Technical Support Development. This includes items such as the communication approaches to be used: leased vs. dedicated lines, half vs. full duplex operation, synchronous vs. asynchronous, band widths, and error rates. The communications protocols to be used must also be determined in detail. The importance of this network design cannot be minimized because of the ramifications it will have on the design of the application programs.

Data Base. The general data base design is reviewed and defined in detail for the particular application. The types of relationships per various schema are defined. Pointer structure and logical relationships, as well as utilities for such functions as loading, unloading, backing out, listing, dumping, modifying, and reorganizing are also specified.

The data base management structure, and the data base management system itself, are finalized in this activity. Integration of these two concepts and related software with the communications network design is also considered.

General-Purpose Software. Detailed specifications for any new general-purpose software required for the Systems Development and Implementation phases of the project are finalized in this activity. Included are operating system software, on-line communications system software, network communications software, data base management, other systems software, and utility software.

Finalize System Design The key output of this activity is a detailed systems design document. This document will be used in Technical Support Development, Step 2, as well as in Applications Specifications, Step 3. Its components include:

User Dialogues and Human Engineering Interfaces. Specific documents are defined in detail in this step. They include both inputs and outputs to the system. Emphasis is placed on understanding how the user will input data to the system and use the imformation provided. This is the point at which the data base and files are initially defined at the data element level. This also is a point at which systems naming conventions are identified for the new system. Sample output reports are defined and reviewed with the user to ensure that what is being designed is fully compatible with requirements as defined in Phase II; similarly, detailed consideration is given to data capture and entry or "inputs." This is an interactive process, and specifications do change. The key is obtaining user agreement and commitment to what will be produced. To this end, it is important to provide both users and management with a general systems description — an overview of what the system will be doing and how it will do it.

System Linkages and Processing. A system flowchart is produced. This flowchart describes two systems components: the manual system and the

136

mechanized computer system. Major processing module functions and interfaces with other systems are defined. The design takes into account the human engineering interfaces as defined in the previous task.

Systems Specifications. The project team in this activity works with previously developed documentation that defines a business problem and its solution. The end product produced by the team is the documentation necessary to implement the solution to the business problem, utilizing technical resources. The work structure follows a top-down pattern. Technical design begins with higher level functions within the new system and moves downward to a series of functions and subfunctions, adding depth and detail at every level.

Data element definitions initiated earlier are expanded at this point. Once the data element definitions are updated, the project team also updates the data dictionary. In projects that do not involve a data base, all new system master files are completely designed in this activity. Care is taken to allow for future changes that will impact file design. The File Contents and Characteristics form is used for listing all information normally associated with the Cobol file definition statement. In addition, by providing spaces for appropriate entries, this form helps apply the discipline necessary to gather information needed for decisions on time frames and storage media or file retention, backup, recovery, security, and privacy.

For systems using a data base, each data base segment is specified in this activity, in terms of:

— Its data elements (as defined above).
— Its hierarchical or other relationships with other data base records.

The key end item produced involving the data is a glossary of terms, as well as a cross-referenced index listing where each data element is used.

Detailed telecommunications specifications are defined in this activity. This includes network specifications, hardware specifications, communications specifications, and the test checklist that will be used in the next activity.

Systems security and control features are then defined. This definition includes a summary of the control design for the system, specific security measures, and control specifications. A test checklist is generated to identify those areas requiring extensive testing during the Systems Test (Step 9). Backup, recovery, and restart specifications are also defined. The specifications are oriented in terms of the technical approach selected, users' operational needs, and the specific risks associated with each type of failure. In developing these specifications, overheads and other implementation costs must be considered and weighted against the related risk; not all systems need to be duplexed, nor do all transactions or files need to be duplicated.

Prepare System
Software Specifications

Any additional design documentation which is necessitated by a technical support approach is defined in this activity.

Data Base Design. The data base design is completed in this activity. The types of items to be included are the data base maps, the access specifications, and the performance measurement criteria.

Also, a set of specifications is developed for programs necessary to test the data base approach selected. This includes:

— Initially building the data base.

— Adding, deleting, and changing the data base records.

— Retrieving individual records.

— Reorganizing the data base.

— Debugging utility programs.

— Collecting statistics in addition to vendor-supplied statistics.

Network Design. As was the case with the data base design, the network design and detailed specifications are defined in this activity. Included are specifications necessary to define the environment and the checklist of items to be tested.

Review and Finalize Performance Estimates

Based upon the statistics developed in the Systems Requirements phase and the performance data developed in the general design of this step, performance criteria are finalized. This includes detailed definitions of response time, storage space, and any other factors that will affect human engineering and technical resource requirements. Throughout the remainder of the project, these estimates are used as the base measuring points, although they may be reviewed and updated.

Review and Finalize Hardware, Software and Communication Commitments

With completion of the design and detailed specifications for the selected approach, the remaining project work plans and time charts are updated. Specific emphasis is placed on finalizing the availability of hardware, software, and communications networks. Since these are all normally long lead-time items, a commitment is obtained for each component's operational availability.

Finalize Development and Implementation Costs and Commitments

Cost comparisons and resource requirements are now updated. This includes a complete reevaluation of manpower and equipment requirements, as well as a reassessment of ongoing cost and staffing requirements necessary to maintain the system. The economic evaluation summary is updated to reflect the new information. A management summary is developed and reviewed with the steering committee, if significant changes have occurred.

Review with Steering Committee

The new economic evaluation summary, time charts, detailed work plans, and management summary are reviewed with the steering committee, emphasizing any changes resulting from the development of the systems technical specifications.

KEY CONSIDERATIONS

Up-Front Management

The purpose of this step is to discern and control the purely technical factors that will impact the system. By emphasizing the placement of these technical components in this early step, management of the technical problem can be initiated as quickly as its components are understood. If a major problem is encountered, decisions at this point can minimize its impact on the system as perceived by users.

How Do You Know When You Are Done?

As each additional level of detail is developed, specific items produced by each activity and task are defined and documented. As these end items are produced and reviewed, management is assured that the project team is accomplishing what had been planned.

Systems design efforts involve a high degree of afterthought. Any system that has been designed or is in use will be subject to innumerable suggestions for improvement, modification, or refinement. Many systems analysts are tempted to incorporate changes as they are suggested. This is often done without sufficient consideration of costs or delays that may be incurred.

Insofar as possible, the systems design should be halted at the conclusion of this step. Unless major flaws come to light, changes should be deferred until after the system's implementation. Any proposed improvements and changes that appear valid are documented and carried forward to the Post-Implementation Review in Phase IV, at which time they are considered seriously and scheduled.

Containing the End Product (Scope)

Project teams should keep the business problems they were originally asked to solve in mind as they work on the technical design of a new system. One technical thought too often leads to another and, almost without thinking, the original problem is redefined in its most complex manifestation. Care must be taken to avoid losing the problem in a labyrinth — or having the designer deliver a limousine when the user wanted an economy compact. This can best be done by continued reference to pragmatic management concerns and to the subsequent statements of user requirements that guided determination of objectives and the allocation of resources in the first place.

Avoiding End-Item Drift

End-item drift is related to the problem of containment — or scope. There is often a tendency on the part of EDP technicians to become intrigued by technical niceties or "what the system could do" at the expense of specific business problems and opportunities to be addressed by the developing system. In other words, technicians may be carried away by the challenge of making the system more sophisticated, to the point where the end product may drift away from its original objective. Thus, for example, the accounts receivable objective may become lost as the focus shifts to on-line order entry and inventory management as a source of receivable data. Again, continued reference to earlier documentation — particularly the user requirements — can keep the focus on target and the costs and deadlines within sight.

STANDARD ACTIVITIES/END ITEMS

TOUCHE ROSS

ID/TITLE SYSTEMS TECHNICAL SPECIFICATIONS

PROJECT NO.

ORGANIZATION PHASE III,

STEP 1

SYSTEM DEVELOPMENT

USER REP

☐ PHASE ☑ ACTIVITY ☐ SUBTASK

☐ STEP ☒ TASK ☐

PREPARED BY MWJ SH

REVIEWED BY CB CB

DATE 3/29/80 11/1/80

PHASE III-1 III-1

NUMBER	PHASE/STEP/ACTIVITY/TASK/SUBTASK NAME	END ITEM	FORM NO.	PERFORMED BY	DUE DATE	APPROVED BY	DATE
A.	Review Requirements History File	Project Plan	102				
B.	Prepare Detailed Work Plan	Work Outline	101				
C.	Finalize General Software Approaches						
C.1	- Network	Network Approach	127, 128, 142				
C.2	- Data Base	Data Base Approach	127, 128, 142				
C.3	- General Purpose Software	Systems Software Approach	142				
D.	Finalize System Design						
D.1	- User Dialogues and Human Engineering Interfaces	Document Definition	132				
		VDT Screen Layout	161				
		VDT Support	162				
		Output Report Layout	164				
		Computer Output Report	163				
		Multiple Card Layout	160				
		System Naming Control	170				
		Data Base/File Contents	152				

STANDARD ACTIVITIES/END ITEMS

TOUCHE ROSS

ID/TITLE __SYSTEMS TECHNICAL SPECIFICATIONS__

ORGANIZATION __PHASE III,__
STEP __1__
SYSTEM __DEVELOPMENT__
USER REP _____

☐ PHASE   ☒ ACTIVITY   ☐ SUBTASK
☐ STEP   ☒ TASK   ☐ _____

PREPARED BY	MVJ	SH
REVIEWED BY	CR	CR
DATE	3/29/80	11/1/80
PHASE	III-1	III-1

PHASE/STEP/ACTIVITY/TASK/SUBTASK		END ITEM	FORM NO.	PERFORMED BY	DUE DATE	APPROVED BY	DATE
NUMBER	NAME						
		Record Contents	153				
		Data Base Record Layout	154				
		Transaction/Data Base Activity	155				
D.2	– System Linkages and Processing	System Flow Chart	127, 128				
		Transaction/Data Base File Activity	155				
		System Naming Control	170				
		Program/Module Function	171				
		Sort Program Parameter	174				
		Decision Tables	176				
		Table Forms	177				
		Module Table/Function	172, 173				
		Code Tables	178				
		File Split/File Merge	175				
		Test Checklist	185				

STANDARD ACTIVITIES/END ITEMS

TOUCHE ROSS

ID/TITLE SYSTEMS TECHNICAL SPECIFICATIONS

ORGANIZATION PHASE III,
STEP 1
SYSTEM DEVELOPMENT
USER REP

☐ PHASE   ☒ ACTIVITY   ☐ SUBTASK
☐ STEP   ☒ TASK

			PREPARED BY	MVJ	SH
			REVIEWED BY	CB	CB
			DATE	3/29/80	11/1/80
			PHASE	III-1	III-1	III-1

NUMBER	PHASE/STEP/ACTIVITY/TASK/SUBTASK NAME	END ITEM	FORM NO.	PERFORMED BY	DUE DATE	APPROVED BY	DATE
D.3	- System Specifications						
		Glossary of Terms	122				
		Data Element Definition	150				
		Data Element Cross Reference	151				
		Network Specification	142				
		Hardware Specifications	142				
		Communication Specifications	142				
		Module Cross Reference	151				
		Summary of Controls	141				
		Security Specification	141				
		Technical Constraints	140				
		Test Checklist	185				
		Backup Specifications	127, 128				
		Recovery Specifications	127, 128				
		Restart Specifications	142				
		Test Checklist	185				

142

STANDARD ACTIVITIES/END ITEMS

TOUCHE ROSS

ORGANIZATION _____
SYSTEM _____
USER REP _____

PHASE III,
STEP 1
DEVELOPMENT

ID/TITLE __SYSTEMS TECHNICAL SPECIFICATIONS__

☐ PHASE ☐ STEP ☒ ACTIVITY ☒ TASK ☐ SUBTASK ☐ _____

	PREPARED BY	REVIEWED BY	DATE	PHASE
	MVJ	CB	3/29/80	III-1
	SH	CB	11/1/80	III-1

NUMBER	PHASE/STEP/ACTIVITY/TASK/SUBTASK NAME	END ITEM	FORM NO.	PERFORMED BY	DUE DATE	APPROVED BY	DATE
E.	Prepare Systems Software Specifications						
E.1	– Data Base Design	Data Base Maps	127, 128, 142				
		Access Specifications	150, 152, 142				
		Data Base Contents and Characteristics	152				
		Test Checklist	185				
		Performance Measurements	142				
E.2	– Network Design	Network Specifications	127, 128, 142				
		Test Checklist	185				
		Performance Measurements	142				
F.	Review and Finalize Performance Estimates	Performance Estimates	142, 177				
G.	Review and Finalize Hardware Software and Communication Commitments	Project Plan	102				
H.	Finalize Development and Implementation Costs and Commitments	Development Cost Measurement	105				
		Programming Estimate	104				
		Operating Cost Summary	145				
		Staffing Requirements	126				
		Economic Evaluation Summary	148				
I.	Review with Steering Committee	Management Summary	149				

THE SYSTEMS DEVELOPMENT PROCESS

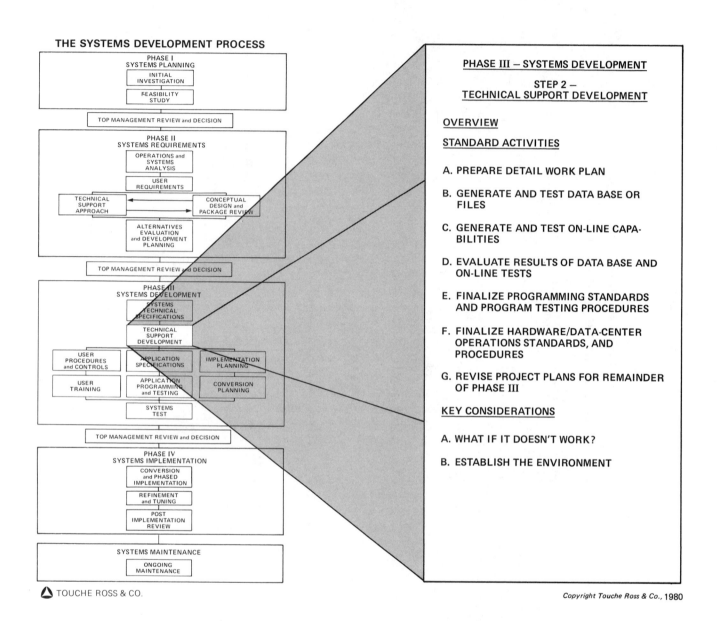

PHASE I
SYSTEMS PLANNING

INITIAL INVESTIGATION

FEASIBILITY STUDY

TOP MANAGEMENT REVIEW and DECISION

PHASE II
SYSTEMS REQUIREMENTS

OPERATIONS and SYSTEMS ANALYSIS

USER REQUIREMENTS

TECHNICAL SUPPORT APPROACH ← → CONCEPTUAL DESIGN and PACKAGE REVIEW

ALTERNATIVES EVALUATION and DEVELOPMENT PLANNING

TOP MANAGEMENT REVIEW and DECISION

PHASE III
SYSTEMS DEVELOPMENT

SYSTEMS TECHNICAL SPECIFICATIONS

TECHNICAL SUPPORT DEVELOPMENT

USER PROCEDURES and CONTROLS | APPLICATION SPECIFICATIONS | IMPLEMENTATION PLANNING

USER TRAINING | APPLICATION PROGRAMMING and TESTING | CONVERSION PLANNING

SYSTEMS TEST

TOP MANAGEMENT REVIEW and DECISION

PHASE IV
SYSTEMS IMPLEMENTATION

CONVERSION and PHASED IMPLEMENTATION

REFINEMENT and TUNING

POST IMPLEMENTATION REVIEW

SYSTEMS MAINTENANCE

ONGOING MAINTENANCE

▲ TOUCHE ROSS & CO.

PHASE III – SYSTEMS DEVELOPMENT

STEP 2 –
TECHNICAL SUPPORT DEVELOPMENT

OVERVIEW

STANDARD ACTIVITIES

A. PREPARE DETAIL WORK PLAN

B. GENERATE AND TEST DATA BASE OR FILES

C. GENERATE AND TEST ON-LINE CAPA-BILITIES

D. EVALUATE RESULTS OF DATA BASE AND ON-LINE TESTS

E. FINALIZE PROGRAMMING STANDARDS AND PROGRAM TESTING PROCEDURES

F. FINALIZE HARDWARE/DATA-CENTER OPERATIONS STANDARDS, AND PROCEDURES

G. REVISE PROJECT PLANS FOR REMAINDER OF PHASE III

KEY CONSIDERATIONS

A. WHAT IF IT DOESN'T WORK?

B. ESTABLISH THE ENVIRONMENT

The size of the project team usually increases dramatically as the project moves toward implementation. The major objective of the Technical Support Development step is to finalize procedures and programming policies so that this increased level of effort can be efficiently and effectively managed.

A secondary objective of the Technical Support Development step is to minimize risks inherent in any assumptions made about the operation or efficiency of the software or hardware during the design process.

This step marks a transition from a fact-finding and creative process to one that actually constructs, tests, and implements the system. It represents the last chance to make significant or far-reaching changes to the detailed design without incurring major reprogramming or reimplementation costs.

STANDARD ACTIVITIES

Prepare Detailed Work Plan Technical personnel, if not already part of the original project team, were added to the project during the Systems Technical Specifications step (Phase III, Step 1). As a result, the project team that produced the technical specifications will generally carry through the execution of the Technical Support Development step. It should therefore not be necessary to review prior assumptions or outputs at great length, since this material should be very clear in the minds of the project team. The first activity is to review the project plan and develop a detailed work plan to establish all necessary conventions, verify the operation of the hardware and software, and establish the environment for programming policies and testing procedures.

Define and Assess Data Base or File Structures If a data base management system is to be employed, it is particularly critical that the project team build a prototype data base. There are three reasons for building a test data base:

— First, it allows the technical support staff to test all access paths through the data base to make sure they function as designed.

— Second, the test should include enough data to enable the technical support team to verify the operational characteristics of the finished system. For example, it is important to determine at this time whether or not access time requirements can be achieved and to make sure that individual processing time requirements are not excessive.

— A third reason for building the test data base at this time is to make it available to programmers during application program development and testing. Because of this, it is sometimes desirable to design a specific version of the data base that can provide the variety of conditions and records needed to achieve thorough testing. For this reason, the final "test" data base may be slightly different in content from the one used to verify access timing or system performance.

It is necessary to build standard files for program testing and to create and test any unusual or exotic file-accessing techniques, even if the system does not employ a data base management system. In any case, at the completion of this activity, prototype file and/or data bases should be created, listed, and controls established and catalogued along with standard procedures for their use in application program testing and development. All files, records and data base segments should be fully defined with standard field names ready for inclusion in programming specifications and in programs themselves. A copy library is thus one possible result of this activity.

Define and Assess On-Line Capabilities

If the system to be developed either employs a standard communications handler or requires that special software be developed to handle on-line transactions, the on-line software and hardware configuration should be generated and tested. As was the case with the data base development activity, the major objective of this phase is to define and test all standard input/output protocol and procedures. Not only is it necessary to verify all operating characteristics and efficiencies of the hardware and software prior to the development of program specifications, but it is also necessary to establish standard linkages and coding conventions instead of leaving it up to the individual programmer. As a general rule, it is also desirable to finalize and implement terminal or on-line security software or procedures during this step.

Evaluate Results of Data Base and On-Line Assessments

Once data base or on-line software has been generated, the technical support team should be able to verify virtually all the critical operating assumptions and characteristics of the system before starting the major application program specification and programming tasks. For example, if the system includes both on-line communications and a data base manager, a few small programs may be generated quickly and easily to exercise the data base manager and the on-line software together in order to determine the effectiveness of the interaction and demands on the total computer configuration. If the interaction causes excessive thrashing or places severe demands on a component (such as a channel or disk), it is now possible to adjust the approach, hardware, or software without making complete sections of the system obsolete. If the system cannot perform to operational specification under test conditions, it certainly will not do so in full operation.

Confirm Programming Standards and Program Testing Procedures

When key operating assumptions about the configuration and the software have been verified, the result of that effort must be formalized by specifying standard input/output procedures and naming conventions. All programming standards and testing procedures should also be defined. Standard procedures already exist in many data processing environments, and this exercise will primarily be one of integrating those standards that are specific to this particular project with those that are the existing installation standards. However sophisticated the EDP organization, it is now up to the project manager to assure that all necessary development and testing procedures and policies have been reviewed and accepted by data processing operations management and programming supervisors. It should never be necessary for an individual programmer to define procedures, establish test policies, or negotiate with operations management at some later stage. The procedures required to generate, test, and document a computer program should be established by the time this activity is completed.

Confirm Hardware/Data Center Operations Standards and Procedures

At this stage of the developmental process, the technical support team must know enough about the operating requirements of the system to first define data center operating procedures and standards. Critical system timings and hardware and software support requirements should be reviewed with operations management to assure that deadlines can be met and to avoid operational conflicts. It now becomes possible to familiarize operating personnel with performance characteristics of the system as it develops and to begin to outline and define operating procedures required by data center management to support the system in its final form. Data center management is thus able to begin training operations personnel as the system moves into the testing stage. If necessary, the fact that special procedures and documentation are required can now be highlighted and planned for in the development of manual procedures and training plans in subsequent steps in this phase.

Revise Project Plans for the Remainder of Phase III, as Required

The systems development project is now about to enter the most expensive and intense part of the sytems development process. It is not unusual to expand the project team at this time. Specialized personnel may be brought in to create program specifications, write programs, develop procedures, and train personnel. For the first time, the project may place significant demands on computing resources for program development and testing.

It is therefore very important to the success of the project to manage all of these activities carefully. One objective of the first two steps in this phase is to assure that the design of the system be as complete and as simple as possible. Another is to assure that individual programs or modules are logically independent. The project team must be able to proceed with the definition and programming of any program or module in the system without affecting the logic or performance of any other program or module. In other words, it is now desirable to maximize flexibility in assigning and scheduling units of work in order to minimize the time required to build the system and the complexity of the programs to be written and tested.

As a general rule, it is desirable to keep the Application Specification and Programming steps as short as possible in order to reduce the time during which the project team essentially loses user contact.

At this point in the project, most contingencies should be resolved and the project leader should be in a position to develop a detailed schedule allowing for maximum overlap in the following steps of this phase. If all of the above activities have been completed and all the issues resolved, this schedule is detailed enough to maximize the output of the project team with a minimum amount of risk.

KEY CONSIDERATION

What If It Doesn't Work?

Once it has completed the systems technical specifications, the project team has defined what the system is to do and how it is to do it. If the team were to now proceed directly into programming and implementation, errors would only be discovered in the finished product. A major objective of the Technical Support Development step is to isolate any technical assumptions or constraint critical to the success of the system and to confirm it before implementation.

A computer system is more likely to fail because of an incorrect assumption about the operation or performance of the software than because of a programming error. The design team has a better overall grasp of the system and its design vulnerabilities and therefore understands those assumptions best. At this point, the strategy is to minimize the probability of failure for the rest of the effort. In fact, major conflicts and problems within any of the activities in this step are best discovered now. It is entirely possible that the project team will have to go back and modify the original design. At this time, only the design will be changed. If discovered later, errors would be far more costly.

Establish the Environment

Project teams are often too eager to probe the programming process, leaving it to each programmer to finalize testing conventions and procedures. In such cases, not only is maintenance made difficult by nonstandard programming practices, but each programmer will also tend to make the same set of mistakes with regard to input/output procedures and the use of specialized software. Time is inevitably wasted and unusual program logic structures result from misconceptions about the hardware and software. It is therefore highly desirable at this time to expend additional effort to finalize the environment in which the programs must be developed. This effort usually saves a great deal of time during later steps and makes the lives of technician and programmer alike a lot easier.

STANDARD ACTIVITIES/END ITEMS

TOUCHE ROSS

ORGANIZATION __PHASE III,__
__STEP 2__
SYSTEM __DEVELOPMENT__
USER REP _____

ID/TITLE __TECHNICAL SUPPORT DEVELOPMENT__

☐ PHASE   ☒ ACTIVITY   ☐ SUBTASK
☐ STEP   ☒ TASK   ☐ _____

PAGE __1__ OF __2__
PROJECT NO. _____

	PREPARED BY	MVJ	SH
REVIEWED BY		CB	CB
DATE		3/29/80	11/1/80
PHASE		III-2	III-2

NUMBER	PHASE/STEP/ACTIVITY/TASK/SUBTASK NAME	END ITEM	FORM NO.	PERFORMED BY	DUE DATE	APPROVED BY	DATE
A.	Prepare Detailed Work Plan	Work Outline	101				
		Project Plan	102				
B.	Define and Assess Data Base or File Structures	Test Checklist	185				
		System Test Checklist	180				
		Data Base/File Test Plan	190				
		Parameter Test Plan	190				
		Computer Test Plan	194				
		Walkthru Log	186				
		Test Data					
		Test Data Base/Files					
		Results Form	198				
		Problem/Request Control	111				
		Approval Form	199				
C.	Define and Assess On-Line Capabilities	Test Checklist	185				
		System Test Checklist	180				
		On-Line Test Plan	190				
		Parameter Test Plan	190				

STANDARD ACTIVITIES/END ITEMS

TOUCHE ROSS

ID/TITLE: TECHNICAL SUPPORT DEVELOPMENT

ORGANIZATION: PHASE III,
STEP 2
SYSTEM: DEVELOPMENT
USER REP: _____

☐ PHASE ☒ ACTIVITY ☐ SUBTASK
☐ STEP   ☒ TASK   ☐ _____

PAGE 2 OF 2

PROJECT NO.: _____

	PREPARED BY	MVJ	SH
	REVIEWED BY	CB	CB
	DATE	3/29/80	11/1/80
	PHASE	III-2	III-2

NUMBER	PHASE/STEP/ACTIVITY/TASK/SUBTASK NAME	END ITEM	FORM NO.	PERFORMED BY	DUE DATE	APPROVED BY	DATE
		Computer Test Plan	194				
		Walkthru Log	186				
		Test On-Line System and Data					
		Results Form	198				
		Problem/Request Control	111				
		Approval Form	199				
D.	Evaluate Results of Data Base and On-Line Assessments	Management Summary	149				
E.	Confirm Programming Standards and Program Testing Procedures	Standards					
		Test Checklist	185				
F.	Confirm Hardware/Data Center Operations Standards and Procedures	Standards					
		Operation Checklist	183				
G.	Revise Project Plans for Remainder of Phase III, As Required	Work Outline	101				
		Project Plan	102				
		Programming Estimate	104				
		Standard Activities/End Items	106				

© Touche Ross & Co., 1980
All Rights Reserved

150

Phase III - Systems Development
Step 3 - Application Specifications

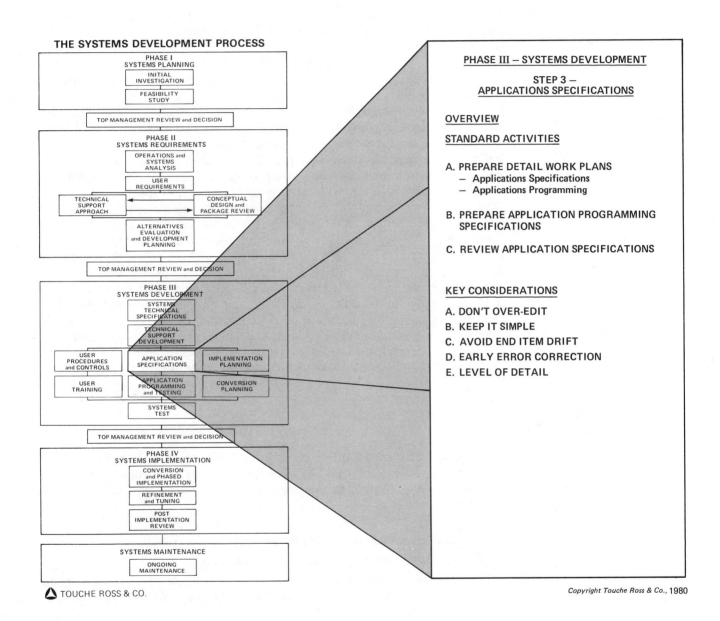

THE SYSTEMS DEVELOPMENT PROCESS

PHASE I
SYSTEMS PLANNING
INITIAL INVESTIGATION
FEASIBILITY STUDY

TOP MANAGEMENT REVIEW and DECISION

PHASE II
SYSTEMS REQUIREMENTS
OPERATIONS and SYSTEMS ANALYSIS
USER REQUIREMENTS
TECHNICAL SUPPORT APPROACH
CONCEPTUAL DESIGN and PACKAGE REVIEW
ALTERNATIVES EVALUATION and DEVELOPMENT PLANNING

TOP MANAGEMENT REVIEW and DECISION

PHASE III
SYSTEMS DEVELOPMENT
SYSTEMS TECHNICAL SPECIFICATIONS
TECHNICAL SUPPORT DEVELOPMENT
USER PROCEDURES and CONTROLS
APPLICATION SPECIFICATIONS
IMPLEMENTATION PLANNING
USER TRAINING
APPLICATION PROGRAMMING and TESTING
CONVERSION PLANNING
SYSTEMS TEST

TOP MANAGEMENT REVIEW and DECISION

PHASE IV
SYSTEMS IMPLEMENTATION
CONVERSION and PHASED IMPLEMENTATION
REFINEMENT and TUNING
POST IMPLEMENTATION REVIEW

SYSTEMS MAINTENANCE
ONGOING MAINTENANCE

TOUCHE ROSS & CO.

PHASE III – SYSTEMS DEVELOPMENT
STEP 3 –
APPLICATIONS SPECIFICATIONS

OVERVIEW
STANDARD ACTIVITIES

A. PREPARE DETAIL WORK PLANS
– Applications Specifications
– Applications Programming

B. PREPARE APPLICATION PROGRAMMING SPECIFICATIONS

C. REVIEW APPLICATION SPECIFICATIONS

KEY CONSIDERATIONS

A. DON'T OVER-EDIT
B. KEEP IT SIMPLE
C. AVOID END ITEM DRIFT
D. EARLY ERROR CORRECTION
E. LEVEL OF DETAIL

Copyright Touche Ross & Co., 1980

151

Basic activities associated with the Application Specifications step involve the conversion of detailed system specifications (prepared as part of Step 1 of this phase) to programming specifications oriented to the specific hardware and software environment. This step is conducted in parallel with developing user procedures and controls, as well as with implementation planning activities.

Personnel needed to carry out this step are primarily experienced specialists with a detailed knowledge of this system's application, hardware, and software requirements. In particular, these specialists must be able to anticipate constraints and potential difficulties that may be imposed by the technical environment. Close liaison is maintained by the applications specifications personnel with the systems technical specifications team (Phase III, Step 1) and, where appropriate, with the technical support and package review teams used in Phase II; this minimizes any tendencies to "reinvent the wheel," or otherwise lead to project budget overruns.

Specification activities include finalization of the input/output record and file layouts prepared during Step 1 of this phase, plus any detail required in the definition video terminal displays. Earlier documentation relating to individual program modules is finalized, and processing details related to decision logics, coding structure and limits, and exception processing are worked out. A systems test checklist, a test plan, and test data are prepared. Finally — and perhaps most importantly — commitments are finalized for personnel and equipment required for program development and testing.

STANDARD ACTIVITIES

Prepare Detailed Work Plans As does virtually every other step, this also begins with a review of the project work files. Plans for both the specification and programming steps are now updated. Several factors are considered in the preparation of these plans:

- The scope and nature of the system to be developed.
- The hardware and software to be employed.
- The capabilities of the personnel to be assigned. This includes prior experience of the staff in both technical and nontechnical aspects of the system.
- The programming standards and convention to be used including:
  - Language conventions.
  - Allowable instruction subsets.
  - Naming conventions.
  - Programming rules.
  - Test procedures.
  - Catalogued procedures.
  - Standard routines/modules.
  - Other programming needs, tools, and techniques.

Organize Specification/ Development Teams and Conduct Structured Walkthrus

This activity begins with the assignment of specific personnel and responsibilities for developing application program specifications needed by the programmers. In organizations where a "constant project team" is employed and all activities from Systems Requirements through Systems Implementation are performed by the same people, this activity is relatively straightforward. In organizations where analysts and programmers are separated or where a development resource pool is employed, it is necessary to carefully consider the nature of the system to be implemented and to use considerable care in securing available resources from the pool.

Once the appropriate team is assembled, a structured walkthru is conducted. As used here, this process is a joint, in-depth review of detailed system specifications by the analysts who prepared them and the programmers or others who will use them as inputs in the preparation of applications specifications.

This process provides a quality control check point and an opportunity to ensure that all parties understand one another. It is one of the most important concepts of the IPT (Improved Programming Techniques) process.

The walkthrus are an iterative process. Similar reviews take place during this and the following step, Applications Programming and Testing. A better understanding of specifically how the system should function is obtained through each of these reveiws. This understanding process always begins at the start of the next activity, preparing the application programming specification.

Prepare Applications Programming Specifications

The purpose of this activity is to create documents that communicate specifications for technical solutions to business problems. As indicated earlier, input to this activity originates from the system design produced in the Systems Technical Specifications step (Phase III, Step 1). This activity provides essentially the same types of documentation, but does so in greater levels of technical detail necessary to guide programming.

A flowchart prepared as an output of Phase III, Step 1 usually represents an editing module or program as a single processing block to which one or more transaction types are presented as input, one or more files are used for lookup, and from which a work file may be prepared as output. While Step 1 may have specified the transactions and files in almost complete detail, the number, types, severity and interrelationships of the editing processes are not normally defined in a form or detail level suitable to guide programming. During the Applications Specification step, it is necessary to "explode" the flowchart for this module or program into one or more detailed flowcharts or decision tables (possibly one for each transaction type) or — if the editing is very complex — one for each data element within a transaction type. As a means of ensuring adequate, yet inexcessive detail, many experienced managers have found it helpful to implement standards. For example, the processing block or design statement in applications specifications will produce a specific range of executable source code statements: 4 to 12 statements, or 5 to 20 statements, etc.

At the applications specifications level, consideration is given not only to the full range of expected transaction types and data element values, but also to the unexpected or "possible" values and value interrelationships. It may also be necessary to go back to the intended users to ensure that editing or other processing does not become so restrictive as to bring about unrealistic demands for data perfection. Such demands can exasperate the users and can increase the workload by causing unnecessary corrections.

Finally, it should be noted that the flowcharts and/or design statements are usually not sufficient by themselves to provide the documentation needed by programmers. As discussed below, additional documentation is usually necessary.

The General-Purpose Chart Description form should always be used to support a flowchart. The form refers back to a corresponding flowchart in two ways. First, the form heading contains spaces entering the identification of the corresponding chart. Second, a column in which to enter coordinate numbers referencing specific locations on the chart is provided; this column is used before each narrative description or statement of a program function in order to relate that function to the specific input, processing step, or output on the flowchart.

In situations where the processing logic is too complex or lengthy to be effectively described on a flowchart, a decision table may be prepared. This simply provides a graphic format to facilitate the presentation of logic rules for a program or module. As was the case with the chart description form, spaces are provided for references that tie back to the corresponding flowchart.

For programs or modules that require detailed edit rules, a table form may be prepared. This table correlates data elements with the edit rules that will be applied to them. This graphically and concisely provides a tool that the programmer can use in identifying areas within a program where common subroutines can be developed and applied. If a program will need work files, they too are designed during this activity.

As indicated earlier, this step marks the point at which the work of the technical specifications and programming teams begin to overlap. To gain maximum leverage from this overlap, care should be taken in establishing a sequence in which program functions are specified. For example, functions related to file maintenance, file integrity, and common modules to be used at several points in an application should be specified first. In this way, requirements for special utility programs (e.g., building master files) are either reduced or eliminated. The common modules prioritized at this point include in-core sorts, end-of-job control reports (including file reconciliation analysis and control totals), common headings and field descriptions, and abort logic — along with processing descriptions on how to handle each. Once a function has been thoroughly and completely documented, only an appropriate reference is required to prepare subsequent documentation for the application specification.

In addition to the specification of program structure or logic and the completion of input/output and file definitions, test checklists and plans should be prepared for each program or module. This process ensures that each program or module is thoroughly checked and tested at three levels: as a stand-alone entity, as part of any program that may use or reference it, and as part of the total system.

Finally, the forecasted requirements for personnel and equipment are updated with each application specification to ensure that adequate resources are available for the compilation and testing of programs or modules that have already been defined. Proper completion of this last piece of documentation can be crucially important in ensuring that realistic implementation schedules are set and costly implementation delays are avoided.

Review Applications Specifications

Although identified as a separate activity, these reviews overlap the writing of applications specifications. Several reviews are scheduled, beginning early in the specifications-writing activity, including an important analyst and programmer review of all mainline logic and calculation specifications.

In planning a session, key program functions critical to the application are emphasized. Copies of selected specifications are predistributed to all those who are to participate in the review meeting. Every participant may then study these specifications in detail and list questions and discrepancies in advance of the meeting. During the review, each specification author directs the other attendees in discussing questions and resolving discrepancies, so that the team is assured that all requirements are adequately fulfilled. Any significant specification rework is normally done after the review session is concluded, rather than as a group effort.

For overall quality control, procedures should exist to ensure that technical managers responsible for the project are advised about questions, discrepancies, and resolutions. The sooner problems and discrepancies are identified and corrected, the more cost effective the development process becomes.

KEY CONSIDERATIONS

Don't Over-Edit

The Applications Specifications step may be the first one to realize some of the detailed ramifications of "computerization." As indicated earlier, the documentation resulting from this step provides not only what is expected, but also for what is unexpected or "impossible." Good systems and programming specialists are characterized by thoroughness and great attention to detail; there is often a tendency to over-edit application specifications. Uncontrolled, this search for data purity and perfection leads to an unexpectedly high rate of data rejection and/or flagging of "errors."

In an operational environment, over-editing results in a high level of frustration on the part of the user. In a conversion environment (where resources are frequently already strained), it can lead to systems collapse or total user rejection. This is a problem, because all defined error data must be trapped, collected, corrected, and reentered — which increases user workload. Until the error correction is done, the data usefulness may be of questionable value.

To minimize these problems, the tendency to over-edit should be avoided. In fact, to maximize user acceptance and usability of the system, it may be desirable to "relax" the editing logic and make every effort to minimize unnecessary data rejection. As users gain discipline, familiarity, and confidence in the system, additional editing can be effectively added with full user support and cooperation.

Keep It Simple

The same stimuli that causes over-editing can also lead to other excesses in complexity or sophistication. Programmers seem to have a natural tendency to exploit the full capabilities of the hardware and software resources available to them. However, unless response time requirements or other constraints make it absolutely essential, unnecessarily clever or complex programming should be avoided. Cost-effective program maintenance requires simple and understandable designs.

Avoid End-Item Drift

During the previously described detailed analysis of the System Technical Specifications (which is essential in preparing Applications Specifications for programming), virtually the entire development process and related systems logic are reviewed. This gives the original designers an opportunity to rethink and improve the problem and, if programming specialists have been added to the team, the added resources can provide new insights into the technical solutions to the business problem. The result is often a tendency to completely rework material prepared to that point, and perhaps make unnecessary changes to the proposed system's basic functioning. Unnecessary changes in system function are defined as "end-item drift."

Minimizing end-item drift is similar in nature to managing maintenance. Each proposed change must be evaluated in terms of criticality, costs and benefits, and — for new systems — in terms of impact on the project schedule. In effect, good management requires a disciplined approach that separates necessary change from "nice" ones. It also involves continued liaison with the intended users to ensure that original objectives are neither subverted nor overelaborated.

Early Error Correction

Structured walkthrus and peer reviews can contribute significantly to the overall productivity of the systems implementation effort. To be most effective, however, these reviews are conducted as soon as possible after the more creative activities have been completed. If too much time passes, the designer tends to forget the reasoning and rationale used to support the approach, or the particular techniques used to document it.

Once an error has been noted as a result of a review or a walkthru, the correction process is managed to ensure quick remedial action. A Walkthru Log form that lists every required action may be used to help the manager follow up on the action taken.

Level of Detail

The level of detail required in the output of this step depends to some degree on the organization of the development team and the strength and depth of the programming team. Where there is organizational separation between analysts and programmers, or where the programming team is small or consists essentially of coders, the level of detail has to be much greater. The size or complexity of the system and of the language(s) used also impacts the level of detail. A powerful report writer language requires less detail than an exhaustive assembler language editing routine. At the very least, sufficient detail is provided to convey the systems intent and to avoid end-item drift or overelaboration of the technical solution compared to the business problem. It may be useful to define the level of detail in terms of the number of expected lines of program code (for example, 10 to 15 lines of executable source code for each unit of specification).

A greater level of detail usually pays off during the testing and conversion steps because an inadequately defined program invariably leads to redefinition and may delay the implementation of an entire system. Further, as this step leads to the allocation of specific programming tasks to individual programmers or coders, as well as to the preparation of data center resource requirements, it is useful for project management to have a clear written statement of the actual programming requirements. Finally, there are the countless examples of project overruns caused by project management's attempt to bypass or abbreviate the Applications Specifications step and to begin coding directly from the documentation of user requirements and system specifications.

STANDARD ACTIVITIES/END ITEMS

TOUCHE ROSS

ORGANIZATION: PHASE III,
STEP 3
SYSTEM: DEVELOPMENT
USER REP:

ID/TITLE: APPLICATION SPECIFICATIONS

☐ PHASE ☐ STEP ☒ ACTIVITY ☒ TASK ☐ SUBTASK ☐

PREPARED BY	MVJ	SH
REVIEWED BY	CB	CB
DATE	3/29/80	11/1/80
PHASE	III-3	III-3

NUMBER	PHASE/STEP/ACTIVITY/TASK/SUBTASK NAME	END ITEM	FORM NO.	PERFORMED BY	DUE DATE	APPROVED BY	DATE
A.	Prepare Detailed Work Plans	Programming Estimates	104				
A.1	- Applications Specification	Work Outline	101				
		Project Plan	102				
A.2	- Applications Programming	Work Outline	101				
		Project Plan	102				
B.	Organize Specification/Development Teams and Conduct Structured Walkthrus	Walkthru Log	186				
C.	Prepare Application Specifications	Data Base/File Contents and Characteristics	152				
		Program/Module Function	171				
		Module Function Support	172				
		Module Table	173				
		Sort Program Parameter	174				
		File Split/File Merge	175				
		System Naming Control	170				
		Multiple Card Layout	160				
		VDT Screen Layout	161				
		VDT Support	162				

STANDARD ACTIVITIES/END ITEMS

TOUCHE ROSS

ID/TITLE __APPLICATION SPECIFICATIONS__

PREPARED BY	MVJ
REVIEWED BY	CB
DATE	3/29/80
PHASE	III-3

	SH
	CB
	11/1/80
	III-3

ORGANIZATION __PHASE III,__

__STEP 3__

SYSTEM __DEVELOPMENT__

USER REP ____

☐ PHASE ☒ ACTIVITY ☐ SUBTASK

☐ STEP ☒ TASK ☐ ____

NUMBER	PHASE/STEP/ACTIVITY/TASK/SUBTASK NAME	END ITEM	FORM NO.	PERFORMED BY	DUE DATE	APPROVED BY	DATE
		Output Layout	164				
		Print Program	165				
		Print Control	166				
		Decision Logic	176				
		Tabular Relationships	177				
		Detailed Flow Charts	127, 128				
		General Descriptions	142				
		Code Tables	178				
		File Layouts	154				
		Module Cross Reference	151				
		Test Checklist	185				
		System Test Checklist	180				
		Computer Test Plan	194				
		Additional Test Data					
		Additional Test Data Base/Files					
		Personnel and Equipment Plan	193				

STANDARD ACTIVITIES/END ITEMS

TOUCHE ROSS

ORGANIZATION ___PHASE III,___

STEP 3

SYSTEM ___DEVELOPMENT___

USER REP ___

ID/TITLE ___APPLICATION SPECIFICATIONS___

☐ PHASE ☒ ACTIVITY ☐ SUBTASK
☐ STEP   ☒ TASK   ☐ ___

PAGE ___3___ OF ___3___
PROJECT NO. ___

		PREPARED BY	MVJ	SH
		REVIEWED BY	CB	CB
		DATE	3/29/80	11/1/80
		PHASE	III-3	III-3

PHASE/STEP/ACTIVITY/TASK/SUBTASK		END ITEM	FORM NO.	PERFORMED BY	DUE DATE	APPROVED BY	DATE
NUMBER	NAME						
		Work Outline	101				
		Detailed Schedule	102				
D.	Review Application Specifications						

© Touche Ross & Co., 1980
All Rights Reserved

159

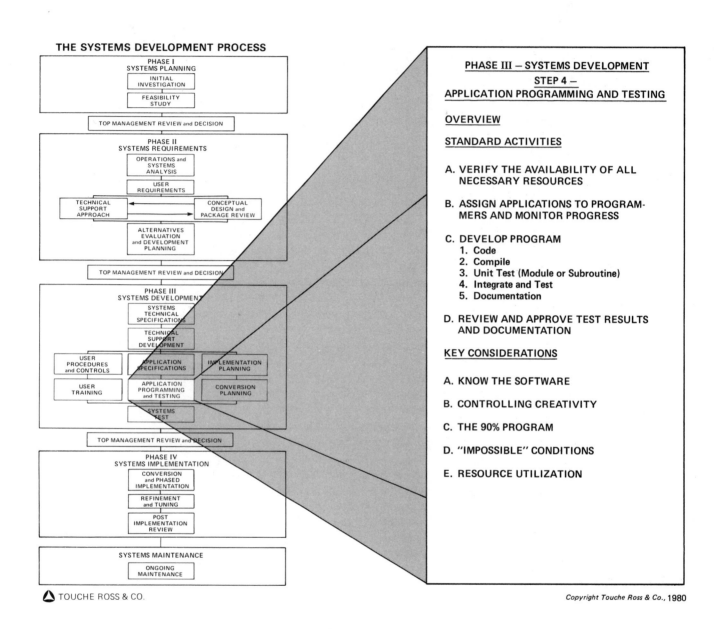

THE SYSTEMS DEVELOPMENT PROCESS

PHASE I
SYSTEMS PLANNING

INITIAL
INVESTIGATION

FEASIBILITY
STUDY

TOP MANAGEMENT REVIEW and DECISION

PHASE II
SYSTEMS REQUIREMENTS

OPERATIONS and
SYSTEMS
ANALYSIS

USER
REQUIREMENTS

TECHNICAL
SUPPORT
APPROACH

CONCEPTUAL
DESIGN and
PACKAGE REVIEW

ALTERNATIVES
EVALUATION
and DEVELOPMENT
PLANNING

TOP MANAGEMENT REVIEW and DECISION

PHASE III
SYSTEMS DEVELOPMENT

SYSTEMS
TECHNICAL
SPECIFICATIONS

TECHNICAL
SUPPORT
DEVELOPMENT

USER
PROCEDURES
and CONTROLS

APPLICATION
SPECIFICATIONS

IMPLEMENTATION
PLANNING

USER
TRAINING

APPLICATION
PROGRAMMING
and TESTING

CONVERSION
PLANNING

SYSTEMS
TEST

TOP MANAGEMENT REVIEW and DECISION

PHASE IV
SYSTEMS IMPLEMENTATION

CONVERSION
and PHASED
IMPLEMENTATION

REFINEMENT
and TUNING

POST
IMPLEMENTATION
REVIEW

SYSTEMS MAINTENANCE

ONGOING
MAINTENANCE

TOUCHE ROSS & CO.

PHASE III – SYSTEMS DEVELOPMENT
STEP 4 –
APPLICATION PROGRAMMING AND TESTING

OVERVIEW

STANDARD ACTIVITIES

A. VERIFY THE AVAILABILITY OF ALL
   NECESSARY RESOURCES

B. ASSIGN APPLICATIONS TO PROGRAM-
   MERS AND MONITOR PROGRESS

C. DEVELOP PROGRAM
   1. Code
   2. Compile
   3. Unit Test (Module or Subroutine)
   4. Integrate and Test
   5. Documentation

D. REVIEW AND APPROVE TEST RESULTS
   AND DOCUMENTATION

KEY CONSIDERATIONS

A. KNOW THE SOFTWARE

B. CONTROLLING CREATIVITY

C. THE 90% PROGRAM

D. "IMPOSSIBLE" CONDITIONS

E. RESOURCE UTILIZATION

OVERVIEW   This step requires conversion of applications specifications into machine executable instructions, unit and string testing of those instructions, preparation of documentation, and delivery of the completed operational programs or modules to the project management team for systems test. This is the most directly hardware- and systems software-related activity in the development phase, both because hardware instructions are being prepared and because considerable hardware and system software resources are typically required for program compilation and testing.

The Applications Programming and Testing step is carried on simultaneously with other activities in the areas of user procedures, training, and conversion planning. A great deal of applications programming and testing can be done in parallel with its predecessor, the Applications Specifications step, particularly where a top-down systems design approach has been followed. The overlap provides an opportunity for project managers to save time, since applications specifications and applications programming and testing account for a very substantial portion of the total time in the Systems Development phase.

Personnel required during this step of the development phase must have a working knowledge of the appropriate programming language(s) and must be able to read and understand detailed applications specifications. They should also be familiar with the applicable programming standards and should observe the necessary thoroughness and level of detail to produce a maintainable and reliable program product. Although many programming teams composed of relatively inexperienced coders can survive, someone on the team must have a good appreciation of the hardware and systems (non-applications) software (such as the operating system, data base management system, applicable programming language(s), programming aids, debugging aids and utilities). Strong technical support is also required if an applications software package is being used as a basis for the application development.

The primary activity in this step is to use a compiler and other basic programming aids to produce computer-executable instructions. The other activities are related closely to this function and include the preparation of data for testing the modules and programs and the formalization of acceptance criteria for each module or program. Where necessary, additional hardware and/or software may have been installed during the Technical Support Development step to accommodate the new system. Finally—so that the programming team can hand over the finished product—a review and approval process must be included.

The level of detail required by this step is usually the highest encountered in the entire project. During testing and debugging, for example, it may be necessary to view, record, and analyze the output of specific hardware registers or storage addresses or review the execution of object code on an instruction-by-instruction basis. In addition, during testing, the processing of data is reviewed on a data element-by-element basis to ensure that all applicable codes, limits, and data element combinations have been appropriately considered and can be accommodated by the new applications programs. Finally, because maintenance is inevitable, the documentation provided in support of each module or program must be complete.

Documentation resulting from applications programming must include at least a cross-reference to all applications specifications documentation.

The compiler input (source code) and output (object code) are also essential parts of documentation. Programming standards should specify that liberal use be made of comments within the source code to document the logic and structure of the program. Test data input and output are other essential components of programming documentation and should be retained for use during subsequent program maintenance. Finally, operations instructions should be prepared to direct the computer operator in properly setting up and running each program or module. Where appropriate, operations instructions should also be outlined for users who will be providing data to the system. These instructions will subsequently become part of the user operations and controls manual.

STANDARD ACTIVITIES

Verify the Availability of All Necessary Resources

As applications specifications are completed for various modules and programs, a clear picture of the magnitude and complexity of the programming requirements emerges. The project manager assesses total resource requirements in terms of personnel, hardware, and system (nonapplications) software. Where the new application is being added to an existing data center operation, potential conflicts between compilation and testing for the new application and ongoing operations for existing applications must be given close attention.

As mentioned earlier, it may be possible to obtain considerable overlap between the Applications Specifications step and Applications Programming and Testing, particularly where a top-down design approach is used. In an overlapped situation, it will be necessary to update resource requirements and repeat the verification of resource availability as each group of the specifications is completed.

Assign Applications to Programmers and Monitor Progress

The assignment of programs and modules to specific programmers is a critical function, especially if high productivity is to be achieved. The largest and most complex programs are typically assigned to the most experienced programmers. However, this approach overlooks several key considerations, including:

— It may be more productive to complete the most frequently used modules early in the programming cycle, even though they may not be the largest and most complex.
— Small programs may contain complex logic that is best coded by more experienced programmers.
— Large, complex programs may only require relatively straightforward coding for which the use of highly experienced programmers may not be productive.
— A one-programmer-per-program approach ignores the potential benefits of team-building by the sharing of experience from assignments on a module-by-module basis.

When a programming group follows a top-down approach and establishes programming assignments by module, programming experience may be deployed more effectively. The most complex functions can be assigned to the most experienced people. Less experienced programmers can be assigned to modules involving functions such as data manipulation, data movement, and less complex logic.

Using this approach, it is possible to begin testing the higher-level modules before coding the lower-level functions. When this is done, stubs are inserted in place of the lower-level functions. A number of studies have established that this modular approach to coding and testing actually reduces the amount of testing time required to check out programs as they are being written. However, the top-down approach also has its costs. One is that it requires a greater amount of management time because modularizing programs creates a greater number of work units to be assigned and controlled (although individual work units are smaller). If carefully done, this investment in management is generally more than offset by improved programmer productivity and the high quality of the end products. Numerous studies have shown that quality can be enhanced by the use of structured coding techniques within an overall, top-down approach to programming management. A detailed discussion of structured coding cannot be included here. However, many experienced project managers strongly recommend combining top-down approaches to programming management with structured coding techniques.

In addition to assigning specific modules to individual programmers, the project manager must also be concerned with adherence to standards. An indication of the areas in which standards are helpful was given in the previous chapter. It is worth pointing out that the proper use of standards will tend to minimize both program development and maintenance costs and should simplify the interfacing of the various modules assigned to the individual programmers. Standards should not be so rigid nor so inflexibly applied, however, as to stifle programmer creativity and productivity.

Develop Program Modules

This activity consists of several distinct tasks: coding, compilation, module or unit testing, integration or string testing, and documentation. Each work unit has its own due dates and budgets as it is assigned.

Code. This task begins with the assignment of specific tasks to programmers. In most cases, the programmer(s) should review specifications with the analyst who prepared them. Specifications should permit a programmer to approach the task of coding in an individual way. Thus, some discussion between programmer and analyst is constructive. Based on these discussions, a programmer may wish to supplement the specifications for an individual module with additional documentation, such as supplementary flowcharts or decision tables.

Once specifications are reviewed and understood by the programmer, the coding begins. This consists of the translating specifications into a handwritten (or terminal-entered) series of compiler statements that can be understood by the compiler program in order to produce machine language instructions. It may often be productive to have the compiler statements desk checked and subjected to a peer or management review so as to detect logical inconsistencies before machine resources are committed.

Compile. The second task is the conversion of the handwritten compiler statements into machine-readable form (e.g., key entry), and the submission of this data to the computer for compilation. Compiler processing produces machine language instructions and program listings, including a number of diagnostic statements to help correct errors. These diagnostics should be analyzed and the compiler statements revised to produce what is known as a "clean compile" prior to the initiation of testing.

Unit Test (Module or Subroutine). This task consists of processing by the module of a variety of predetermined data values and data combinations. Test data should be meticulously prepared so that a full range of data values and combinations are considered, and all instruction paths within the module are thoroughly tested. It is very important to proceed through as many paths and conditions as possible during each test. The alternative is to abort the testing with the first error and then recompile the module to make the appropriate corrections. This is extremely expensive and can lead to extensive delays in implementation because of the number of correction cycles and the turnaround time required for each such cycle.

Testing can also be made more productive through the selective use of debugging aids generally provided by the computer manufacturer. Selective use is important because many of these aids generate substantial quantities of diagnostic listings which cannot be justified for the detection of a minor programming deficiency. It is extremely important that the programming manager properly supervise the programming team to ensure that their time, machine time, and other resources are efficiently utilized.

Integrate and String Test.   The fourth task is to integrate the individual modules and string test them as a program entity. Given proper programming management and well-defined module interfaces, integration should be possible with a single recompile or link edit. Testing must comprise not only the full range of test data applied to the individual modules earlier, but should also include a reasonable subset of valid transaction data. Again, significant effort must be made to see that every possible data combination and every instruction path in the program is tested.

Documentation.   The fifth task is to prepare the documentation. Several types of documentation may be involved: documentation of the program and its component modules, operator documentation for running the program, user documentation, and control documentation. Of these, program documentation is usually the most voluminous. It includes the original application specifications prepared in the previous step, plus any supplemental logic documentation developed by the programmers. Samples of machine-readable or machine-produced input and output data should be provided, and so should complete source and object code listings from the compiler. Complete listings of test data and test results are to be included and will be needed during subsequent program modification or maintenance.

The type of computer operator documentation provided depends on the prevailing standards at the installation that will run the program. At the very least, however, sufficient documentation must be developed to allow the operator to link or initiate and run the program without analyst or programmer supervision. A complete description of all files required for computer operation and of the retention treatment to be accorded to both input and output files must be provided. A full description of all normal and abnormal terminations possible during the execution of the program, and of the restart and recovery procedures to be taken in each case must be given. Samples of the external labeling to be affixed to newly created files should be provided.

User documentation will be required for the preparation of input, error corrections detected by editing, and external controls. In most cases, this documentation should be prepared in consultation with users responsible for departmental training and operations. This documentation should serve both as a training vehicle for new employees and as a reference for more experienced ones. The major point to be made in connection with user documentation is that it should relate to business operations and user practices rather than to the hardware or the idiosyncrasies of the programmer. This documentation is usually provided by the programmers to a nontechnical project team for expansion and inclusion in the user procedures and controls documents (Phase III, Step 5).

The control documentation defines the types of controls designed in the program or module. It can be as simple as input and output record counts, or it can be as complex as a mechanized balancing procedure that matches and reconciles with a mechanized control file. In any case, the external controls to be maintained by the user should always be defined.

Review and Approve Test Results and Documentation

This function should initially be carried out by senior members of the project management team. The purpose of this initial review is to see that the program is complete, thoroughly tested, and ready for integration with other programs for the purposes of systems testing (Phase III, Step 9).

A detailed documentation review should be performed by those who will be primarily concerned with its use. In the case of the program documentation, the review should be performed by someone who will be accepting responsibility for program maintenance. Operating documentation should be reviewed by the operations manager or his designee. User documentation should be reviewed by user supervisors responsible for operations, controls, and training. Other reviews may be performed by persons in administration or elsewhere responsible for the control and maintenance of clerical procedures manuals. It is also desirable for reviews to be performed by the internal and external auditors.

KEY CONSIDERATIONS

Know the Software

Before assigning programming tasks and the start of coding, it is extremely important that the manager — and, ideally, all programmers — be thoroughly familiar with the system software to be used. For example, procedures that are easy to implement and operate efficiently using one operating system or one compiler may be relatively ineffective using another. In addition, almost all software has "default options," some of which are extremely expensive in terms of their resource utilization. For example, if no disk extents are specified, the system software may assume that an entire disk is required — which in turn can cause severe operating bottlenecks.

If an application software package is to be used as a basis for implementation, additional care must be exercised. Few packages will provide an ideal fit for any given user. It is important for programmers to know precisely what package features must be extended or elaborated on and, in particular, which parts of the package must be left alone to avoid degrading the package's throughput or operating efficiency. Most packages contain features that are not needed, but great care must be exercised to avoid undermining the basic architecture of the package when deleting unnecessary features.

It may even prove desirable to have a technical support person specialize in the use of software utilities. For example, the efficiency of a sort may frequently be optimized to maximize the throughput for a given batch of data, configuration of hardware, and operating environment. Finally, as mentioned earlier, the selected use of system software debugging aids can materially improve programmer productivity.

Controlling Creativity

Creative people often express themselves through their work. In the case of programmers, this may mean attempting to make the hardware and/or software perform in unique ways that are not necessarily productive. Stylized or clever programming can often lead to operating inefficiencies and to extreme difficulties in subsequent program maintenance. For this reason, it is important for the manager to effectively control the level and results of programmer creativity.

Control begins during the preparation of applications specifications. Ideally, specifications will not be overly detailed so as to reduce the programming activity to one of routine coding. Avoiding excessive detail in the application specifications is another reason to adopt a standard that indicates that each "functional" specification should translate to some specific range of lines of source code.

Unproductive programmer creativity also may be curtailed through the adoption and enforcement of programming standards. Further, as suggested earlier, a peer review of coding prior to compilation may also be effective in ferreting out the overly clever solutions. Finally, the review and approval of test results and documentation (which precedes the approval of the program for systems testing) should be thorough enough to disclose unproductive creativity, particularly as it may impact the program maintenance function.

On a post-implementation basis, hardware and software monitoring techniques may be utilized to detect modules or programs that are particularly unbalanced or inefficient. Where results consistently show a recurrent problem from a particular individual, training and discipline may be required. The systematic sampling of programmer output by senior EDP management, a software specialist, or even a hardware supplier's representative may aid in effecting corrective action.

The 90% Complete Program

Managers, users, and others reviewing a project's progress in anticipation of conversion are frequently told that the applications programming is almost done, or "90% complete." This status may continue for some time until—in exasperation—the offending program or system is reassigned, or additional programming resources are applied. This may result in having to start over, often virtually from scratch. In the meantime, deadlines are missed, costs mount, and nerves get frayed.

The "90% complete program" can be avoided. This begins with proper systems design, including a thorough definition of all user requirements and anticipation of the things that supposedly can't happen. The process follows through to an appropriate level documentation of applications specification —e.g., one functional statement should *not* result in a programmer writing hundreds of lines of source code. Finally, assignment of technically qualified programming resources, the application of programming standards and effective management of programming can play an important part in minimizing the risks of coming up with a "90% complete program."

The earned-hours concept may also be useful in minimizing the "90% complete" problem. Under this concept, the applications programming task is broken into discrete units (perhaps logical modules) and a time estimate is arrived at for each unit. Programmers are then only given credit for their budgeted hours for fully completed units. With an earned-hours approach, programmers will tend to assure that the time allotment is reasonable before they start, and that problems with specifications are quickly brought to management attention. Although difficult to implement and tough on novice programmers, the earned-hours approach quickly develops a strong productivity orientation throughout the systems and programming managers and staff.

If the "90% complete" problem persists, it may be necessary to establish an error management system that defines each problem in writing, identifies its cause, assigns and takes corrective action, and follows up where appropriate with corrective training. Such a system can pinpoint the cause(s) of continued delays and provides the basis for preventing a recurrence.

"Impossible" Conditions Sometimes — possibly months or years after implementation — a program "blows up" or malfunctions inexplicably. All too often, this happens because a situation is encountered that users, systems analysts, and programmers thought "impossible." While the "impossible" condition may not be prevented, it should be possible to minimize program blowups.

Avoidance of most "impossible" situations begins with the user and the analyst whose job it is to predict or anticipate such events. For example: goods no longer in the current sales catalogue or on the active inventory file will continue to be returned by customers for credit; salesmen will make nonstandard adjustments to prices in order to obtain an order; or dimensions will become metric and file size limits will have to be increased. The structured walkthru and review processes can also be instrumental in anticipating "impossible" conditions and seeing that they are provided for in the applications specifications. Finally, the programmer must anticipate and provide for these "impossible" conditions with orderly halts for unexpected codes, values beyond expected ranges, or other conditions. In short, every effort must be made to ensure that when the "impossible" condition arises, corrective action can be taken in a timely manner.

Resource Utilization During the programming step of systems development, there is often a tendency to squander or waste resources. This most frequently occurs when the programmers are given uncontrolled access to the computer, either directly or via terminals, to do "machine debugging." In this situation the programmer generally concentrates on debugging a single error at a time. Upon finding an error, the programmer corrects the code, recompiles the program, rechecks the error condition and then searches for the next error. In its attempts to substitute machine power for brain power, this process generally results in increasing machine testing and recompile time, programmer time and total elapsed time for testing, debugging, and completing the program.

There are a number of techniques for minimizing poor utilization of resources. The first is to tightly control programmers' direct access to the machine. The second is to require some minimum amount of elapsed time (e.g., four hours unless approved by the project manager) between tests so that ample time is available to the programmer for "desk checking" and correction of multiple error conditions before recompilation and further testing. Another is to provide a standard rapid turnaround time for compiling and testing that is reasonably responsive to programmer needs. This will avoid the temptation to rush the "desk checking" and corrections in order to quickly resubmit the program because of the lengthy turnaround time. In addition, assigning work units to programmers in a way that allows them to productively use the turnaround time on one program for work on another may also contribute to the programmer's effectiveness by providing a change of scene, stimulating fresh insight when debugging the problem program.

STANDARD ACTIVITIES/END ITEMS

TOUCHE ROSS

ID/TITLE APPLICATION PROGRAMMING AND TESTING

ORGANIZATION __PHASE III,__
STEP 4
SYSTEM __DEVELOPMENT__
USER REP

☐ PHASE ☒ ACTIVITY ☐ SUBTASK
☐ STEP   ☒ TASK   ☐

PAGE __1__ OF __2__
PROJECT NO.

	PREPARED BY	REVIEWED BY	DATE	PHASE
	MVJ	CB	3/29/80	III-4
	SH	CB	11/1/80	III-4

NUMBER	PHASE/STEP/ACTIVITY/TASK/SUBTASK NAME	END ITEM	FORM NO.	PERFORMED BY	DUE DATE	APPROVED BY	DATE
A.	Verify the Availability of all Necessary Resources	Work Outline	101				
B.	Assign Applications to Programmers and Monitor Progress	Detailed Schedule	102				
		Walkthru Log	186				
		Review Notes					
C.	Develop Program Modules						
C.1	– Code	Walkthru Log	186				
		Code					
C.2	– Compile	Walkthru Log	186				
		Clean Compile					
		Test Checklist	185				
		Test Data					
		Test Data Base/File					
C.3	– Unit Test (Module or Subroutine)	Unit Test Results					
C.4	– Integrate and String Test	String Test Results					
C.5	– Documentation	Documentation					

© Touche Ross & Co., 1980 All Rights Reserved

168

STANDARD ACTIVITIES/END ITEMS

TOUCHE ROSS

ORGANIZATION ___PHASE III,___

STEP 4

SYSTEM ___DEVELOPMENT___

USER REP ____

ID/TITLE ___APPLICATION PROGRAMMING AND TESTING___

☐ PHASE	☒ ACTIVITY	☐ SUBTASK
☐ STEP	☒ TASK	☐ _____

	PREPARED BY	MVJ	SH
	REVIEWED BY	CB	CB
	DATE	3/29/80	11/1/80
	PHASE	III-4	III-4

NUMBER	PHASE/STEP/ACTIVITY/TASK/SUBTASK NAME	END ITEM	FORM NO.	PERFORMED BY	DUE DATE	APPROVED BY	DATE
D.	Review and Approve Test Results and Documentation	JCL, WFL (etc.)					
		Results Form	198				
		Approval Form	199				
		Program/Module Maintenance Control	113				

THE SYSTEMS DEVELOPMENT PROCESS

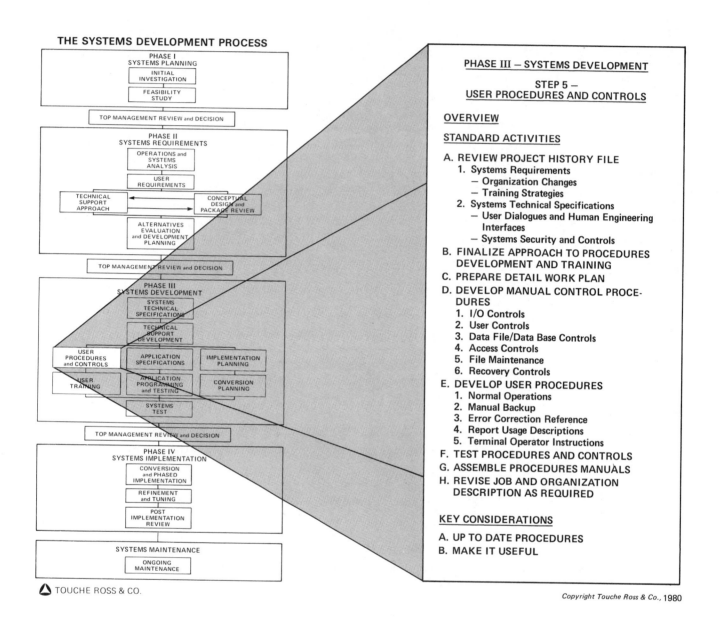

PHASE I
SYSTEMS PLANNING

INITIAL
INVESTIGATION

FEASIBILITY
STUDY

TOP MANAGEMENT REVIEW and DECISION

PHASE II
SYSTEMS REQUIREMENTS

OPERATIONS and
SYSTEMS
ANALYSIS

USER
REQUIREMENTS

TECHNICAL
SUPPORT
APPROACH

CONCEPTUAL
DESIGN and
PACKAGE REVIEW

ALTERNATIVES
EVALUATION
and DEVELOPMENT
PLANNING

TOP MANAGEMENT REVIEW and DECISION

PHASE III
SYSTEMS DEVELOPMENT

SYSTEMS
TECHNICAL
SPECIFICATIONS

TECHNICAL
SUPPORT
DEVELOPMENT

USER
PROCEDURES
and CONTROLS

APPLICATION
SPECIFICATIONS

IMPLEMENTATION
PLANNING

USER
TRAINING

APPLICATION
PROGRAMMING
and TESTING

CONVERSION
PLANNING

SYSTEMS
TEST

TOP MANAGEMENT REVIEW and DECISION

PHASE IV
SYSTEMS IMPLEMENTATION

CONVERSION
and PHASED
IMPLEMENTATION

REFINEMENT
and TUNING

POST
IMPLEMENTATION
REVIEW

SYSTEMS MAINTENANCE

ONGOING
MAINTENANCE

PHASE III — SYSTEMS DEVELOPMENT

STEP 5 —
USER PROCEDURES AND CONTROLS

OVERVIEW

STANDARD ACTIVITIES

A. REVIEW PROJECT HISTORY FILE
1. Systems Requirements
   – Organization Changes
   – Training Strategies
2. Systems Technical Specifications
   – User Dialogues and Human Engineering Interfaces
   – Systems Security and Controls
B. FINALIZE APPROACH TO PROCEDURES DEVELOPMENT AND TRAINING
C. PREPARE DETAIL WORK PLAN
D. DEVELOP MANUAL CONTROL PROCE-DURES
1. I/O Controls
2. User Controls
3. Data File/Data Base Controls
4. Access Controls
5. File Maintenance
6. Recovery Controls
E. DEVELOP USER PROCEDURES
1. Normal Operations
2. Manual Backup
3. Error Correction Reference
4. Report Usage Descriptions
5. Terminal Operator Instructions
F. TEST PROCEDURES AND CONTROLS
G. ASSEMBLE PROCEDURES MANUALS
H. REVISE JOB AND ORGANIZATION DESCRIPTION AS REQUIRED

KEY CONSIDERATIONS

A. UP TO DATE PROCEDURES
B. MAKE IT USEFUL

△ TOUCHE ROSS & CO.

170

OVERVIEW   This step is conducted in parallel with the Applications Specifications (Phase III, Step 3) and Programming and Testing (Phase II, Step 4), concentrating on the noncomputer processing aspects of the system. It utilizes previously completed User Requirements (Phase II) and the Systems Technical Specifications (Phase III, Step 1) to develop and test the detailed manual processes that must be performed in conjunction with computer processes to make the system complete. A classic failure in many systems development projects has been to ignore or improperly address the user procedures portion of the system. This failure results in a high degree of risk that the new system will not work or not provide the expected benefits.

In the Applications Specifications and Programming steps, several general types of computer programs are identified and developed. For example, programs are usually required for input/edit, main-line processing, error recovery, special reporting, internal data and file control, security control, and others. Similarly, in this step, a variety of procedures and control documents are generally required to assure adequate operation of the entire system. This chapter therefore includes discussions of manual control procedures for input/output, data files, system access, file maintenance, and recovery; as well as user procedures for normal operations, manual backup, error correction, report usage, and terminal operations.

This step and the next (User Training) should be performed primarily by user members of the project team. However, both analyst time and computer operations staff time are also usually required to coordinate and integrate the manual and computer processes. Since these steps are completed simultaneously with the applications specifications and programming steps, they are typically not a limiting factor in the overall elapsed timing of the project. They can become critical, however, since the project must not proceed to the Systems Test step (Phase III, Step 9) until these two steps have been satisfactorily completed.

STANDARD ACTIVITIES

Review Project History File   Several previous steps and end products of this project have resulted in documents that are now used to develop user procedures and controls. This documentation provides the basis for describing what the system will do and how it will do it in the user environment. As such, it is vitally important that project team members assigned to this step be intimately familiar with these documents and the rationale that supports them in order to create useful and usable procedures and controls. The documentation should be in the following files:

Systems Requirements.   This file contains descriptions of the system's objectives and of the processes that are to be performed. Thus, it must be well understood prior to initiating the subsequent activities of this step. The requirements document includes functional descriptions of the new system operation with the general flow of information throughout the user areas, the interactions of users with computer processing for inputs and outputs, and the approach to system security and controls. Also of major importance is the identification of any organization changes required with the new system. The project team must understand both the structure and the skill-level requirements of the new organization. Otherwise, the team (consisting mainly of user personnel in the current organization) may inadvertently create inefficient procedures which attempt to utilize the new system and computer programs in the present organizational environment. This error could make achievement of benefits related to personnel reduction substantially more difficult to attain.

Finally, the requirements phase documentation should describe the general strategies to be used in training personnel and testing the system. These must also be understood by the project team, since the next major activity within this step is to finalize the approach for both procedures development and user training.

Systems Technical Specifications. This file consists primarily of the technical documents required to develop the computer programs for the new system. However, it also contains detailed information that must be utilized by the project team in this step. First are specifications for user dialogues and human engineering interfaces that identify the specific technical methods by which the users and computer will communicate. For example, if on-line data entry and edit is part of the new system, the systems technical specifications file will contain such items as screen formats, entry sequences, edit rules, and error messages. Procedures developed in this step will include the instructions on how to use these features.

Second, this file contains the technical details of how systems security and controls are to be implemented in the new system. For example, this includes the approach to passwords used to gain access to terminal inquiries, the specific internal editing and balancing rules, and the reported control totals that are to be programmed into the new system. Each of these features must be understood and incorporated into the new user procedures and controls manuals.

Finalize Approach to Procedures Development and Training

At this point, the project team should have a thorough understanding of the new system concepts and technical specifications. However, before developing any procedures, a standard approach to formats should be defined to maximize the usefulness of the end products in user operations.

Many organizations have their own formats and techniques for the development of procedures manuals. Where these exist, they should be applied consistently to cover the manual portions of the new system. If there are no standards in place, the use of a modified "scenario" is generally effective. This involves use of clear headings for tasks, jobs, or functions, and then listing the steps to be performed by each responsible person or "player," usually with indented margins for each change in responsibility. Vocabulary and writing style should be geared to the level of the audience.

An effective procedures manual should also be useful as a ready-reference document. Thus, the manual should be indexed and segmented so that user personnel can quickly find sections that apply to their jobs. The manual should be sufficiently complete not to require constant assistance from the EDP organization or a reliance on memory or tradition.

Materials used to train user personnel are often byproducts of the writing and testing of procedures manuals. Training materials include references, overview descriptions, and case studies or practice sets. These items are required largely because people often cannot understand procedures manuals without performing the procedures described in these manuals. Thus, specific training sessions as well as supplementary training materials are usually needed to teach employees what they must know about new or modified jobs.

The development of an outline covering the contents of the new manuals is often helpful at this point. Items that may be included in an effective procedures manuals are:

— A sufficiently detailed *table of contents* to allow references to be pinpointed. Instead of simply listing chapters, major titles and subtitles should be identified and page references should be cited.
— A brief *overview* or *outline summary* to be used at the beginning of training sessions.
— Detailed *procedure descriptions*, in individual sections and chapters and appropriate to specific work assignments, addressing each procedure and control topic discussed in this chapter.
— *Revision* and *updating* procedures and responsibilities.
— An alphabetic topical *index*.

Prepare Detailed Work Plan

Based on the project team's understanding of the project history file and the formalized approach to procedures development, the detailed work plan for this step should now be prepared. Key user personnel who will train, test, and operate the new system should be identified and used as much as possible in this step. Enough analyst time should be made available to assure appropriate integration of the manual procedures with the computer programs. If the organization has an internal methods department, a training division, or both, these groups could be called upon to participate in this phase. To the extent feasible, internal and external auditors might also be involved at appropriate review points to assure that the system's manual and automated controls are acceptable. Unless a clear commitment of all project participants' time is obtained as part of finalizing the detailed work plan, procedures are not likely to be completed in a timely and acceptable manner.

Develop Manual Control Procedures

The procedures manuals, as previously outlined, contain sections or chapters about various types of system controls directed to the various groups or functions involved in the operation of the new system. The purpose of these controls is to assure the valid and proper entry and maintenance of data in the system and to prevent the classic "garbage in, garbage out" problem typical of poorly developed systems. Manual controls and associated procedures are usually developed around the following topics:

I/O Controls. These control forms and procedures are used by the data control function either at the user or within data processing operations. Control documents and checklists are developed for assembling data and requesting jobs to be completed by both the data preparation and computer operations functions. Forms, checklists, and procedures are similarly developed for data control to make sure the jobs requested were performed and the output(s) requested were produced.

User Controls. These consist of control documents and procedures required by the user departments in submitting and receiving information from data processing operations. Examples are preparation of input data batch controls, verification of report totals, control over the correction and resubmission of rejected data, preparation of special requests, and other necessary user balancing and control functions. Other measures may include assignment of batch control numbers, use of data and time stamps, or use of prenumbered documents, as appropriate for tight control.

Data File/Data Base Controls. These consist of procedures required by the data control or librarian function to assure that file integrity is maintained, that the proper files are used in requested runs, and that appropriate backup and historical file retention is established. In addition, these controls include procedures that allow the users to verify consistency of file or data base totals through record counts, hash totals, or similar processes.

Access Controls. These consist of security procedures that restrict use of the computer programs to authorized parties. This may involve establishing a function to issue and control passwords for terminal access. Also, the designation of specific functions for certain key data entry should be set up through authorized passwords or signatures. For some systems, controls may be required to ensure that access to certain output reports (e.g., checks, sensitive personnel data, etc.) is restricted to authorized users.

File Maintenance. Designed to ensure that maintenance transactions are properly handled, these procedures and controls normally occur on a nonregular basis. They may cause significant changes to computer files, such as code changes for edit rules or historical data changes. Thus, they must be carefully developed to address levels of authorization, separation of responsibilities, verification that desired changes have taken place, correction of wrong or rejected entries, and verification that unplanned additional changes did not occur.

Recovery Controls. This set of controls consists of a logical and thorough approach to reestablishing a current, balanced system after destruction of files (manual or computer) or identification of previously undetected computer program errors. These controls may be developed by simulating such situations and then documenting the steps to be followed to recover from the specified problem. This technique may uncover weaknesses in other controls, audit trails, or processing approaches that need to be corrected during this systems development phase. Needless to say, it is not appropriate to wait until a problem occurs to determine a reasonable approach for its correction. Conversely, an attempt to build in "ultimate" controls may result in the inability to effectively process the normal workload in a timely fashion.

Develop User Procedures

In addition to the manual control forms, checklists, and procedures described above, several types of user procedures are also required for proper system operation. Their purpose is to describe the workflow through the various manual processing steps in the user departments and to provide a reference guide to assist in explaining specific parts of the system. The types of user procedures usually address the following topics:

Normal Operations. These procedures consist of a step-by-step instructional description of the work to be performed by users in a normal mode of operation. They include the user tasks required to record, distribute, communicate, and file information. The procedures should reference the appropriate control steps as previously described, and should be accompanied by a workflow diagram that ties together the various functions and controls. Procedures for normal operations are generally organized by job or function and are in a modified scenario format.

Manual Backup. A secondary set of user procedures is required to describe the workflow and manual processing steps in the event the computer processing portion of the system is inoperative. The manual backup approach will vary considerably, depending on the nature of the system and the degree of user dependence on real-time or on-line computer operations. It may sometimes be necessary to develop alternative manual backup approaches which vary based on the anticipated downtime of the computer. In addition, creation of these procedures may identify the need for special computer reports or controls to prevent a complete business shutdown in the event the computer is out of service for an extended period of time. In such cases, the additional systems development and programming work required should be completed in this project phase or management should be advised of the degree of risk before approving the start of implementation (Phase IV).

Error Correction Reference.   Completed procedures manuals should contain sections that provide ready references aiding in the correction of errors. These references are normally organized by error type and describe what caused the error and what actions should be taken. The types of errors include: error messages on rejected data entry; out-of-balance batches or other control total mismatches; user-generated maintenance and historical data changes; and other nonroutine situations.

Report Usage Descriptions.   The procedures manual should describe the contents and intended usage of each system report. This normally involves inserting a "live" copy of each output (including video displays) with attached narrative describing its purpose, the meaning of each data element, and expected action, based on report contents. This documentation can prove to be extremely valuable in maintaining report usability and system effectiveness.

Terminal Operator Instructions.   These procedures, both in step-by-step and reference format, are developed to assist operators in the use of computer terminals. Each form used for data entry is included to show how each data element is entered from the form on the terminal. Likewise, each video display format or option is included for all types of data entry, error correction, and terminal inquiry. A subsection may include the standard vendor instructions to initiate terminal operations, perform normal on-site cleaning and maintenance, change paper, and similar functions. These procedures will vary in complexity, depending on the type of application and the amount of terminal-based intelligence or temporary mass storage.

Test Procedures and Controls   Once all procedures and controls for the new system have been drafted, they should each be tested for completeness and understandability. Testing should be performed by members of the project team to facilitate making changes and corrections as the testing progresses. The testing process should include a walkthru of the manual operation, both in normal and manual backup mode, to verify that the manual functions fit properly together. In addition, sample control documents and checklists are completed both correctly and incorrectly to test the error detection and correction procedures. These processes are continued through all portions of the manual system until the project team is satisfied that the procedures are ready for user training.

Assemble Procedures Manuals   This activity is primarily administrative, involving the production of procedures manuals and associated forms and documents in a manner acceptable for user training and systems test. Ideally, manuals should be in almost final form, requiring only minor revisions in the event of any subsequent systems test discrepancies. At this time, the detailed table of contents and the topical index are also reviewed and completed. Enough time must be allowed for this activity to avoid project delays while waiting for the typing, proofing, and reproduction process to be completed.

Revise Job and Organization Description as Required

As a final activity in this step, job or position descriptions within the user departments are reviewed and updated to reflect the new system operations described in the procedures manuals. If organization manuals also exist, they should be updated to reflect the revised organization and staffing levels. These documents are then reviewed and approved by user management prior to publication.

KEY CONSIDERATIONS

Up-to-Date Procedures

An outdated procedures manual is a useless document. It is essential to designate who will maintain the procedures manuals and related training materials after the new system is operational. Responsibilities for changing programs and program documentation are usually well documented and understood by the systems and programming staff. However, this is often not the case with procedures manuals. The result is that interviews with six people may produce six different versions of undocumented changes to the procedures manual. To avoid built-in obsolescence, the procedures manual should contain a specific section describing how it is to be maintained and by whom. This section should also assign responsibilities for transmitting revisions, including a current distribution list, to show who should receive notice of maintenance changes. A master list of all persons who have a copy of the procedures manual should also be kept to ensure that revisions are completely distributed.

Some sources of information about needed changes may be overlooked during this task. For example, clerks may have developed their own cross-references to important topics which could be consolidated and incorporated into the manual. A review procedure should be established to make sure that these handy references are identified and added to the manual.

Make It Useful

In order to be useful, the procedures manual must be up to date, organized, and written in a manner that encourages its use. Typical problems of ineffective procedures manuals include:

— Inability to quickly locate answers to common questions.
— Inability to understand the answers provided.
— Inability to determine what action steps to take once the problem has been identified.
— Voluminous detail must be read in order to perform a simple task.
— Awkward formatting, such as scenarios that are indented to such an extent that only two or three words appear on each line, thereby requiring several pages to describe a single function.
— Insufficient copies or inconvenient locations of copies of the procedures manuals.

These problems can be minimized through effective planning and execution of both this step and the next (User Training).

STANDARD ACTIVITIES/END ITEMS

TOUCHE ROSS

ORGANIZATION _____

SYSTEM _____ PHASE III,

STEP 5

DEVELOPMENT

USER REP _____

ID/TITLE __USER PROCEDURES AND CONTROLS__

- ☐ PHASE
- ☐ STEP
- ☒ ACTIVITY
- ☒ TASK
- ☐ SUBTASK _____

	PREPARED BY	MVJ	SH
	REVIEWED BY	CB	CB
	DATE	3/29/80	11/1/80
	PHASE	III-5	III-5

NUMBER	PHASE/STEP/ACTIVITY/TASK/SUBTASK NAME	END ITEM	FORM NO.	PERFORMED BY	DUE DATE	APPROVED BY	DATE
A.	Review Project History File	Procedures Checklist and Plan	182, 195				
B.	Finalize Approach to Procedures Development and Training	Standards	142				
C.	Prepare Detailed Work Plan	Work Outline	101				
		Project Plan	102				
D.	Develop Manual Control Procedures	Summary of Controls	141				
		Control Procedures Manuals*					
E.	Develop User Procedures	User Procedures Manuals*					
F.	Test Procedures and Controls	Test Checklist	185				
		Results Form	198				
		Approval Form	199				
	*Source Material for Manuals Includes:	Multiple Card Layout	160				
		VDT Screen and Support	161, 162				
		Output Report and Layout	163, 164				
		Decision Logic (Edits)	176				
		Code Tables	178				
		Summaries of Controls	141				

STANDARD ACTIVITIES/END ITEMS

TOUCHE ROSS

ORGANIZATION ___PHASE III,___
       ___STEP 5___

SYSTEM ___DEVELOPMENT___

USER REP _____

ID/TITLE ___USER PROCEDURES AND CONTROLS___

☐ PHASE   ☒ ACTIVITY   ☐ SUBTASK

☐ STEP   ☒ TASK   ☐ _____

PREPARED BY __MWJ__ | __SH__

REVIEWED BY __CB__ | __CB__

DATE __3/29/80__ | __11/1/80__

PHASE __III-5__ | __III-5__

NUMBER	PHASE/STEP/ACTIVITY/TASK/SUBTASK NAME	END ITEM	FORM NO.	PERFORMED BY	DUE DATE	APPROVED BY	DATE
G.	Assemble Procedures Manuals	Assembled Manuals					
		Distribution List	142				
H.	Revise Job and Organization Description, As Required	Job Descriptions					
		Summary of Functions	125				
		Organization Chart	142				

THE SYSTEMS DEVELOPMENT PROCESS

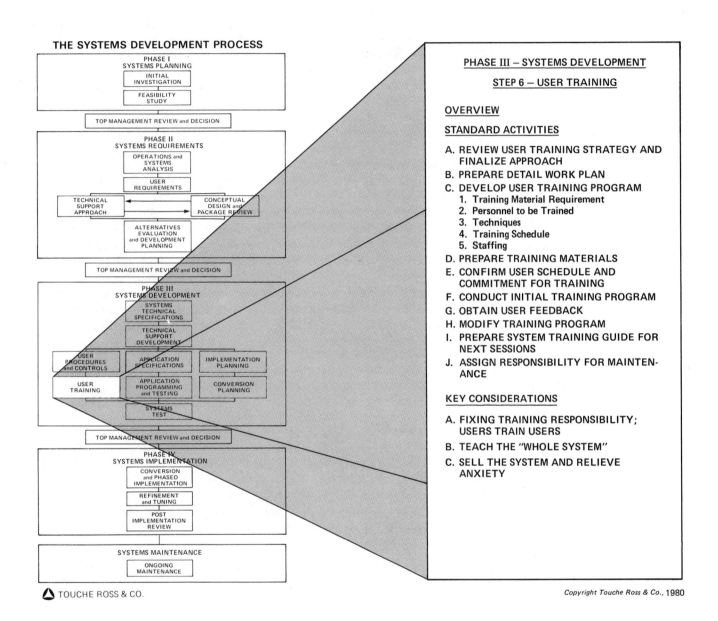

PHASE I
SYSTEMS PLANNING

INITIAL
INVESTIGATION

FEASIBILITY
STUDY

TOP MANAGEMENT REVIEW and DECISION

PHASE II
SYSTEMS REQUIREMENTS

OPERATIONS and
SYSTEMS
ANALYSIS

USER
REQUIREMENTS

TECHNICAL
SUPPORT
APPROACH

CONCEPTUAL
DESIGN and
PACKAGE REVIEW

ALTERNATIVES
EVALUATION
and DEVELOPMENT
PLANNING

TOP MANAGEMENT REVIEW and DECISION

PHASE III
SYSTEMS DEVELOPMENT

SYSTEMS
TECHNICAL
SPECIFICATIONS

TECHNICAL
SUPPORT
DEVELOPMENT

USER
PROCEDURES
and CONTROLS

APPLICATION
SPECIFICATIONS

IMPLEMENTATION
PLANNING

USER
TRAINING

APPLICATION
PROGRAMMING
and TESTING

CONVERSION
PLANNING

SYSTEMS
TEST

TOP MANAGEMENT REVIEW and DECISION

PHASE IV
SYSTEMS IMPLEMENTATION

CONVERSION
and PHASED
IMPLEMENTATION

REFINEMENT
and TUNING

POST
IMPLEMENTATION
REVIEW

SYSTEMS MAINTENANCE

ONGOING
MAINTENANCE

△ TOUCHE ROSS & CO.

PHASE III – SYSTEMS DEVELOPMENT

STEP 6 – USER TRAINING

OVERVIEW

STANDARD ACTIVITIES

A. REVIEW USER TRAINING STRATEGY AND FINALIZE APPROACH
B. PREPARE DETAIL WORK PLAN
C. DEVELOP USER TRAINING PROGRAM
　1. Training Material Requirement
　2. Personnel to be Trained
　3. Techniques
　4. Training Schedule
　5. Staffing
D. PREPARE TRAINING MATERIALS
E. CONFIRM USER SCHEDULE AND COMMITMENT FOR TRAINING
F. CONDUCT INITIAL TRAINING PROGRAM
G. OBTAIN USER FEEDBACK
H. MODIFY TRAINING PROGRAM
I. PREPARE SYSTEM TRAINING GUIDE FOR NEXT SESSIONS
J. ASSIGN RESPONSIBILITY FOR MAINTENANCE

KEY CONSIDERATIONS

A. FIXING TRAINING RESPONSIBILITY; USERS TRAIN USERS
B. TEACH THE "WHOLE SYSTEM"
C. SELL THE SYSTEM AND RELIEVE ANXIETY

The User Training step immediately follows the User Procedures and Controls step (Phase III, Step 5) in order to prepare users for the Systems Test (Phase III, Step 9) and subsequent Implementation (Phase IV). The purpose of this step is twofold: (1) to prepare an organized training program and supporting training material, and (2) to train an initial group of trainers and users. For systems which have only a small group of users located in one department, this step may include all the required training. However, for systems that impact many users and involve multiple departments or physical locations, this step may only include the initial training and a detailed plan for the remaining training. It is essential to coordinate the timing of this training program with other steps of the systems development and implementation process.

As described in the previous step, the absence of complete user procedures and controls may result in a high degree of risk that the new system will not function properly. Likewise, the absence of properly trained users may negate all the benefits of well-constructed procedures, controls, and computer programs.

The User Training step is generally performed by the same project team that produced the user procedures and controls. However, if the organization has a training department, individuals from that department may become more directly involved in this step.

STANDARD ACTIVITIES

Review User Training Strategy and Finalize Approach

The approach used for both procedures development and training was finalized in the previous step. The project team should now review that approach for understanding and agreement. Any appropriate changes based on the newly completed procedures manual should be made at this time. In addition, the schedules for initial training and full user training should be updated to reflect the current status of the programming effort and the planned timing of systems test and implementation activities.

Prepare Detailed Work Plan

Based on the updated schedule for all user training sessions, the project team now plans the detailed activities and tasks required in this step. Timing and effort required to complete each task also are determined. Responsibilities and personnel assignments must be clearly stated and commitments of all participants' time must be obtained as part of finalizing the detailed work plan. If this is not done, the training program and materials are not likely to be completed in an acceptable manner.

Develop User Training Program

The first major activity in this step is the development of a formalized user training program. Although this program will vary depending on the type of system and the type and quantity of user personnel, it generally contains several common elements:

Training Material Requirement. The training program specifies in detail the requirements for training materials. These requirements are documented for

180

each user group and major function in the system. Differing requirements generally exist for user staff in data preparation, data entry, error control and correction, report usage, and others. Some training material may already exist, having been created as part of the User Procedures and Controls step and other development activities. Other materials may be required to address each section of the procedures and control manuals. It is important to include materials that sell the system and its benefit to users as well as instruct them in its use.

Personnel to be Trained. For each user group involved in the system, the training program also includes identification of the specific personnel to be trained and the sequence of training within each group. In some cases, the new system may require that new personnel be hired for certain new functions. Any required orientation programs should be planned for these personnel prior to specific training on the new system. The new user organization charts developed during User Requirements (Phase II) are reviewed to ensure that all personnel who should receive training have been included in the program.

Techniques. The training program also identifies specific techniques to be used in conducting user training sessions. These techniques may include slide presentations, overhead transparencies, sample case studies, role playing, open practice times with new terminal equipment, and other approaches. Video recording can also be useful to package parts of the training program and to provide feedback to participants during the training sessions. The techniques selected should be those most appropriate to both the type of user personnel and the systems tasks which the users will be required to perform.

Training Schedule. Now that the material requirements, techniques, and personnel to be trained have been determined, the actual schedule for the specific training sessions is prepared. This schedule must not only reflect training program requirements, but also constraints outside the system project. These include workload requirements within current user operations, vacation and holiday schedules, overtime considerations, availability of special facilities and equipment availability. Another critical factor in establishing the training schedule is the overall plan for systems testing, conversion, and phased implementation. Training sessions—no matter how well prepared—which occur too long before the new system is available for personnel to use, are ineffective. They may, in fact, result in negative reactions from users who made special efforts to understand and prepare for the new system. Alternatively, training sessions scheduled after implementation may be complicated by users who have learned erroneous or ineffective methods of working with the new system.

Staffing. Finally, the training program includes specific staffing assignments for conducting the scheduled training sessions. Whenever possible, staffing should be organized so that members of the project team conduct the initial training sessions to train users who then will be the trainers for the actual user training program. If the new system changes operations substantially and users are not sure they can cope with it, it may be useful to have an organization development specialist or a psychologist participate in the training process. Selection of staff to conduct the sessions is critical to achieving a proper understanding of the new system by the users. This task should therefore receive careful attention.

Prepare Training Materials   At this point, preparation of training materials simply involves creation of material requirements as determined in the previous activity. Sufficient time should be allocated to this activity to allow printing special control forms, typing, reproducing training packets, creating slides, and similar administrative tasks. Care should be taken to test draft materials so that errors can be corrected and modifications can be incorporated before assembling the final materials.

Confirm User Schedule and Commitment for Training   As developed in a previous activity, the training program must be reviewed and committed to by management of all affected user areas before training can begin. This review and commitment includes training approach, schedule, staffing, and personnel to be trained. It is critical for user management to understand the need for training and the proposed program, since training sessions usually disrupt normal operations. It may not be assumed that user management will be receptive of the new system just because they requested it. Rather, the project team should plan to spend some time reselling the new system concepts and benefits. Further, they should be flexible in adjusting schedules to reflect significant user management concerns regarding current operations workloads, overtime requirements, vacation schedules, and similar problems. However, the project team should not compromise the potential success of the system by avoiding an adequate training program simply because it disrupts normal operations. It is generally advisable to confirm the schedules and commitments in writing with user management to minimize any misunderstandings.

Conduct Initial Training Program   As indicated earlier, the initial training program is generally conducted by project team members to train users who will subsequently be the trainers of the remaining users. Thus, this activity has two primary objectives: to test the adequacy of training materials and techniques and to prepare the staff who will conduct the training sessions. This does not suggest that this initial training program should be inadequately prepared or conducted informally. To the contrary, it should be conducted as a prototype for the subsequent sessions. This approach allows the training activity to be most meaningful.

Obtain User Feedback   Obtaining feedback from the users who attend the initial training session is essential to derive maximum effectiveness from the program. This feedback should be obtained at two points: (1) immediately at the end of the training session, and (2) several days after the training session has been conducted. This is important since the project team needs to obtain information on both initial reaction and retention. The training program must leave the users with the enthusiasm and desire to implement and use the new system. Thus, the feedback on initial reaction is designed to understand the effectiveness of the selling portion of the training program. If the training material is difficult to understand or is not relevant, if the session is dull or boring, or if the techniques used tend to detract from instead of add to the presentation, then an important element of training has failed.

Conversely, retention can best be measured through a delayed feedback approach. Potentially, this can be accomplished with a carefully structured test which is directed at the most significant aspects of each user group and major function involved in the new system. This test should attempt to determine if the users understand both the basic principles of the new system and the methods in which available procedural reference manuals may be utilized. It is not necessary for users to recall all the details of exception item handling, balancing controls, and so forth. Rather, it is critical that they

182

generally understand the functions and tasks required and where to find answers to specific questions or problems.

Modify Training Program

The project team may now use the feedback obtained above to modify the training program. Adequate time should be allocated for this activity to maximize both the learning and selling aspects of the program. If possible, users who attended the initial session and who will assist in future training sessions should participate in making these modifications. This approach improves users' capabilities to conduct and instruct the remaining training sessions.

Prepare System Training Guide for Next Sessions

The end product of the feedback and modification activities described above is an updated training program and training guide to be used by the instructors. This guide should be complete and easily understood by the instructors, since it will be their responsibility to complete the training based on the schedule without continuous direct participation by the project team. Absence of an adequate training guide may require continued full time involvement of project team members rather than allowing them to concentrate their efforts on the remaining steps in the development and implementation process.

Assign Responsibility for Maintenance

Finally, before the project team leaves this step, it must turn over the training program to those who will be responsible for its ongoing maintenance. The training program may be required for use over a long period of time when many similar users (e.g., branch offices) are scheduled for a phased implementation of the new system. Subsequent to full system installation, the training program may be required for new employees or for periodic refresher sessions. Responsibility for maintaining the training program is often assigned to the group that has responsibility for maintaining the user procedures manuals.

KEY CONSIDERATIONS

Fixing Training Responsibility; Users Train Users

We have frequently pointed out that users need to be heavily involved in the training step. The project team is primarily composed of users. This user team first develops the training program, materials, and schedules. It then conducts an initial session to train a group of users who become the trainers for the remaining sessions. Finally, users are assigned responsibility for maintaining the training program and the procedures manuals. This is ideal in a complex system environment involving many users. In the smallest of new systems, an analyst may work with one or two users to document procedures and controls, and no other users may have to be trained. However, in either extreme, users should be directly involved and responsible for assuring that their procedures are complete and that all necessary personnel have been trained. In organizations with minimal systems experience, this approach has historically been difficult or impossible to pursue. However, in those instances, the project manager must question whether users who are not ready to assume responsibility for training are in fact ready to assume responsibility for using the new system.

Teach the Whole System

A classic failure in many training programs has been to ignore the whole system. This occurs whenever the project team mistakenly believes either that the users already understand the whole system or that they have no need to know the whole system. Both assumptions are incorrect. Even where users generally understand the workflow, the functions performed, and the role of computer processing in the new system, there is a need to include such overviews in the training program. This will correct any misunderstandings that may exist and will also serve to ensure that at least a minimum level of knowledge exists among all user personnel. Obviously, this does not imply that the intricate details of data entry or error correction should be taught to every user. Rather, this suggests that the training program include for all users an overview in sufficient depth to explain the new system scope, objectives, workflow, primary functions of each user group, major computer processing components, use of new terminal equipment, and other similar topics. This type of overview allows each user to better understand his or her role in the overall system. Further, it increases awareness of the impact — both positive and negative — that the work of one user can have on all the other users.

Sell the System and Relieve Anxiety

As mentioned earlier in this subsection, the training program should be constructed to both teach and sell. The project team all too often fails to adequately consider the anxiety that develops when an imminent change is not well understood. No one likes change to the unknown. Thus the major emphasis at the beginning of the training sessions and throughout the program should be to sell the concepts and positive aspects of the new system. Users will emphasize the negative side — the extra work required for conversion, error correction, or batch control. They need to be sold and reminded of the positive side and of the expected benefits to the whole organization. Once they understand the system and their role and responsibility, they should begin to accept ownership of the new system.

STANDARD ACTIVITIES/END ITEMS

TOUCHE ROSS

ORGANIZATION __PHASE III__
STEP 6
SYSTEM __DEVELOPMENT__
USER REP _____

ID/TITLE ___USER TRAINING___

☐ PHASE ☑ ACTIVITY ☐ SUBTASK
☐ STEP   ☒ TASK   ☐ _____

PAGE 1 OF 2
PROJECT NO. _____

	PREPARED BY	REVIEWED BY	DATE	PHASE
	MVJ	CB	3/29/80	III-6
	SH	CB	11/1/80	III-6

NUMBER	PHASE/STEP/ACTIVITY/TASK/SUBTASK NAME	END ITEM	FORM NO.	PERFORMED BY	DUE DATE	APPROVED BY	DATE
A.	Review User Training Strategy and Finalize Approach	Training Checklist and Plan	182,195				
B.	Prepare Detailed Work Plan	Work Outline	101				
		Project Plan	102				
C.	Develop User Training Program	Training Material Outline	183				
		Training List	142				
		Visual Aids Outlines	183				
		Personnel and Equipment Plan	193				
D.	Prepare Training Materials	System Training Guides					
		Visual Aids					
		Handouts					
E.	Confirm User Schedule and Commitment for Training	Training Schedule	102,195				
		Confirmation Letter					
F.	Conduct Initial Training Program	Training Material					
G.	Obtain User Feedback	Written Critique	111				
H.	Modify ...ning Program						

TOUCHE ROSS

STANDARD ACTIVITIES/END ITEMS

PAGE __2__ OF __2__
PROJECT NO. _____

ORGANIZATION __PHASE III,__
STEP 6
SYSTEM __DEVELOPMENT__
USER REP _____

ID/TITLE __USER TRAINING__

☐ PHASE   ☒ ACTIVITY   ☐ SUBTASK
☐ STEP   ☒ TASK   ☐ _____

PREPARED BY __MVJ__ __SH__
REVIEWED BY __CB__ __CB__
DATE __3/29/80__ __11/1/80__
PHASE __III-6__ __III-6__

NUMBER	PHASE/STEP/ACTIVITY/TASK/SUBTASK NAME	END ITEM	FORM NO.	PERFORMED BY	DUE DATE	APPROVED BY	DATE
I.	Prepare System Training Guide for Next Sessions	System Training Guide					
		Visual Aids					
		Handouts					
J.	Assign Responsibility for Maintenance	Job Description	103				

All Rights Reserved

186

THE SYSTEMS DEVELOPMENT PROCESS

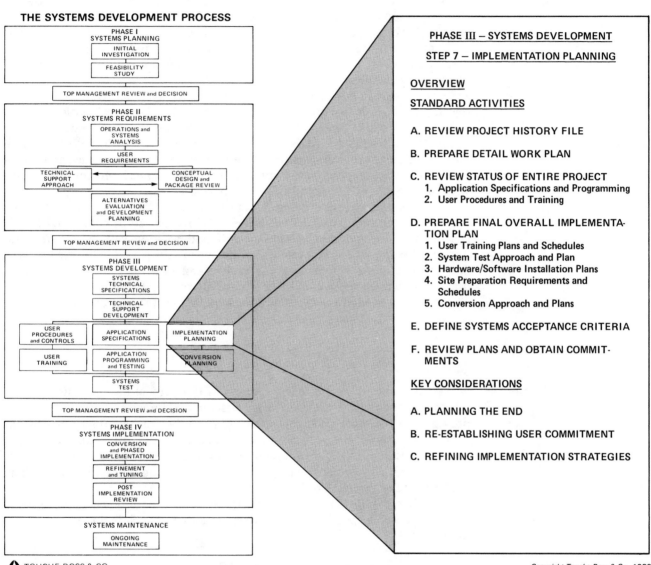

PHASE I
SYSTEMS PLANNING

INITIAL
INVESTIGATION

FEASIBILITY
STUDY

TOP MANAGEMENT REVIEW and DECISION

PHASE II
SYSTEMS REQUIREMENTS

OPERATIONS and
SYSTEMS
ANALYSIS

USER
REQUIREMENTS

TECHNICAL
SUPPORT
APPROACH

CONCEPTUAL
DESIGN and
PACKAGE REVIEW

ALTERNATIVES
EVALUATION
and DEVELOPMENT
PLANNING

TOP MANAGEMENT REVIEW and DECISION

PHASE III
SYSTEMS DEVELOPMENT

SYSTEMS
TECHNICAL
SPECIFICATIONS

TECHNICAL
SUPPORT
DEVELOPMENT

USER
PROCEDURES
and CONTROLS

APPLICATION
SPECIFICATIONS

IMPLEMENTATION
PLANNING

USER
TRAINING

APPLICATION
PROGRAMMING
and TESTING

CONVERSION
PLANNING

SYSTEMS
TEST

TOP MANAGEMENT REVIEW and DECISION

PHASE IV
SYSTEMS IMPLEMENTATION

CONVERSION
and PHASED
IMPLEMENTATION

REFINEMENT
and TUNING

POST
IMPLEMENTATION
REVIEW

SYSTEMS MAINTENANCE

ONGOING
MAINTENANCE

△ TOUCHE ROSS & CO.

PHASE III — SYSTEMS DEVELOPMENT

STEP 7 — IMPLEMENTATION PLANNING

OVERVIEW

STANDARD ACTIVITIES

A. REVIEW PROJECT HISTORY FILE

B. PREPARE DETAIL WORK PLAN

C. REVIEW STATUS OF ENTIRE PROJECT
 1. Application Specifications and Programming
 2. User Procedures and Training

D. PREPARE FINAL OVERALL IMPLEMENTA-
 TION PLAN
 1. User Training Plans and Schedules
 2. System Test Approach and Plan
 3. Hardware/Software Installation Plans
 4. Site Preparation Requirements and
 Schedules
 5. Conversion Approach and Plans

E. DEFINE SYSTEMS ACCEPTANCE CRITERIA

F. REVIEW PLANS AND OBTAIN COMMIT-
 MENTS

KEY CONSIDERATIONS

A. PLANNING THE END

B. RE-ESTABLISHING USER COMMITMENT

C. REFINING IMPLEMENTATION STRATEGIES

OVERVIEW   Implementation Planning, in conjunction with the following step, Conversion Planning, is conducted as a final preparation before initiating Phase IV, Systems Implementation. Previous steps throughout the development process have included conceptual approaches and strategies for conversion and implementation. These two steps are now required to finalize the plans and obtain clear commitments from all affected areas as to both required effort and schedules.

This step is initiated after completion of systems technical support development. It is conducted in parallel with the technical project team's effort to complete applications specifications and programming, and the nontechnical team's activities in user procedures and training. Both of these two planning steps are performed primarily by project management personnel interfacing with the technical and nontechnical project teams and with management of user and EDP departments.

The Implementation Planning and Conversion Planning step should not take very long compared to the other development steps conducted simultaneously. However, they should be initiated as soon as possible after the Technical Support Development step has been completed. This gives everyone the maximum opportunity to understand both role and responsibility during implementation and to complete all required preparation activities. The systems test cannot begin until these planning steps are completed.

STANDARD ACTIVITIES

Review Project History File   Several previous steps and end products of this project have produced documents that contain implementation plans and strategies. These documents provide the basis for finalizing the details of the forthcoming implementation. Since these initial plans and strategies were critical in developing economic evaluations and obtaining management approvals to proceed with development, the project managers must be thoroughly familiar with their contents and supporting rationale.

During the final step of Phase II, Systems Requirements, the project team developed a specific implementation strategy which included considerations of:

— Implementation timing of multiple system segments.
— Implementation timing of multiple locations.
— Need for a pilot implementation and site.
— Need to simultaneously process both the old and the new systems, or to use control approaches if not required.
— New system acceptance criteria.
— Approach to phasing out current operations and realigning personnel.

In addition, at the end of the Systems Technical Specifications step, the implementation costs and commitments were updated to reflect the project team's improved understanding of the technical aspects of the system. Finally, the Technical Support Development step may have resulted in some

188

adjustments to schedules or to specific implementation considerations involving data base loading and on-line operations.

Prepare Detailed Work Plan

A project plan for this step was prepared near the conclusion of Phase II. This plan outlined major activities and resources required to complete implementation planning. Since this step is basically performed by the project managers, specific identification of resources to assign to activities and tasks is only minimally required. Instead, it is critical to ensure that all persons to be contacted and all schedules to be coordinated are identified and included as activities and tasks.

Review Status of Entire Project

As indicated earlier, this step is performed simultaneously with both a technical project team effort and a nontechnical project team effort. Project managers must avoid finalizing the implementation plans in a vacuum. Thus, at this point, they should formally review the status and schedules of the concurrent development steps as follows:

Applications Specifications and Programming. The technical project team is now involved in developing detailed applications specifications, and applications programming may have been initiated. In any case, this team's first activities involved preparing a detailed work plan for both steps and conducting a structured walkthru of the entire system. This technical review is therefore designed to update the project manager's understanding of the technical work plans, status, and any overall project implications of technical work to date. This information will be used in subsequent activities to plan the systems test and detail acceptance criteria.

User Procedures and Training. The nontechnical project team is now involved in developing manual control procedures and may have begun to develop a training program. At the very least, however, this team has finalized its approach to procedures development and training and has prepared a detailed work plan for completing the procedures manuals. The project manager's review identifies any overall project schedule or other required activity changes resulting from the approaches and work plan developed to date.

Prepare Final Overall Implementation Plan

The previously developed implementation plans and strategies, together with information regarding current project schedule and status, are now used to prepare a finalized overall implementation plan. This plan addresses user training, systems test, hardware and software installation, site preparation, and conversion. Much of this planning process requires direct interfaces with user management, EDP management, vendors, and others.

User Training Plans and Schedules. This plan component is primarily the responsibility of the nontechnical members of the project team and is produced as part of the User Training step. It is also included in this step as a reminder that project managers must also be directly involved in developing training plans and schedules. It is essential that training sessions and timing of new system availability be well coordinated.

System Test Approach and Plan. This plan component provides the detailed approach and tasks required to conduct the Systems Test step. It is critical that this testing plan be carefully and thoroughly constructed so that it will lead to a controlled environment for testing the entire new system. All participants will be requested to sign-off on the new system at the conclusion of systems test, indicating acceptance of test results and approval to proceed with implementation. Thus, sufficient testing must be included in the plan to provide each participant with results on which to base approval. More details regarding this testing process are given in Step 9 of this phase, Systems Test, which should be reviewed before preparing this component of the plan.

The systems test is an integrated test of the computer programs, manual controls, and procedures as they will exist in the new system environment. It is performed by trained user and EDP operations personnel who will be using the system (in addition to project team members). Thus, the schedule for the systems test must be coordinated with the existing schedules for user training and applications programming and testing.

Three critical areas to be addressed when constructing the systems test plan are:

— Adequate testing must be planned to verify that the system (programs and procedures) accomplishes its desired objectives and does not fail when unanticipated events occur.

— Adequate personnel and equipment resources must be allocated to conduct test runs, check-out test results, and correct programs, procedures, forms, and controls.

— Adequate time must be allocated to permit continued testing until all necessary conditions have been checked and corrected, and all participants are satisfied with the new operations.

A Computer Test Plan form and System Test Checklist are recommended to assist in preparing this plan.

Hardware/Software Installation Plans. This plan component addresses the installation of all new central and remote equipment and systems software required by the new system. The plan includes those activities necessary for physical installation, vendor checkout, and customer acceptance. Schedules must be coordinated with the project needs during applications programming, user training, systems test, conversion, and phased implementation. Care should be taken to avoid unnecessary costs that result from installing hardware or software either significantly prior to or after the time required by the overall project schedule. A review of vendor contracts is also necessary at this time to verify that the plan is consistent with contractual commitments regarding acceptance timing and criteria, warranty provisions, notification procedures, and payment timing. Any conflicts between these contract provisions and the project plan should be immediately reviewed with the responsible user or EDP manager and resolved with the vendor if required. To the extent that vendor shipment notifications are necessary, they should be prepared at this time but not actually sent until all reviews and commitments have been obtained.

Site Preparation Requirements and Schedules. This planning activity is actually an extension of the previous hardware/software installation plans. The site preparation requirements and schedules reflect all the other physical space and equipment preparation for the new system, including power, air conditioning, controls over security access, and furniture. Physical specification manuals supplied by the vendors should be reviewed and discussed with the appropriate department managers. As in all planning processes, the impact of schedule changes should be analyzed and contingency approaches should be identified and documented at this time.

Conversion Approach and Plans. Development of detailed plans for conversion constitute the major activities of the next step — Conversion Planning. However, at this point it is necessary to review the previously developed strategies and general plans for conversion, modify them where appropriate, and incorporate them into the current overall plans and schedules for implementation. If commitments are obtained for the overall implementation plan at the end of this step, details of the required conversion activities will be specified in the next step. This does not imply that conversion approaches and plans are ignored at this point — simply that the specific details regarding conversion activities and tasks are not necessarily determined at this time.

Define Systems Acceptance Criteria

The overall implementation plan developed above indicates two major points where systems acceptance is required: at the conclusion of systems test; and at the conclusion of each aspect of a phased implementation. At each point, success must be measurable with sufficient objectivity to determine whether or not the new system should be accepted. Thus, criteria must be defined that are both objective and measurable. These criteria may generally be developed by reviewing the requirements and systems technical specifications documents and may address such characteristics as:

— Response times for various types of transactions are within prescribed time limits.

— The types of input data that must be entered and properly handled by the system.

— Every report specified in User Requirements has been produced and is usable.

— Manual control procedures and forms are usable and fulfill their required functions.

— The system flows through its cycle within specified time constraints.

— Procedures reference manuals are easy to use and accurately describe report contents and error correction procedures.

— All backup and recovery methods and procedures operate properly.

The systems acceptance criteria are specified on a formalized document that includes checklists and other appropriate methods for indicating each item with eventual evidence of its acceptance. The specified benefits of the new system are often inappropriate for inclusion as acceptance criteria. This occurs whenever elapsed time is required after implementation before any benefits can be realized. The Post-Implementation Review (Phase IV, Step 3) includes analysis of realized benefits in addition to the other system review topics.

Review Plans and Obtain Commitments

The overall implementation plan, with its component plans and systems acceptance criteria, is now assembled and prepared for review. This may include distribution of complete copies for detailed review and preparation of summary charts for presentation and discussion. Whatever methods are used, the plans must effectively communicate each participant's role, responsibility, and schedule. Plans are not final until understood and committed to by all parties. This review and commitment process may be difficult to complete, but should not be avoided. Implementation of new systems may be very disruptive to user and data processing organizations. If some areas do not fulfill assigned responsibilities, the implementation process can become even more difficult and may result in long-term negative attitudes toward the new system.

KEY CONSIDERATIONS

Planning the End

One of the most difficult criteria to define within a system development project can be the determination of when the project is over. Failure to develop such a definition, and to have it understood explicitly by both user and EDP managers, can dramatically add to costs and schedules of a project. Unless there is a clear definition of a termination point, a project can literally drag on indefinitely. The challenge lies in securing agreement among members of the project team, user personnel, and EDP operations, on exactly when a system should be considered operational and therefore subject to maintenance rather than continuing development. An important element in this picture is a commitment by the user that once the predetermined conditions have been met, existing systems will be discontinued and the new system will be considered accepted.

Misunderstandings frequently arise over the projected handling of system enhancements identified following completion of the design during the Systems Technical Specifications step. There is a tendency for user management to assume that the project team will remain intact until all new opportunities have been implemented. On the other hand, members of the project team tend to assume that enhancements will be handled as part of ongoing maintenance for the new system.

The potential problem — if this misunderstanding is not resolved during implementation planning — is that the user, at the close of the project, may refuse to accept the new system until all changes have been implemented.

This same misunderstanding can have an impact on budget presentations made to the steering committee. The project team may present budget estimates based on the assumption that system enhancements will be handled as maintenance assignments, while users assume that they are included within the project structure. Such misunderstandings could ultimately lead to substantial variances in costs, schedules, and return on investment for individual projects.

Reestablishing User Commitment

A new dimension and degree of user commitment is demanded during this step. In earlier steps, discussions centered primarily around benefits and improved results. In this step, the project reaches a point where the user must understand that sacrifices and inconveniences will be necessary to realize improvements. Thus, it becomes important to clarify the degree of commitment requested and to renew or modify assurances of user participation. Any reduction in user commitment should be understood and resolved. Significant reductions in user commitment level should be reported to the steering committee as a problem requiring resolution before proceeding with implementation.

Refining Implementation Strategies

The key word here is refining. This is not the place in the project to *begin* thinking about setting implementation strategy. If strategies are considered for the first time during this step, the requirements they might impose can have a serious impact upon the costs and schedules of the project. For example, if the concept for phased implementation is introduced for the first time during this step, extensive reworking of the system's technical design may be necessary. This, in turn, could severely impact the project's costs and schedules.

Implementation strategies should have been planned on a preliminary basis during Systems Planning and Systems Requirements (Phases I and II). During this step, emphasis should be on updating and fine-tuning implementation strategies.

STANDARD ACTIVITIES/END ITEMS

TOUCHE ROSS

ORGANIZATION __PHASE III,__
STEP __7__
SYSTEM __DEVELOPMENT__
USER REP _____

ID/TITLE __IMPLEMENTATION PLANNING__

☐ PHASE   ☒ ACTIVITY   ☐ SUBTASK
☐ STEP   ☒ TASK   ☐

	PREPARED BY	MVJ	SH
	REVIEWED BY	CB	CB
	DATE	3/29/80	11/1/80
	PHASE	III-7	III-7

NUMBER	PHASE/STEP/ACTIVITY/TASK/SUBTASK NAME	END ITEM	FORM NO.	PERFORMED BY	DUE DATE	APPROVED BY	DATE
A.	Review Project History File						
B.	Prepare Detailed Work Plan	Work Outline	101				
		Project Plan	102				
C.	Review Status of Entire Project						
C.1	- Application Specifications and Programming						
C.2	- User Procedures and Training						
D.	Prepare Final Overall Implementation Plan						
D.1	- User Training Plans and Schedules	User Training Plan	182, 195				
		Work Outline	101				
		Detailed Schedules	102				
		Personnel and Equipment Plan	193				
D.2	- System Test Approach and Plan	System Test Checklist	180				
		System Test Plan	190				
		Personnel and Equipment Plan	193				
D.3	- Hardware/Software Installation Plans	Installation Plan	183				
		Personnel and Equipment Plan	193				

STANDARD ACTIVITIES/END ITEMS

TOUCHE ROSS

ORGANIZATION ___PHASE III,___
    ___STEP 7___
SYSTEM ___DEVELOPMENT___
USER REP _____

ID/TITLE ___IMPLEMENTATION PLANNING___

☐ PHASE   ☒ ACTIVITY   ☐ SUBTASK
☐ STEP   ☒ TASK   ☐ _____

PAGE _2_ OF _2_
PROJECT NO. _____

	PREPARED BY	MWJ	SH
REVIEWED BY	CB	CB
DATE	3/29/80	11/1/80
PHASE	III-7	III-7

NUMBER	PHASE/STEP/ACTIVITY/TASK/SUBTASK NAME	END ITEM	FORM NO.	PERFORMED BY	DUE DATE	APPROVED BY	DATE
		Summary Personnel and Equipment Plan	193				
D.4	- Site Preparation Requirements and Schedules						
D.5	- Conversion Approach and Plans	Outline Conversion Planning Checklist	181				
		Outline Conversion Plan	191				
		Outline Data Acquisition Plan	192				
		Outline Personnel and Equipment Plan	193				
E.	Define Systems Acceptance Criteria	Acceptance Criteria	190, 142				
F.	Review Plans and Obtain Commitments	Implementation Plans	102, 190 193, 195				
		Management Summary	149				

© Touche Ross & Co., 1980
All Rights Reserved

195

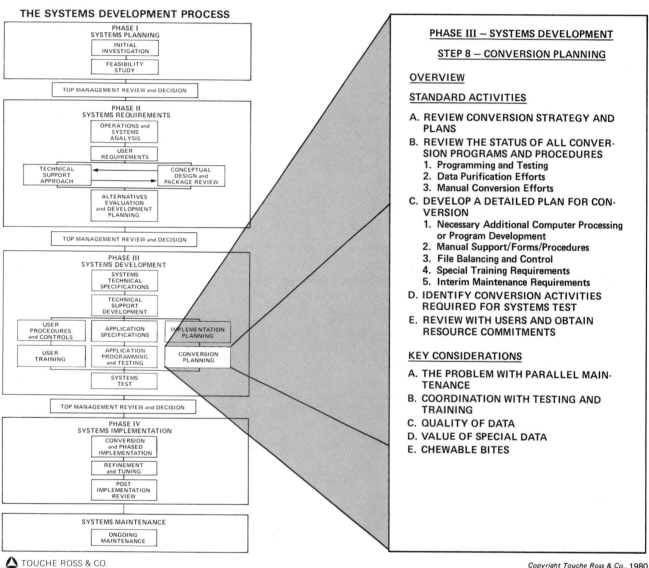

OVERVIEW   The Conversion Planning step is the second major planning step conducted in preparation for Phase IV, Systems Implementation. Previous steps throughout the development process have included conceptual approaches and strategies for conversion. They may also have included identification of special conversion programs and manual procedure requirements which are in process of development. This step is now required to review the status of special activities and to finalize detailed plans for converting to the new system.

Conversion planning is initiated immediately after completion of the final overall implementation plans. All participants are now aware of their implementation responsibilities and are committed to perform their activities within the published implementation schedules.

This step, like its predecessor, is performed primarily by project management personnel interfacing with the technical and nontechnical project teams and with management of user and EDP departments. Conversion planning should not require much time compared to the programming, procedures, and training steps conducted simultaneously. However, it should be completed as soon as possible to allow maximum time for any conversion preparation activities. Since some conversion activities may be required for testing, this step must be completed before the systems test can begin.

STANDARD ACTIVITIES

Review Conversion
Strategy and Plans

Several previous activities within this project have resulted in documents that contain conversion strategies and plans. The most significant of these documents was the result of the last step of Phase II, Systems Requirements. At that time, the tasks necessary for conversion of files, preparation of data collection forms, and creation of conversion programs were outlined. Also identified were the desired sequence of conversion and the need to purify data before acceptance into the new system. This document was modified wherever appropriate in the previous step and was then incorporated into the current overall implementation schedules.

For this activity, project managers must assure themselves that they are thoroughly familiar with defined strategies and plans, including the supporting rationale.

Review the Status of All
Conversion Programs
and Procedures

As indicated above, previously developed conversion strategies and plans may have identified the need for special conversion programs and procedures. If so, these activities should currently be in process as part of the work plans for the technical and nontechnical project teams. Thus, at this point project managers should formally review the status of these activities.

Programming and Testing. The technical project team is now involved in developing detailed applications specifications and programs. In the previous step, project managers conducted a formal technical review to understand the technical work plans and current status of the programming and testing efforts. They now need to conduct a more specific review of the approach and status of those programs intended for use in conversion. This may or may not include special programs. However, careful consideration should be made of any regular programs that are planned to be used for conversion.

For example, the normal input/edit program may be planned for use in entering data to build new master records. This review should determine if the edits require certain data fields that are not initially available due to time constraints or lack of historical information. If so, a special version of this edit program may be required for conversion to bypass the normal input requirements. Also, the initial file build may be planned to result from the normal file maintenance program. Again, this approach should be carefully reviewed. The file maintenance program may be designed to very efficiently add or change a limited number of records projected to change on each production cycle. However, this design could be extremely inefficient when presented with a large volume of records. If so, a complete new file build program may be required. Finally, the planned conversion effort may require various special listings or control reports which have not been specified as required in the normal ongoing system. In this case, the project managers' review should ascertain the status and adequacy of these special report programs.

Data Purification Efforts.   During the analysis of current operations within Phase II, Systems Requirements, the project team may have encountered major errors or omissions in existing manual files that are now to be converted to computer-based operations. Once systems requirements were finalized and approved, a significant data purification effort should have been initiated to prepare these files for conversion. This effort may not be included within the direct management of the systems development project. However, its completion may well be critical to the overall timing and success of the upcoming conversion activities. It is therefore vital that a formal review be conducted at this point to determine the status and completion targets for all data purification efforts. The review may result in revised plans for the amount of data to be initially converted or new approaches for phasing in purified data once implementation has been completed. The impact of such revisions must be fully understood and documented, and other affected schedules must be changed to reflect new approaches.

Manual Conversion Efforts.   In addition to the data purification described above, certain other manual conversion efforts may be required in preparation for the new system. This may involve copying data on new system forms or capturing and storing information through new data entry terminals. In these instances, the nontechnical project team may be directly involved because of requirements for new forms, procedures, controls, and training programs. Thus, this review should determine the status and adequacy of the activities intended to develop these items. Any special conversion programs may require special forms, procedures, and controls. Furthermore, the availability of these materials and trained personnel must be timed so as to be consistent with the overall schedules for conversion and implementation.

Develop a Detailed Plan for Conversion   The previously developed conversion strategies and plans, together with new information regarding the current status of all conversion programs and procedures, are now used to prepare a finalized detailed plan for conversion. This plan addresses special program development, necessary computer processing workloads, manual support requirements, special forms and procedures, file balancing and control considerations, special training programs, and interim file maintenance requirements. The end result of this planning activity is a formal document that is the basis for obtaining necessary commitments at the end of this step.

Necessary Additional Computer Processing or Program Development. The preceding review of conversion programming status may have identified the need for additional one-time programs or special one-time modifications to certain other programs. If so, these items are now documented in the conversion plan. Documentation should adequately describe the rationale for any additional programs and should also list program requirements in sufficient detail so that, once approved, they can be developed by the technical project team. The second major portion of this task involves planning computer processing resource requirements. Based on the project managers' current understanding of the manual conversion effort and conversion program approach, the requirements for conversion processing are now documented. This involves working with management of user and computer operations departments to develop workload estimates and processing schedules. Allowances should be made in the plan for multiple cycles of the conversion data to enter corrections and verify results. All data processing overtime and special shift operations requirements must also be identified and documented at this time.

Manual Support/Forms/Procedures. The review of current and required data purification and manual conversion efforts may have identified the need to devote additional personnel to these activities for timely completion. Estimates of the number and type of support and the required time frames are now documented. Any additional forms or procedures to be developed are also noted, with appropriate activities incorporated into the conversion plan. Requirements for manual support, including overtime and temporary personnel needs, must also be consistent with the conversion processing schedules developed in the previous task.

File Balancing and Control. One important aspect of the conversion process is the need for initial computer files in the new system to contain accurate and balanced data. Thus, the conversion plan should document the detailed requirements for controlling conversion data input and balancing the new files as they are established in the computer system. Activities required to develop these balancing and control procedures are identified and incorporated into the appropriate work plans. Staffing requirements to perform the actual balancing and control functions during the conversion process are also identified and documented.

Special Training Requirements. The conversion process includes many one-time activities, and as such are not among the normal training programs being developed by the nontechnical project team. Some of these activities, such as data purification efforts, may currently be in process and on schedule. As such, they do not require any additional training considerations. Other activities — such as conversion data entry and file balancing and control — may not have been initiated and may require developing and setting up special training programs before they may begin. New systems involving large file conversions may require hiring temporary additional personnel for short periods of time to complete the conversion preparation activities. These personnel also require special training programs if they are to accomplish the desired results. Training requirements for all these situations must be documented. Activities required to develop training materials and programs are identified and incorporated into the appropriate work plans. Conversion schedules are prepared so as to allow enough time for the completion of all necessary special training.

Interim Maintenance Requirements. Manual conversion efforts in the preparation and entry of data into the new system's files may extend over a period of time during which the old system is still operating and normal file changes are occurring. Procedures and controls must therefore be established that will permit all such changes made to the old files to be incorporated into the new files. The conversion plan must reflect the requirements for instituting these procedures and controls at the same time as manual file conversion efforts are initiated.

Identify Conversion Activities Required for Systems Test

Up until now, the planning process has been primarily concerned with identifying the activities and schedules required for full conversion during the Systems Implementation phase. Supplementing these plans are the additional conversion activities required to conduct a systems test. To identify these activities, project managers must first review the detailed plans for systems test prepared in the previous step (Implementation Planning). Those systems test plans may indicate several levels of testing, each implying a different requirement for special conversion data. Initial systems tests may be planned with a limited amount of data and may thus have little, if any, requirement for file conversions. Later on, the testing plans may require virtually the entire converted files in simulations of normal new operations, or in volume or stress testing. The conversion activities required to support these systems tests are then identified and incorporated into the overall conversion plans. In systems that involve large or complex conversions requiring many new programs and procedures, a separate systems test of the conversion should also be developed and included in the overall plans.

Review with Users and Obtain Resource Commitments

The detailed conversion plans, including all preparation activities and all conversion requirements for testing and implementation, are now assembled and prepared for review. This process may include distribution of complete copies for review and preparation of summary charts for presentation and discussion. Whatever methods may be used to present the plans must effectively communicate each participant's role, responsibility, and schedule. In the previous step, detailed implementation plans were reviewed and approved by many of these same participants. These conversion plans now present the details of the activities, schedules, and resource plans. In some cases, the process of developing detailed conversion plans may bring about changes to the overall implementation plans. If so, it is critical for all parties to understand not only the conversion plans, but also the revised implementation plans.

None of the plans may be considered final until all parties are committed to their own required activities. As with the implementation plan review process, obtaining commitments for conversion activities and schedules may be difficult to complete but cannot be avoided. Conversion resource requirements may strain the capacities of user and computer operations departments. They may result in excessive overtime and other out-of-pocket expenses that managers are reluctant to authorize. Nevertheless, new systems cannot be successful if the required conversions do not result in new system files that are complete, accurate, and in balance.

The Problem with Parallel Maintenance

One of the most complicated logistics and control problems involved in conversions is the parallel maintenance of files in the old and new systems. This problem occurs at two points in the project. First, while manual conversion preparation activities are in process, new system files are being created while the old system continues to operate. Second, if the implementation strategy includes parallel operation of the old and new systems after conversion, normal maintenance transactions must be applied to both systems in order to maintain parallel or consistent files. This second point can be avoided by developing an implementation strategy which avoids parallel processing. The absence of a parallel operation may be most reasonable in many systems that are not really computerized approaches for previous manual operations.

It is usual in new systems to retain different types of data with different criteria for acceptance than were applicable in the old system. This situation complicates the parallel maintenance process because the same maintenance transaction presented to both systems often produces different results.

Coordination with Testing and Training

The systems test and implementation process is a point at which many systems development projects appear to be out of control. There are many reasons for this. One of the more critical shortcomings, however, is a lack of adequate planning for the conversion requirements. Conversion plans that are not adequately coordinated with training programs and schedules result in untrained staff creating data for the new system. This in turn results in incomplete and inaccurate new files and often leads to a situation where the actual status of the new files is unknown. Major efforts are then required to determine what data has been accepted, what data is missing, and where out-of-balance conditions exist.

Similarly, conversion plans that are not coordinated with testing needs and schedules result in the inability to adequately complete systems tests because of the lack of data or the absence of files. Coupled with the inevitable pressures to get a new system implemented, this problem may result in proceeding with conversion without first completing sufficient systems testing. The risk that major errors will occur during initial operations of the new system then becomes much higher.

Quality of Data

The use of computer-based files often implies a much higher level of accuracy in the data than that required in corresponding manual files. Thus, it is extremely critical for the project team to understand the quality of existing data early in the development project. If major data purification efforts are required prior to conversion, but are not recognized until Conversion Planning, then major delays in implementation are likely to occur.

The minimum quality level of the data required for a new system to produce adequate results is ultimately a judgment issue. There is often a point at which the effort required to purify data becomes significantly greater than the improvement in operations expected to result.

Value of Special Data

A common fallacy in the preparation of conversion plans is to assume that every data element maintained in the new system must be converted. This generally occurs where files contain several years of historical information. The collective judgment of user and project management must be applied to determine the value of converting this special data. If users are expected to initially concentrate on obtaining maximum benefit from current information maintained in the system, then initial conversions of historical information could be virtually useless. In such cases, the new system would automatically generate historical information with the passage of time. This same judgment process should be applied to all data in developing the conversion requirements.

Chewable Bites

Plans may specify conversion of all files at one time, or phased-in conversions of portions of files over an extended time period. The term "chewable bites" here means that the plans should reflect the abilities of organizations to accomplish the proposed tasks. This may require creative approaches to address the needs of conversion. In any case, plans that place an undue burden on user organizations or computer operations and cause them to "choke" when they are trying to be executed are not practical.

STANDARD ACTIVITIES/END ITEMS

ID/TITLE CONVERSION PLANNING

☐ PHASE ☒ ACTIVITY ☐ SUBTASK
☐ STEP   ☒ TASK   ☐

TOUCHE ROSS

ORGANIZATION PHASE III,
STEP 8
SYSTEM DEVELOPMENT
USER REP

PROJECT NO. _____

	PREPARED BY	REVIEWED BY
	MVJ	SH
	CB	CB
DATE	3/29/80	11/1/80
PHASE	III-8	III-8

NUMBER	PHASE/STEP/ACTIVITY/TASK/SUBTASK NAME	END ITEM	FORM NO.	PERFORMED BY	DUE DATE	APPROVED BY	DATE
A.	Review Conversion Strategy and Plans	Conversion Checklist and Plans	181, 191				
B.	Review Status of all Conversion Programs and Procedures						
B.1	- Programming and Testing	Operational Code and Status	108				
B.2	- Data Purification Efforts	Status Report	108				
B.3	- Manual Conversion Efforts	Status Report	108				
C.	Develop a Detailed Plan for Conversion	Conversion Checklist and Plans	181, 191				
C.1	- Necessary Additional Computer Processing or Program Development	Program Specifications	III-3				
C.2	- Manual Support/Forms/Procedures	Personnel and Equipment Plan	193				
C.3	- File Balancing and Control	Summary of Controls	141				
C.4	- Special Training Requirements	User Procedures and Training Checklist	182				
		User Procedures and Training Plan	195				
C.5	- Interim Maintenance Requirements	Work Definition	125, 126, 142				
D.	Identify Conversion Activities Required for Systems Test	Checklist and Plans	181, 191				
E.	Review With Users and Obtain Resource Commitments	Conversion Plans	191				
		Management Summary	149				

THE SYSTEMS DEVELOPMENT PROCESS

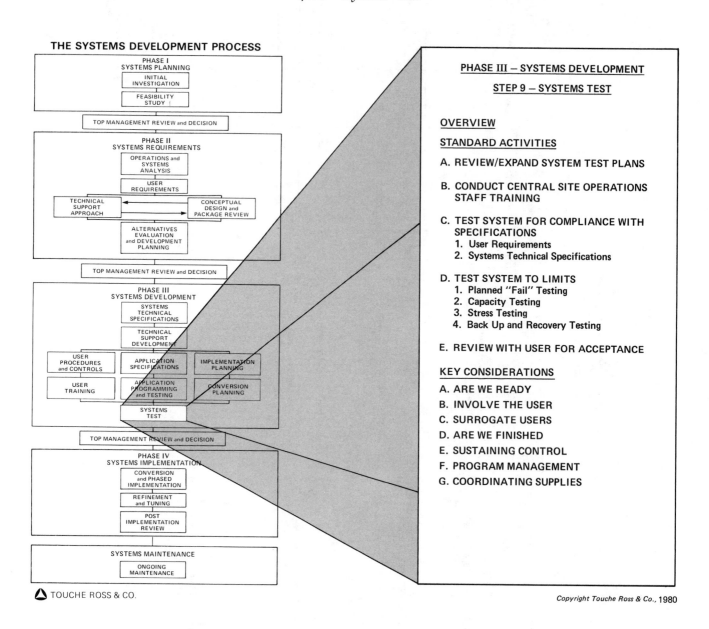

PHASE I
SYSTEMS PLANNING

INITIAL INVESTIGATION

FEASIBILITY STUDY

TOP MANAGEMENT REVIEW and DECISION

PHASE II
SYSTEMS REQUIREMENTS

OPERATIONS and SYSTEMS ANALYSIS

USER REQUIREMENTS

TECHNICAL SUPPORT APPROACH

CONCEPTUAL DESIGN and PACKAGE REVIEW

ALTERNATIVES EVALUATION and DEVELOPMENT PLANNING

TOP MANAGEMENT REVIEW and DECISION

PHASE III
SYSTEMS DEVELOPMENT

SYSTEMS TECHNICAL SPECIFICATIONS

TECHNICAL SUPPORT DEVELOPMENT

USER PROCEDURES and CONTROLS

APPLICATION SPECIFICATIONS

IMPLEMENTATION PLANNING

USER TRAINING

APPLICATION PROGRAMMING and TESTING

CONVERSION PLANNING

SYSTEMS TEST

TOP MANAGEMENT REVIEW and DECISION

PHASE IV
SYSTEMS IMPLEMENTATION

CONVERSION and PHASED IMPLEMENTATION

REFINEMENT and TUNING

POST IMPLEMENTATION REVIEW

SYSTEMS MAINTENANCE

ONGOING MAINTENANCE

PHASE III — SYSTEMS DEVELOPMENT

STEP 9 — SYSTEMS TEST

OVERVIEW

STANDARD ACTIVITIES

A. REVIEW/EXPAND SYSTEM TEST PLANS

B. CONDUCT CENTRAL SITE OPERATIONS STAFF TRAINING

C. TEST SYSTEM FOR COMPLIANCE WITH SPECIFICATIONS
1. User Requirements
2. Systems Technical Specifications

D. TEST SYSTEM TO LIMITS
1. Planned "Fail" Testing
2. Capacity Testing
3. Stress Testing
4. Back Up and Recovery Testing

E. REVIEW WITH USER FOR ACCEPTANCE

KEY CONSIDERATIONS

A. ARE WE READY
B. INVOLVE THE USER
C. SURROGATE USERS
D. ARE WE FINISHED
E. SUSTAINING CONTROL
F. PROGRAM MANAGEMENT
G. COORDINATING SUPPLIES

△ TOUCHE ROSS & CO.

OVERVIEW The purpose of this step is to perform an efficient, accurate, and complete test of all components of the system. This includes all the computerized and manual procedures in an integrated fashion.

In Step 4, Applications Programming, program modules were tested individually and there was some "string testing" of the related program modules. In Step 6, User Training, procedures were tested in a training environment. Throughout these earlier steps, errors were dealt with as they were identified. Thus, to the best of the project team's knowledge, the system to be tested consists of a series of valid and proven programs and procedures.

In the systems development process, there are multiple interrelationships between programs that can be tested only under volume conditions. The testing that occurred earlier is not sufficient to guarantee that the system will work properly (any more than the performance of an assembled engine can be guaranteed when all of its parts have been tested individually). Actual operational considerations are the key to the systems test because they place the system under the same kind of daily conditions and stresses encountered during regular operations, including both technical and human stresses. To fully test these conditions, the systems test includes deliberately caused errors and difficulties specifically intended to force the system to fail so as to test its error detection and recovery capabilities. Both human and physical types of failures are introduced. These erroneous transactions are purposely inserted in the processing scheme to see how the system handles them. Moreover, computer operations are deliberately interrupted to determine how the system will handle such problems as hardware failures and system software failures. In each case, the objective is to ensure that the risks have been anticipated and that the system can recover from failure.

STANDARD ACTIVITIES

Review/Expand Systems
Test Plans
A series of tasks is structured within this activity to update the systems test plan and systems test checklist developed in earlier steps. The test plan is reviewed in light of all changes which have taken place since it was initiated. Plan components are expanded to the level of detail necessary for close control of testing activities and the evaluation of results. The test plan defines all the necessary steps for the comprehensive testing of the new system, including those steps necessary both for conversion and ongoing production. This work is performed by the systems development personnel on the project team, users, auditors, EDP operations, and the standards compliance group.

The team reviews, evaluates, and updates the test plans for individual programs. This work centers around a series of individual program test plans developed in the Applications Programming step. During the concluding portions of applications programming, some of the programs may have been revised on the basis of reviews of test results. These revisions may alter the expected results of the revised programs and of other programs. If so, the test plan is modified accordingly. Further, in the context of a full systems test within this step, it may be desirable to add some dimensions or criteria to the program test plan. At the conclusion of this activity, the project team has a series of test plans that cover all the known or expected conditions and results to be produced by the programs within the new system.

The testing of the computerized and the manual portions of the system takes place in a series of processing cycles. These cycles are carefully structured according to functional characteristics. For example, it is generally desirable for the test to cover several working days in the life of a system. This is planned to bring all of the reporting programs into play. By scheduling test cycles to represent the last two days of one month and the first day of the next, the test encompasses all conditions expected to be encountered during daily processing, including end-of-month or period changes. Inclusion of multiple days over a month-end provides an opportunity to test the cumulative reporting functions built into a month-end program.

Multiple test cycles are also needed because it is normally impossible to interject all the error failure conditions to be tested in a single cycle. Thus, a major function performed during this activity is the identification of error or failure conditions to be introduced by specific test cycles. All these conditions and their expected results are documented on systems test worksheets. One worksheet is prepared for each cycle to be run.

As the systems test checklists are reviewed, it may become apparent that additional test cycles must be added. Based upon the work performed in completing the test checklist, it will probably be necessary to alter the systems test work plan to accommodate newly identified cycles.

One of the key end products of this activity is the personnel and equipment plan necessary to complete the systems test. A significant amount of resources — both equipment and personnel — is normally required to perform an adequate systems test. This should be reviewed in detail, and commitments should be obtained from all appropriate organizations.

Conduct Central Site Operations Staff Training

Up to this point, the applications programs have been running in a test mode. The operations staff has been executing them with fairly rudimentary instructions. As the systems test begins, the operations staff is trained in the proper operation of the system. This provides the added benefit of a check on the procedures, run instructions, and other operating documentation.

Test System For Compliance With Specifications

The systems test plan must provide a vehicle to ensure that the features of the system, as defined in Systems Requirements (Phase II), are implemented in the intended way. The tasks that follow are oriented toward reviewing actual results versus anticipated results.

As test outputs are reviewed, differences between planned and actual results are noted. For each such difference or discrepancy, a Control form is initiated. This document serves as the primary tool for tracking the problem and its resolution throughout the remainder of the systems test. The following items are noted on the form:

— Priority (as discussed below).

— Unique sequential number.

— Brief description of discrepancy symptoms.

— Person who identified the error.

— Date of the discovery.

Supporting documentation such as copies of test outputs and operator logs are attached to the form as appropriate. During the logging of errors and test results, the team must take care not to involve itself in excessive fine-tuning. This will be performed after the system becomes operational. Changing procedures for the sake of minor improvements prolongs the systems test unnecessarily.

Where discrepancies have been identified and noted on a Control form, a detailed review of each discrepancy is required. This involves determining the causes for the discrepancies and finding their solution. When causes are identified and solutions prescribed, appropriate entries are added to the Control form. In addition, each item to be changed is identified at this time. An item may consist of a program, a user procedure, program documentation, or other systems elements. Responsibility for making the change is assigned, an estimate of the time required is entered, and a new working document is created — a Change Request form.

The Change Request form is designed to provide a detailed description of the change for the guidance of the person who will handle its implementation. Note that spaces in the form cross-refer to the sequential number of the Control form as well as the specific change item number. This important process helps ensure that documentation is current and that the project team has thought out all corrections necessary to fix a specific problem. (This technique is also useful in systems maintenance.)

The testing process can get bogged down by a tendency to regard all problems identified during the systems test as being equally critical. This practice can result in the inefficient use of program resources. For example, if report format changes are always considered as serious as errors in the updating of master files, there could be serious delays in completing the Systems Test step, which could in turn impact the entire project schedule.

To prevent delays, each discrepancy must be assigned a priority number as it is identified, such as that shown below:

Level A: Must be fixed before the next system test cycle.
Level B: Must be fixed before the subsystem will be approved by the user.
Level C: Must be fixed prior to implementation.
Level D: Will be fixed after implementation.

In practice, "A" priority changes are made immediately. "B" priority changes can be made in a block. Thus, if there are multiple "B" level changes for a single program, it becomes necessary to open that program only once. This conserves time and cost, since there is a relatively high fixed price to be paid each time a program is changed, no matter how many lines of code are changed. "C" level changes can be made at the programmer's convenience, as long as they are completed before the start of implementation. By setting this priority level, it becomes possible to proceed with systems test and conversion without schedule delays. Priority "D" gives recognition to the Refinement and Tuning Step (Phase IV, Step 2) in the overall development plan.

Once established, priorities are recorded on the appropriate Control form and on the corresponding Change Request forms. This allows all discrepancies to be monitored (regardless of priority level) and assists in maintaining control of those making the changes. Copies of these updated Change Request forms are then distributed to the people who will act upon them. As a final documentation step for the work in this task, the test checklist is updated to reflect the status of completed test cycles.

The programming of changes resulting from systems test discrepancies should proceed in the same manner as that for routine program maintenance assignments. That is, separate program and data files are maintained for preliminary and systems testing. When a programmer determines that changes have been made correctly, the project team coordinator is notified and the updated program is shifted to the systems test library. After several changes have been made, additional systems test cycles can be scheduled.

No subsystem can be considered fully tested until all supporting documentation has been updated. For each change item processed, minimum documentation should include:

— Change Request forms with documentation for the program.
— Control sheet signed off by the reviewer.
— Effective user procedures revised as necessary.
— Operating instructions or any other supporting documentation updated accordingly.

There are two major areas in which compliance may initially be tested. They are User Requirements (as defined in Phase II) and Systems Technical Specifications (as defined in Phase III).

User Requirements. Results anticipated in the test that normally relate to the user are output reports and the results of computations. These items were defined in detail in the Systems Requirement (Phase II). Specifically, the required features should be included in the systems test plan, as defined, for approval and sign-off by the users.

Systems Technical Specifications. These relate to the data base, data communications, and other technical features used to implement specified user requirements. Testing should include a review to ensure that all technical components work as anticipated and as designed in the earlier steps of this development phase. When working with data bases in particular, data element relationships can be complex, but it is important to test thoroughly enough to ensure that not only anticipated processing occurs, but also that unintended side effects do not impact the structure and content of the data base.

Test System to Limits   The focus of this activity is to test a system to its limits in order to determine both its real limits and its ability to fail in an orderly manner and to subsequently recover. In rigorously planned or critical systems, failure points and limits may be defined as part of the specifications. In this case, limit testing will focus on the extent to which implementation of the system has met specifications. Where limits have not been specified, it is still useful to determine them so that growth limits or critical operation conditions can be anticipated and unexpected blowups can be avoided.

Testing a system to its limits involves four major tasks or areas of activity:

Planned "Fail" Testing. All systems have areas in which failure can be anticipated. For a batch system, it may be a data sequence error or the overflow of a table or counter as a result of excessive data volumes. For a communications system, it may be receiving an endless stream of garbled characters as a result of an open line condition or an output line problem causing a queue overflow. Failures such as these can be anticipated and it is the responsibility of the test group to predict how failures will occur and, in particular, to keep data losses to a minimum (or, ideally, to zero). Each failure condition should be specified on the appropriate test form, be subjected to one or more test runs on the computer, and have the test results noted as part of the system's permanent documentation. In every case, the system must come to an orderly and expected halt.

Capacity Testing. Capacity testing can take many forms. For batch systems, testing is primarily oriented toward meeting throughput or turnaround requirements; that is, using the resources available and the anticipated data volumes, ensuring that production schedules can be met. For on-line systems, the capacity test will be primarily oriented toward ensuring that the system can meet required demand levels (e.g., that it can properly cope with all terminals being simultaneously active). As with fail testing, capacity testing involves careful planning and execution and the permanent documentation of test results for each measure of capacity.

Stress Testing. Perhaps the most difficult, stress testing involves an increasingly severe progression of tests incorporating different combinations of events. The objective remains to ensure that the system will not "blow up" at a time and in a manner which is unanticipated.

Stress testing requires particularly careful planning. Like *all* tests, it should be possible to rerun the test later with the same results. A comprehensive stress test plan will include the simulation of hardware malfunctions, extreme data volumes and combinations of data designed to provide the maximum utilization of all hardware, software and communications facilities.

Backup and Recovery Testing. No limit test can be considered complete without an exhaustive test of backup and recovery procedures. This includes specific tests of audit trails and transaction logging routines and of the manual procedures involved in operating while the data processing and/or communication system are degraded or inoperative. In the case of critical on-line systems, the effectiveness of manual backup procedures can be an important factor in maintaining credibility with customers or users. They may also be important in limiting financial liability (as in the case of orders in process at the time of system malfunction).

As critical as backup procedures, systems and procedures for restarting a system may involve such activities as the repositioning of magnetic tapes, the restoration of communications or other queues, and/or the manual reentry of missed transactions while ensuring that their execution is not duplicated. All capabilities required to recover completely from any type of malfunction must be thoroughly tested and the results documented. Furthermore, many of these tests should be repeated on a regular basis, like a fire drill, to ensure that all personnel are thoroughly familiar with backup and recovery roles.

Review with User
for Acceptance

As described earlier, subsystems are tested individually in a series of iterations. Once these subsystem tests are completed, the entire package is merged into a single system and a complete test of the entire system is conducted. This complete run-through of the system also serves as a basis for final approval prior to the preparation of a report for the steering committee. Each system's output is reviewed again to verify that every report and cycle is producing the expected results. For each output and cycle, review and approval is noted on the Approval form. In addition, a narrative memorandum is prepared indicating that the systems test is complete and the programs and procedures are ready for implementation. This memo should be prepared and/or approved by all affected parties.

Are We Ready? As a project nears the systems test, there is a great inclination to begin testing. It is important to understand when the system is, in fact, ready for a test. A premature start can cause problems. For example, if special test data and files have to be created and adequate procedures are not established for their backup, significant additional effort and costs may be incurred.

Involve the User Encouraging the users who will actually operate the system to participate in the systems test provides an excellent opportunity to instill in them valuable confidence in the evolving system. This confidence can be a vital asset during Systems Implementation (Phase IV), boosting the spirit of cooperation during the inevitable rough spots.

To help build user confidence, it is important at the outset of the systems test to educate users to the fact that errors and discrepancies will take place. By the end of the step, users who have participated in the identification and correction of errors are able to sign off with confidence that the system is in a state of operational readiness.

To minimize the shock effect that can result if users encounter a large number of discrepancies during this step, programs should be tested as thoroughly as possible during the Applications Programming and Testing step. Any temptation to debug programs for the first time during the systems test should be resisted.

No matter how strongly users are urged to participate in a systems test, there are occasions when the desired level of participation simply cannot be arranged. When this happens, systems analysts may act as the surrogate users. In adopting this role, the analyst must make every effort to participate as though devoid of technical background or vested interest in the project.

At the very least, users should be exposed to the results of the systems test and be asked to approve the outputs and procedures. However, it should be recognized that such a reduction in user involvement can cause potential problems, since the educational benefits normally achieved during the systems test will not be present during Systems Implementation (Phase IV). Therefore, when it is impossible to secure full user participation, additional time should be budgeted for hand-holding during the ensuing steps. In addition, users should be forewarned that their failure to participate at this juncture may lead to implementation problems.

Are We Finished? As users encounter the evolving system face-to-face they will inevitably recognize opportunities for improvement. With recognition will come a desire to add features to the system immediately. Project team management must set guidelines that will determine what changes are mandatory (to overcome discrepancies or major omissions in the definition of requirements or specifications) and which are optional (not immediately necessary for proper system performance). Each situation is different. Considerable judgment must be applied in determining when to incorporate changes and when to insist that the system be allowed to "settle down" and that changes be put off until the Refinement and Tuning Step (Phase IV, Step 2), or handled as maintenance items.

At a minimum, before committing to a change, the project team must reach an understanding with users about how to handle change requests. The user must recognize the impact of every change on the system and on implementation schedules. This understanding should be documented in the project file. Many so-called necessary changes are downgraded in priority or deferred once users are exposed to consequences of their immediate implementation.

Sustaining Control Documenting systems test procedures and results can be tedious. People get tired of continuing requirements to execute and update a mountain of control documentation. As the step proceeds, there is a tendency to minimize or ignore some of the specified documentation. When this happens, the ability to control testing activities and their impact on the quality and timeliness of the finished system diminishes. As a consequence, more discrepancies may appear during the implementation phase for subsystems that went through the systems test last.

To guard against this problem, the project manager should review systems test documentation periodically and take appropriate action when a lack of completeness is identified.

Program Management Although a number of forms have already been described in this chapter for use in identifying and tracking discrepancies and the status of test cycles, the addition of just one more can enhance a manager's ability to control the project. This additional form is a blackboard, used to list and show the status of change items requiring program modification.

When using this approach, it may be best to list change items according to programs to be modified. This gives the manager a graphic overview of program maintenance activities and minimizes the number of times each program must be opened for modification.

Coordinating Supplies Checking the supplies needed to support the systems test may seem a trivial consideration. At least it appears this way until a project actually experiences a shortage of disk packs or other necessary items. Such shortages are commonplace because of a failure to allow for exceptional interim supply needs and, in particular, for the large number of backup files maintained during this step. In fact, a project can come to a halt for lack of routine supplies. Supply requirements should therefore be reviewed in advance, allowing sufficient lead time to secure items that may be in short supply.

STANDARD ACTIVITIES/END ITEMS

▲ TOUCHE ROSS

ID/TITLE _____ SYSTEMS TEST

ORGANIZATION __PHASE III,__

STEP 9

SYSTEM __DEVELOPMENT__

USER REP _____

☐ PHASE   ☒ ACTIVITY   ☐ SUBTASK

☐ STEP   ☒ TASK   ☐

PREPARED BY	MVJ	SH
REVIEWED BY	CB	CB
DATE	3/29/80	11/1/80
PHASE	III-9	III-9

NUMBER	PHASE/STEP/ACTIVITY/TASK/SUBTASK NAME	END ITEM	FORM NO.	PERFORMED BY	DUE DATE	APPROVED BY	DATE
A.	Review/Expand Systems Test Plans	System Test Checklist	180				
		System Test Plan	190, 194				
		Personnel and Equipment Plan	193				
B.	Conduct Central Site Operations Staff Training	Training Plan	195				
C.	Test System for Compliance with Specifications						
C.1	– User Requirements	Results Log	198				
C.2	– Systems Technical Specifications	Results Log	198				
		Problem/Request Control	111				
		Change Request	112				
		Work Outline	101				
		Updated Documentation Program/Module Maintenance Control	113				

212

STANDARD ACTIVITIES/END ITEMS

TOUCHE ROSS

ORGANIZATION __PHASE III,__
STEP __9__
SYSTEM __DEVELOPMENT__
USER REP ____

ID/TITLE __SYSTEMS TEST__

☐ PHASE ☒ ACTIVITY ☐ SUBTASK
☐ STEP   ☒ TASK   ☐

	PREPARED BY		
PREPARED BY	MVJ	SH
REVIEWED BY	CB	CB
DATE	3/29/80	11/1/80
PHASE	III-9	III-9

NUMBER	PHASE/STEP/ACTIVITY/TASK/SUBTASK NAME	END ITEM	FORM NO.	PERFORMED BY	DUE DATE	APPROVED BY	DATE
D.	Test System to limits	Results Log	198				
		Problem/Request Control	111				
		Change Request	112				
		Work Outline	101				
		Updated Documentation					
		Program/Module Maintenance Control	113				
E.	Review With User for Acceptance	Approval Form	199				
		System Certification Checklist	115				

THE SYSTEMS DEVELOPMENT PROCESS

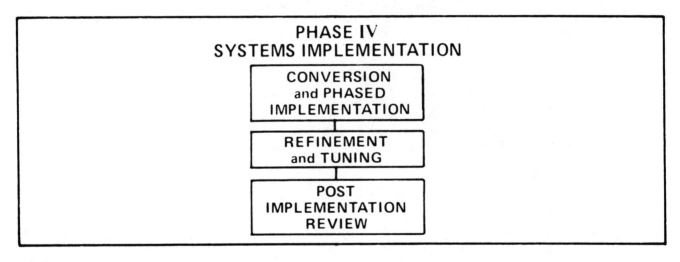

PHASE IV
SYSTEMS IMPLEMENTATION

CONVERSION
and PHASED
IMPLEMENTATION

REFINEMENT
and TUNING

POST
IMPLEMENTATION
REVIEW

 TOUCHE ROSS & CO.

THE SYSTEMS DEVELOPMENT PROCESS

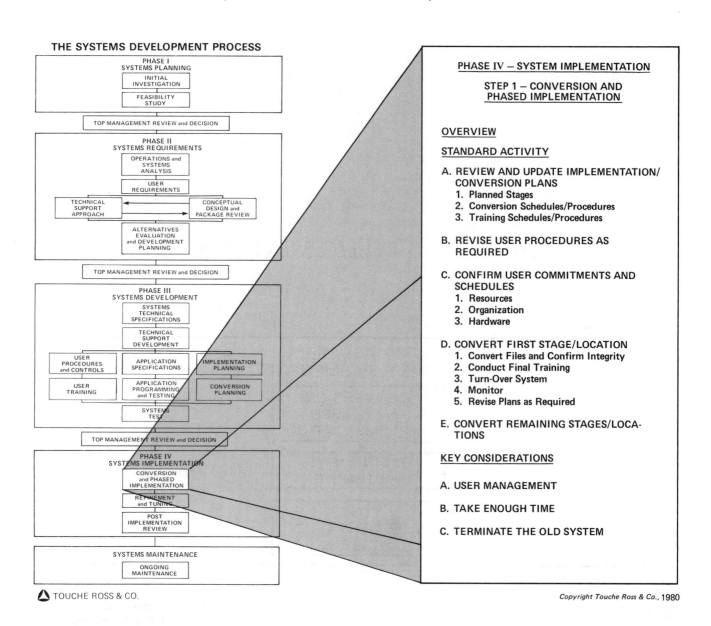

PHASE I
SYSTEMS PLANNING
INITIAL INVESTIGATION
FEASIBILITY STUDY

TOP MANAGEMENT REVIEW and DECISION

PHASE II
SYSTEMS REQUIREMENTS
OPERATIONS and SYSTEMS ANALYSIS
USER REQUIREMENTS
TECHNICAL SUPPORT APPROACH
CONCEPTUAL DESIGN and PACKAGE REVIEW
ALTERNATIVES EVALUATION and DEVELOPMENT PLANNING

TOP MANAGEMENT REVIEW and DECISION

PHASE III
SYSTEMS DEVELOPMENT
SYSTEMS TECHNICAL SPECIFICATIONS
TECHNICAL SUPPORT DEVELOPMENT
USER PROCEDURES and CONTROLS
APPLICATION SPECIFICATIONS
IMPLEMENTATION PLANNING
USER TRAINING
APPLICATION PROGRAMMING and TESTING
CONVERSION PLANNING
SYSTEMS TEST

TOP MANAGEMENT REVIEW and DECISION

PHASE IV
SYSTEMS IMPLEMENTATION
CONVERSION and PHASED IMPLEMENTATION
REFINEMENT and TUNING
POST IMPLEMENTATION REVIEW

SYSTEMS MAINTENANCE
ONGOING MAINTENANCE

PHASE IV – SYSTEM IMPLEMENTATION

STEP 1 – CONVERSION AND PHASED IMPLEMENTATION

OVERVIEW

STANDARD ACTIVITY

A. REVIEW AND UPDATE IMPLEMENTATION/ CONVERSION PLANS
1. Planned Stages
2. Conversion Schedules/Procedures
3. Training Schedules/Procedures

B. REVISE USER PROCEDURES AS REQUIRED

C. CONFIRM USER COMMITMENTS AND SCHEDULES
1. Resources
2. Organization
3. Hardware

D. CONVERT FIRST STAGE/LOCATION
1. Convert Files and Confirm Integrity
2. Conduct Final Training
3. Turn-Over System
4. Monitor
5. Revise Plans as Required

E. CONVERT REMAINING STAGES/LOCA-TIONS

KEY CONSIDERATIONS

A. USER MANAGEMENT

B. TAKE ENOUGH TIME

C. TERMINATE THE OLD SYSTEM

OVERVIEW The project is now ready for the final phase of the systems development process — Systems Implementation. This phase is initiated only after top management has reviewed and approved the results of the development phase (III), as evidenced by the successful systems test. Much of the planning for this step occurred during Phase III. These efforts are described in Implementation Planning (Phase III, Step 7) and Conversion Planning (Phase III, Step 8).

The goal of the conversion portion of this step is to attain a state of operation of the new system that includes:

— Installation, testing, and acceptance of the equipment required to implement the system.
— Construction and validation of the new data files.
— Final training of user and data processing operations personnel for their new or modified job functions.

In many systems projects, this step occurs several times and may occur simultaneously with portions of the previous phase. Overlap is necessary in situations such as these:

— Systems implemented at multiple sites on a staggered schedule.
— Systems phased into use through a series of functional cycles.
— Systems implemented at pilot sites as a test prior to final decisions for implementation within all units of the organization.

In addition, some conversion activities may actually have been initiated very early in the project. For example, major data purification efforts may be required. These in-process activities were formally reviewed for progress and completion plans during the Conversion Planning step (Phase III, Step 8).

The effort required to complete this step varies widely depending on the nature of the system and the strategies used. For example, if conversion is from manual to computer-based files and the accepted approach requires initially recording a significant amount of purified data in these new files, the effort may be extensive. Conversely, if source files are already computer-based and are highly reliable the effort will be modest.

This step also includes implementation of the new system. Its basic purpose is to bring the newly converted system to the point where it is a routine, ongoing part of the operations of both user and data processing operations departments. In reaching that point, monitoring functions are included to ensure that problems associated with startup activities are quickly identified, diagnosed and resolved. Implementation is not complete for the Project Team until the next step — Refinement and Tuning (Phase IV, Step 2) — is complete. Only at that point is technical responsibility for the new system turned over to the programming maintenance group.

The time required to complete implementation varies widely and is somewhat dependent on the severity of operating problems encountered in the new system. At the very least, it should extend through several production cycles.

Review and
Update Implementation/
Conversion Plans

The first activity in this step is to perform a complete review and update of the detailed conversion and implementation plans. These plans are finalized during Steps 7 and 8 of Phase III. User training, programming, and the systems test have since been completed. In addition, top management has reviewed development results to date and has decided to proceed with implementation. These activities may have resulted in a requirement to change the time schedules in the plans for both starting dates and elapsed time. Further, results may suggest some adjustments in both types and sequence of required activities. Thus, review and update are necessary for planned stages of implementation, conversion schedules and procedures, and training schedules and procedures.

Planned Stages. Conversion and implementation plans may specify multiple stages of effort due to a multiplicity of locations or segments of the systems. These basic approaches are not likely to be changed at this point, but adjustments of the detail may be appropriate. For example, systems tests may have indicated that a particular segment scheduled for one stage of implementation is too large or complex for a single stage. Conversely, multiple segments may now appear as reasonable candidates for combined implementation, based on a very successful systems test. (However, in this situation, caution should be exercised to avoid overly optimistic estimates of implementation efforts.)

In many cases, the pilot test site or initial implementation location is directly involved in the Systems Test step. The results of such efforts may now indicate that an alternate pilot or initial site should be selected for improved environmental or human relations considerations.

Finally, project schedule slippages may have occurred during the later steps of the Systems Development phase. These delays could affect the availability of locations to be implemented in the planned sequence. Systems segments could be combined or rearranged because of noncontrollable deadlines or other outside constraints.

Conversion Schedules/Procedures. The conversion plans specify the detailed schedules required to accomplish the conversion. Some subsets of these activities were performed during the systems test. They may indicate that planned schedules or procedures are inadequate or unrealistic in light of the upcoming conversion. If so, it is critical that the schedules and procedures be updated at this point before launching the actual conversion efforts. Ignoring this task greatly increases the risk of an uncontrolled conversion.

Training Schedules/Procedures. Like the previous task, the training schedules and procedures are now reviewed and updated. This task includes the training requirements for both conversion and ongoing operations. In this case, however, the User Training step in Phase III should have covered basic training for a core group of user personnel. Final training may now be planned for remaining personnel, locations, or systems segments. In addition, retraining may be necessary due to inadequate original training programs and procedures or to systems changes made during the systems test. Training schedules and procedures are now updated with final training conducted in a subsequent activity of this step.

Revise User Procedures
as Required

The completed Systems Test step identified many discrepancies in computer programs and user procedures. Normally, the project team corrects or otherwise disposes of all program-related discrepancies before the end of the systems test. This occurs for the simple reason that a new system cannot be implemented if computer programs do not function properly. Less obvious in many projects is the inability of a system with inaccurate or incomplete user procedures and controls to operate smoothly. In fact, the failure of many systems projects results from ignoring the procedural deficiencies and proceeding with implementation. This action often prevents the expected benefits of the new system from being achieved. Thus, this activity is specifically included as a reminder that user procedures must be revised now — before implementation.

Depending on the extent of revisions required, this activity could take several weeks to complete. In addition to creating procedural modifications, the associated administrative tasks of typing, duplicating, and reissuing manuals must also be completed. Adjustments to training programs and materials may also be necessary to make them consistent with revised procedures or to highlight changes to previously trained personnel.

Confirm User Commitments and Schedules

The updated conversion and implementation plans for both resource requirements and schedules must now be reconfirmed with all users. Since these plans were finalized and approved by users in the previous phase, the basic activities and schedules should be well understood. The primary tasks at this time are to ensure that all users understand and accept the revisions and to make sure that they are committed to accomplishing their required activities. The commitments and schedules that pertain to resources, organization, and hardware are particularly important. Confirmation between the project team and the responsible departmental managers should be in writing.

Resources. Conversion and implementation activities generally require efforts that exceed normal workloads in user departments and EDP operations. For conversion, this may include data purification, input preparation and control, and file balancing. For implementation, it may involve maintaining some portions of both the old and new systems until the old system is completely phased out. Even where parallel operation is not planned, some additional effort will be required during the new system's initial operation simply because personnel are not as familiar (and therefore not as productive) with the new operations. Also, the new system will inevitably encounter unexpected problems. Estimates of these nonrecurring efforts are identified in the resource requirement plans. Initial commitments must now be reconfirmed as to the availability of appropriate resources at specified times.

Organization. The Systems Requirements documents specify organizational revisions associated with the new system. These changes may include staff reductions, new reporting relationships and adjustments to the mix of capabilities within user areas. A new system often requires the addition of data entry, control, and error correction personnel. Procedures manuals created during the Systems Development phase are oriented to these new organizations. Schedules to phase in these new organizations must be consistent with implementation plans, the political and emotional environment, and appropriate human behavior considerations. Changing organizational structures at the same time as new systems are implemented is a difficult task and requires considerable management attention. Contingency plans should be prepared and reviewed so that the organization may cope with unexpected problems that could arise during the initial implementation period. Caution should be exercised, however, to assure that the new organizational alignments are committed to be implemented. If not, benefits associated with the new system may not be realized.

Hardware. The finalized implementation plans prepared during the previous phase contain specific sections on hardware/software installation and site preparation. Since the programming, user training, and systems test steps have now been completed, the hardware/software initially required by the new system is likely to be already installed. For example, this could include a limited number of data entry or communications terminals, or a new data base management system.

The process of updating conversion and implementation plans (as previously completed in this step) may imply changes to the hardware requirements plan, that must now be reconfirmed. Adjustments to the sequence of planned stages or locations could significantly impact the central computer run time requirements or the need for mass storage. Schedules for acquisition of new disk drives, disk packs, or tapes could have changed. Availabilities of new preprinted forms may be critical. All of these items must now be carefully reviewed and confirmed by the appropriate managers before proceeding with the conversion.

Convert First Stage/Location

The project team, all users, and EDP operations are now prepared to begin the final conversion and implementation tasks. Where multiple stages or locations are involved, these tasks become repetitive — that is, a specified set of tasks, performed in a defined sequence, is completed for each stage or location involved in the system. In general, the primary tasks involve completion of all file conversions, confirmation of initial file integrity, final training, turnover of the new system to the users, and monitoring new operations. Finally, plans for the next stage or location are revised to reflect the actual results of the completed tasks. The next conversion/implementation is then initiated.

Convert Files and Confirm Integrity. Planning activities included in this developmental process are extensive and are intended to provide a thorough approach to the problems of converting and controlling new system files. The conversion process is too often disorganized or incomplete and results in unplanned overtime, schedule slippages, and dissatisfaction with the operations of the new system. If the planning, review, and revision process discussed in this and previous steps has not been adequately performed, this is likely to fail. This is not to imply that extensive plans and preparation result in simple conversions: they only increase the probability of attaining controlled and orderly conversions. Even then, they only do so with proper management execution of committed activities and schedules. Managing change is difficult at best, and new systems often involve significant change.

The activities and tasks performed during conversion involve completing the data purification efforts, coding new transactions, building and maintaining files, and evaluating and correcting results. All of these activities require close supervision and generally suggest use of a formal checklist or tracking mechanism to ensure a timely and accurate completion.

Purification of existing files assures that data created for the new system is accurate and complete. The approach varies, depending on whether the existing files are manual or computer-based. If current files are manual, the records should be reviewed, corrected, and validated before actual data capturing begins. If existing files are computerized, two approaches may be feasible.

The first alternative for converting computerized files consists of building the new files directly from the old ones, then using a file integrity program to identify data discrepancies. An advantage of this approach is that it reduces the amount of time necessary to identify errors. This is particularly true where procedures in the old system were unreliable. This approach then requires new procedures for reviewing file integrity reports and for assuring that discrepancies are resolved. Failure to have adequate controls over the error resolution process can allow errors to pass into the new files.

The second alternative for converting computerized files is to update existing files before building the new ones. This approach may provide greater inherent accuracy if the old system is known to produce reliable results. However, this approach may require some team members to learn two sets of file maintenance procedures, which may increase the amount of time necessary to complete this task.

Data undergoing conversion generally needs to be transcribed onto new forms using existing, previously tested new procedures. During transcription, a number of questions and problems inevitably arise. The ideal way to handle questions would be to deal with them as they are identified, and then to communicate both questions and answers to all the members of the conversion team. However, because the supervisor of the conversion effort must balance productivity and the thoroughness of troubleshooting, an evolutionary approach may be best. That is, at the early stages of the task, problems are dealt with as they arise and information is disseminated immediately. Later, as the conversion team gains experience, it may prove workable to identify questionable items and deal with them collectively at designated times. In any case, legitimate questions and their answers should be documented and added to the procedures.

Completed data forms are now converted to machine-readable media. Although this process is generally straightforward, certain precautions are appropriate. For example, transaction listings should be produced and reviewed by both technical project team members and responsible users to verify that no major errors exist. In addition, reviews should cover samples of work performed by each person and samples of each type of record being converted.

Whenever possible, building new files or data-base segments is accomplished with programs that will become an integral part of the implemented system. The program functions involved include editing, updating, listing, and verifying. As each conversion program is run, the EDP operations staff should note the results of every cycle on a Results Log, which includes comments identifying the input data sets used during the processing cycle as well as the last step processed. This Results Log, a copy of the operator's log, and all printed outputs should be reviewed by the Project Team. A set of backup files of the data should be maintained in a secure place to make recovery possible if failure occurs.

Almost without exception, the new master files or data base segments will be subjected to a variable volume of change transactions during the course of the conversion. It is essential that all relevant changes be reflected in the converted files. For example, in developing a customer order-processing system, one of the files or data segments to be converted would include customer master information. Suppose conversion started in early December, with a January 1 implementation target. Transactions handled under the existing system throughout December could impact the new master files. The organization may acquire new customers, or old ones may move. Credit ratings may vary, shipping instructions may change, etc. Reliable procedures that assure that the new master files are updated to reflect all such transactions are required. One such procedure is to conduct periodic and final reconciliation of existing and converted files prior to implementation. Another technique is to withhold all file maintenance documents after the specified, initial conversion effort. They can then be batch-processed against the converted files, which are subsequently rebalanced against the old system files. This should make it possible, at some point before the new files are put into productive use, to assure that they are correctly updated. While differences between old and new master files cannot always be completely reconciled, the project team still has the responsibility to make sure data balances between the two systems.

If a file is expected to undergo a particularly high level of change during conversion, it may be useful to use a special-purpose program that identifies and displays any differences between file content of the new and the old systems. This is especially effective when running parallel systems.

Each file conversion should include a confirmation of file integrity and an evaluation of computer processing results. The starting point for this task is a careful review of outputs produced by regular file maintenance, such as input transaction reports and file control reports. Periodically, these outputs should be supplemented with reviews of comprehensive file listing and/or formatted printouts of selected master records. These supplementary reports should particularly be used during the early portions of the conversion.

The objective of all of these reviews is to achieve concurrence by users, project team members and the computer operations staff that the new files are complete, accurate, and ready to use. Any discrepancies identified during this activity should be documented and prioritized. Corrective actions should then relate to the severity of each problem. Alternative actions could range from halting conversion activities until correction takes place to deferring corrective maintenance until convenient programming time becomes available.

Conduct Final Training.   Completion of training of personnel who are to use and operate the system must occur prior to running the new system on a production basis. This final training provided for EDP operations and user personnel is essentially the same as that presented to key personnel and trainers during the previous phase. If implementation involves parallel system processing, training programs should include presentations on how to handle overlapping responsibilities. Mechanisms should have been designed to resolve conflicts that arise over the allocation of resources between the new and the old systems.

Turn Over System.   Once all files have been converted and verified and final training has been completed, the new system may begin to function through regular production cycles. At this point, project team members begin to withdraw from active involvement in the new operations. Ideally, if users have actively participated in the systems testing and conversion activities this process should be smooth and straightforward. In virtually all cases, however, project team personnel become directly involved in some portion of the new operations and must now discontinue that participation. Strong leadership by both user management and project management is usually required to accomplish this process successfully. If the proper emphasis on selling the new system has occurred throughout the entire development process, this turnover task should be easy.

Monitor.   Having turned over the system to the users, the technical project staff cannot simply disappear. They must now be actively involved in a monitoring role until the new system is operating as a routine, ongoing part of the user and data processing operations functions. This does not imply that any necessary refinement activities will now be performed. Those activities are best deferred until the new system "settles in" and are therefore addressed in the next step. Instead, the effort here is to assure that the new system survives the startup period. Only then will it be possible to perform any refinement and tuning.

At a minimum, the monitoring activities must continue through the first few processing cycles. It is at this point that any undiscovered program bugs emerge and are identified. Problems of user inexperience will be most acute during these first few cycles. Therefore, special attention and/or precautions are usually in order. These typically include:

— File and data base backup runs are generally called for more frequently during these initial cycles. It is assumed that adequate backup and recovery procedures have been developed. However, since the new system is more vulnerable at this point, it may be desirable to prepare backup copies of the files after each processing cycle.

   In this way, when problems are encountered, recovery and restart efforts are limited to a single cycle, rather than covering an extended period.

— File integrity programs should be used more frequently during the early stages of implementation than would be considered normal at later stages. For example, routine procedures may require running a file integrity program weekly or monthly. At the point of system startup, however, it may be desirable to run this program on a daily basis. Programs of this kind unfortunately require a significant amount of computer processing time. However, the additional overhead usually is justified because these programs are excellent tools for detecting system discrepancies.

— In addition to running file integrity programs, it is usually worthwhile to generate file listings which are useful in the diagnosis of problems identified by the file integrity programs or normal system outputs.

— It is a sound practice to ask EDP operations personnel to prepare Results Logs for several production cycles. These logs can be valuable diagnostic tools, since they provide a consolidated list of all processing on a given application or system. By contrast, entries are usually widely separated and hard to find if a normal operator's log is used. In a system using a data base, the normal operator's log is not generally useful for these diagnostic techniques.

Throughout implementation, there should be periodic reviews of system results aimed at identifying and dealing with system-generated errors and processing bottlenecks. Participants in these reviews should include EDP operations personnel, user representatives and project team members. Although similar to reviews conducted during the systems test, these reviews emphasize user understanding and acceptance of the new system and the quick identification and resolution of problems.

During implementation, it is important to establish practices for prioritizing problems or change requests as they are identified. Under the structure used in a workable three-level approach, a priority of "A" indicates that identified changes must be made before the next cycle is processed. A priority of "B" identifies a change that should be completed before the end of this implementation step. A "C" priority indicates a change that should be incorporated within the Refinement and Tuning step or within maintenance.

Revise Plans as Required. An extensive amount of learning occurs during the conversion of the first stage or location for a new system. This knowledge should not be ignored—it can be a valuable input to plans for converting and implementing the remaining stages and locations. This revision process is essential to the production of realistic plans for completing the project. Critical assessments of each of the conversion and implementation activities performed should be made. Some of these activities will proceed more smoothly the next time simply because of the "learning curve" process. But this should not be overemphasized. Subsequent stages or locations will have new personnel or new programs, or both. Thus the learning process will be repeated.

Convert Remaining Stages/Locations

Finally, the remaining stages and locations may be converted and implemented. The same types of activities and tasks described for the first stages or location are required for each. And after each is completed, plans for those that remain should be reviewed and revised so that they continue to reflect the total accumulated experience to date.

KEY CONSIDERATIONS

User Management

It should be obvious that conversion and implementation of a new system cannot be successful without direct management from the user organizations. However, the technical staff is often so anxious to complete the project that the user managers are either not required or not given the opportunity to assume control. When this occurs, the desire for early completion generally backfires. That is, the technical staff finds itself involved for a longer period of time until user management finally takes charge and runs the new system.

Take Enough Time

The early stages of implementation can be trying times for the user organization. This is to be expected because:

— Personnel are performing functions at which they are inexperienced. For many clerical personnel, implementation may be the first exposure to the workings of the new system.
— User personnel are frequently required to perform duplicate functions that may seem pointless, even with some explanation from the team.
— Some — possibly most — user personnel may be comfortable with existing procedures and unenthusiastic about the prospects of changing established practices.

Under pressures such as these, project team members must exhibit a great deal of patience. They should be careful to establish an environment that encourages user personnel to ask questions and offer suggestions. When questions and suggestions are received, responses should be clear, courteous, and prompt. The project team should budget enough time to assure extensive interaction with the user organization.

In addition, periodic reviews between members of the project team and user management should be held. They should be dedicated to discussions of implementation status. As appropriate, user management should be asked for support and assistance in dealing with resistance that may materialize at lower levels of the user organization.

Terminate the Old System

Some overlap between old and new system processing is inevitable. It is likewise inevitable that questions will arise as to when to discontinue the old system and let the new one take over.

On the one hand, user management will tend to continue processing under the old system until all discrepancies have been dealt with and all enhancements for the new system have been implemented. Users tend to assume that if they "buy" the new system before all changes and enhancements have been made, those changes will never take place. On the other hand, members of the project team — who have been involved in a long and arduous development cycle — are anxious to discontinue the old system as soon as possible and to place the new one into operation.

While it is impossible to draw hard and fast rules on when to discontinue the old system, these guidelines may be helpful:

— Before the old system is discontinued, the new one should have operated through several production cycles without uncovering any new "A" or "B" priority problems. This guideline refers, of course, to daily processing cycles. If discrepancies are noted on monthly cycles, they may have to be resolved through testing by the project team, with followup responsibility turned over to the maintenance group.

— All outstanding "B" priority discrepancies should be resolved.

— User personnel should be able to handle routine processing functions without assistance from project team members.

As discussed earlier, policies covering these decision criteria should be established well before the problems arise. It is altogether impractical to try to formulate policy under the pressures of disagreement.

TOUCHE ROSS

ID/TITLE __CONVERSION AND PHASED IMPLEMENTATION__

ORGANIZATION __PHASE IV,__
STEP 1

SYSTEM __IMPLEMENTATION__

USER REP

☐ PHASE ☒ ACTIVITY ☐ SUBTASK
☐ STEP ☒ TASK ☐

PAGE __1__ OF __2__

PROJECT NO.

	PREPARED BY	MVJ	SH
	REVIEWED BY	CB	CB
	DATE	3/29/80	11/1/80
	PHASE	IV-1	IV-1

NUMBER	PHASE/STEP/ACTIVITY/TASK/SUBTASK NAME	END ITEM	FORM NO.	PERFORMED BY	DUE DATE	APPROVED BY	DATE
A.	Review and Update Implementation/ Conversion Plans	Conversion Plan	191				
		Data Acquisition Plan	192				
		Implementation Plan	III-7				
		Personnel and Equipment Plan	193				
		Work Outline	101				
		Project Plan	102				
B.	Revise User Procedures As Required	Control Procedures	III-5				
		User Procedures	III-5				
C.	Confirm User Commitments and Schedules	Confirmation Letter					
D.	Convert First Stage/Location						
D.1	- Convert Files and Confirm Integrity	Converted Files					
D.2	- Conduct Final Training	Trained Users					
D.3	- Turn-Over System	Operational System					
D.4	- Monitor						
D.5	- Revise Plans As Required	Work Outline	101				
		Project Plan	102				
		Development Cost Comparison	105				

STANDARD ACTIVITIES/END ITEMS

TOUCHE ROSS

ID/TITLE CONVERSION AND PHASED IMPLEMENTATION

☐ PHASE   ☒ ACTIVITY   ☐ SUBTASK
☐ STEP   ☒ TASK   ☐ ___

ORGANIZATION PHASE IV,
              STEP 1
SYSTEM IMPLEMENTATION
USER REP

PAGE 2 OF 2
PROJECT NO.

	PREPARED BY	REVIEWED BY	DATE	PHASE
	MVJ	CB	3/29/80	IV-1
	SH	CB	11/1/80	IV-1

NUMBER	PHASE/STEP/ACTIVITY/TASK/SUBTASK NAME	END ITEM	FORM NO.	PERFORMED BY	DUE DATE	APPROVED BY	DATE
E.	Convert Remaining Stages/Locations	Operational System					
		Development Cost Comparison	105				
		Project Plan	102				

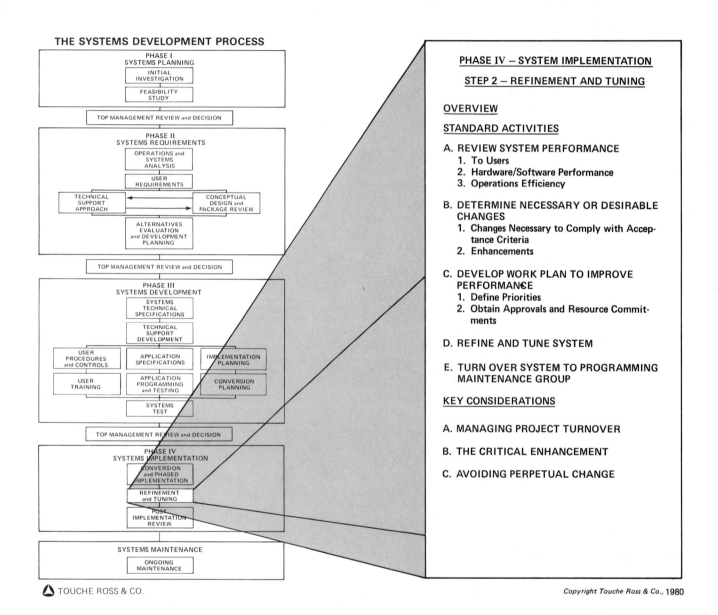

THE SYSTEMS DEVELOPMENT PROCESS

PHASE IV – SYSTEM IMPLEMENTATION

STEP 2 – REFINEMENT AND TUNING

OVERVIEW

STANDARD ACTIVITIES

A. REVIEW SYSTEM PERFORMANCE
   1. To Users
   2. Hardware/Software Performance
   3. Operations Efficiency

B. DETERMINE NECESSARY OR DESIRABLE CHANGES
   1. Changes Necessary to Comply with Acceptance Criteria
   2. Enhancements

C. DEVELOP WORK PLAN TO IMPROVE PERFORMANCE
   1. Define Priorities
   2. Obtain Approvals and Resource Commitments

D. REFINE AND TUNE SYSTEM

E. TURN OVER SYSTEM TO PROGRAMMING MAINTENANCE GROUP

KEY CONSIDERATIONS

A. MANAGING PROJECT TURNOVER

B. THE CRITICAL ENHANCEMENT

C. AVOIDING PERPETUAL CHANGE

TOUCHE ROSS & CO.

Copyright Touche Ross & Co., 1980

Refining and tuning the system that has just been implemented is a critical, but frequently ignored, step in the systems development process. As users become familiar with the new system's design, they can and do identify areas that need to be changed and corrected.

The first major activity is the complete review of actual versus estimated systems performance. Changes that are necessary and desirable, but which have not yet been recorded are then documented, and priorities are established. The system is then changed through a refinement and tuning process that helps it to meet the performance and requirements criteria defined in the Systems Requirements phase. The last activity in this step is the turnover of the system to the programming maintenance group to assume ongoing maintenance responsibilities.

STANDARD ACTIVITIES

Review System Performance

As the Conversion and Phased Implementation step is completed, a series of performance statistics are available. The purpose of this activity is to review those statistics and correlate them with the estimated performance as stated in the systems requirements documentation in each of the following areas:

Users. Various volume and timing statistics were estimated in the User Requirements step. The purpose of this task is to review the estimated versus actual volumes and timings recorded in the implementation documentation. For example, the entry of data may have been estimated at 30 documents per operator/hour, but the throughput may actually turn out to be half that. In addition, some reports may require modifications or expansion in order to increase their usability. The objective is to identify those types of problem areas.

Hardware/Software Performance. The hardware on which the system is running is defined to have a specific set of performance characteristics. For example, a six-second response time might have been specified for an on-line system; if the actual response time is ten seconds, serious problems can result in the user organization. Similarly, a batch program estimated to require 45 minutes of processing may actually require several hours, and thereby cause severe scheduling problems.

Hardware/software performance problems must be thoroughly documented and carefully defined; their solution may involve software specialists, vendor maintenance personnel, and others—both inside and outside the organization.

Operations Efficiency. As the system operates in both the user and data processing organizations, operation inefficiencies are identified. These can be caused by technical deficiencies in the procedures that actually run the programs, or they may result from an inadequate understanding of the cut-off times and paper flow of the organization. The objective is to identify areas that are critical to obtaining the results and benefits necessary from the system.

Determine Necessary or Desirable Changes

With the review of the systems performance and comments from users, a number of changes are identified. The key consideration will be the impact of changes on the achievement of benefits and effective utilization of the system, and should address the following:

Changes Necessary to Comply with Acceptance Criteria. As part of the Implementation Planning step a series of acceptance criteria was finalized. It is necessary to identify those areas where changes are to be implemented in order to comply with acceptance criteria as defined and to provide users with the system that meets their requirements. These can be changes designed to improve response time, modify reports, expand recovery procedures, change schedules, and other such items.

Enhancements. These are features that were not identified in the requirements, but that the user now recognizes to be essential parts of the system. This is a normal event resulting from actually using the system. During this process the user will normally do a secondary, in-depth evaluation of the system that may disclose requirements not previously recognized. Also, with experience, the user's sophistication and level of expectation may increase, resulting in new demands on the system.

Develop Work Plan to Improve Performance

Each of the changes from the previous activity, and those from the previous steps that have a low priority, (i.e., to be implemented after the initial Implementation Step), are reviewed in order to develop a detailed work plan for improvements. This plan takes into account overlapping changes and their relative urgency. In essence, all the needed improvements are considered and prioritized.

Define Priorities. As the detailed work effort is defined and the coordination between multiple changes is identified, a specific work plan establishes the priorities necessary to improve the system. These priorities are established on the basis of the most benefit for the least cost (as the entire systems development process was initially established). In many cases it may prove desirable to defer requested changes.

A key activity in this work plan is the reexecution of the systems test. The purpose of the test is to ensure the proper implementation of the changes.

Obtain Approvals and Resource Commitment. With priorities established and the detailed work plan prepared, the resources necessary to implement these changes to improve the system are identified and committed.

Refine and Tune System

Actually refining and tuning the system requires a significant amount of effort and coordination between various elements of the organization. The active involvement of the user and the data processing operations staff are essential to the efficient and timely implementation of these changes.

The systems test is reexecuted, the performance of the system is remeasured, and a complete review of all changes in output reports, processing logic, and processing flows is made. Before the start of this activity, it is important to identify when the activity is to be considered complete. If this is not done, the refinement and tuning process can continue indefinitely. Segregation of this activity from maintenance is important.

230

Turn Over System
to Programming
Maintenance Group
The system which is complete to a defined level and certified for production is now turned over to the maintenance group. At this point, all changes and requests for changes are directed to the maintenance group. Any further requests for changes will follow the normal request procedures for maintenance. This activity is intended to assure a complete understanding of the system and the proper continuation of documentation and the implementation of changes. The business world is not static, nor are the systems on which it depends for support.

KEY CONSIDERATIONS

Managing Project Turnover
A successful systems implementation results from the proper application of cumulative experience. It is impossible for all of the knowledge of every member on a project team to be fully documented for turnover to the maintenance group. Therefore, the maintenance group will not initially understand and be able to react to discrepancies or enhancement requests quite as well as members of the original project team. This condition will probably be apparent to user managers who may experience and show some irritation over this transition period.

It is therefore a project management challenge to plan and implement a smooth turnover to program maintenance personnel. This transition can be accomplished evenly by keeping several key points in mind:

— Training sessions between members of the project team and maintenance personnel should supplement the turnover of documentation. Any new maintenance personnel that are going to be needed should be hired during the systems test to give them enough time to familiarize themselves both with the organization and with the developing system.

— When change assignments for a new system are picked up by maintenance personnel, time estimates should be extended to compensate for their lack of familiarity.

— If a substantial backlog of changes and enhancements is turned over, it may be desirable to phase out project team assignments gradually, providing for a period of overlap in assignments between project management and maintenance personnel.

— Proposed solutions to problems should be reviewed by qualified members of the project team before additional programming modifications are undertaken.

The Critical Enhancement
As implementation responsibilities are executed, users become increasingly familiar with the new system and its potential. As they do, they are apt to identify increasing numbers of potential changes and enhancements. These can either build upon or lead to reconciliation with earlier change requests which have been deferred as maintenance items. The project team should orient itself and understand those enhancements and new requirements that will truly help to realize the original system's objectives.

Under such pressures, project team members should be extremely patient. They should be careful to establish an environment that encourages user personnel to ask questions and offer suggestions. When questions and suggestions are received, responses should be clear, courteous, and prompt. The project team should budget sufficient time to ensure adequate interaction with the user. As a result of this, the team will become aware of those enhancements that are really necessary in the short term, and are thus top-priority items.

Avoiding Perpetual Change

In attempting to maintain constructive rapport with users, systems personnel may sometimes have a tendency to continually agree to the implementation of all suggested enhancements as part of the Refinement and Tuning step. This implementation of perpetual change is a very costly process. While it is impossible to draw hard and fast rules about which changes to make and which to defer, it can be profitable to address and answer some pointed questions concerning each change request.

— Is the change essential to meet the originally defined and agreed system objectives?
— What will be the impact of the proposed change on other functions of the new system, including both those to be implemented in the future and those already in operation?
— To what degree will users who are still gaining familiarity with the system be able to cope with early changes?
— Are the benefits of the change (both economic and intangible) commensurate with its costs?
— What impact will the change have upon the organization's ability to reconcile old and new systems?

In general, the new system should be allowed to settle down, and changes should possibly be deferred for implementation during normal on-going maintenance. One mechanism that may prove useful to determine how and when to put into effect enhancements identified during implementation is to establish a review meeting with all interested groups. This meeting should define needed enhancements and prioritize them. A final list of priorities should be the product of the user department.

STANDARD ACTIVITIES/END ITEMS

TOUCHE ROSS

ORGANIZATION PHASE IV, STEP 2
SYSTEM IMPLEMENTATION
USER REP _____

ID/TITLE REFINEMENT AND TUNING

☐ PHASE ☐ STEP ☒ ACTIVITY ☐ SUBTASK ☒ TASK ☐ _____

	PREPARED BY	REVIEWED BY	DATE	PHASE
	MVJ	CB	3/29/80	IV-2
	SH	CB	11/1/80	IV-2

NUMBER	PHASE/STEP/ACTIVITY/TASK/SUBTASK NAME	END ITEM	FORM NO.	PERFORMED BY	DUE DATE	APPROVED BY	DATE
A.	Review System Performance						
A.1	– Users	Status Report					
A.2	– Hardware/Software Performance	Status Report					
A.3	– Operations Efficiency	Status Report					
B.	Determine Necessary or Desirable Changes						
B.1	– Changes Necessary to Comply With Acceptance Criteria	Problem/Request Control	111				
		Program/Module Maintenance	113				
		Change Request	112				
		Work Outline	101				
B.2	– Enhancements	Problem/Request Control	111				
		Program/Module Maintenance	113				
		Change Request	112				
		Work Outline	101				
C.	Develop Work Plan to Improve Performance						
C.1	– Define Priorities	Problem/Request Control	111				
		Change Request	112				
		Work Plan	102				

STANDARD ACTIVITIES/END ITEMS

TOUCHE ROSS

ORGANIZATION __PHASE IV,__
__STEP 2__
SYSTEM __IMPLEMENTATION__
USER REP _____

ID/TITLE __REFINEMENT AND TUNING__

☐ PHASE   ☒ ACTIVITY   ☐ SUBTASK
☐ STEP   ☒ TASK   ☐

		PREPARED BY	MVJ	SH
		REVIEWED BY	CB	CB
		DATE	3/29/80	11/1/80
		PHASE	IV-2	IV-2

NUMBER	PHASE/STEP/ACTIVITY/TASK/SUBTASK NAME	END ITEM	FORM NO.	PERFORMED BY	DUE DATE	APPROVED BY	DATE
C.2	- Obtain Approvals and Resource Commitments	Approval Letter					
D.	Refine and Tune System	Refined and Tuned System					
E.	Turn Over System to Programming Maintenance Group	Development Cost Comparison	105				
		Program Module/ Maintenance Control	113				
		Outstanding Change Requests	112				

Phase IV - Systems Implementation
Step 3 - Post Implementation Review

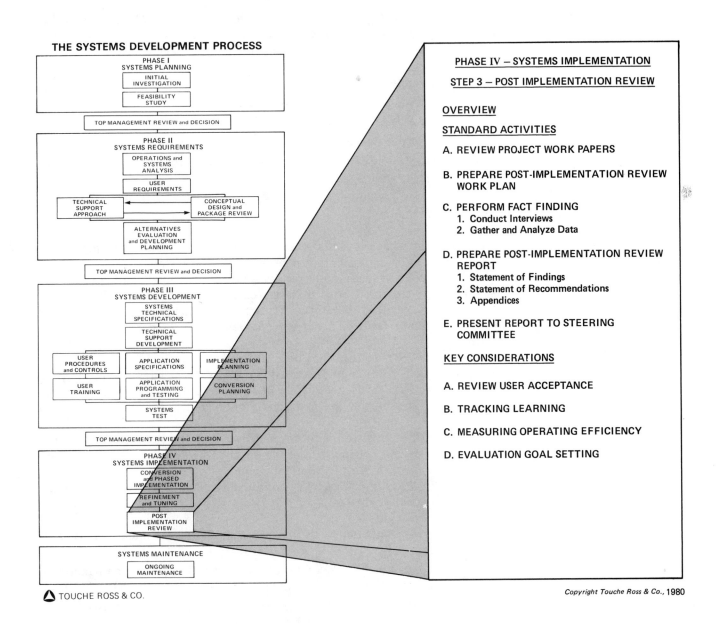

THE SYSTEMS DEVELOPMENT PROCESS

PHASE I
SYSTEMS PLANNING

INITIAL INVESTIGATION

FEASIBILITY STUDY

TOP MANAGEMENT REVIEW and DECISION

PHASE II
SYSTEMS REQUIREMENTS

OPERATIONS and SYSTEMS ANALYSIS

USER REQUIREMENTS

TECHNICAL SUPPORT APPROACH

CONCEPTUAL DESIGN and PACKAGE REVIEW

ALTERNATIVES EVALUATION and DEVELOPMENT PLANNING

TOP MANAGEMENT REVIEW and DECISION

PHASE III
SYSTEMS DEVELOPMENT

SYSTEMS TECHNICAL SPECIFICATIONS

TECHNICAL SUPPORT DEVELOPMENT

USER PROCEDURES and CONTROLS

APPLICATION SPECIFICATIONS

IMPLEMENTATION PLANNING

USER TRAINING

APPLICATION PROGRAMMING and TESTING

CONVERSION PLANNING

SYSTEMS TEST

TOP MANAGEMENT REVIEW and DECISION

PHASE IV
SYSTEMS IMPLEMENTATION

CONVERSION and PHASED IMPLEMENTATION

REFINEMENT and TUNING

POST IMPLEMENTATION REVIEW

SYSTEMS MAINTENANCE

ONGOING MAINTENANCE

△ TOUCHE ROSS & CO.

PHASE IV — SYSTEMS IMPLEMENTATION

STEP 3 — POST IMPLEMENTATION REVIEW

OVERVIEW

STANDARD ACTIVITIES

A. REVIEW PROJECT WORK PAPERS

B. PREPARE POST-IMPLEMENTATION REVIEW WORK PLAN

C. PERFORM FACT FINDING
   1. Conduct Interviews
   2. Gather and Analyze Data

D. PREPARE POST-IMPLEMENTATION REVIEW REPORT
   1. Statement of Findings
   2. Statement of Recommendations
   3. Appendices

E. PRESENT REPORT TO STEERING COMMITTEE

KEY CONSIDERATIONS

A. REVIEW USER ACCEPTANCE

B. TRACKING LEARNING

C. MEASURING OPERATING EFFICIENCY

D. EVALUATION GOAL SETTING

Copyright Touche Ross & Co., 1980

235

This step is conducted after the new system has been implemented so that management may assess the successes and shortcomings of the systems development work. Two specific areas are included in the review:

— System performance.
  · Have system operating expectations been met?
  · Have benefits been achieved?
— Project performance.
  · Was the systems project performed in a professional and satisfactory manner?
  · Were developmental costs and schedules met within forecast parameters?

Since the objective is assessment, timing is important. It is impractical to perform a post-implementation review until the system has operated long enough to produce measurable results. During Systems Planning (Phase I), benefits were projected both in terms of value and the time within which they would be realized. Whatever this time frame may be—and it will vary with individual systems or benefits—a review should be performed to evaluate results.

Since the project team has been disbanded, responsibility for initiating the post-implementation review must be assigned elsewhere. Typically, the EDP manager calls this scheduled event to the attention of the steering committee. The committee itself retains responsibility for authorizing and supervising each review.

The work of this step is performed by a high-level group of individuals independent of the original project team and the user organization. Composite skills for this group should be similar to those applied during the Initial Investigation and Feasibility Study steps. That is, individuals assigned to these reviews should have:

— Extensive experience and proven capabilities for management judgment.
— An understanding of corporate plans (both strategic and tactical), and supporting plans of operating divisions and the EDP function.
— An understanding of the environment as it currently exists for the EDP function and the user departments involved.

In some situations, task forces are assembled specifically to review individual projects. In others, there is a quality assurance function that handles this responsibility, frequently in cooperation with an internal audit group.

STANDARD ACTIVITIES

Review Project Work Papers Selected key documents developed as standard end items throughout the course of the project are reviewed to establish a perspective for this step. These include primarily the reports presented to the steering committee at the conclusion of Systems Planning (Phase I), Systems Requirements (Phase II), and Systems Development (Phase III). The statements of benefits and economic evaluations with their supporting rationale are particularly important. Any additional, significant status reports that may have been presented to the steering committee are also reviewed.

Prepare Post-Implementation Review Work Plan

The general activities and time frame required to complete this step, along with those for all other steps, were prepared as part of the feasibility study. At this point, the objective is to prepare a detailed work plan, including identification of individuals to be interviewed and assignment of responsibilities for gathering data and evaluating findings. The task force leader for this step concentrates on identifying personnel within the user and EDP groups who can contribute meaningful information and critiques of results. Within the user organization, persons to be interviewed include:

— Management personnel who are making decisions on the basis of outputs from the new system, including both top-level and operating management.
— Persons responsible for achieving the benefits.
— Selected clerical personnel who either provide data to the new system or work with operating reports generated by it.

Within the EDP organization, persons selected for interviewing include:

— Computer operators.
— Data control personnel.
— Program maintenance staff.
— Original project team members.

Perform Fact-Finding

During this activity the task force gathers data on actual system performance and system development results and compares them with plans and forecasts established during the initial steps of the project. This is accomplished through a combination of interviews, reviews of reports and files, observations of actual operations and, as appropriate, data sampling.

More specifically, two tasks are structured within this activity: interviews, and data gathering and analysis. These tasks are repetitive, since analysis of available data often leads to the scheduling of additional interviews to fill in gaps or enhance understanding.

Conduct Interviews. Interview techniques applied during this task are basically the same as those described earlier in connection with the Initial Investigation step. At this point, however, it is particularly important that specific questions be developed and reviewed carefully prior to interviewing. These questions should be directed at the specific areas of system performance under evaluation.

Wherever possible, task force members should review and confirm comments or data provided during the course of the actual interview. This minimizes the requirements for additional interview sessions.

Gather and Analyze Data. A substantial body of documentation is accumulated in the course of a properly conducted systems development project. However, in evaluating results, it is most efficient to concentrate the review on four types of documentation: (1) system change requests; (2) estimates of benefits; (3) estimates of development costs and timing; and (4) current and projected operating statistics and costs.

Systems change requests should have been completed to cover each system change initiated in the course of developing the system. All changes, regardless of origin (user request, program specification error, program error, etc.), should be documented. A review of these requests and subsequent dispositions can be extremely useful in identifying potential weaknesses in the new system. For example, if extensive changes have been required to modify certain programs, a subsequent investigation may show weaknesses either in program specifications or in the actual coding. Analyses of these changes could lead to a recommendation that the program be rewritten to improve operational or program maintenance efficiencies.

Another effective analysis technique for deriving data from these documents is to sort or segregate them according to types of change — application scope, system design, program specification, and so on. Such analysis can provide some strong clues about the causes of possible problems or project overruns. For example, if change requests centered around altering the scope of the system, it would be suspected that the project ran into problems with the definitions of user requirements or inadequate communication between user and project team personnel. Excessive changes in scope could also mean that the project team spent too little time or functioned ineffectively in defining and understanding the business problem to be solved.

Estimates of benefits were originally made as part of the feasibility study in Phase I and later updated at the end of Phase II, Systems Requirements. At this point, the task force should review each identified benefit to determine actual results and compare them with forecasts. Criteria for identifying and measuring the extent of benefits should have been incorporated in the initial Statement of Benefits. Should methods or approaches for measuring benefits be changed at this point, all such changes should be documented. The reasons for selecting alternate methods should be explained. Variances between estimated and actual benefits should be carefully analyzed. Some variances may result from inflationary differences. Others may be due to operating or transaction volume changes.

Estimates of development costs and timing may be compared to actual results by reviewing project control reports. It may be necessary to accumulate actual time records in order to compare total costs with projected costs. Since several projections are made during different phases of most projects, several comparisons should be performed to evaluate forecasting accuracy attained by the project team as their work progressed. The projection prepared at the end of Systems Requirements (Phase II) will, in most instances, be the one used by the steering committee to evaluate the effectiveness of the project team in this area. However, by comparing actual results to other projections, and then comparing these with similar forecasts from other projects, the steering committee can develop an improved understanding of the credibility of forecasts at different stages in the project.

Finally, data on operating statistics and costs in the old system and as they presently exist with the new system are carefully gathered and analyzed. Again, the same basis or approach and assumptions used initially in the project must be used now in order to generate meaningful comparisons. Variances resulting from volume, cost rates, quality of service, and mix of work should be identified and explained. In all cases where possible, the organization's standard accounting system should be used to obtain actual cost data. If this is not possible, the alternative approach and rationale used should be clearly documented.

| Prepare Post-Implementation Review Report | The task force should prepare a report in the form of a management level synopsis for the steering committee. Contents should include statements of findings and recommendations along with supporting appendices. |

Statement of Findings. This is a concise narrative identifying and describing major variances between actual and projected performance in the development project and the new system operation. Variances identified should include discussions of both positive and negative aspects, as appropriate.

Statement of Recommendations. This is a recommended plan of action conveying any significant deficiencies that have been identified. For each of these recommendations, there should be an identification of who should be responsible for implementation, the level of effort involved and the resources required. Further, recommendations should be prioritized, using the same method utilized to develop priorities for change requests processed during Step 1 of Systems Implementation.

Appendices. These should support the major findings of the report. Charts comparing planned and actual figures should be provided in the following areas:

— Benefits.
— Development costs.
— Operating costs.
— Operating statistics.
— Return on investment or other financial criteria applied.

The report should be reviewed with all affected parties prior to submission to the steering committee, including the original project manager, user management, and EDP systems and operations management. Any disagreements over the findings and recommendations should be analyzed and corrected as necessary.

| Present Report to Steering Committee | A summary of the highlights of the report should be presented to the steering committee by the manager of the task force responsible for the post-implementation review. This session should include task force members, the original project manager, and appropriate user and EDP systems management. These individuals should be available to answer questions, provide supplementary information, or express dissenting opinions. |

Acceptance of this report marks the conclusion of the systems development project.

KEY CONSIDERATIONS

| Reviewing User Acceptance | Although a post-implementation review may show a system to be highly successful in terms of quantitative results, evaluations should determine whether the company is, in fact, deriving all expected benefits from the system. Specifically, it is possible for an implemented system to match quantitative forecasts while delivering less than optimum impact upon the actual conduct of the business. For example, this is frequently the case when users perform their responsibilities without enthusiasm, as might happen when |

users feel they are only doing what the EDP organization tells them to do. They regard the system as something imposed upon them rather than as an integral part of their day-to-day operations. If it is apparent that this attitude is prevalent, it should be brought to the attention of all responsible parties — EDP management, user management, and the steering committee.

Problems such as these are sometimes easily remedied. It may simply be a matter of building a better understanding of the rationale behind some of the functions being performed. On the other hand, unenthusiastic users could be the symptom of a more serious and deeper problem. For example, user personnel may not be relying upon the output of the new system in their day-to-day decision making, but are instead applying intuitive judgment or utilizing data from other sources. Investigation may show that this results from concern over a lack of adequate controls within the new system, or from poorly designed reports. In either situation, prompt attention should be given to identifying and solving the problems.

Tracking Learning

It is quite possible that a post-implementation review will uncover a situation in which management feels that a new system is highly successful while members of the project team are unimpressed or unenthusiastic.

This could identify a situation in which members of the project team have performed in a perfunctory way, with little understanding of the impact of their work upon the organization as a whole. In other words, there may have been a failure to inform members of the project team of the "big picture." Another possibility is that this project seemed no different to project team members than several others that preceded it. They may view their work as repetitive and boring.

The task force should be sensitive to these possibilities. Where they occur, they could indicate that the organization is not developing or advancing the skills of valuable technical personnel. If this is the case, the organization may either be threatened with the imminent turnover of valuable people or with stagnation that can prevent the full contribution of its technical staff.

Measuring Operating Efficiency

An implemented system may be meeting stated objectives and yet not perform as efficiently as it might. Members of the task force should be sensitive to this possibility when reviewing system performance. They should encourage operations and user personnel to identify ways in which additional improvements may be realized. It is important to do this now, because the longer the system is in use, the less likely it is that suggestions for improvement will be put forward.

For example, many systems that use remote data entry are designed for inexperienced users. That is, data entry displays provide highly detailed instructions that, though they offer guidance, also serve to slow down personnel as they gain experience. If this proves to be the case, it may be desirable to provide an alternative data entry format curtailing tutorial content while increasing data entry productivity.

Evaluating Goal-Setting

It is usually assumed, in the course of evaluating the results of a newly implemented system, that initial goals were realistic: neither too high nor too low.

The task force may in fact find evidence to the contrary. In the course of comparing planned and actual results, the task force should be prepared to challenge the goals or projections of the project team. The task force may conclude that attainment or failure to attain a given goal resulted from ineffective goal-setting rather than project team performance.

STANDARD ACTIVITIES/END ITEMS

TOUCHE ROSS

ORGANIZATION: PHASE IV, STEP 3
SYSTEM: IMPLEMENTATION
USER REP: _____

ID/TITLE: POST IMPLEMENTATION REVIEW

☐ PHASE ☑ ACTIVITY ☐ SUBTASK
☐ STEP ☑ TASK ☐ _____

	PREPARED BY	REVIEWED BY	DATE	PHASE
	MVJ	CB	3/29/80	IV-3
	SH	CB	11/1/80	IV-3

NUMBER	PHASE/STEP/ACTIVITY/TASK/SUBTASK NAME	END ITEM	FORM NO.	PERFORMED BY	DUE DATE	APPROVED BY	DATE
A.	Review Project Work Papers	Work Outline	101				
B.	Revise Post Implementation Review Work Plan	Work Plan	102				
		Interview Schedules	120				
C.	Perform Fact Finding	Interviews					
C.1	- Conduct Interviews	Interview Summaries	121				
C.2	- Gather and Analyze Data	Performance Statistics					
D.	Prepare Post Implementation Review Report	Statement of Findings					
		Statement of Recommendations					
		Appendices					
		Management Summary	149				
E.	Present Report to Steering Committee						

THE SYSTEMS DEVELOPMENT PROCESS

SYSTEMS MAINTENANCE
ONGOING MAINTENANCE

 TOUCHE ROSS & CO.

THE SYSTEMS DEVELOPMENT PROCESS

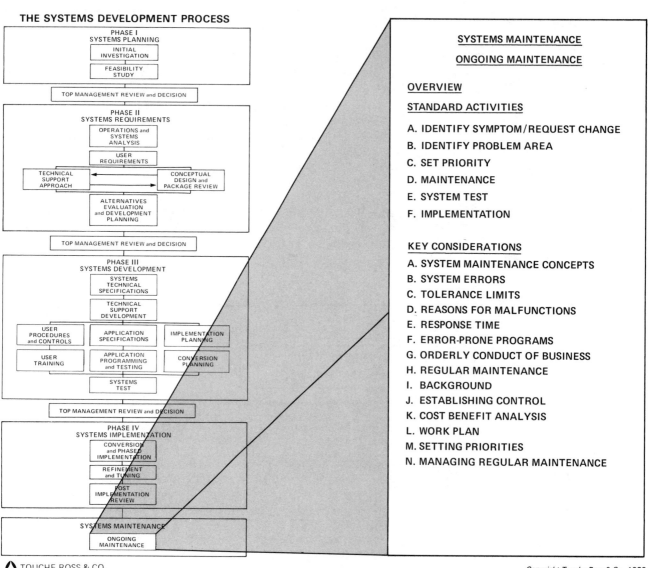

PHASE I
SYSTEMS PLANNING
INITIAL INVESTIGATION
FEASIBILITY STUDY

TOP MANAGEMENT REVIEW and DECISION

PHASE II
SYSTEMS REQUIREMENTS
OPERATIONS and SYSTEMS ANALYSIS
USER REQUIREMENTS
TECHNICAL SUPPORT APPROACH
CONCEPTUAL DESIGN and PACKAGE REVIEW
ALTERNATIVES EVALUATION and DEVELOPMENT PLANNING

TOP MANAGEMENT REVIEW and DECISION

PHASE III
SYSTEMS DEVELOPMENT
SYSTEMS TECHNICAL SPECIFICATIONS
TECHNICAL SUPPORT DEVELOPMENT
USER PROCEDURES and CONTROLS
APPLICATION SPECIFICATIONS
IMPLEMENTATION PLANNING
USER TRAINING
APPLICATION PROGRAMMING and TESTING
CONVERSION PLANNING
SYSTEMS TEST

TOP MANAGEMENT REVIEW and DECISION

PHASE IV
SYSTEMS IMPLEMENTATION
CONVERSION and PHASED IMPLEMENTATION
REFINEMENT and TUNING
POST IMPLEMENTATION REVIEW

SYSTEMS MAINTENANCE
ONGOING MAINTENANCE

SYSTEMS MAINTENANCE

ONGOING MAINTENANCE

OVERVIEW

STANDARD ACTIVITIES

A. IDENTIFY SYMPTOM/REQUEST CHANGE

B. IDENTIFY PROBLEM AREA

C. SET PRIORITY

D. MAINTENANCE

E. SYSTEM TEST

F. IMPLEMENTATION

KEY CONSIDERATIONS

A. SYSTEM MAINTENANCE CONCEPTS

B. SYSTEM ERRORS

C. TOLERANCE LIMITS

D. REASONS FOR MALFUNCTIONS

E. RESPONSE TIME

F. ERROR-PRONE PROGRAMS

G. ORDERLY CONDUCT OF BUSINESS

H. REGULAR MAINTENANCE

I. BACKGROUND

J. ESTABLISHING CONTROL

K. COST BENEFIT ANALYSIS

L. WORK PLAN

M. SETTING PRIORITIES

N. MANAGING REGULAR MAINTENANCE

△ TOUCHE ROSS & CO.

244

OVERVIEW Maintenance is playing an increasingly important role in most EDP installations as more and more systems are put into production. The complex relationships among systems in a typical EDP environment calls for an ever-increasing maintenance overhead. Meeting these maintenance needs is an important challenge and a vital extension of the systems development process.

Resources devoted to maintain existing applications have expanded to a major systems analysis and programming effort in many organizations. A number of factors are responsible for this rise and create some attendant problems. As the number of applications increases, so do demands for maintenance. Maintenance groups are typically recruited from the less-experienced personnel ranks because organizations do not accord these functions the stature of new development. No matter how logical the trend toward increased maintenance may appear, top managers tend to concern themselves with the negative impact of maintenance activities on resource availabilities and planning constraints. They view conditions with increased irritation, particularly the following:

— Steadily increasing maintenance costs for existing systems.
— Lack of systems and programming resources required to implement new EDP systems.

The systems department effort attributed to maintenance may be misleading. Maintenance often has a negative connotation, indicating that something is wrong or that it needs fixing. However, maintenance requirements actually caused by system deficiencies are only part of the total effort. Many requirements that fall under the heading of maintenance are necessary for other reasons:

— Enhancements requested by users. These may include adding new functions or new outputs to existing systems.
— Changes in governmental regulations. For example, a FICA change usually requires modifying the payroll system.
— The business itself undergoes changes—a new pricing structure, perhaps, or a new product line—that require adjusting EDP systems.

Many problems associated with systems maintenance are controllable, but three key situations must be recognized to assure effective control:

— *Poorly designed systems.* Maintenance assignments are often the result of inadequately defined systems requirements. If the business environment is not clearly understood before the start of technical design and programming, major portions of maintenance projects are devoted to simply identifying business problems.
— *Poorly designed programs.* Programmers may code programs instead of structuring them. In addition, technical management may focus on computer outputs, taking little time to review the programs. This results in a wide range of coding styles among active programs.

— *Insufficient maintenance efforts.* Too little time and effort may be devoted to managing the maintenance function because management's attention is allocated to operations and new projects. This inevitably leads to inadequate maintenance assignments.

Occurrences of the first two situations can be substantially reduced by using the systems development process described in this book. The third situation calls for allocating management resources consistent with demand for EDP department services.

Ongoing maintenence often includes a number of separate processes that may be categorized as follows:

— *System errors.* These include abnormal program terminations. inability to execute a job, incorrect reports, etc. No matter what the causes may prove to be, systems and programming resources are needed at once to deal with these errors.

— *Normal business needs.* These are systems changes brought about by changes in business activities, such as price changes, demands by regulatory agencies, the addition of product lines, etc. Because this type of maintenance requirement usually involves deadlines, and because changes are often mandatory, cost justification is not a primary decision factor (although cost estimates are developed).

— *Enhancements.* These are changes that improve the efficiency of a system or its value to users. Requests for changes in this category are initiated either by users or by EDP personnel and usually require cost justification and prioritization.

Although there are other ways to categorize systems maintenance, these three are useful because they correspond to appropriate management control techniques. Once approved for maintenance and placed in a work queue, a job should be subject to the project control techniques described in the subsection on project management.

Systems maintenance management requires techniques and tools that vary with the type of work involved. In the case of system errors, management's greatest impact is made by detecting abnormal operating trends, reacting to them with specific plans, and reducing them to acceptable levels. When dealing with mandatory changes, management should be able to forecast legislative and organizational requirements. These projections should permit a reasonably accurate allocation of systems and programming resources. By considering enhancement requirements to be discretionary, they can by brought under existing project management techniques. Management is thereby able to create a mechanism to ensure that jobs are dealt with in order of their importance to the organization. Managing maintenance requirements allows an organization to optimize its return from investment in ongoing maintenance.

STANDARD ACTIVITIES

Prepare Request for Change

As described in the Initial Investigation (Phase I, Step 1), requests for systems changes are generated by a variety of users. In many organizations, these requests are first reviewed by the systems department manager to determine if only minor changes or enhancements are involved. For new systems or major enhancements, requests are sent to the steering committee for assignment of priority and resources. Other requests are sent to the appropriate maintenance group.

The preparation of these requests is covered in Phase I, Step 1. In addition, backup documentation should be attached to each request. Upon receipt, control should be established by assigning a number to and logging in the request. The status of requests received, in process, or disposed of should be reported periodically to the steering committee. This gives the committee perspective in its examination of ongoing maintenance activities.

Identify Problem Area

Procedures for changing existing systems are consistent with those applied in systems development. The same approaches, techniques, and forms described in earlier subsections apply to maintenance and involve analyzing requests, preparing economic evaluations (except for emergency maintenance or correcting system errors), and developing work plans. These activities require the same level of skills used in systems planning — senior systems analysts and user managers. Initial maintenance requests should not be routinely turned over to programmers.

Analyze Request. The appropriate maintenance group reviews each request and identifies the technical problems and changes required. Depending on the type of request, this analysis may only require a review of technical documentation, such as program design and systems specifications. More complex requests may require a more extensive analysis, including:

— Review of project history files, such as the systems requirements manual.
— Interviews with affected user personnel.
— Analysis of workflows and operating statistics within user departments and data processing operations.
— Preparation of new systems requirements documentation.

One item that requires careful analysis during the examination of any maintenance request is the identity of the user departments of the system being modified. Large and complex business environments usually include many users besides those who requested maintenance. This can become a complicated matter if there have been organizational changes or if applications involve closely interrelated functions.

For example, in an insurance company, a change to a private passenger insurance system may also impact premium systems, claims processing, actuarial systems, statutory management reporting, and other systems. When evaluating a request for a maintenance change, it is often difficult to determine who the user really is. Great care must be taken to identify all the organizational elements that might be affected by a specific service request.

Prepare Economic Evaluation. Earlier discussions of systems development projects suggested that resources be allocated in the same general manner used for capital budgeting. In many organizations, an officer-level committee typically reviews and approves large capital expenditures. These usually involve all requests exceeding a predetermined amount and extent of risk or commitment involved. The capital-budgeting mechanism may also refer requests for smaller expenditures to a lower-level committee of operating managers. The second group usually has authority to decide on commitments up to an established cutoff point or level of consequences. Alternatively, some organizations have delegated decision authority and responsibility for smaller capital-budgeting decisions to line managers who have responsibility for the segment of the business affected by the decision.

Whether made by committees or individuals, these capital decisions should follow the same general guidelines and decision criteria. That is, the organization typically has policies covering return-on-investment and other decision criteria for the review and approval of capital-budgeting commitments. The same type of policy should be established in the EDP area. Since major systems development decisions are a capital-budgeting commitment, a top-level EDP Steering Committee should be given authority for approving and monitoring systems development projects. Since maintenance projects correspond closely to lower-level capital-budgeting commitments, they too should be handled in either of the following ways:

— A lower-level committee of operating managers can be established to allocate resources and monitor maintenance projects.

— A qualified executive, often the EDP director, can be given line responsibility and authority for approving and monitoring maintenance projects.

The method used should follow the policies and approaches used to make capital-budgeting decisions within the organization. Whichever procedure is followed, the elements of the systems development methodology discussed earlier are appropriate for establishing and maintaining control.

For example, let's assume that an in-depth cost analysis or economic evaluation was prepared during the Systems Planning phase of a developmental project. This estimate was subsequently modified as the project team gained a better understanding of the user requirements and technologies involved. By the time a project reaches the end of Systems Requirements (Phase II), the project team is expected to be able to predict costs and benefits within close tolerances.

The same type of economic evaluation is appropriate for maintenance projects, although some variables should be noted. The same forms can be used and the same general approaches are appropriate. However:

— Personnel are expected to have a better, more detailed knowledge of requirements and technical factors in a maintenance project. This is because the system exists and is understood in detail by both the user and systems organizations.

— Because the scope of maintenance work is better known and understood, the analysis of costs and benefits should require considerably less effort.

A single estimate should be sufficient to pinpoint the costs and benefits of a maintenance project. In addition, estimates for maintenance work should be accurate.

The working and control forms used for cost and benefit analyses of maintenance projects should be the same as those completed during systems development. Using the same forms makes use of existing experience and allows comparison within the organization. Projected benefits, operating cost changes, and development costs for a maintenance project should be documented with forms described earlier in the feasibility study.

The analyst who uses these tools to forecast costs and benefits should keep in mind the fact that they are time-related. That is, an economic evaluation spreads anticipated costs and savings over a predictable period, sometimes involving several years. In preparing these forecasts, the analyst should be aware that different time spans may be involved than those used for a systems development project, where a useful life span of five to seven years may have been assumed. In a maintenance project, some of this useful life span may be dissipated. Therefore, economic projections for a maintenance project must be limited to the system's remaining useful life. For example, a system that is four years old may be a candidate for replacement in one to three years. This could obviously impact the projected return on investment, and thus require a faster payoff from a maintenance project than from a systems development project if the same rate of return is to be realized.

After economic evaluations have been completed, some maintenance projects will be dropped because they simply do not deliver sufficient return on investment. Others are eliminated for the same reasons used to drop systems development projects:

— A given maintenance project may be inconsistent with plans for the organization, specific operating division, or EDP function.
— A systems development project under active consideration or development may be found to duplicate the intended effect of the proposed maintenance project.

This last point illustrates the rationale for having the EDP director participate in the evaluation of regular maintenance requests, either through sole responsibility or as member of a committee. The director has a thorough knowledge of existing EDP plans. Thus, if a maintenance request is to be superseded by a pending systems development project, the EDP director will be in a position to assess the projected life of the change realistically. A short life span does not necessarily mean that a maintenance request will be dropped (although that can be one of the consequences). In some cases, short-term benefits will be great enough to overcome the short life span involved.

Develop Work Plan. In some organizations, maintenance projects have been organized into two specific activities: programming and program testing. Comparatively little time has been spent on overall systems considerations, with the following consequences:

— Changes have failed to produce desired results. This happens primarily because of failure to take the necessary time to understand the problems and objectives at the outset. As a result, many maintenance projects have gone through multiple cycles to refine the definitions of changes to conform with what the user really wanted.
— Other areas of the system have been impacted by unforeseen errors or efforts of maintenance projects because of the inadequate integration of changes into the system as a whole.
— As systems change because of uncoordinated maintenance, they gradually become less efficient and more difficult to maintain.
— By emphasizing programming and testing for the changed areas only, the cost of regular maintenance is consistently underestimated. When this happens to a whole series of maintenance projects, the impact upon programming resources may become significantly distorted.

An effective method of planning maintenance projects is required to avoid these problems. This can be done by treating each maintenance request as a miniature systems development effort. In doing this, the analyst preparing an estimate for a maintenance project should briefly review all activities from Systems Requirements (Phase II) through Systems Implementation (Phase IV). The level of effort necessary to complete the maintenance assignment must be determined for each activity. Activities that do not apply to the maintenance project can be disposed of at once. In other cases, consideration of the basic activity structure leads to a better understanding and to improved planning, because the analyst recognizes that certain standard activities that may ordinarily have been overlooked in a maintenance project are necessary to assure a quality end product.

By approaching the planning of maintenance projects in a reasonable degree of detail, the following benefits can be realized:

— Forecasts of time requirements are more realistic.
— The likelihood of overlooking or leaving out a significant task or step in a maintenance project is reduced significantly.
— The quality of the finished work is almost surely higher than if the maintenance project had been allowed to proceed directly to the programming step. In addition, the likelihood that documentation will become outdated shortly after its completion is distinctly reduced.

This work plan approach controls maintenance projects within the existing project management system. Maintenance requirements may be included in operating reports and forecasts delivered to EDP management and the steering committee. Thus, a single set of reports provides a complete picture of resource requirements and workloads.

After completing the analysis, economic evaluation, and work plan, a meeting should take place with the initiator of the request and other affected users. This review assures that all parties agree with the planned approach and its projected economic consequences. User approval is required before proceeding to the next activity.

Establish Priorities

The final activity before performing maintenance is the prioritization of projects. Criteria for this process vary from organization to organization. However, the approach described in the Initial Investigation (Phase I, Step 1) is usually appropriate.

One major difference concerns small changes. There is a relatively high fixed cost associated with opening any program. Therefore, the more changes that can be implemented when a given program is opened for modification, the lower the cost per change. Therefore, as part of the process for establishing queues for maintenance projects, a report on pending maintenance requests should be produced and reviewed periodically as part of the priority-setting procedure. All job requests that impact any given program are displayed and their priority ratings are identified. Another consideration especially important to user management is the timing of changes. This factor can alter user priorities—a fact to be taken into consideration by EDP personnel performing the maintenance tasks.

Establishing priorities also requires consideration of the three basic categories of maintenance requests—system errors, normal business needs, and enhancements.

System Errors. This category of maintenance involves system malfunctions that must be diagnosed and solved by the maintenance group. System errors can obviously neither be planned nor scheduled, but they do occur and responsiveness is necessary. Therefore, sufficient resources must be available to ensure that corrective action can be taken in time to prevent business interruptions. Establishing priorities in this case only involves the allocation of adequate standby resources. However, other priority considerations are also required to properly address system errors.

Excessive system errors create severe problems for any EDP unit. Establishing a threshold level beyond which errors are unacceptable is a major challenge that may involve establishing parameters or tolerance limits for each individual system. When the number of system errors exceeds that limit, management review is triggered automatically and a new maintenance request is generated. Tracing an abnormal number of system errors to specific causes may indicate a need for corrective action.

When reviews of system errors indicate that the incidence of change for individual programs exceeds predetermined limits, consideration should be given to rewriting those programs. For example, it could be determined that a program that has been opened more than ten times since the start of ongoing maintenance is a candidate for reprogramming. Another method that may be available to identify error-prone programs is the use of automated source statement librarian packages. These keep track of the number of lines of code that have been changed within a given program. Parameters may be established to flag programs once these limits are exceeded. For example, it may be determined that whenever over half the lines of code in a given program have been changed, it should be a candidate for a complete rewriting.

These diagnostic techniques help pinpoint the frequency and location of recurring system errors. When they indicate that errors persist in an identifiable area, EDP management may determine that extensive corrective action is necessary. This can be implemented with a request for regular maintenance of a program, a series of programs, or an entire system. When this happens, the request is similar to a routine user request for maintenance or enhancement. As such, it must be cost-justified and prioritized with other routine maintenance projects.

Normal Business Needs. The second category of maintenance resembles regular enhancements in most respects. Its requirements are known in advance; it can be planned for and scheduled. There are differences in timing and cost considerations, however. Many maintenance jobs in this category have implementation deadlines. For example, price changes or changes in tax rates must be made by specific dates. Similarly, personnel or operations reports must be submitted to government agencies by certain deadlines. Changes such as these are not required to be cost-justified. Once requirements are identified, jobs are automatically placed in queues and scheduled.

To supplement regular maintenance reports, an analysis of open mandatory changes should be prepared. Late jobs, or those close to targeted completion dates, should be highlighted for management review. Since deadlines are mandatory, other priorities may be adjusted to assure that these requests are completed.

Enhancements. Management can do little to control the mix or scheduling of jobs when it is dealing with maintenance brought about by system errors or normal business needs. In these first two areas of maintenance, establishing priorities is limited to meeting shcedules while assuring a high quality of work performed. However, in the area of enhancements, management gains a large measure of discretionary control. Individual request priorities should be established jointly with analysts and user management. Relative priorities may then be determined for all requests in the systems department backlog. These relative priorities take several factors into consideration:

— The volume of system errors and mandatory change requests.

— The economic impact of the enhancements.

— The degree to which requests may be grouped for more efficient scheduling and control.

Perform Maintenance

Individual maintenance projects are assigned from the request backlog according to current relative priorities. Except for high-priority system errors, this assignment process takes place whenever resources are freed from development or other maintenance projects.

At this point, the initial analysis of requests and development of work plans has been done. Thus, the first activity involves reviewing the project files and updating plans to reflect current schedules and personnel assignments. When completed, the plans may be executed to perform maintenance. This may involve many activities from the Systems Requirements, Development, and Implementation phases of the standard systems development process. The same approaches and forms used in new systems development apply to maintenance, as does the project management process.

The systems test conducted in the Systems Development phase is designed to ensure that changes have not in any way adversely affected the system. If any new features have been added to the system or if a particular error condition is being tested, test data should be added to show that the proper result has occurred. All the documentation described in the Systems Test step applies in the ongoing maintenance.

After the user has approved the results, modifications are implemented, and the appropriate documentation is updated and placed in the program and systems history files. This entire package should then be reviewed by a quality assurance group to ensure proper implementation of the change.

KEY CONSIDERATIONS

Report by Type of Mainenance

Every maintenance activity should be recorded and assigned within its proper category. It is important that resource allocation and cost information take place uniformly and accurately. This type of detailed reporting is necessary for proper management evaluation of the effectiveness of maintenance activities. In addition, reporting categories should correspond to those used for overall project management. This is necessary to enable management to tie its evaluations and decisions in the maintenance area back to overall systems development projects.

Test the System

Too often, maintenance projects fail to test the entire system. This omission can easily lead to undetected errors that subsequently require emergency maintenance. Any maintenance project that involves file manipulation, input data, or computational logic requires a new systems test. If the original test step was conducted properly, this new test should consist of resubmitting all the pertinent test data and verifying that the expected results have not changed.

Maintaining test files, data, procedures, and expected results may appear to be cumbersome and time-consuming. However, it assures that maintenance changes (that will continue throughout the life of the system) are properly applied. It also minimizes the disruption and high costs associated with emergency maintenance.

STANDARD ACTIVITIES/END ITEMS

TOUCHE ROSS

ORGANIZATION _____

SYSTEM ___MAINTENANCE___

USER REP _____

ID/TITLE ___ONGOING MAINTENANCE___

☐ PHASE ☒ ACTIVITY ☐ SUBTASK

☐ STEP   ☒ TASK   ☐ _____

PREPARED BY   MVJ   SH

REVIEWED BY   CB   CB

DATE   3/29/80   11/1/80

PHASE

NUMBER	PHASE/STEP/ACTIVITY/TASK/SUBTASK NAME	END ITEM	FORM NO.	PERFORMED BY	DUE DATE	APPROVED BY	DATE
A.	Prepare Request for Change	Change Request	112				
B.	Identify Problem Area						
B.1	- Analyze Request	Interview Summaries	121				
		Work Flows	127, 128				
		Document Definitions	132				
		Data Element Definitions and Uses	150, 151 152, 154				
		Constraints and Controls	140, 141				
B.2	- Prepare Economic Evaluation	Development Costs	104, 105				
		Operating Costs	145				
		Benefits	146, 147				
		Economic Evaluation	148				
B.3	- Develop Work Plan	Work Plan	101, 102				
		Management Summary	149				
C.	Establish Priorities	Maintenance Project Plans	102				

STANDARD ACTIVITIES/END ITEMS

TOUCHE ROSS

ORGANIZATION _____

SYSTEM __MAINTENANCE__

USER REP _____

PREPARED BY __MVJ__ __SH__
REVIEWED BY __CB__ __CB__
DATE __3/29/80__ __11/1/80__
PHASE

ID/TITLE __ONGOING MAINTENANCE__

☐ PHASE ☒ ACTIVITY ☐ SUBTASK
☐ STEP ☒ TASK ☐ _____

NUMBER	PHASE/STEP/ACTIVITY/TASK/SUBTASK NAME	END ITEM	FORM NO.	PERFORMED BY	DUE DATE	APPROVED BY	DATE
D.	Perform Maintenance	Data Element and File Changes	150-155				
		Input and Output Changes	160-166				
		Program and Logic Changes	170-178				
		Program/Module Maintenance Control	113				
		Test Checklists and Plans	180-195				
		Results Form	198				
		Approval Form	199				
		System Certification Checklist	115				

254

3

Systems Development Standard Forms

This section contains a comprehensive set of standard forms which are to be used in conjunction with Section II. These forms aid in structuring documentation and in realizing the end-product orientation of the systems development process. Other benefits derived from using standard forms include:

— The forms provide a reminder of information to be gathered or analytical work to be done.

— The forms provide a consistent documentation approach among multiple projects within one systems or user department.

— The forms encourage complete and thorough analytical work.

— The ability to review completed work by project managers and users is enhanced through standard forms for development.

— Project managers have improved capabilities to estimate effort required by defining discrete tasks with standard format structures for end products.

— A structured approach to systems development combined with standard forms for documentation improves the ability to change project staff during the development process.

— Documentation on standard forms results in a useful history file through subsequent phases and steps and for systems maintenance.

The standard forms do not explain what systems requirements are or how a system should be developed and implemented. They only provide a structured format for recording results. As such, they do not preclude or inhibit the creative process necessary in any systems project.

Forms such as those included in this book have been used by many organizations on a multitude of projects for a number of years. They have been updated to reflect the experience gained from actual use and the methodology presented in Section Two. However, they should not be considered absolute requirements or totally applicable for every project environment. Rather, they are presented as guidelines and suggestions for project documentation.

Systems departments should use these format examples as guidelines for developing their own comprehensive set of standard forms. Then, for each specific project, the project manager should select from the comprehensive set those forms that appear applicable and useful in that situation. The selected forms may also require minor modifications to fulfill the unique needs of the project. Rarely, if ever, will the complete set of forms be used on any one project.

Within Section Two — the systems development process — a standard activities/end item matrix has been included with each step. This matrix outlines the standard activities and tasks described in the step, the potential end products to be developed from each activity and task, and the suggested forms to be used in recording the end products. In many cases, a particular form may be utilized in several steps. This illustrates the cumulative documentation approach whereby additional detailed data is added to the same forms throughout the development process as more information is gathered and analyzed.

The forms and instructions contained in this section are divided into four general categories: project management, user-oriented activities, technically-oriented activities, and development planning and testing. However, as shown in the standard activities/end item matrices, these forms are used throughout the process and not strictly limited to their general category.

Forms for Project Management

100	Index of Forms
101	Work Outline Form
102	General-Purpose Gantt Chart
103	Job Description
104	Programming Estimate
105	Development Cost Measurement
106	Standard Activities/End Items
107	Time Report
108	Status Report
111	Problem/Request Control
112	Change Request
113	Program/Module Maintenance Control
115	System Certification Checklist

Forms for User-Oriented Activities

120	Interview Schedule
121	Interview Summary
122	Glossary of Terms
125	Summary of Functions
126	Staffing Requirements
127	General-Purpose Chart
128	General-Purpose Chart Description
130	Input/Output Index
131	Input/Output Identification
132	Document Definition
133	File Description and Inquiry
134	Data Element Description
140	Assumptions and Constraints
141	Summary of Controls
142	Multi-Purpose Forms
145	Operating Cost Summary
146	Statement of Benefits
147	Measurable Benefits Evaluation
148	Economic Evaluation Summary
149	Management Summary

Forms for Technically-Oriented Activities

150	Data Element Definition
151	Data Element/Module Cross Reference
152	Data Base/File Contents and Characteristics
153	Record/Document Contents
154	Data Base Record/File Layout
155	Transaction/Data Base/File Activity
160	Multiple Card Layout
161	VDT Screen Layout
162	VDT Support
163	Computer Output/Report
164	Output Report Layout
165	Print Report Program/Printer Support
166	Print Control
170	System Naming Control
171	Program/Module Function
172	Module Function Support
173	Module Table
174	Sort Program Parameter
175	File Split/File Merge
176	Decision Table
177	Table Form
178	Code Table

Forms for Development Planning and Testing

FORMS FOR PROJECT MANAGEMENT

FORM NUMBER	FORM NAME
100	Index of Forms
101	Work Outline Form
102	General-Purpose Gantt Chart
103	Job Description
104	Programming Estimate
105	Development Cost Measurement
106	Standard Activities/End Items
107	Time Report
108	Status Report
111	Problem/Request Control
112	Change Request
113	Program/Module Maintenance Control
115	System Certification Checklist

INDEX OF FORMS
FORM 100

PURPOSE: To list all forms used in a particular set of documentation and to record approvals and revisions to the forms in that set of documentation.

PROCEDURE FOR COMPLETING:

INFORMATION	ACTION
1. Heading	Complete and check appropriate boxes.
2. Form Name Form Number	Complete for each form used.
3. Approval	Indicate initials and date of original approval to a completed form in the documentation package.
4. Revision Completed	Indicate initials and date of latest revision to a completed form in the documentation package.

INDEX OF FORMS

TOUCHE ROSS

ID/TITLE _____

PAGE _____ OF _____

PROJECT NO. _____

ORGANIZATION _____

SYSTEM _____

USER REP _____

☐ CURRENT   ☐ PROPOSED
☐ SYSTEM   ☐ PROGRAM
☐ OTHER _____

PREPARED BY _____

REVIEWED BY _____

DATE _____

PHASE _____

FORM NAME	FORM NUMBER	APPROVAL COMPLETED	REVISION COMPLETED

WORK OUTLINE FORM
FORM 101

PURPOSE: To provide a means for recording the required work and estimated effort to complete all major activities and tasks.

PROCEDURE FOR COMPLETING:

INFORMATION	ACTION
1. Heading	Complete and check appropriate boxes.
2. Number	Indicate the number of phase, step, activity, task, etc.
3. Work definition	Describe the work to be performed.
4. Responsibility	Identify the responsible individual and organization.
5. Personnel type	Identify the type of skills or organization required to do the specific work.
6. Work days required	Determine the estimated number of work days required to complete the work.
7. Budget	Indicate the dollar budget available to complete the work.
8. Start date	Indicate the planned start date.
9. Target date	Indicate the planned completion date.
10. Total	Indicate the total estimated days and budget to complete the phase, step, activity, etc.

WORK OUTLINE FORM

TOUCHE ROSS

ORGANIZATION _____

SYSTEM _____

USER REP _____

ID/TITLE _____

☐ PROJECT   ☐ ACTIVITY

☐ PHASE   ☐ TASK

☐ STEP   ☐ SUB-TASK

PREPARED BY _____

REVIEWED BY _____

DATE _____

PHASE _____

NO.	WORK DEFINITION	RESPONSI-BILITY	PERSONNEL TYPE	WORK DAYS REQUIRED	BUDGET	START DATE	TARGET DATE
TOTAL							

FORM NO. 101

263

GENERAL-PURPOSE GANTT CHART
FORM 102

PURPOSE: To graphically display activities and tasks with start and end dates.

PROCEDURE FOR COMPLETING:

INFORMATION	ACTION
1. Heading	Complete.
2. Body	List the required activities and tasks with calendar dates across the form. Draw lines to display the calendar start and end of each activity and task.

GENERAL-PURPOSE GANTT CHART

TOUCHE ROSS

ORGANIZATION

SYSTEM

USER REP

ID/TITLE

PAGE _____ OF _____

PROJECT NO. _____

PREPARED BY

REVIEWED BY

DATE

PHASE

JOB DESCRIPTION
FORM 103

PURPOSE: To define and document the role and responsibility of each project team member.

PROCEDURE FOR COMPLETING:

INFORMATION	ACTION
1. Heading	Complete and check appropriate boxes for summary, objectives, and scope.
2. Description	Describe the project role and responsibility of the specific team member to the level required for adequate communication to all concerned parties.

TOUCHE ROSS

ORGANIZATION _____

_____

SYSTEM _____

USER REP _____

☐ SUMMARY
☐ OBJECTIVES
☐ SCOPE

PAGE _____ OF _____

PROJECT NO. _____

PREPARED BY _____

REVIEWED BY _____

DATE _____

PHASE _____

DESCRIPTION _____

PROGRAMMING ESTIMATE
FORM 104

PURPOSE: To record estimates of programming effort for a project.

PROCEDURE FOR COMPLETING:

INFORMATION	ACTION
1. Heading	Complete. Check appropriate box to indicate if estimate is based on requirements-level documentation or detail specifications-level documentation.
2. Program number and name	Enter the specific program name or the general program type.
3. Type	Indicate the type of program from the standard classifications.
4. Frequency	Indicate the frequency planned for this program to execute.
5. Module number and module name	Enter each module within the identified program, if appropriate.
6. Available in Library	Indicate (Y or N) if this program or module currently exists in the installation library.
7. Complexity	Indicate the degree of complexity within the standard classification type of program or module.
8. Work effort	Enter the standard time estimate for this type and complexity of program or module.
9. Computer time	Enter estimates for required computer time in development (programming and systems test) and ongoing operations (recurring), if appropriate.

PROGRAMMING ESTIMATE

TOUCHE ROSS

ORGANIZATION _____

SYSTEM _____

USER REP _____

☐ REQUIREMENTS LEVEL
☐ SPECIFICATIONS LEVEL

PAGE _____ OF _____

PROJECT NO. _____

PREPARED BY _____

REVIEWED BY _____

DATE _____

PHASE _____

PROGRAM NO.	PROGRAM NAME	TYPE	F R E Q	Mod. No.	MODULE NAME OR FUNCTION TYPE	Avail In Lib.	COMPLEXITY 1	2	3	4	WORK EFFORT Anal.	Sr. Pro.	Prog.	Total	COMPUTER TIME Prog.	Sys Tst	Recur.

TOTALS

COST SUMMARY	DEVELOPMENTAL Work Effort	Work $	Computer Hours	Computer $	Total $	RECURRING Hours Mo.	$/Mo.
ANALYST							
SR. PROGRAMMER							
PROGRAMMER							
TOTALS							

COPYRIGHT 1980   FORM NO. 104
TOUCHE ROSS & CO.

269

DEVELOPMENT COST MEASUREMENT
FORM 105

PURPOSE: To provide a summary-level comparison of the plan versus actual dollars or hours for the development of a system.

PROCEDURE FOR COMPLETING:

INFORMATION	ACTION
1. Heading	Complete and check the appropriate box.
2. Number	Indicate the number associated with each line item.
3. Phase/step/activity/task	Check the appropriate box and briefly describe the phase, step, activity, or task.
4. Reference	Indicate the backup documentation.
5. Time period	Record the plan and actual hours or dollars by period and line item.

DEVELOPMENT COST MEASUREMENT

TOUCHE ROSS

PAGE _____ OF _____

PROJECT NO. _____

ID/TITLE _____

ORGANIZATION _____ DATE FROM _____ TO _____ PREPARED BY _____

_____ PERIOD SIZE _____ REVIEWED BY _____

SYSTEM _____ ☐ HOURS   ☐ DOLLARS   DATE _____

USER REP _____ INFLATION FACTOR _____ PHASE _____

TIME PERIOD

NO. | ☐ PHASE ☐ ACTIVITY | ☐ STEP ☐ TASK | REF | PLAN | ACTUAL | PLAN | ACTUAL | PLAN | ACTUAL | PLAN | ACTUAL | PLAN | ACTUAL | PLAN | ACTUAL | PLAN | ACTUAL | PLAN | ACTUAL | PLAN | ACTUAL | PLAN | ACTUAL | PLAN | ACTUAL | PLAN | ACTUAL | PLAN | ACTUAL | PLAN | ACTUAL | PLAN | ACTUAL | PLAN | ACTUAL | PLAN | ACTUAL | PLAN | ACTUAL | PLAN | ACTUAL | PLAN | ACTUAL | PLAN | ACTUAL | PLAN | ACTUAL | PLAN | ACTUAL | PLAN | ACTUAL | TOTAL PLAN | TOTAL ACTUAL | VARIANCE |

STANDARD ACTIVITIES/END ITEMS
FORM 106

PURPOSE: To record activities with specified end products, dates, responsibilities, and approvals.

PROCEDURE FOR COMPLETING:

INFORMATION	ACTION
1. Heading	Complete.
2. Body	Complete as appropriate. This form may be used to supplement the Work Outline Form (101) in order to assure that specific end products are identified and produced with each unit of work. Where appropriate, the standard form numbers are entered to indicate that the specific end product should be documented in a consistent and standard format.

STANDARD ACTIVITIES/END ITEMS

TOUCHE ROSS

ORGANIZATION _____

SYSTEM _____

USER REP _____

PAGE _____ OF _____

PROJECT NO. _____

PREPARED BY _____

REVIEWED BY _____

DATE _____

PHASE _____

ID/TITLE _____

☐ PHASE   ☐ ACTIVITY   ☐ SUBTASK
☐ STEP   ☐ TASK   ☐ _____

PHASE/STEP/ACTIVITY/TASK/SUBTASK		END ITEM	FORM NO.	PERFORMED BY	DUE DATE	APPROVED BY	DATE
NUMBER	NAME						

TIME REPORT
FORM 107

PURPOSE: To record all time spent on a project.

PROCEDURE FOR COMPLETING:

INFORMATION	ACTION
1. Heading	Complete.
2. Activity/task	List each activity and task this time report represents.
3. Description	Briefly describe the activity and task.
4. Hours	Record the number of hours for each activity and task by day and total.
5. Earned hours	Indicate the earned hours for each completed activity and task. Earned hours are equal to planned hours (not actual hours) for the activity or task when the work is completed. In process activities and tasks have no earned hours.
6. Hours to complete	Indicate the estimated hours to complete each activity and task.
7. Estimated date	Indicate the estimated completion date for each activity and task.
8. Comments	Enter comments as appropriate.

274

TIME REPORT

TOUCHE ROSS

ID/TITLE _____

ORGANIZATION _____

_____

SYSTEM _____

USER REP _____

NAME _____

NUMBER _____

WEEK ENDING _____

PAGE _____ OF _____

PROJECT NO. _____

PREPARED BY _____

REVIEWED BY _____

DATE _____

PHASE _____

TASK	DESCRIPTION	HOURS M	T	W	TH	F	S	S	TOTAL	EARNED HOURS	HOURS TO COMPLETE	EST. DATE	COMMENTS
TOTAL													

PURPOSE: To report the status of a project measuring the current plan and actual completion versus the original plan.

PROCEDURE FOR COMPLETING:

INFORMATION	ACTION
1. Heading	Complete and check the appropriate boxes.
2. Description	Briefly describe the phase, step, activity or task being reported.
3. Original plan	Enter the date the original plan was prepared, including the start date, completion date, and budget. This plan should not change through the life of the project except with top-management approval.
4. Actual or last current plan	When items are actually started and completed, record the actual start date, completion date, and budget. If the actuals do not occur, the last presented current plan and date are entered.
5. Current plan	When changes in the plan occur, indicate the date the plan is revised and the start date, completion date, and budget of the current plan.
6. Change	Check this box if there is a difference between the original plan, actual or last current plan, and the current plan.

STATUS REPORT

TOUCHE ROSS

ID/TITLE _____

PAGE _____ OF _____

PROJECT NO. _____

ORGANIZATION _____
_____

SYSTEM _____
USER REP _____

☐ PROJECT   ☐ ACTIVITY
☐ PHASE   ☐ TASK
☐ STEP   ☐ _____

PREPARED BY _____
REVIEWED BY _____
DATE
PHASE

CHANGE																						

CURRENT PLAN — DATE REVIEWED—: BUDGET / COMP. DATE / START DATE

ACTUAL OR LAST CURRENT PLAN — DATE REVIEWED—: BUDGET / COMP. DATE / START DATE

ORGINAL PLAN — DATE SET—: BUDGET / COMP. DATE / START DATE

DESCRIPTION

PROBLEM/REQUEST CONTROL
FORM 111

PURPOSE: To record problems and changes to a system during systems testing or maintenance.

PROCEDURE FOR COMPLETING:

INFORMATION	ACTION
1. Heading	Complete.
2. Symptom/request	Describe the symptom or change request, sign, and date.
3. Problem/reason	Record the analysis of the problem or change modification, sign, and date.
4. Solution/disposition	Summarize the solution or disposition, sign, and date.
5. Change request(s) issued	Indicate the items to be changed, persons assigned, and dates required. Also complete Change Requests (Form 112), sign and date.
6. Date of completion	Enter the date this item was completed.

PROBLEM/REQUEST CONTROL

TOUCHE ROSS

ORGANIZATION _____

_____

SYSTEM _____

USER REP _____

NUMBER [   ]

PRIORITY _____

COMMITMENT DATE _____

COMPLETE? [   ] DATE _____

PAGE _____ OF _____

PROJECT NO. _____

PREPARED BY		
REVIEWED BY		
DATE		
PHASE		

SYMPTOM/REQUEST

SUBMITTED BY _____   DATE _____

PROBLEM/REASON

DIAGNOSED BY _____   DATE _____

SOLUTION/DISPOSITION

SOLVED BY _____   DATE _____

CHANGE REQUEST(S) ISSUED

NO.	ITEM TO BE CHANGED	ASSIGNED TO	DATE REQUIRED	DATE OF ACTUAL COMPLETION

APPROVED BY _____   DATE _____

CHANGE REQUEST
FORM 112

PURPOSE: To communicate to various responsible parties a change to be made to a system during systems test or maintenance.

PROCEDURE FOR COMPLETING:

INFORMATION	ACTION
1. Heading	Complete.
2. Reason for change	Describe the reason for the change.
3. Description of change	Describe the proposed solution or change to be made.
4. Documentation attached	List the documentation that is attached.
5. Changes required	Check the appropriate items to be changed.
6. Comments	Enter comments as appropriate.
7. Signature and date	Sign and date.

CHANGE REQUEST

TOUCHE ROSS

ORGANIZATION _____

SYSTEM _____

USER REP _____

NUMBER [_____]

PROBLEM/REQUEST CONTROL NO. _____

ASSIGNED TO_____

DATE REQUIRED_____

COMPLETE? ☐ DATE_____

PAGE _____ OF _____

PROJECT NO. _____

PREPARED BY _____

REVIEWED BY _____

DATE _____

PHASE _____

REASON FOR CHANGE

DESCRIPTION OF CHANGE

DOCUMENTATION ATTACHED

CHANGES REQUIRED

ITEM	PERFORMED BY	DATE COMPLETED	ITEM	PERFORMED BY	DATE COMPLETED
☐ PROGRAM _____	_____	_____	☐ RUN INSTRUCTIONS	_____	_____
☐ PROGRAM DOCUMENTATION	_____	_____	☐ USER PROCEDURES	_____	_____
☐ FILE _____	_____	_____	☐	_____	_____
☐ FILE DOCUMENTATION	_____	_____	☐	_____	_____
☐ PRINTER LAYOUT	_____	_____	☐	_____	_____
☐ DATA ELEMENT DICTIONARY	_____	_____	☐	_____	_____
☐ TEST DATA & RUN	_____	_____	☐	_____	_____

COMMENTS

REQUESTED BY	DATE	CHANGED BY	DATE	APPROVED BY	DATE

PROGRAM/MODULE MAINTENANCE CONTROL
FORM 113

PURPOSE: To record the history of a program from development through maintenance.

PROCEDURE FOR COMPLETING:

INFORMATION	ACTION
1. Heading	Complete.
2. Programming specifications	
A. Description of program module.	Briefly describe the program or module.
B. Programming estimate	Enter the estimated hours to code and test the program or module.
C. Date required	Enter the date that is needed for systems test.
D. Language	Specify the programming language to be used.
E. Specifications	Obtain all required signatures.
3. Programming assignment	Enter the name and date of assignment and any appropriate comments.
4. Certification	Complete all data at program test, systems test, and implementation.
5. Maintenance history change request	Complete for each change or problem occurrence after systems test.
A. Control number	Fill in from Change Request (Form 112).
B. Changed by	Identify programmer's name.
C. Date	Enter date completed. A supplemental form may be initiated if more than 12 maintenance changes are made to the program before it is rewritten or discontinued.

PROGRAM/MODULE MAINTENANCE CONTROL

PAGE _____ OF _____

PROJECT NO. _____

ID/TITLE_____

ORGANIZATION _____

_____

SYSTEM_____

USER REP _____

PREPARED BY _____ |_____|_____

REVIEWED BY _____ |_____|_____

DATE _____ |_____|_____

PHASE _____ |_____|_____

PROGRAMMING SPECIFICATIONS

DESCRIPTION OF PROGRAM/MODULE:

PROGRAMMING HOUR ESTIMATE _____ DATE REQUIRED _____ LANGUAGE _____

SPECIFICATIONS COMPLETED BY _____ DATE _____ SPECIFICATIONS APPROVED BY _____ DATE

PROGRAMMING ASSIGNMENT

PROGRAM/MODULE ASSIGNED TO: _____ SCHEDULED COMPLETION DATE_____

ASSIGNED BY_____ DATE _____

COMMENTS

CERTIFICATION

PROGRAM/MODULE WRITTEN BY _____ DATE _____ DOCUMENTATION COMPLETED BY _____ DATE

PROGRAM/MODULE QUALITY ASSURANCE BY _____ DATE _____ PROJECT ACCEPTANCE BY _____ DATE

MAINTENANCE HISTORY

NO.	CHANGE REQUEST NO.	CHANGED BY	DATE	NO.	CHANGE REQUEST NO.	CHANGED BY	DATE
1.				7.			
2.				8.			
3.				9.			
4.				10.			
5.				11.			
6.				12.			

SYSTEM CERTIFICATION CHECKLIST
FORM 115

PURPOSE: To record the necessary reviews and approvals for a new system prior to acceptance for ongoing operations.

PROCEDURE FOR COMPLETING:

INFORMATION	ACTION
1. Heading	Complete.
2. Body	Enter the initials and date of each individual reviewing and approving a new system for documentation standards, technical quality, and management acceptance.

SYSTEM CERTIFICATION CHECKLIST

TOUCHE ROSS

ORGANIZATION_____

_____

SYSTEM _____

USER REP_____

PAGE_____ OF _____

PROJECT NO. _____

PREPARED BY ____	
REVIEWED BY ____	
DATE ____	
PHASE ____	

DOCUMENTATION REVIEW:

	MAINTENANCE		OPERATIONS	
	Reviewed By	Date	Reviewed By	Date
1. System Requirements Book				
2. Program Specifications				
3. Program Test Data and Results				
4. System Test Plan and Results				
5. Control Procedures				
6. Operating Instructions				
7. Run Books				
8. Run Schedule				
9.				

TECHNICAL REVIEW:

1. Programming Standards				
2. Error Recovery Procedures				
3. File Handling Techniques				
4.				

MANAGEMENT REVIEW AND ACCEPTANCE:

1. Programming				
2. Operations				
3.				

FORMS FOR USER-ORIENTED ACTIVITIES

FORM NUMBER	FORM NAME
120	Interview Schedule
121	Interview Summary
122	Glossary of Terms
125	Summary of Functions
126	Staffing Requirements
127	General-Purpose Chart
128	General-Purpose Chart Description
130	Input/Output Index
131	Input/Output Identification
132	Document Definition
133	File Description and Inquiry
134	Data Element Description
140	Assumptions and Constraints
141	Summary of Controls
142	Multi-Purpose Forms
145	Operating Cost Summary
146	Statement of Benefits
147	Measurable Benefits Evaluation
148	Economic Evaluation Summary
149	Management Summary

INTERVIEW SCHEDULE
FORM 120

PURPOSE: To plan and document the list of all people interviewed and the subject areas covered in those interviews.

PROCEDURE FOR COMPLETING:

INFORMATION	ACTION
1. Heading	Complete.
2. Interviewee/title	List the name and title of each person to be interviewed.
3. Interviewer	Enter the intitals of the interviewer.
4. Date/time/location	Indicate the date, time, and location of the interview.
5. Topics to be discussed	Summarize in a few words the subject matter of the interview.
6. Interview summary preparation date.	Enter the date the Interview Summary (Form 121) is completed. This column may be used to monitor the timely completion of Interview Summaries by the project team members.

INTERVIEW SCHEDULE

TOUCHE ROSS

ID/TITLE _____

PAGE _____ OF _____

PROJECT NO. _____

ORGANIZATION _____

SYSTEM _____

USER REP _____

PREPARED BY _____

REVIEWED BY _____

DATE

PHASE

Interview Summary Preparation Date																					
Topics to be discussed																					
Location																					
Time																					
Date																					
Interviewer																					
Interviewee/Title																					

INTERVIEW SUMMARY
FORM 121

PURPOSE: To summarize in an orderly format the topics discussed with the interviewee. This form is generally completed after the interview in order to organize and expand on the raw notes taken during the interview session.

PROCEDURE FOR COMPLETING:

INFORMATION	ACTION
1. Heading	Complete.
2. Interviewee/position/ organization	Indicate the name, position held, and organizational unit of this interviewee.
3. Body	Complete the body and cover the points listed:

A. The functional responsibilities of the organizational unit and interviewee.

B. The organization's objectives.

C. Problems and deficiencies in the current operations and systems that impact the organizational unit.

D. A brief description of the current manual and computerized systems from the interviewee's perspective.

E. Summary of pertinent budget information to be used in cost and benefit analyses.

F. Existing short- and long-range plans for improvements to operations and systems.

G. General information required for the organization and interviewee to effectively perform their functions.

H. Other general comments.

INTERVIEW SUMMARY

TOUCHE ROSS

PAGE _____ OF _____

PROJECT NO. _____

ID/TITLE _____

ORGANIZATION _____

_____

SYSTEM _____

USER REP _____

PREPARED BY		
REVIEWED BY		
DATE		
PHASE		

INTERVIEWEE:	POSITION:	ORGANIZATION:

A. FUNCTIONAL RESPONSIBILITIES
B. OBJECTIVES
C. PROBLEMS AND DEFICIENCIES
D. CURRENT SYSTEMS

E. BUDGETS
F. PLANNED SYSTEMS
  SHORT AND LONG RANGE PLANS
G. INFORMATION REQUIREMENTS
H. GENERAL COMMENTS

291

GLOSSARY OF TERMS
FORM 122

PURPOSE: To identify and define all unique terms used by an organization.

PROCEDURE FOR COMPLETING:

INFORMATION	ACTION
1. Heading	Complete and check the appropriate box.
2. Term	Enter the term to be defined.
3. Meaning	Define the term in its usage relative to this organization. All terms that may communicate unique legal, policy, procedural, timing, or technical information should be included in this glossary.

GLOSSARY OF TERMS

ID/TITLE _____

ORGANIZATION _____

□ CURRENT   □ PROPOSED

SYSTEM _____

USER REP _____

PAGE _____ OF _____

PROJECT NO. _____

PREPARED BY _____

REVIEWED BY _____

DATE

PHASE

MEANING																			
TERM																			

PURPOSE: To document by organizational unit the functions performed with associated time requirements, volumes, and costs.

PROCEDURE FOR COMPLETING:

INFORMATION	ACTION
1. Heading	Complete and check appropriate box for current or proposed functions.
2. Function number	Assign a reference number for the function.
3. Hours per day/week/month	Enter the hours required to perform the function on a daily, weekly, or monthly basis.
4. Volume	Note any volume indicators that relate to the amount of work performed.
5. Cost	Determine the personnel cost of each function by applying the cost of salaries and fringes of assigned personnel to the percent of hours spent to total available hours.
6. N/C/O	Indicate if the function is new, changed, or ongoing if this form contains proposed functions.
7. Personnel	List names of personnel involved in the function.
8. Function description	Describe the functional operations.

SUMMARY OF FUNCTIONS

PAGE _____ OF _____

PROJECT NO. _____ —

ORGANIZATION _____

_____

SYSTEM _____

USER REP _____

ID/TITLE _____

☐ CURRENT   ☐ PROPOSED

PREPARED BY _____

REVIEWED BY _____

DATE _____

PHASE _____

FUNC-TION NO.	HOURS PER			VOLUME	COST	N C O	PERSONNEL	FUNCTION DESCRIPTION
	DAY	WEEK	MONTH					
TOTAL								

NO. OF EMPLOYEES _____

APPROVED BY _____

DATE _____

COMMENTS:

295

STAFFING REQUIREMENTS
FORM 126

PURPOSE: To time phase the staffing requirements for functions within an organization or project.

PROCEDURE FOR COMPLETING:

INFORMATION	ACTION
1. Heading	Complete and check the appropriate box for current or proposed functions.
2. Period	Indicate the time period being described on this time phasing.
3. Function	List the functions within the organization.
4. Reference	Reference the supporting documentation, such as Summaries of Functions (Form 125).
5. Total hours	Enter the number of hours required to perform each function.
6. Number of equivalent people	Calculate the number of equivalent people required to perform each function.
7. Total budget	Determine the total personnel budget to perform each function.

STAFFING REQUIREMENTS

TOUCHE ROSS

ID/TITLE _____

ORGANIZATION _____

SYSTEM _____

USER REP _____

☐ CURRENT   ☐ PROPOSED

DATE FROM _____ TO _____

PERIOD SIZE _____

INFLATION FACTOR _____

PAGE _____ OF _____

PROJECT NO. _____

PREPARED BY _____

REVIEWED BY _____

DATE

PHASE

TOTAL BUDGET																							
NO. EQUIV. PEOPLE																							
TOTAL HRS.																							
TOTAL BUDGET																							
NO. EQUIV. PEOPLE																							
TOTAL HRS.																							
TOTAL BUDGET																							
NO. EQUIV. PEOPLE																							
TOTAL HRS.																							

PERIOD	REF.																						TOTAL
FUNCTION																							

COPYRIGHT 1980   FORM NO. 126
TOUCHE ROSS & CO.

GENERAL-PURPOSE CHART
FORM 127

PURPOSE: To show in pictorial form a manual systems flow, computer run-to-run flow, data base map, organization chart, etc.

PROCEDURE FOR COMPLETING:

INFORMATION	ACTION
1. Heading	Complete and check appropriate boxes. Normally, two boxes will be checked. First, a check will indicate if this chart depicts a manual systems flow or a computer (run-to-run) flow or other (e.g., a data base map, organization chart). Second, a check will indicate if this chart pertains to current operations or proposed operations.
2. Body	Complete as necessary. Generally, this form is used in conjunction with the General-Purpose Chart Description (Form 128) in order to provide a narrative description of the pictorial display on this chart.

298

GENERAL-PURPOSE CHART

TOUCHE ROSS

ORGANIZATION _____
SYSTEM _____
USER REP _____

NOTES

ID/TITLE _____

☐ MANUAL
☐ COMPUTER RUN TO RUN
☐ OTHER _____
☐ CURRENT
☐ PROPOSED
☐ OTHER _____

PAGE _____ OF _____
PROJECT NO. _____

PREPARED BY	
REVIEWED BY	
DATE	
PHASE	

	A	B	C	D	E	F	G	H
9								
8								
7								
6								
5								
4								
3								
2								
1								
0								

GENERAL-PURPOSE CHART DESCRIPTION
FORM 128

PURPOSE: To provide a narrative supplement to the work flows, operations, etc. pictured on the General-Purpose Chart (Form 127).

PROCEDURE FOR COMPLETING:

INFORMATION	ACTION
1. Heading	Complete and check appropriate boxes, indicating either current or proposed operations for either manual workflows or computer runs.
2. Coordinate Number	Identify the specific section of the General-Purpose Chart to be described, such as A4, or C2, or F3, etc.
3. Description	Describe the processes, activities, functions, purposes, etc. related to the identified coordinate.

GENERAL-PURPOSE CHART DESCRIPTION FORM

TOUCHE ROSS

ORGANIZATION _____

_____

SYSTEM _____

USER REP _____

ID/TITLE _____

page _____

☐ CURRENT   ☐ PROPOSED

☐ MANUAL   ☐ COMPUTER

☐ OTHER _____

PAGE _____ OF _____

PROJECT NO. _____

PREPARED BY		
REVIEWED BY		
DATE		
PHASE		

COORDINATE NUMBER	DESCRIPTION

INPUT/OUTPUT INDEX
FORM 130

PURPOSE: To list the input or output documents associated with the current operations or proposed new system. This list is often supported by attached copies of documents and descriptions on the Input/Output Identification (Form 131).

PROCEDURE FOR COMPLETING:

INFORMATION	ACTION
1. Heading	Check if input or output. Check if current system or proposed system.
2. Document number and document name	List each document with the organization's assigned document number (or sequentially number the documents for cross reference purposes).
3. Volume	Enter the volume of these documents related to a specified time period.
4. Source	Indicate the organization, department, individual, etc. that generates this document.
5. Distribution	Indicate the organization, department, individual, etc. that receives the completed document.

302

☐ INPUT
☐ OUTPUT **INDEX**

▲

TOUCHE ROSS

ORGANIZATION_____

_____

SYSTEM_____

USER REP_____

☐ CURRENT
☐ PROPOSED

PAGE_____ OF_____

PROJECT NO. _____

PREPARED BY			
REVIEWED BY			
DATE			
PHASE			

Doc. No.	Document Name	Volume	Source	Distribution

▲ COPYRIGHT 1980   FORM NO. 130
TOUCHE ROSS & CO.

INPUT/OUTPUT IDENTIFICATION
FORM 131

PURPOSE: To describe the general contents of input or output documents used in a current operation or proposed new system. A summary list of all the documents is often recorded on the Input/Output Index (Form 130).

PROCEDURE FOR COMPLETING:

INFORMATION	ACTION
1. Heading	Check if input or output. Check if current system or proposed system.
2. Document name and number	Enter the name and organization's assigned number or use a sequential number appropriate for cross reference.
3. Content	Describe in general the contents of the document.
4. Source	List the organizations, departments, etc. that generate this document.
5. Use	Briefly describe the purpose or uses of this document.
6. Preparation	List major steps involved to prepare this document.
7. Distribution	List the organizations, departments, etc. who receive the completed document.
8. Frequency	Indicate the volume related to a time period (frequency).

Document Name	Document No.

Content	Source

Use:

Preparation	Distribution

Frequency	Volume

DOCUMENT DEFINITION
FORM 132

PURPOSE: To organize the important information pertaining to a specific document in the current or proposed system. This form may be used in place of the Input/Output Identification (Form 131) whenever additional levels of detail are required — especially for computer-related input forms.

PROCEDURE FOR COMPLETING:

INFORMATION	ACTION
1. Heading	Complete and check appropriate boxes for current or proposed system.
2. Description	Describe the document's purpose or general use.
3. Document name and form number	Enter the document name and form number.
4. Present input form	Check the appropriate box to show the current media of this document.
5. Document converted to	Indicate how this document is converted into machine-readable format.
6. Manual process and edit steps	Describe the manual process and edit steps performed within the department. Reference any additional documentation. Specify by whom these steps are performed.
7. Distribution flow	List the department name and number to which each copy of the document is distributed. Reference any additional documentation. Indicate the day of week and time the document is scheduled in and/or out of the department.
8. Control	Describe the controls on this document within all departments. Reference any additional documentation. Specify by whom the controls are performed.
9. Volume	Identify the season or period of unusual volumes — e.g., day's, week's, month's range. Indicate in the frequency column the cycle (daily, etc.) and the minimum, average, and maximum volumes.
10. Key strokes	Enter the number of key strokes by period, if applicable.

DOCUMENT DEFINITION

▲ **TOUCHE ROSS**

ID/TITLE _____

☐ CURRENT   ☐ PROPOSED

PAGE _____ OF _____

PROJECT NO. _____

ORGANIZATION _____

_____

DOCUMENT NUMBER _____

PREPARED BY _____

REVIEWED BY _____

SYSTEM _____

COPY ATTACHED   ☒ Y   ☒ N

DATE _____

USER REP _____

PHASE _____

DESCRIPTION:

DOCUMENT NAME: _____   FORM NUMBER: _____

PRESENT INPUT FORM:
☐ PUNCHED CARDS   ☐ MARKED/SENSE FORM   ☐ DISK   ☐ DOES NOT EXIST
☐ PREPRINTED FORM   ☐ MAGNETIC TAPE   ☐ MEMO   ☐ OTHER _____

DOCUMENT CONVERTED TO:
☐ CARD   ☐ KEY-TO-TAPE   ☐ KEY-TO-DISK   ☐ DEMAND INQUIRY   ☐ OTHER _____

MANUAL PROCESS AND EDIT STEPS	REF.	PERFORMED BY
1.		
2.		
3.		
4.		
5.		
6,		
7.		

DISTRIBUTION FLOW	REF.	DATE DUE IN	DATE DUE OUT
1.			
2.			
3.			
4.			
5.			
6.			
7.			

CONTROL	REF.	PERFORMED BY
1.		
2.		
3.		
4.		
5.		
6.		
7.		
8.		

VOLUME					KEY STROKES					
PERIOD	FREQ.	MIN.	AVE.	MAX.	Strokes / Period					
					PUNCH					
					VERIFY					
					TOTAL					

COMMENTS

▲ COPYRIGHT 1980   FORM NO. 132
TOUCHE ROSS & CO.

307

FILE DESCRIPTION AND INQUIRY
FORM 133

PURPOSE: To describe the general contents and characteristics of each file used in the current operations or proposed new system.

PROCEDURE FOR COMPLETING:

INFORMATION	ACTION
1. Heading	Complete and check if current or proposed system.
2. File number and name	Enter the name and organization's number or use a sequential number appropriate for cross reference.
3. File characteristics	Complete each section for update interval (e.g., daily, monthly), number of records in file, volume of transactions presented to the file, file media (card, disk, etc.), security requirements, existing or required backup, retention, and file sequence.
4. Access requirements	Describe requirements for accessing this file including purpose, how fast, how often, by whom, when, and where.
5. Control and update procedure	Document methods used to control file integrity and to update the file.

FILE DESCRIPTION AND INQUIRY

TOUCHE ROSS

ORGANIZATION_____

_____

SYSTEM_____

USER REP_____

☐ CURRENT

☐ PROPOSED

PREPARED BY _____

REVIEWED BY _____

DATE _____

PHASE _____

| | FILE NUMBER | FILE NAME:_____ | COPY ATTACHED | Y | N |

UPDATE INTERVAL:	SECURITY:
RECORDS IN FILE:	BACKUP:
TRANSACTIONS:	RETENTION:
MEDIA:	SEQUENCE:

ACCESS REQUIREMENTS

PURPOSE:

HOW FAST:

HOW OFTEN:

BY WHOM:

WHEN:

WHERE:

CONTROL AND UPDATE PROCEDURE

COMMENTS:

DATA ELEMENT DESCRIPTION
FORM 134

PURPOSE: To describe the essential data elements that are of importance during requirements analysis. The major data elements are defined, documented for proper values and edit criteria, and cross-referenced to input/output documents and files. A more detailed technical orientation to data elements may be found in the Data Element Definition (Form 150) that is an alternative to this form.

PROCEDURE FOR COMPLETING:

INFORMATION	ACTION
1. Heading	Complete with ID or Title, if appropriate.
2. Element name, ID, and number	Assign unique values for the data element — not necessarily within technical system constraints or conventions.
3. Definition, values, and size	Provide a concise and understandable identification of this data element.
4. Edit criteria	Specify the methods to test validity.
5. Input/output document/file usage	List all inputs, outputs, and files in which this data element appears.

DATA ELEMENT DESCRIPTION

TOUCHE ROSS

ID/TITLE_____

PROJECT NO._____

ORGANIZATION_____

_____

SYSTEM_____

USER REP_____

PREPARED BY _____

REVIEWED BY _____

DATE   _____

PHASE   _____

ELEMENT NAME	
ELEMENT ID	ELEMENT NUMBER

DEFINITION	
VALUES	SIZE

EDIT CRITERIA

INPUT/OUTPUT DOCUMENT/FILE USAGE					
NAME	NUMBER	I/O/F	NAME	NUMBER	I/O/F

COMMENTS

311

ASSUMPTIONS AND CONSTRAINTS
FORM 140

PURPOSE: To document for future reference and approval, four major classifications of requirements which impact the systems design and implementation.

PROCEDURE FOR COMPLETING:

INFORMATION	ACTION
1. Heading	Complete.
2. Body	Describe the schedule, timing, policy, legislative, and technical feasibility considerations that impact the system. Indicate the document number relating to any supporting data as well as the applicable function and transaction.
3. Approved By	Obtain approvals as appropriate from the:

— User organization.

— Systems group.

— EDP organizations.

— Project leader.

Note: Additional approvals may be required (internal audit, etc.).

ASSUMPTIONS AND CONSTRAINTS

ID/TITLE _____

PAGE _____ OF _____

PROJECT NO. _____

ORGANIZATION _____

_____

SYSTEM _____

USER REP _____

PREPARED BY		
REVIEWED BY		
DATE		
PHASE		

FUNCTION TRANSACTION	A. SCHEDULE TIMING B. POLICY C. LEGISLATIVE D. TECHNICAL FEASIBILITY	DOCUMENT NUMBER

APPROVED BY:

USER ORGANIZATION	DATE	SYSTEMS GROUP	DATE	EDP OPERATIONS	DATE	PROJECT LEADER	DATE

SUMMARY OF CONTROLS
FORM 141

PURPOSE: To record all controls established for a system.

PROCEDURE FOR COMPLETING:

INFORMATION	ACTION
1. Heading	Complete and check the appropriate box.
2. Function/transaction	Indicate the function or transaction being controlled.
3. Description of controls	Describe all controls by type (e.g., input, output, processing, etc.).
4. Document and added function reference	Indicate the relevant documentation. A copy of it should be attached for each control.

SUMMARY OF CONTROLS

▲ TOUCHE ROSS

ID/TITLE _____

ORGANIZATION _____

_____

SYSTEM _____

USER REP _____

☐ CURRENT   ☐ PROPOSED

PAGE _____ OF _____

PROJECT NO. _____

PREPARED BY		
REVIEWED BY		
DATE		
PHASE		

FUNCTION TRANSACTION	DESCRIPTION OF CONTROL	DOCUMENT AND ADDED FUNCTION REFERENCE

MULTI-PURPOSE FORM
FORM 142

PURPOSE: To document those situations in which a fixed format is not appropriate or where a general-purpose chart is too large.

PROCEDURE FOR COMPLETING:

INFORMATION	ACTION
1. Heading	Complete.
2. Body	Complete as required for such items as:

— Organization chart.

— Macro flowchart.

— Data base map.

— Description of operational characteristics.

— Narrative of specific processing logic.

— Description of major system functions.

— Tables of contents.

316

TOUCHE ROSS

ORGANIZATION _____

SYSTEM _____

USER REP _____

ID/TITLE _____

PREPARED BY _____

REVIEWED BY _____

DATE _____

PHASE _____

OPERATING COST SUMMARY
FORM 145

PURPOSE: To show all operating costs associated with a current or proposed system for EDP and non-EDP operations.

PROCEDURE FOR COMPLETING:

INFORMATION	ACTION
1. Heading	Complete and check the appropriate boxes, for current or proposed system and for EDP or non-EDP.
2. Cost element	Describe each cost element, such as:
	— Hardware (e.g., CPU, peripherals, terminals, storage devices):
	· Purchase.
	· Lease.
	· Depreciation.
	· Taxes.
	· Maintenance.
	— Software.
	— Site preparation.
	— Salaries, fringes, travel.
	— Data entry, data conversion.
	— Office equipment.
	— Supplies.
	— Consultants.
3. Reference	Refer to any documentation that is appropriate (budgets, contracts, etc.).
4. Capital; expense	Check if this is a capital or expense item.
5. Unit	Describe the unit of measurement (if applicable).
6. Rate	Enter the rate per each unit.
7. Periods	Distribute the costs in units and dollars across the periods.
8. Approved by	Obtain approvals as required from the:
	— User organization.
	— Systems group.
	— EDP operations.
	— Project leader.

318

OPERATING COST SUMMARY

TOUCHE ROSS

ORGANIZATION _____

_____

SYSTEM _____

USER REP_____

ID/TITLE_____

☐ CURRENT   ☐ PROPOSED

DATE FROM_____TO_____

PERIOD SIZE _____

INFLATION FACTOR _____

☐ EDP   ☐ NON-EDP

PAGE _____ OF _____

PROJECT NO. _____

PREPARED BY _____

REVIEWED BY _____

DATE _____

PHASE _____

COST ELEMENT	REF.	CAP	EXP	UNIT	RATE	QTY.	$	QTY.	$	QTY.	$	QTY.	$	QTY.	$	QTY.	$

TOTAL CAPITAL $ $

TOTAL EXPENSE $ $

APPROVED BY:

PROJECT LEADER _____ DATE

EDP OPERATIONS _____ DATE

SYSTEMS GROUP _____ DATE

USER ORGANIZATION _____ DATE

STATEMENT OF BENEFITS
FORM 146

PURPOSE: To describe the appropriate facts concerning benefits to be achieved through installation of the new system.

PROCEDURE FOR COMPLETING:

INFORMATION	ACTION
1. Heading	Complete.
2. Body	Use one sheet for each major benefit identified. In outline format indicate:

— How the benefit will be achieved.
— When the benefit will be achieved.
— Value of the benefit (attach schedule — Form 147).
— Method of calculation.
— Responsibility for achieving the benefit.
— Account number effected (in the organization's general ledger).

STATEMENT OF BENEFITS

TOUCHE ROSS

PAGE _____ OF _____

PROJECT NO. _____

ID/TITLE _____

ORGANIZATION _____

_____

SYSTEM _____

USER REP _____

PREPARED BY _____

REVIEWED BY _____

DATE _____

PHASE _____

DESCRIBE THE BENEFIT LISTING THESE POINTS

A. HOW BENEFIT WILL BE ACHIEVED
B. WHEN BENEFIT WILL BE ACHIEVED

C. VALUE OF BENEFIT
D. METHOD OF CALCULATION

E. RESPONSIBILITY FOR ACHIEVING BENEFIT
F. ACCOUNT NUMBER EFFECTED

MEASURABLE BENEFITS EVALUATION
FORM 147

PURPOSE: To show the summary of all benefits to be achieved. All of these items should be described on separate Statements of Benefits (Form 146).

PROCEDURE FOR COMPLETING:

INFORMATION	ACTION
1. Heading	Complete.
2. Benefit description	Enter a summary level description of each benefit.
3. Reference	Refer to the corresponding Statement of Benefits (Form 146).
4. Cash flow by period	Distribute by period the benefit dollars.
5. Total	Total all periods.
6. Approved by	Obtain approvals as required from the:

    — User organization.

    — Systems group.

    — EDP operations.

    — Project leader.

MEASURABLE BENEFITS EVALUATION

TOUCHE ROSS

ID/TITLE _____

ORGANIZATION _____

_____

SYSTEM _____

USER REP _____

DATE FROM _____ TO _____

PERIOD SIZE _____

INFLATION FACTOR _____

PAGE _____ OF _____

PROJECT NO. _____

PREPARED BY _____

REVIEWED BY _____

DATE _____

PHASE _____

BENEFIT DESCRIPTION	REFERENCE	CASH FLOW BY PERIOD																			
TOTAL																					

APPROVED BY:

USER ORGANIZATION	DATE	SYSTEMS GROUP	DATE	EDP OPERATIONS	DATE	PROJECT LEADER	DATE

COPYRIGHT 1980   FORM NO. 147
TOUCHE ROSS & CO.

ECONOMIC EVALUATION SUMMARY
FORM 148

PURPOSE: To provide a comparison of benefits and costs of proposed and present systems. This form is also used to record actual versus plan costs and benefits achievement.

PROCEDURE FOR COMPLETING:

INFORMATION	ACTION
1. Heading	Complete.
2. Proposed system	Distribute all costs and benefits across the periods. Include:
	— Development costs (Form 105).
	— Operating costs:
	• Non-EDP (Form 145).
	• EDP (Form 145).
	— Measurable benefits (Form 147).
	— Gross cost (benefit): computed by adding costs and subtracting benefits.
3. Present system	Distribute all costs across the periods. Include:
	— Operating cost:
	• Non-EDP (Form 145)
	• EDP (Form 145)
	— Total is computed by adding present system costs.
4. Net savings (Cost)	Subtract the proposed system gross cost (benefit) from the present system costs.
5. Return on investment	Computed by dividing the development cost by the net savings (cost).
6. Imputed annual value of unmeasured benefits	Estimate a dollar value, if appropriate.
7. Cash flow	Indicate actual and plan cash flow by period as the periods elapse.
8. Actual return on investment	Compute when periods elapse.

ECONOMIC EVALUATION SUMMARY

△ TOUCHE ROSS

PAGE _____ OF _____

PROJECT NO. _____

ID/TITLE_____

ORGANIZATION _____

_____ DATE: FROM_____ TO_____

SYSTEM_____ PERIOD SIZE _____

USER REP _____ INFLATION FACTORS _____

PREPARED BY _____|_____|_____

REVIEWED BY _____|_____|_____

DATE _____|_____|_____

PHASE _____|_____|_____

PROPOSED SYSTEM:	REFERENCE	PERIOD 1	PERIOD 2	PERIOD 3	PERIOD 4	TOTAL
DEVELOPMENT COSTS	PLAN					
	ACTUAL					
OPERATING COSTS – NON EDP	PLAN					
	ACTUAL					
EDP RECURRING COSTS	PLAN					
	ACTUAL					
MEASURABLE BENEFITS	PLAN					
	ACTUAL					
GROSS COST (BENEFIT) PROPOSED SYSTEM	PLAN					
	ACTUAL					

PRESENT SYSTEM:						
OPERATING COSTS – NON EDP	PLAN					
EDP RECURRING COSTS	PLAN					
TOTAL PRESENT SYSTEM	PLAN					

NET SAVINGS (COST)	PLAN					
	ACTUAL					

RETURN ON INVESTMENT (BASED ON MEASURABLE COSTS AND BENEFITS)				%
IMPUTED ANNUAL VALUE OF UNMEASURED BENEFITS TO ACHIEVE REQUIRED ROI %	$			%
PLAN	CUMULATIVE				
	CASH FLOW				
PERIOD 1 ACTUAL WITH REVISED PLAN	CUMULATIVE				
	CASH FLOW				
PERIOD 2 ACTUAL WITH REVISED PLAN	CUMULATIVE				
	CASH FLOW				
PERIOD 3 ACTUAL WITH REVISED PLAN	CUMULATIVE				
	CASH FLOW				
PERIOD 4 ACTUAL WITH REVISED PLAN	CUMULATIVE				
	CASH FLOW				
		ACTUAL RETURN ON INVESTMENT		%

MANAGEMENT SUMMARY
FORM 149

PURPOSE: To describe in a narrative, nontechnical fashion how the new system will operate.

PROCEDURE FOR COMPLETING:

INFORMATION	ACTION
1. Heading	Complete and check the appropriate box, for current or proposed system.
2. Body	Describe in summary each point:

- General description.
- Benefits.
- Costs.
- Processing cycle.
- System outputs.

MANAGEMENT SUMMARY

TOUCHE ROSS

PAGE _____ OF _____

PROJECT NO. _____

ID/TITLE_____

ORGANIZATION _____

_____

SYSTEM_____

USER REP_____

☐ CURRENT   ☐ PROPOSED

PREPARED BY _____|_____|_____

REVIEWED BY _____|_____|_____

DATE _____|_____|_____

PHASE _____|_____|_____

A. GENERAL DESCRIPTION   B. BENEFITS   C. COSTS   D. PROCESSING CYCLE   E. SYSTEM OUTPUTS

327

FORMS FOR TECHNICALLY-ORIENTED ACTIVITIES

FORM NUMBER	FORM NAME
150	Data Element Definition
151	Data Element/Module Cross Reference
152	Data Base/File Contents and Characteristics
153	Record/Document Contents
154	Data Base Record/File Layout
155	Transaction/Data Base/File Activity
160	Multiple Card Layout
161	VDT Screen Layout
162	VDT Support
163	Computer Output/Report
164	Output Report Layout
165	Print Report Program/Printer Support
166	Print Control
170	System Naming Control
171	Program/Module Function
172	Module Function Support
173	Module Table
174	Sort Program Parameter
175	File Split/File Merge
176	Decision Table
177	Table Form
178	Code Table

DATA ELEMENT DEFINITION
FORM 150

PURPOSE: To document the technical characteristics of each data element within the system. A more general form that may be used for major data elements during requirements analysis is the Data Element Description (Form 134).

PROCEDURE FOR COMPLETING:

INFORMATION	ACTION
1. Heading	Complete and check appropriate box for current or proposed system.
2. Data element name, picture and source	Element number must agree with Data Element Cross Reference (Form 151).
3. Classification	Check appropriate box:
	— Indicative-Key information utilized in searches.
	— Descriptive-Alphabetic nonindicative field.
	— Quantitative-Numeric nonindicative field normally used in arithmetic calculations.
4. Description	Briefly describe or define the data element.
5. Edit criteria	Specify the desired edits.
6. Control	Describe the applicable data controls.
7. User synonyms and technical synonyms	Indicate the various data names used interchangeably for this data element by user or EDP personnel.
8. Data dependencies	Identify the required relationships between this data element and any others.
9. Maintenance responsibility	Identify name of position or department responsible for data input, control, and maintenance.
10. Coding attributes	Indicate the implied meaning of coding, or expand on a Multipurpose Form (Form 142).
11. Comments	Include any other information about this data element, as needed.

DATA ELEMENT DEFINITION

TOUCHE ROSS

ID/TITLE _____

PAGE _____ OF _____

PROJECT NO. _____

ORGANIZATION _____

_____

SYSTEM _____

USER REP _____

ELEMENT
NUMBER

☐ CURRENT   ☐ PROPOSED

PREPARED BY			
REVIEWED BY			
DATE			
PHASE			

DATA ELEMENT NAME	PICTURE	SOURCE

CLASSIFICATION: ☐ INDICATIVE   ☐ DESCRIPTIVE   ☐ QUANTITATIVE

DESCRIPTION

EDIT CRITERIA

CONTROL

USER SYNONYMS

TECHNICAL SYNONYMS

DATA DEPENDENCIES

AUDIT/ERROR NAME

MAINTENANCE RESPONSIBILITY

CODING ATTRIBUTES

COMMENTS

COPYRIGHT 1980   FORM NO. 150
TOUCHE ROSS & CO.

331

DATA ELEMENT/MODULE CROSS REFERENCE
FORM 151

PURPOSE: To record the various files and programs (or modules) in which a given data element may be found. Primary cross references may be included on the Data Element Descriptions (Form 134).

PROCEDURE FOR COMPLETING:

INFORMATION	ACTION
1. Heading	Complete.
2. Data element number and data element/module name	Complete.
3. Usage	List each instance in which a data element is used and describe that usage by using the appropriate code.
A. CD	Enter the codes which explain how this data element is used for this identifier. Add descriptions to codes 05 thru 10 for any desired usage.
B. Identifier	Enter the name, as defined on the System Naming Control (Form 170).

DATA ELEMENT/MODULE CROSS-REFERENCE

TOUCHE ROSS

ORGANIZATION _____

SYSTEM _____

USER REP _____

APPLICATION NAME _____

STRUCTURE ID _____

PREPARED BY _____
REVIEWED BY _____
DATE _____
PHASE _____

CODES
01—ADD
02—REPLACE
03—DELETE
04—EXTRACT
05 _____
06 _____
07 _____
08 _____
09 _____
10 _____

ELEMENT NO.	DATA ELEMENT/MODULE NAME	CD	IDENTIFIER	USAGE	CD	IDENTIFIER	USAGE	CD	IDENTIFIER	USAGE	CD	IDENTIFIER	USAGE	CD	IDENTIFIER	USAGE	CD	IDENTIFIER	USAGE	CD	IDENTIFIER	USAGE	CD	IDENTIFIER	USAGE	CD	IDENTIFIER	USAGE	CD	IDENTIFIER	USAGE

DATA BASE/FILE CONTENT AND CHARACTERISTICS
FORM 152

PURPOSE: To record the contents and characteristics of a data base or a file.

PROCEDURE FOR COMPLETING:

INFORMATION	ACTION
1. Heading	Complete and check the appropriate boxes (current or proposed; physical or logical; permanent or transient).
2. Data base/file description	Briefly describe the data base or file.
3. Data base/file characteristics	Fill in only applicable areas:

— Name of the library and identifier for use by programmers.
— Type of labels.
— Storage media (disk, tape, etc.).
— Number of volumes the data base or file takes.
— Number of devices it takes to use this data base or file.
— How the data base or file is organized and can be accessed.
— Estimated number of records on the data base or file.
— Fixed or variable length.
— Minimum physical record length.
— Maximum physical record length.
— Minimum block size.

4. Data base/file sequence	Fill in only applicable areas:

— Data element number of the key as shown on the Data Element Definition (Form 150).
— Data element name of the key as shown on the Data Element Definition (Form 150).
— Ascending or a descending key field.

5. Blank	Enter the title for this section as:

— Record types contained.
— Segment types contained.

A. Name and description	Enter the name, description, and size of each record or segment type.
B. Support document	Refer to the Record/Document Contents (Form 153) or other documentation which describes this record or segment type.
C. Identifying/key fields	Enter the data element number and name of the key of this item as defined on the Data Element Definition (Form 150). Also include the key length, value if it is constant, and whether ascending or descending.
6. Data base/file retention security	Describe the retention and security approaches to be used for future processing, backup and recovery, audit trail, and legal requirements. Refer to support sheets if additional documentation is required.
7. Controls	Describe controls used on the data base or file.

334

DATA BASE/FILE CONTENT AND CHARACTERISTICS

▲ **TOUCHE ROSS**

PAGE _____ OF _____

DATA BASE/FILE ID _____ PROJECT NO. _____

DATA BASE/FILE TITLE _____

ORGANIZATION _____

☐ CURRENT ☐ PROPOSED
☐ PHYSICAL ☐ LOGICAL
☐ PERMANENT ☐ TRANSIENT
☐ SUPPORT ATTACHED

SYSTEM _____

USER REP _____

PREPARED BY		
REVIEWED BY		
DATE		
PHASE		

DATA BASE/FILE DESCRIPTION

DATA BASE/FILE CHARACTERISTICS

LIBRARY/IDENTIFIER:	ESTIMATED NO. OF RECORDS:
FILE LABELS:	FIXED OR VARIABLE:
MEDIA:	RECORD LENGTH: MIN MAX
NO. OF VOLUMES:	BLOCK SIZE: MIN MAX
NO. OF DRIVES:	COMMENTS:
ORGANIZATION:	

DATA BASE/FILE SEQUENCE

FILE SEQUENCE	ELEM. NO.	KEY FIELDS DATA ELEMENT NAME	A/D	FILE SEQUENCE	ELEM. NO.	KEY FIELDS DATA ELEMENT NAME	A/D
MAJOR							
↓				↓ MINOR			

NAME	DESCRIPTION	SUPPORT DOCUMENT	RECORD SIZE	IDENTIFYING/KEY FIELDS				
				ELE. NO.	DATA ELEMENT NAME	LEN	VALUE	A/D

DATA BASE/FILE RETENTION/SECURITY

PURPOSE	DESCRIPTION	PERIOD	MEDIA	SUPPORT SHEETS
FUTURE PROCESSING				
BACK UP/RECOVERY				
AUDIT TRAIL				
LEGAL REQUIREMENT				
COMMENTS				

CONTROLS:

RECORD/DOCUMENT CONTENTS
FORM 153

PURPOSE: To record the contents and characteristics of a record or a document.

PROCEDURE FOR COMPLETING:

INFORMATION	ACTION
1. Heading	Complete and check the appropriate box for current or proposed system.
2. Support of document number	Reference the Data Base/File Content and Characteristics (Form 152) FD number.
3. Name	Identify the record name.
4. Description	Include a brief description.
5. Length	Specify the record length.
6. Occurrences	Indicate the minimum, maximum, common, and average number of occurrences.
7. Data base/file ID	Enter the Data Base/File ID from the Data Base/File Content and Characteristics (Form 152).
8. Library identifier	Indicate the name of the library and the member's name for use by programmers.
9. Key field information	Enter the data element number and name of the key of this record as shown on the Data Element Definition (Form 150). Also enter the value if it is constant.
10. Contents	List each data element contained in the record or document with associated information as indicated on the form.

RECORD/DOCUMENT CONTENTS

TOUCHE ROSS

ID/TITLE _____

ORGANIZATION _____

☐ CURRENT   ☐ PROPOSED

SYSTEM _____

USER REP _____

PAGE _____ OF _____

PROJECT NO. _____

PREPARED BY			
REVIEWED BY			
DATE			
PHASE			

SUPPORT OF DOCUMENT NO. [_____]   NAME _____

RECORD/DOCUMENT CHARACTERISTICS

DESCRIPTION:

LENGTH:	KEY FIELD INFORMATION		
	ELEM. NO.	NAME	VALUE
OCCURRENCES: MIN:			
MAX: COMMON: AVE:			
DATA BASE/FILE ID:			
LIBRARY IDENTIFIER:			
COMMENTS:			

ELE. NO.	STANDARD DATA ELEMENT NAME	STD. ABBR. DATA NAME	FD LEVEL	ELEMENT SIZE/ PICTURE	LENGTH	US- AGE	START POSITION	COMMENTS/SOURCE

DATA BASE RECORD/FILE LAYOUT
FORM 154

PURPOSE: To picture graphically a data base record or file on a file layout.

PROCEDURE FOR COMPLETING:

INFORMATION	ACTION
1. Heading	Complete.
2. Body	Complete as appropriate. This form may be replaced by vendor-supplied forms for specific data base structures or file types. Usage of high-level language program coding generally eliminates the need for this form.

338

DATA BASE RECORD/FILE LAYOUT

TOUCHE ROSS

ORGANIZATION _____

SYSTEM _____
USER REP _____

DATA BASE RECORD/FILE ID _____
DATA BASE RECORD/FILE NAME _____

PAGE _____ OF _____
PROJECT NO. _____

PREPARED BY _____
REVIEWED BY _____
DATE _____
PHASE _____

COPYRIGHT 1980 TOUCHE ROSS & CO.

FORM NO. 154

339

TRANSACTION/DATA BASE/FILE ACTIVITY
FORM 155

PURPOSE: To show how a transaction impacts a field (in a data base or file) and what programs cause that impact.

PROCEDURE FOR COMPLETING:

INFORMATION	ACTION
1. Heading	Complete and check the appropriate box for current or proposed system.
2. Transaction/ID	Enter the appropriate identification.
3. Transaction description	Briefly describe the transaction.
4. By whom	Identify the function or department responsible for this transaction.
5. Frequency	Specify how often this transaction is completed (e.g., daily, weekly).
6. Volume	Estimate the volume relative to the frequency (e.g., 500 transactions per day).
7. Transaction data element	List each data element in the transaction that will impact a field in the data base or file.
8. Data element impacted	Associate the transaction data elements with their corresponding fields in the data base or file.
9. How impacted	Describe as: — Replacement. — Added. — Subtracted. — Other.
10. Program ID/title	Identify the program that performs this activity.

TRANSACTION/DATA BASE/FILE ACTIVITY

TOUCHE ROSS

ORGANIZATION _____

_____

SYSTEM _____

USER REP _____

DATA BASE/FILE ID _____

DATA BASE/FILE TITLE _____

☐ CURRENT   ☐ PROPOSED

PAGE _____ OF _____

PROJECT NO. _____

PREPARED BY _____

REVIEWED BY _____

DATE _____

PHASE _____

PROGRAM ID/TITLE	HOW IMPACTED	DATA ELEMENT IMPACTED	TRANSACTION DATA ELEMENT	VOLUME	FRE-QUENCY	BY WHOM	TRANSACTION DESCRIPTION	TRAN/ ID

MULTIPLE CARD LAYOUT
FORM 160

PURPOSE: To graphically picture the contents of data for specific card formats.

PROCEDURE FOR COMPLETING:

INFORMATION	ACTION
1. Heading	Complete.
2. Body	Enter all captions, titles, and headings on the appropriate cards. Draw vertical lines representing each card field and label the field. Reference each card layout to its appropriate documentation.

TOUCHE ROSS

ID/TITLE _____

ORGANIZATION _____

_____

SYSTEM _____

USER REP _____

PREPARED BY _____

REVIEWED BY _____

DATE _____

PHASE _____

1   1 2 3 4 5 6 7 8 9 10 11 12 13 14 15 16 17 18 19 20 21 22 23 24 25 26 27 28 29 30 31 32 33 34 35 36 37 38 39 40 41 42 43 44 45 46 47 48 49 50 51 52 53 54 55 56 57 58 59 60 61 62 63 64 65 66 67 68 69 70 71 72 73 74 75 76 77 78 79 80

2   1 2 3 4 5 6 7 8 9 10 11 12 13 14 15 16 17 18 19 20 21 22 23 24 25 26 27 28 29 30 31 32 33 34 35 36 37 38 39 40 41 42 43 44 45 46 47 48 49 50 51 52 53 54 55 56 57 58 59 60 61 62 63 64 65 66 67 68 69 70 71 72 73 74 75 76 77 78 79 80

3   1 2 3 4 5 6 7 8 9 10 11 12 13 14 15 16 17 18 19 20 21 22 23 24 25 26 27 28 29 30 31 32 33 34 35 36 37 38 39 40 41 42 43 44 45 46 47 48 49 50 51 52 53 54 55 56 57 58 59 60 61 62 63 64 65 66 67 68 69 70 71 72 73 74 75 76 77 78 79 80

4   1 2 3 4 5 6 7 8 9 10 11 12 13 14 15 16 17 18 19 20 21 22 23 24 25 26 27 28 29 30 31 32 33 34 35 36 37 38 39 40 41 42 43 44 45 46 47 48 49 50 51 52 53 54 55 56 57 58 59 60 61 62 63 64 65 66 67 68 69 70 71 72 73 74 75 76 77 78 79 80

5   1 2 3 4 5 6 7 8 9 10 11 12 13 14 15 16 17 18 19 20 21 22 23 24 25 26 27 28 29 30 31 32 33 34 35 36 37 38 39 40 41 42 43 44 45 46 47 48 49 50 51 52 53 54 55 56 57 58 59 60 61 62 63 64 65 66 67 68 69 70 71 72 73 74 75 76 77 78 79 80

VDT SCREEN LAYOUT
FORM 161

PURPOSE: To show the format of a video display (e.g., data entry, inquiry) in the proposed system. The form should be modified for the actual VDT screen size (rows and columns) in use. Additionally, this form may be used with lines in the screen display area to use as a worksheet.

PROCEDURE FOR COMPLETING:

INFORMATION	ACTION
1. Heading	Complete.
2. Transaction name and code	Enter the general name and technical code of the transaction (entry, inquiry, etc.).
3. Screen number	Assign a unique reference number for the screen format.
4. Description	Describe the purpose and general operation of this screen and how it relates to other screen formats.
5. Controls or restrictions	Describe the edit controls and access restrictions.
6. Screen layout	Complete the layout with the screen information in the correct relative (row, column) locations.

TOUCHE ROSS

ORGANIZATION _____

VDT
SCREEN LAYOUT

PREPARED BY _____
REVIEWED BY _____

SYSTEM _____
USER REP _____

DATE _____
PHASE _____

TRANSACTION NAME	TRANSACTION CODE	SCREEN NUMBER
DESCRIPTION		

CONTROLS OR RESTRICTIONS

	0	1	2	3	4	5	6	7
	1234567890	1234567890	1234567890	1234567890	1234567890	1234567890	1234567890	123456789
1								
2								
3								
4								
5								
6								
7								
8								
9								
10								
11								
12								
13								
14								
15								
16								
17								
18								
19								
20								
21								
22								
23								
24								

VDT SUPPORT SHEET
FORM 162

PURPOSE: To document the fields included on a VDT screen format (from Form 161).

PROCEDURE FOR COMPLETING:

INFORMATION	ACTION
1. Heading	Complete. Use the "ID/Title" to cross reference the VDT Screen Format (Form 161).
2. Field name	List each field on the screen format.
3. Data element reference number	Reference the data element source for each field.
4. Starting position	Enter the beginning row and column number of each field.
5. Length	Specify the character length of each field.
6. Special characters	Indicate any special characteristics of each field (based on the Codes list on the form).
7. Comments or references	Include any other pertinent comments for each field.

VDT SUPPORT SHEET

TOUCHE ROSS

ORGANIZATION _____

SYSTEM _____

USER REP _____

ID/TITLE _____

PAGE _____ OF _____

PROJECT NO. _____

PREPARED BY _____

REVIEWED BY _____

DATE _____

PHASE _____

FIELD NAME	DATA ELEMENT REFERENCE NO.	STARTING POSITION ROW	STARTING POSITION COL.	LENGTH	SPECIAL CHARACTERS	COMMENTS OR REFERENCES

TOTAL FORMAT CHARS. _____

TOTAL DATA CHARS. _____

SPECIAL CHARACTERISTICS CODES

1. BLINKING
2. INTENSIFIED
3. INVISIBLE
4. WRITE PROTECTED
5. REVERSED DISPLAY
6. _____

N. NUMBER ONLY
A. ALPHABETIC
X. EITHER

COPYRIGHT 1980   FORM NO. 162
TOUCHE ROSS & CO.

347

COMPUTER OUTPUT REPORT
FORM 163

PURPOSE: To describe the contents and characteristics of each report produced by a system.

PROCEDURE FOR COMPLETING:

INFORMATION	ACTION
1. Heading	Complete and check the appropriate box for current or proposed system.
2. Document number	Assign a document reference number.
3. Report name and report number	Indicate the computer report name and number.
4. Distribution flow	Identify the various departments and locations that will receive this report.
5. Sequence key	Specify the data elements on which the report is sequenced and totaled.
6. Frequency	Indicate the report frequency.
7. Due to data control	State the time this report is due to data control.
8. Due to departments	State the time this report is due to the user departments.
9. Data control functions	Briefly describe all data control functions for this report including control, bursting, deleaving, and special instructions.
10. Per page print line	Estimate under each volume column the minimum, average, and maximum number of lines for each item.
11. Output other than printed document	Estimate the volume for outputs which are other than printed reports.

COMPUTER OUTPUT/REPORT

TOUCHE ROSS

ID/TITLE _____

ORGANIZATION _____
_____

☐ CURRENT   ☐ PROPOSED

SYSTEM _____

PROGRAM ID _____

USER REP _____

PAGE _____ OF _____

PROJECT NO. _____

PREPARED BY		
REVIEWED BY		
DATE		
PHASE		

DOCUMENT NUMBER	COPY WITH RD _____ ATTACHED ☐ Y ☐ N

REPORT NAME: REPORT NUMBER:

DISTRIBUTION FLOW

DEPARTMENT NAME/TITLE	LOCATION
1.	
2.	
3.	
4.	
5.	
6.	

ELE. NO.	SEQUENCE KEY / DATA ELEMENT NAME	SUM ON	
			MAJOR
			↓
			MINOR

FREQUENCY

			DUE TO DATA CONTROL _____
DAILY ☐	MONTHLY ☐	DEMAND INQUIRY ☐	
WEEKLY ☐	ANNUAL ☐	_____ OTHER ☐	DUE TO DEPTS. _____

DATA CONTROL FUNCTIONS

CONTROLS	BURSTING & DELEAVING	SPECIAL INSTRUCTIONS

PER PAGE PRINT LINE

	VOLUME		
	MIN.	AVE.	MAX.
HEADER LINES			
DETAIL LINES			
SUMMARY LINES			
LINE TOTAL			
SPACE			
SKIP			
TOTAL LINES ACCOUNTED FOR			
TOTAL LINES AVAILABLE ON			

NO. COPIES REQUIRED _____ A _____ SIZE PAPER [   ]   NO. OF PAGES [   ] [   ] [   ]

OUTPUT OTHER THAN PRINTED DOCUMENT

MEDIA:	CARD	MAG. TAPE	DISK	DISPLAY	MICROFILM	8½ x 11 COPY	OTHER		
VOLUME OF RECORDS:									

COPYRIGHT 1980   FORM NO. 163
TOUCHE ROSS & CO.

OUTPUT/REPORT LAYOUT
FORM 164

PURPOSE: To define the specific spacing of an output.

PROCEDURE FOR COMPLETING:

INFORMATION	ACTION
1. Heading	Complete.
2. Body	Shade out unused portions of the form (if short or narrow) and fill out:

    — X: Alpha character,

    — Z: Zero suppress,

    — 9: Numeric without zero suppression, and

    — A: Text—literals.

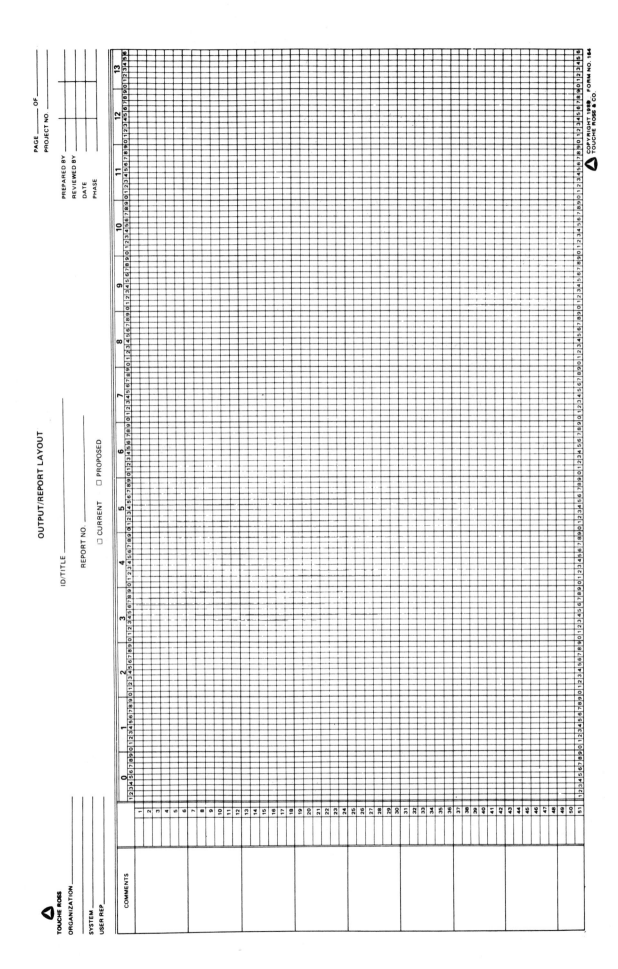

OUTPUT/REPORT LAYOUT

TOUCHE ROSS

ORGANIZATION

SYSTEM

USER REP.

ID/TITLE

REPORT NO.

☐ CURRENT   ☐ PROPOSED

COMMENTS

PAGE _____ OF _____
PROJECT NO. _____

PREPARED BY
REVIEWED BY
DATE
PHASE

PRINT REPORT PROGRAM/PRINTER SUPPORT
FORM 165

PURPOSE: To specify the characteristics and contents of a print report program. This form is supplemented by the Print Control (Form 166) for each print report.

PROCEDURE FOR COMPLETING:

INFORMATION	ACTION
1. Heading	Complete.
2. Input file data (Section I)	Specify the name and characteristics of the input file containing the report data.
3. Print image (Section II)	Complete this section if the report is produced from a print image file.
4. File sequence (Section III)	Identify the data elements used as sequence keys on this report (from major to minor keys).
5. Line control (Section IV)	Identify each type of print line, its spacing, and the condition causing it to be printed.

TOUCHE ROSS

ORGANIZATION _____

_____

SYSTEM_____

USER REP_____

PREPARED BY
REVIEWED BY
DATE
PHASE

REPORT NAME:_____

I. INPUT FILE DATA

FILE NO. _____ NAME _____ MEDIA _____ MULTI REEL _____

CHARACTERS/BYTES PER RECORD_____ RECORDS PER BLOCK _____

BLOCK LENGTH_____ ESTIMATED NUMBER OF RECORDS ON FILE _____

II. IF PRINT IMAGE FILE IS USED, COMPLETE THIS SECTION

FILE GENERATED BY PROGRAM: NO. _____ NAME _____

III. FILE SEQUENCE

		DATA ELEMENT	PICTURE	COMMENT
MAJOR	01			
	02			
	03			
TO	04			
	05			
	06			
MINOR	07			

IV. LINE CONTROL

		CONDITION	PRINT LINE	SPACING	SEE PRINT CONTROL ITEMS
DETAIL(S)	01				THRU
	02				THRU
	03				THRU
	04				THRU
	05				THRU
	06				THRU
TO	07				THRU
	08				THRU
	09				THRU
	10				THRU
	11				THRU
FINAL	12				THRU

V. PRINTER LAYOUTS NOTES:

1. ELEMENTS ARE IDENTIFIED BY NUMERICS

2. LINES ARE IDENTIFIED BY ALPHAS

VI. REQUIREMENTS:

3. IF FORM IS USED FOR PRINT PROGRAM, SECTIONS I, III, AND IV, (OR II) ARE USED.

4. IF USE FOR SUPPORT SECTION, IV IS USED.

PRINT CONTROL SHEET
FORM 166

PURPOSE: To document the data elements contained on each type of print line identified on the corresponding Printer Support Sheet (Form 165).

PROCEDURE FOR COMPLETING:

INFORMATION	ACTION
1. Heading	Complete.
2. Body	For each type of print line, list each data element, its picture, and any relevant comments. Associate the item numbers (list of elements) with the corresponding type of line from the Printer Support Sheet (Form 165).

PRINT CONTROL SHEET

TOUCHE ROSS

ORGANIZATION_____

_____

SYSTEM_____

USER REP_____

PAGE_____ OF_____

PROJECT NO._____

PREPARED BY	
REVIEWED BY	
DATE	
PHASE	

ITEM	DATA ELEMENT	ELE. NO.	PICTURE	COMMENT
1				
2				
3				
4				
5				
6				
7				
8				
9				
0				
1				
2				
3				
4				
5				
6				
7				
8				
9				
0				
1				
2				
3				
4				
5				
6				
7				
8				
9				
0				

COPYRIGHT 1980   FORM NO. 166
TOUCHE ROSS & CO.

355

SYSTEM NAMING CONTROL
FORM 170

PURPOSE: To record and control program, data base, and file ID numbers and naming conventions within a system.

PROCEDURE FOR COMPLETING:

INFORMATION	ACTION
1. Heading	Complete and check appropriate boxes for current or proposed system.
2. Description of system	Briefly describe the system.
3. Program module titles	List the ID number and names of all programs and modules assigned in the system.
4. Data base/file titles assigned	List the ID numbers and names of all data bases and files assigned in the system.

SYSTEM NAMING CONTROL

TOUCHE ROSS

ID/TITLE_____

ORGANIZATION_____

_____ □ CURRENT □ PROPOSED

SYSTEM_____

USER REP_____

PAGE_____ OF_____

PROJECT NO._____

PREPARED BY		
REVIEWED BY		
DATE		
PHASE		

DESCRIPTION OF SYSTEM:

PROGRAM/MODULE TITLES ASSIGNED

PROGRAM/ MODULE ID	PROGRAM/MODULE TITLE	PROGRAM/ MODULE ID	PROGRAM/MODULE TITLE

DATA BASE/FILE TITLES ASSIGNED

DATA BASE/ FIELD ID	DATA BASE/FILE TITLE	DATA BASE/ FIELD ID	DATA BASE/FILE TITLE

357

PROGRAM/MODULE FUNCTION
FORM 171

PURPOSE: To describe the macro functions of a program or module and provide references to the detail documentation.

PROCEDURE FOR COMPLETING:

INFORMATION	ACTION
1. Heading	Complete and check the appropriate box to indicate if a Module Function Support Sheet (Form 172) is attached.
2. Input data/data base records/ files used	List all input files and other sources of data as well as output data files.
A. ID	Enter the system identification for this Program/ Module.
B. Input data/data base records/file name	Enter the descriptive name of the data, file, or data base record.
C. Media	Indicate the media (tape, disk, card, etc.).
D. Organization	Indicate the organization (ISAM, Sequential, etc.).
E. Accessing	Indicate how data is accessed.
F. Update/output	Specify if data is input only, updated (add, change, delete), or output.
3. Functions performed	List the major functions of the program or module and provide references to support sheets such as:

— Narrative descriptions (Form 142).
— Logic charts (Form 127).
— Card input (Form 160).
— Video terminal usage (Forms 161, 162).
— Reports (Forms 163, 164, 165, 166).
— Logic tables (Forms 176, 177).

PROGRAM/MODULE FUNCTION

TOUCHE ROSS

ID/TITLE _____

ORGANIZATION _____

_____

SYSTEM _____

USER REP _____

PAGE _____ OF _____

PROJECT NO. _____

LANGUAGE _____

MODULE SHEET ATTACHED

☐ YES

☐ NO

PREPARED BY			
REVIEWED BY			
DATE			
PHASE			

INPUT DATA/DATA BASE RECORD/FILES USED

ID	INPUT DATA/DATA BASE RECORD/FILE NAME	MEDIA	ORGANIZATION	ACCESSING	UPDATED/ OUTPUT

FUNCTIONS PERFORMED

FUNCTION NUMBER	DESCRIPTION OF FUNCTION	SUPPORT SHEETS

COMMENTS:

MODULE FUNCTION SUPPORT
FORM 172

PURPOSE: To describe called modules and functions in support of another program or module (Form 171).

PROCEDURE FOR COMPLETING:

INFORMATION	ACTION
1. Heading	Complete with identification of program or module on function sheet (Form 171).
2. Called module ID and description	List all modules called by the primary program or module.
3. Parameters passed (with identification of element numbers) or support sheets	Either identify and describe parameters passed to the called module or enter references to support sheets that detail the calling routine.
4. Function description	Describe the purpose of calling each module.

MODULE FUNCTION SUPPORT

TOUCHE ROSS

ORGANIZATION

SYSTEM

USER REP

ID/TITLE

PAGE _____ OF _____

PROJECT NO. _____

PREPARED BY

REVIEWED BY

DATE

PHASE

CALLED MODULE ID	CALLED MODULE DESCRIPTION	PARAMETERS PASSED OR SUPPORT SHEET	ELEMENT NO.	FUNCTION DESCRIPTION

MODULE TABLE
FORM 173

PURPOSE: To record all modules used by a program or a module (Form 171). This is an alternative to using the Module Function Support (Form 172).

PROCEDURE FOR COMPLETING:

INFORMATION	ACTION
1. Heading	Complete with identification of program (Form 171).
2. Called module ID and description	List all modules called by the program or module.
3. Language	Specify the language the called module is written in.
4. Library	Indicate the library the called module is in.
5. Parameters passed on support sheet	Identify the parameters passed or reference the support sheets which describe the calling routine.
6. Element number	Identify the data element number passed to this module.

MODULE TABLE

TOUCHE ROSS

ID/TITLE _____

PAGE _____ OF _____

PROJECT NO. _____

ORGANIZATION _____

_____

SYSTEM _____

USER REP _____

PREPARED BY _____

REVIEWED BY _____

DATE _____

PHASE _____

CALLED MODULE ID	CALLED MODULE DESCRIPTION	LANGUAGE	LIBRARY	PARAMETERS PASSED OR SUPPORT SHEET	ELEMENT NO.

SORT PROGRAM PARAMETER
FORM 174

PURPOSE: To define the input, output, and parameters of a sort.

PROCEDURE FOR COMPLETING:

INFORMATION	ACTION
1. Heading	Complete and check the appropriate boxes.
2. Program/module	Identify the program or module occurring before and after this sort.
3. Input file data	Specify the input file ID, name, media, multivolume status, characters or bytes per record, records per block, block length, and estimated number of records on the file.
4. Output file data	Indicate if the output file is the same as the input file. If it is not, complete the output file section, including file ID, name, media, multivolume status, characters or bytes per record, records per block, block length, and estimated number of records on file.
5. Sequence parameters	Specify the sort sequence from major to minor key. For each key, enter the data element name, picture, record position and ascending/descending sequence.
6. Sort exit routine	Indicate if one is used. If it is, identify the phase, exit point and program or module which describes it (Form 171).
7. Other sort options used	Describe as appropriate.

SORT PROGRAM PARAMETER

▲ TOUCHE ROSS

ORGANIZATION _____

_____

SYSTEM _____

USER REP _____

ID/TITLE _____

☐ CURRENT   ☐ PROPOSED

PAGE _____ OF _____

PROJECT NO. _____

PREPARED BY		
REVIEWED BY		
DATE		
PHASE		

PROGRAM/MODULE BEFORE SORT: PROGRAM/MODULE AFTER SORT:

ID _____ NAME _____ ID _____ NAME _____

INPUT FILE DATA.

FILE ID _____ NAME _____ MEDIA _____ MULTI VOLUME _____

CHARACTERS/BYTES PER RECORD _____ RECORDS PER BLOCK _____

BLOCK LENGTH _____ ESTIMATED NUMBER OF RECORDS ON FILE _____

OUTPUT FILE DATA

SAME AS INPUT?   ☐ YES   ☐ NO   IF NO, COMPLETE THIS SECTION

FILE ID _____ NAME _____ MEDIA _____ MULTI VOLUME _____

CHARACTERS/BYTES PER RECORD _____ RECORDS PER BLOCK _____

BLOCK LENGTH _____ ESTIMATED NUMBER OF RECORDS ON FILE _____

SEQUENCE PARAMETERS

		DATA ELEMENT	PICTURE	RECORD POSITION		A/D	COMMENT
MAJOR ↑	01			FROM:	TO:		
	02			FROM:	TO:		
	03			FROM:	TO:		
	04			FROM:	TO:		
	05			FROM:	TO:		
TO	06			FROM:	TO:		
	07			FROM:	TO:		
	08			FROM:	TO:		
	09			FROM:	TO:		
↓ MINOR	10			FROM:	TO:		

SORT EXIT ROUTINE   USED? ☐ YES   ☐ NO

PHASE _____ EXIT POINT NO. _____ SEE PROGRAM/MODULE FORM _____

PHASE _____ EXIT POINT NO. _____ SEE PROGRAM/MODULE FORM _____

PHASE _____ EXIT POINT NO. _____ SEE PROGRAM/MODULE FORM _____

OTHER SORT OPTIONS USED – EXPLAIN _____

FILE SPLIT/FILE MERGE
FORM 175

PURPOSE: To define any program or module whose function is to split one file into several files or to merge several files into one file.

PROCEDURE FOR COMPLETING:

INFORMATION	ACTION
1. Heading	Complete.
2. Input file data	Specify all input files.
3. Control	Describe the conditions and actions required to split or merge files.
4. Output files	Specify all resulting output files.

FILE SPLIT ☐
FILE MERGE ☐

PAGE_____ OF_____
PROJECT NO._____

ORGANIZATION_____

_____

SYSTEM_____
USER REP_____

PREPARED BY		
REVIEWED BY		
DATE		
PHASE		

INPUT FILE DATA

	FILE NAME	NUMBER	MEDIA
01			
02			
03			
04			
05			
06			
07			
08			

CONTROL

	CONDITION	ACTION
01		
02		
03		
04		
05		
06		
07		
08		
09		
10		
11		
12		

OUTPUT FILES

	FILE NAME	NUMBER	MEDIA
01			
02			
03			
04			
05			
06			
07			
08			

DECISION TABLE
FORM 176

PURPOSE: To describe, in a table form, the decision rules which are necessary to make a function perform correctly.

PROCEDURE FOR COMPLETING:

	INFORMATION	ACTION
1.	Heading	Complete.
2.	Line	Indicate a condition with an alpha character and an action with a numeric character.
3.	Condition/action	Describe each logic condition then list each action to be taken.
4.	Rule	Sequentially number the rules. For each rule, indicate "true" logic conditions ("Y") where appropriate, then check the corresponding actions to be taken.
5.	Go to	Specify the next step to be taken after all actions for a given condition have been performed.
6.	Reviewed	Initial and check all rules which have been reviewed and approved.

TOUCHE ROSS

ORGANIZATION _____

_____

SYSTEM _____

USER REP _____

ID/TITLE _____

PREPARED BY _____

REVIEWED BY _____

DATE _____

PHASE _____

TABLE NAME:

CONDITION/ACTION

RULE →

LINE

GO TO – F (FUNCTION); R (RULE, SAME TABLE); DT (TABLE); MPF (MULTIPURPOSE FORM)

REVIEWED

NOTES

TABLE FORM
FORM 177

PURPOSE: To describe rules and functions or relationships which lend themselves to tabular presentation.

PROCEDURE FOR COMPLETING:

INFORMATION	ACTION
1. Heading	Complete.
2. Body	Label the two sides of the table (in the upper left corner when the form is turned on its side) and enter the desired information in matrix form such as edit requirements by field, update action on master file, counters by transaction record, etc.

TABLE FORM

TOUCHE ROSS

ID/TITLE _____

PAGE _____ OF _____
PROJECT NO. _____

ORGANIZATION _____

_____

SYSTEM _____

USER REP _____

NOTES:

PREPARED BY _____
REVIEWED BY _____
DATE _____
PHASE _____

CODE TABLE
FORM 178

PURPOSE: To describe the elements of a table.

PROCEDURE FOR COMPLETING:

INFORMATION	ACTION
1. Heading	Complete and check the appropriate box for current or proposed system.
2. Table name	Enter the table name.
3. Library name	Identify the library and member name for this table.
4. Description	Briefly describe the table.
5. Data elements using this table	List the data elements using this table.
6. Programs using this table	List the programs using this table.
7. Entry number	Indicate the position of each element in the table.
8. Code value	Specify the code value of each element in the table.
9. Code description	Describe the code of each element in the table.

CODE TABLE

TOUCHE ROSS

ID/TITLE _____

ORGANIZATION _____

_____ ☐ CURRENT ☐ PROPOSED

SYSTEM _____

USER REP _____

PAGE _____ OF _____

PROJECT NO. _____

PREPARED BY		
REVIEWED BY		
DATE		
PHASE		

TABLE NAME	LIBRARY NAME

DESCRIPTION

DATA ELEMENTS USING THIS TABLE	PROGRAMS USING THIS TABLE

ENTRY NO.	CODE VALUE	CODE DESCRIPTION

COPYRIGHT 1980 FORM NO. 178
TOUCHE ROSS & CO.

373

FORMS FOR DEVELOPMENT PLANNING AND TESTING

FORM NUMBER	FORM NAME
180	System Test Checklist
181	Conversion Planning Checklist
182	User Procedures and Training Checklist
183	General-purpose Checklist
185	Test Checklist
186	Walkthru Log
190	System Test Plan
191	Conversion Plan
192	Data Acquisition Plan
193	Personnel and Equipment Plan
194	Computer Test Plan
195	User Procedures and Training Plan
198	Results Form
199	Approval Form

SYSTEM TEST CHECKLIST
FORM 180

PURPOSE: To indicate the responsibility, schedule, and approval of all the major activities which are considered in producing a reliable, well-planned systems test. The Systems Test Checklist is supplemented with detail schedules and descriptions (Systems Test Plan—Form 190) for each major item on the list. The level of detail planning varies; however, each detail activity to be performed appears on a schedule.

PROCEDURE FOR COMPLETING:

INFORMATION	ACTION
1. Heading	Complete.
2. Module number	Identify the program or module number, if appropriate.
3. Module name	Identify the program or module name, if appropriate.
4. Schedule start date	Indicate the scheduled start date.
5. Actual start date	Indicate the actual start date.
6. Scheduled completion	Indicate the scheduled completion date.
7. Actual completion	Indicate the actual completion date.
8. Project leader	Enter the name of the project leader.
9. Activities	For each activity list:
	— Individual responsible.
	— Organization responsible.
	— Scheduled start date.
	— Actual completion date.
	— Approval of the department responsible for the activity.
10. Approved by	Obtain approvals as required from the:
	— User organization.
	— Systems group.
	— EDP operations.
	— Project leader.
	Additional approvals may be required (internal audit, etc.).

SYSTEM TEST CHECKLIST

TOUCHE ROSS

PAGE _____ OF _____

PROJECT NO. _____

ID/TITLE _____

ORGANIZATION _____

_____

SYSTEM _____

USER REP _____

PREPARED BY _____|_____|_____

REVIEWED BY _____|_____|_____

DATE _____|_____|_____

PHASE _____|_____|_____

MODULE NO.	MODULE NAME	SCHEDULED START DATE	ACTUAL START DATE	SCHEDULED COMPLETION	ACTUAL COMPLETION	PROJECT LEADER

DESCRIPTION OF ACTIVITY	INDIVIDUAL RESPONSIBLE	ORGANIZATION RESPONSIBLE	START DATE	COMPLETION DATE	APPROVED BY
1. COMPUTER TEST PLAN					
2. PROCEDURES					
USER ORGANIZATION					
EDP OPERATIONS					
SYSTEMS & PROGRAMMING					
DATA PROCESSING CONTROLS					
3. FORMS					
INPUT TEST DATA					
DATA BASE/FILE CREATION					
DATE BASE/FILE MAINTENANCE					
4. CONTROLS					
USER ORGANIZATION					
EDP CONTROLS					
5. EQUIPMENT					
AVAILABILITY					
EMERGENCY SERVICE					
6. PERSONNEL					
USER ORGANIZATION					
EDP OPERATIONS					
SYSTEMS & PROGRAMMING					
DATA PROCESSING CONTROLS					
7. SUPPLIES					
AVAILABILITY					
8. DATA					
CREATED & VERIFIED					
CONTROLLED					
9. DATA BASES/FILES					
CREATED & VERIFIED					
CONTROLLED					
10. REVIEW/APPROVAL					
11. MISCELLANEOUS					

APPROVED BY:

_____ _____ _____ _____ _____ _____ _____ _____

USER ORGANIZATION   DATE   SYSTEMS GROUP   DATE   EDP OPERATIONS   DATE   PROJECT LEADER   DATE

377

CONVERSION PLANNING CHECKLIST
FORM 181

PURPOSE: To indicate the responsibility, schedule, and approval of all the major activities which are considered in producing a reliable, well-planned systems conversion. The Conversion Planning Checklist is supplemented with detail schedules and descriptions (Conversion Plan—Form 191) for each major item on the list. The level of detail planning varies; however, each detail activity to be performed appears on a schedule.

PROCEDURE FOR COMPLETING:

INFORMATION	ACTION
1. Heading	Complete.
2. Activities	For each activity list:

    — Individual responsible.

    — Organization responsible.

    — Scheduled start date.

    — Actual completion date.

    — Approval of the department responsible for the activity.

10. Approved by	Obtain approvals as required from the:

    — User organization.

    — Systems group.

    — EDP operations.

    — Project leader.

Additional approvals may be required (internal audit, etc.).

TOUCHE ROSS

ID/TITLE _____

ORGANIZATION _____

_____

SYSTEM _____

USER REP _____

PREPARED BY _____

REVIEWED BY _____

DATE _____

PHASE _____

DESCRIPTION OF ACTIVITY	INDIVIDUAL RESPONSIBLE	ORGANIZATION RESPONSIBLE	START DATE	COMPLETION DATE	APPROVED BY
1. CONVERSION PLAN					
2. DATA BASE/FILE/DATA ACQUISITION PLAN					
3. PERSONNEL & EQUIPMENT PLAN					
4. DATA BASES/FILES					
PURIFICATION OF RECORDS					
CODING REQUIREMENTS					
CONTROL					
CONVERSION					
MAINTENANCE					
5. FORMS					
DESIGN					
INTERNAL PRINTING					
EXTERNAL PRINTING					
CONVERSION					
6. PARALLEL PROCESSING					
PROCEDURES					
VERIFICATION REQUIREMENTS					
SCHEDULE					
7. CONVERSION SEQUENCE					
ORGANIZATIONAL SEQUENCE					
SCHEDULE					
8. CONVERSION PROGRAMS					
DEFINITION					
SPECIFICATIONS					
PROGRAMMING					
TESTING					
REVIEW/APPROVAL					
9. INTERFACE WITH OTHER SYSTEMS					
DATA BASES/FILES					
DATA					
PROGRAMS					
TESTING					
REVIEW/APPROVAL					

APPROVED BY:

USER ORGANIZATION   DATE   SYSTEMS GROUP   DATE   EDP OPERATIONS   DATE   PROJECT LEADER   DATE

USER PROCEDURES AND TRAINING CHECKLIST
FORM 182

PURPOSE: To indicate the responsibility, schedule, and approval of all the major activities which are considered in producing a reliable, well-planned systems implementation. The User Procedures and Training Checklist is supplemented with detail schedules and descriptions (User Procedures and Training Plan — Form 192) for each major item on the list. The level of detail planning varies; however, each detail activity to be performed appears on a schedule.

PROCEDURE FOR COMPLETING:

INFORMATION	ACTION
1. Heading	Complete.
2. Activities	For each activity list:
	— Individual responsible,
	— Organization responsible,
	— Scheduled start date,
	— Actual completion date, and
	— Approval of the department responsible for the activity.
10. Approved by	Obtain approvals as required from the:
	— User organization.
	— Systems group.
	— EDP operations.
	— Project leader.
	Additional approvals may be required (internal audit, etc.).

USER PROCEDURES AND TRAINING CHECKLIST

TOUCHE ROSS

ID/TITLE _____

PAGE _____ OF _____

PROJECT NO. _____

ORGANIZATION _____

_____

SYSTEM _____

USER REP _____

PREPARED BY		
REVIEWED BY		
DATE		
PHASE		

DESCRIPTION OF ACTIVITY	INDIVIDUAL RESPONSIBLE	ORGANIZATION RESPONSIBLE	START DATE	COMPLETION DATE	APPROVED BY
1. USER PREPARATION					
2. INTERNAL NOTIFICATION					
EXECUTIVE ANNOUNCEMENT					
EMPLOYEE ANNOUNCEMENT					
3. EXTERNAL NOTIFICATION					
CUSTOMER COORDINATION					
VENDOR COORDINATION					
PUBLIC RELATIONS					
OTHER					
4. POLICY CONSIDERATIONS					
CORPORATE					
DIVISIONAL					
5. PROCEDURES					
CONTENT PLAN					
MANUALS					
PUBLICATION & ISSUANCE					
6. JOB OUTLINES					
7. FORMS					
DESIGN					
INTERNAL PRINTING					
EXTERNAL PRINTING					
8. TRAINING AND ORIENTATION					
PROGRAM PLAN					
PROGRAM INSTRUCTORS MANUAL					
PRESENTATION					
OTHER					
9. SPECIAL EQUIPMENT & FIXTURES					
DETERMINATION OF REQ'MTS.					
ENGINEERING DEPARTMENT					
SUB CONTRACTORS					
10. OFFICE EQUIPMENT REQ.					
11. FLOOR SPACE & LAYOUT					
12. SUPPLIES					
13. PERSONNEL					
RECLASSIFICATION					
HIRING					

APPROVED BY:

_____ _____ _____ _____ _____ _____ _____ _____
USER ORGANIZATION DATE   SYSTEMS GROUP   DATE   EDP OPERATIONS   DATE   PROJECT LEADER   DATE

GENERAL-PURPOSE CHECKLIST
FORM 183

PURPOSE: To indicate the responsibility, schedule, and approval of other major activities sequence of events that are not covered on the other checklists (Forms 180, 181, and 182).

PROCEDURE FOR COMPLETING:

INFORMATION	ACTION
1. Heading	Complete.
2. Activities	For each activity list:
	— Activity description.
	— Individual responsible.
	— Scheduled start date.
	— Actual completion date.
	— Approval of the department responsible for the activity.
10. Approved by	Obtain approvals as required from the:
	— User organization.
	— Systems group.
	— EDP operations.
	— Project leader.
	Additional approvals may be required (internal audit, etc.).

GENERAL-PURPOSE CHECKLIST

ID/TITLE _____

PAGE _____ OF _____

PROJECT NO. _____

ORGANIZATION _____

_____

SYSTEM_____

USER REP_____

PREPARED BY			
REVIEWED BY			
DATE			
PHASE			

DESCRIPTION OF ACTIVITY	INDIVIDUAL RESPONSIBLE		START DATE	COMPLETION DATE	APPROVED BY

APPROVED BY:

_____ _____ _____ _____ _____ _____ _____ _____

USER ORGANIZATION   DATE   SYSTEMS GROUP   DATE   EDP OPERATIONS   DATE   PROJECT LEADER   DATE

TEST CHECKLIST
FORM 185

PURPOSE: To monitor the performance of the systems test.

PROCEDURE FOR COMPLETING:

INFORMATION	ACTION
1. Heading	Complete and check appropriate boxes for systems test or maintenance and for system function or program function.
2. Number and description	Enter the number and description of each test step.
3. Date Responsibility Status Result/Reference Program ID	Indicate as the test is carried out the date each step is completed, the person responsible, the step status and results, (referencing appropriate documentation of the test results), and identify the program.

TEST CHECKLIST FORM

TOUCHE ROSS

ID/TITLE _____

PAGE _____ OF _____

PROJECT NO. _____

ORGANIZATION _____

☐ SYSTEM TEST

☐ MAINTENANCE

☐ SYSTEM FUNCTION

☐ PROGRAM/MODULE FUNCTIONS

_____

SYSTEM _____

USER REP _____

PREPARED BY _____

REVIEWED BY _____

DATE _____

PHASE _____

NO.	DESCRIPTION (TRANSACTION AND CONDITION)	DATE	RESP.	STATUS	RESULTS/REFERENCE	PROGRAM ID

WALKTHRU LOG
FORM 186

PURPOSE: To document the results of walkthru meetings and to monitor subsequent corrective actions.

PROCEDURE FOR COMPLETING:

INFORMATION	ACTION
1. Heading	Complete.
2. Purpose & participants	Record the purpose of the meeting and the names of those attending.
3. Body	Identify each of the programs, modules, or functions discussed. Record any problems identified and the people responsible for correcting them. Enter the date as the problems are corrected.

WALKTHRU LOG

▲ **TOUCHE ROSS**

ID/TITLE _____

ORGANIZATION _____

_____

SYSTEM _____

USER REP _____

PAGE _____ OF _____

PROJECT NO. _____

PREPARED BY		
REVIEWED BY		
DATE		
PHASE		

PURPOSE:	PARTICIPANTS:

PROGRAM/MODULE/ FUNCTION ID	PROBLEM	RESP	CORRECTED BY	DATE

SYSTEM TEST PLAN
FORM 190

PURPOSE: To describe in detail the major activities or specific tasks, action steps or items to be accomplished for each major function of the systems test. This plan supplements the System List Checklist (Form 180).

PROCEDURE FOR COMPLETING:

INFORMATION	ACTION
1. Heading	Complete.
2. Boxes	Check the box(es) this form covers.
3. Body	Complete in narrative or outline format.
4. Approved by	Obtain approvals as required from the:

— User organization.

— Systems group.

— EDP operations.

— Project leader.

Additional approvals may be required (internal audit, etc.).

SYSTEM TEST PLAN

TOUCHE ROSS

ID/TITLE _____

PROJECT NO. _____

ORGANIZATION _____

_____

SYSTEM _____

USER REP _____

PREPARED BY			
REVIEWED BY			
DATE			
PHASE			

DESCRIBE THE FOLLOWING MAJOR ACTIVITIES OR SPECIFIC TASKS, ACTION STEPS OR ITEMS TO BE ACCOMPLISHED FOR EACH MAJOR FUNCTION OF THE SYSTEM.

☐ COMPUTER TEST PLAN   ☐ PERSONNEL AND EQUIPMENT PLAN

☐ USER PROCEDURE AND TRAINING PLAN   ☐ SUPPLIES AND FORMS

☐ CONVERSION PLAN   ☐ DATA ACQUISITION PLAN

☐ CONTROLS   ☐ FILES

☐ EQUIPMENT   ☐ OTHER _____

APPROVED BY:

USER ORGANIZATION	DATE	SYSTEMS GROUP	DATE	EDP OPERATIONS	DATE	PROJECT LEADER	DATE

CONVERSION PLAN
FORM 191

PURPOSE: To describe in detail the major activities, specific tasks, action steps, and items to be accomplished for each major function of the conversion. This plan supplements the Conversion Planning Checklist (Form 181).

PROCEDURE FOR COMPLETING:

INFORMATION	ACTION
1. Heading	Complete.
2. Boxes	Check the box(es) this form covers.
3. Body	Complete in narrative or outline format.
4. Approved by	Obtain approvals as required from the:

— User organization.

— Systems group.

— EDP operations.

— Project leader.

Additional approvals may be required (internal audit, etc.).

CONVERSION PLAN

TOUCHE ROSS

ID/TITLE _____

ORGANIZATION _____

_____

SYSTEM _____

USER REP _____

PREPARED BY _____|_____|_____

REVIEWED BY _____|_____|_____

DATE _____|_____|_____

PHASE _____|_____|_____

DESCRIBE THE FOLLOWING MAJOR ACTIVITIES IN TERMS OF SPECIFIC TASKS, ACTION STEPS, OR ITEMS TO BE ACCOMPLISHED:

☐ DATA ACQUISITION PLAN   ☐ CONVERSION SEQUENCE

☐ **PERSONNEL AND EQUIPMENT PLAN**   ☐ CONVERSION PROGRAMS

☐ FORMS   ☐ INTERFACE WITH OTHER SYSTEMS

☐ PARALLEL PROCESSING

APPROVED BY:

USER ORGANIZATION	DATE	SYSTEMS GROUP	DATE	EDP OPERATIONS	DATE	PROJECT LEADER	DATE

DATA ACQUISITION PLAN
FORM 192

PURPOSE: To describe requirements for creating every data element shown on each Record/ Document Contents (Form 153) in the system. The plan is further organized to reference the records which must be created for each data base or file as well as the conversion programs necessary to create such records.

PROCEDURE FOR COMPLETING:

INFORMATION	ACTION
1. Heading	Complete.
2. Record types on data base/file	Identify the segment or record types to which these elements apply.
3. File maintenance program number	Specify the number of the maintenance program designed for the data base or file acquisition.
4. Analyst responsible	Assign an analyst responsible for creating the data base or file.
5. Element number	List each data element number.
6. Element name	List each data element name.
7. Source converted from	Indicate the source converted from.
8. Input transaction code	Indicate the transaction code.
9. Input record name	Identify the input record.
10. Input record code	Specify the record code this element will update.
11. Field number or card column	Indicate the field number or column this element will be in this record.
12. Description or reference to method of acquisition	Describe the method of acquiring the data element. Reference any additional documentation.
13. Approved by	Obtain approvals as required.

DATA ACQUISITION PLAN

TOUCHE ROSS

ORGANIZATION _____

SYSTEM _____

USER REP _____

DATA BASE/FILE ID _____

DATA BASE/FILE NAME _____

PAGE _____ OF _____

PROJECT NO. _____

PREPARED BY _____

REVIEWED BY _____

DATE _____

PHASE _____

RECORD TYPES ON DATA BASE/FILE		FILE MAINT. PROG. NO.	ANALYST RESPONSIBLE	DESCRIPTION OF OR REFERENCE TO METHOD OF ACQUISITION																				
				CONV. PROG. NO.																				
				FIELD NO. OR C.C.																				
				INPUT RECORD CODE																				
				INPUT RECORD NAME																				
				INPUT TRANS. CODE																				
				SOURCE CONVERTED FROM																				
	ELEMENT NAME																							
ELE. NO.																								

APPROVED BY:

USER DEPARTMENT _____ DATE _____

SYSTEMS GROUP _____ DATE _____

EDP OPERATIONS _____ DATE _____

PROJECT LEADER _____ DATE _____

PERSONNEL AND EQUIPMENT PLAN
FORM 193

PURPOSE: To document the requirements for personnel and equipment necessary to convert from an existing system to a new or revised system. This plan is used as a guide by the departments responsible for the conversion.

PROCEDURE FOR COMPLETING:

INFORMATION	ACTION
1. Heading	Complete and check the appropriate box.
2. Resource	Indicate, under resource, the user departments, data control groups, data entry groups, names of outside service agencies, computer and other resources required.
3. Skill level	Identify the skill levels required for each resource (e.g., typist, clerical).
4. Hours required	Estimate the total hours required by skill level and resource.
5. Schedule	Label and distribute the total hours across the schedule columns by the day, week and month in which the hours will be required.
6. Approved by	Obtain approvals as required from the:

— User organization.

— Systems group.

— EDP operations.

— Project leader.

Additional approvals may be required (internal audit, etc.).

PERSONNEL AND EQUIPMENT PLAN

TOUCHE ROSS

ID/TITLE _____

PAGE _____ OF _____

PROJECT NO. _____

ORGANIZATION _____

_____

☐ CURRENT   ☐ PROPOSED

PREPARED BY _____

REVIEWED BY _____

DATE _____

PHASE _____

SYSTEM _____

USER REP _____

SCHEDULE

RESOURCE	SKILL LEVEL*	HOURS REQ'D.							

1. USER ORGANIZATION

2. DATA CONTROL

3. DATA ENTRY

4. OUTSIDE SERVICES

5. COMPUTER

6. OTHER

*WHEN APPLICABLE

APPROVED BY:

USER ORGANIZATION	DATE	SYSTEM GROUP	DATE	EDP OPERATIONS	DATE	PROJECT LEADER	DATE

COPYRIGHT 1980   FORM NO. 193
TOUCHE ROSS & CO.

COMPUTER TEST PLAN
FORM 194

PURPOSE: To document the approach in which systems, individual programs, or modules are to be tested on the computer.

PROCEDURE FOR COMPLETING:

INFORMATION	ACTION
1. Heading	Complete and check the appropriate box for systems test or maintenance.
2. Test plan	Identify each program or module to be tested, including date scheduled, date planned for completion, operations person responsible, equipment to be used and analyst responsible. Describe in detail the steps required to prepare the data, files, data bases, tables and any other material. Explain the expected output results in a manner in which each output will be evaluated for accuracy and completeness.
3. Approved by	Obtain approvals as required from the:

— User organization.

— Systems group.

— EDP operations.

— Project leader.

Additional approvals may be required (internal audit, etc.).

COMPUTER TEST PLAN

TOUCHE ROSS

ORGANIZATION _____

_____

SYSTEM _____

USER REP _____

ID/TITLE _____

☐ SYSTEMS TEST
☐ MAINTENANCE

PROBLEM/REQUEST NO. _____
CHANGE REQUEST NO. _____
DATE REQUIRED _____

PAGE _____ OF _____

PROJECT NO. _____

PREPARED BY _____
REVIEWED BY _____
DATE _____
PHASE

DESCRIPTION OF PLAN

APPROVED BY:

USER ORGANIZATION	DATE	SYSTEMS GROUP	DATE	EDP OPERATIONS	DATE	PROJECT LEADER	DATE

COPYRIGHT 1980   FORM NO. 194
TOUCHE ROSS & CO.

USER PROCEDURES AND TRAINING PLAN
FORM 195

PURPOSE: To describe in detail the major activities, specific tasks, or items to be accomplished for each major function within user procedures and training. This plan supplements the User Procedures and Training Checklist (Form 182).

PROCEDURE FOR COMPLETING:

INFORMATION	ACTION
1. Heading	Complete.
2. Boxes	Check the boxes this form covers.
3. Body	Complete the narrative or outline format.
4. Approved by	Obtain approvals as required from the:

    — User organization.
    — Systems group.
    — EDP operations.
    — Project leader.

Additional approvals may be required (internal audit, etc.).

USER PROCEDURES AND TRAINING PLAN

TOUCHE ROSS

ID/TITLE _____

ORGANIZATION _____

_____

SYSTEM _____

USER REP _____

PREPARED BY _____|_____|_____

REVIEWED BY _____|_____|_____

DATE _____|_____|_____

PHASE _____|_____|_____

DESCRIBE THE FOLLOWING MAJOR ACTIVITIES IN TERMS OF SPECIFIC TASKS, ACTION STEPS, OR ITEMS TO BE ACCOMPLISHED:

- ☐ USER PREPARATION
- ☐ INTERNAL NOTIFICATION
- ☐ EXTERNAL NOTIFICATION
- ☐ POLICY CONSIDERATIONS
- ☐ PROCEDURES
- ☐ JOB OUTLINES
- ☐ FORMS

- ☐ TRAINING AND ORIENTATION
- ☐ SPECIAL EQUIPMENT AND FEATURES
- ☐ OFFICE EQUIPMENT REQUIREMENTS
- ☐ FLOOR SPACE AND LAYOUT
- ☐ SUPPLIES
- ☐ PERSONNEL
- ☐ OTHER _____

APPROVED BY:

USER ORGANIZATION	DATE	SYSTEMS GROUP	DATE	EDP OPERATIONS	DATE	PROJECT LEADER	DATE

PURPOSE: To control and document the results of all tests.

PROCEDURE FOR COMPLETING:

INFORMATION	ACTION
1. Heading	Complete and check appropriate box for systems test, implementation, or maintenance.
2. Body	Indicate the date and time of each test. Note the module number, operator and analyst responsible. Record the results.

RESULTS FORM

TOUCHE ROSS

ID/TITLE _____

PAGE _____ OF _____

PROJECT NO. _____

ORGANIZATION _____

SYSTEM _____

USER REP _____

☐ SYSTEM TEST
☐ IMPLEMENTATION
☐ MAINTENANCE

PREPARED BY _____
REVIEWED BY _____
DATE _____
PHASE _____

DATE OF TEST	TIME OF TEST	MODULE NO.	OPERATOR RESPONSIBLE	ANALYST RESPONSIBLE	✓	RESULTS

APPROVAL FORM
FORM 199

PURPOSE: To document user and systems approval of the results of all tests.

PROCEDURE FOR COMPLETING:

INFORMATION	ACTION
1. Heading	Complete and check appropriate box for systems test, implementation, or maintenance.
2. Body	Indicate the program ID and output or report names. Initial and date each approval of results by the user and systems personnel.

APPROVAL FORM

TOUCHE ROSS

PAGE _____ OF _____

PROJECT NO. _____

ID/TITLE _____

ORGANIZATION _____

☐ SYSTEM TEST RESULTS
☐ IMPLEMENTATION RESULTS
☐ MAINTENANCE RESULTS

SYSTEM _____

USER REP _____

PREPARED BY _____|_____|_____

REVIEWED BY _____|_____|_____

DATE _____|_____|_____

PHASE _____|_____|_____

PROGRAM ID	OUTPUT/REPORT NAME	USER APPROVAL		SYSTEMS APPROVAL	
		NAME	DATE	NAME	DATE

COPYRIGHT 1980   FORM NO. 199
TOUCHE ROSS & CO.

Index

N

Network design, 136, 138

O

Object code, 162
Operating costs:
  estimating EDP, 72
  estimating, 71
Operations analyst, 7
Operations and systems analysis, 83
  business objectives, 88
  company policies, 85
  describing outputs and inputs, 84
  end product documentation, 87
  evaluating existing systems, 88
  file description, 85
  functions and staffing, 84
  performance data, 85
  project team selection, 88
  review of existing systems, 86
  understanding data content, 87
  workflow, 85
Organizational structure, 64
Organization of project, 27

P

Package review, 15, 114
  contact with vendors, 120
  evaluation of application package,
    117-119
  package features, 116
  user requirements, 116, 120
  vendor proposal, 117
Parallel maintenance, 201
Parallel system operation, 129
PERT, 4
Post-implementation review, 236
  data gathering and analysis, 237-
    238
  documentation review, 237-238
  interviews with users, 237
  operating efficiency, 240
  personnel, 236
  report, 239
  standard activities/end items, 241
  supporting documentation, 236
  user acceptance, 239
Program classifications, 35
Programming:
  applications, 161
  assignments, 162
  documentation, 153-154
  level of detail, 156
  specifications, 152, 153
  standards, 146, 163, 166

Project:
  control, 39
  estimates, 32
  file, 57
  management, 25-27, 42
  organization, 27
  personnel, 19
  plan, 29
  planning, 30
  room, 40
  schedule changes, 42
  status reports, 41
  team, 6, 19
Project estimates, 32
  distribution of effort, 34
Project management, 25-27, 42
  forms, 259-285
Project manager:
  selection of, 27
Project team, 6, 19
  selection of, 28

Q

Quality assurance team, 20

R

Refinement of system, 229
  analysis of change request, 232
  changes to system, 230
  enhancements, 230
  maintenance group, 231
  review of system performance, 229-
    230
  standard activities/end items, 233-
    234
  system improvements, 230
Requests for proposals, 105, 108, 117
Requests for systems development, 52
  steering committee, 56
Results log, 221
Review:
  of application specifications, 154
  of existing systems, 75, 86
  of package, 15, 114
  of system performance, 229-230
  of technical specifications, 138
  of vendor contracts, 190
  post-implementation, 236
  user, 200
Risk exposures, 4

S

Schedule changes in project, 42
Service bureau, 125
Shaw, John C., 3

Skill requirements, 7
Source code, 162
Specifications:
  application, 152
  programming, 153
  technical, 16, 135, 172, 208
  telecommunications, 137
Standard activities, 5
Standard activities/end items matrix,
    47
Standard forms:
  benefits of, 235
  categories of, 256
  for development planning and
    testing, 375-403
  for project management, 259-285
  for technically-oriented activities,
    329-373
  for user-oriented activities, 287-327
  list of, 256-258
  standard activities/end items
    matrix, 256
Standards:
  development, 20-23
  deviation from, 23-24
  manuals, 22
  operations, 146
  programming, 146
Statement of benefits, 238, 320-321
Status:
  measurement of project, 41
  reports, 41
Steering committee, 19
  candidates for, 51
Strategic planning, 5
System flowchart, 136
System proposals:
  evaluation of, 56
System test checklist, 190, 376-377
Systems design:
  determining EDP functions, 15
  interface with users, 136
Systems development, 11, 15-17, 45
  overview, 11, 46
  phases, 11
  project plan revision, 127
  requests for, 52
Systems implementation, 12, 18, 217
  contact with user management, 224
  conversion of files, 220-221
  conversion plans, 218
  discontinuing the old system, 225
  hardware, 220
  monitoring the system, 222-223
  organizational changes, 219
  resource requirements, 219
  standard activities/end items, 226-
    227
  training, 222
  turn-over system, 222
  user commitment, 219